Ohio under COVID

LESSONS FROM AMERICA'S HEARTLAND IN CRISIS

Edited by
Katherine Sorrels, Vanessa Carbonell, Danielle Bessett, Lora Arduser, Edward V. Wallace, and Michelle L. McGowan

UNIVERSITY OF MICHIGAN PRESS
Ann Arbor

Published in the United States of America by the
University of Michigan Press
Manufactured in the United States of America
Printed on acid-free paper
First published May 2023

A CIP catalog record for this book is available from the British Library.

Library of Congress Cataloging-in-Publication data has been applied for.

ISBN 978-0-472-07572-0 (hardcover: alk. paper)
ISBN 978-0-472-05572-2 (paper: alk. paper)
ISBN 978-0-472-90306-1 (open access ebook)

DOI: https://doi.org/10.3998/mpub.12396322

This book is freely available in an open access edition thanks to TOME (Toward an Open Monograph Ecosystem)—a collaboration of the Association of American Universities, the Association of University Presses, and the Association of Research Libraries—and the generous support of the University of Cincinnati.

The University of Michigan Press's open access publishing program is made possible thanks to additional funding from the University of Michigan Office of the Provost and the generous support of contributing libraries.

Cover Image: Portraits from the collection "Faces in the Time of COVID" by Yani Sheng.

Ohio under COVID

Contents

Digital materials related to this title can be found on the Fulcrum platform via the following citable URL: https://doi.org/10.3998/mpub.12396322

Just a Sneeze

Molly Jasina

I remember when a sneeze was just a sneeze
I'd sneeze, excuse myself, and then slip back into invisibility
Maybe I'd rouse a few "bless yous"
But the moment passed, and the onlookers looked on
But now...
Hold it
I feel the stares
Hold it
They lean away
Hhhooollllddd it
I'm rousing suspicion
Achoo
Shit.
"Cover your mouth!"
"Gross!"
"I don't want to get sick!"
But I'm not even sick.
"People like you are responsible for everything!"
I feel the heat of embarrassment. Uncomfortable.
Self-conscious.
I remember when a sneeze was just a sneeze
But perceptions stay the same by changing with time
My sneeze plus your prejudice
Powerful.
The truth about my body
Powerless.
What really has the potential to infect, spread, and destroy

The potential to kill
My virus-free body or hatred and ignorance?
I remember when a sneeze was just a sneeze
Now it's a target on my back
How can I explain the centuries of oppression that led to this
not-so-isolated incident in the middle of the grocery store?
With all eyes on me, how can I seize the day and turn visibility into voice? Into
strength? Into a movement?
How can I *sneeze* the day and reclaim my outbursts?
I remember when a sneeze was just a sneeze. Now it's got me making metaphors,
writing poetry, and participating in activism.
Powerful.

This poem is reprinted from the OPAWL 2020 publication *Quaranzine: 2020 Pandemic Stories* with permission from OPAWL and the author, Molly Jasina. The full zine can be found online at: https://opawl.gumroad.com/l/opawl_zine/dream_devise_disrupt. OPAWL—Building AAPI Feminist Leadership "is a grassroots member-led community that organizes for social justice and elevates the voices, visibility, and progressive leadership of Asian, Asian American, and Pacific Islander (AAPI) women and nonbinary people in Ohio" (opawl.org, 2021).

Jasina writes of this poem: "I joined OPAWL's Writer's Circle during the summer of 2020. With encouragement from the group, I began writing to help process the hate crimes against AAPI people. In "Just a Sneeze," I wanted to explore concepts of invisibility versus hypervisibility and the (in)significance of things and events depending on context. I grew up in southwest Ohio, and with this poem, I wanted to share a way in which the discomfort of racialization affects mundane situations in the predominantly white suburbs of Ohio."

Acknowledgments

This book is a project of the University of Cincinnati's Health Humanities Research Group, a cluster of faculty who collaborate on transdisciplinary scholarship that addresses questions of human health and well-being using humanistic and social-scientific tools and methods. The group is sponsored by the university's Charles Phelps Taft Research Center, and we are very grateful for the center's support and encouragement of this project and of our broader efforts to promote research and community engagement around a broad range of interests, including reproductive health, eugenics, medical ethics, rhetoric of health and medicine, health disparities, trauma, and the allied field of Disability Studies.

This book is freely available in an open access digital edition thanks to Toward an Open Monograph Ecosystem (TOME)—a collaboration of the Association of American Universities, the Association of University Presses, and the Association of Research Libraries—and the generous support of the University of Cincinnati. An oft-repeated maxim in digital humanities says that just because a text is widely available, that does not mean it is broadly accessible. We are deeply grateful to our copy editor, Mary Elizabeth Strunk, for helping make the writing across the whole volume clearer and more compelling. Finally, a big thanks to Taraneh Wilkinson for indexing the book and to our research assistants, Annie McGhee, Katherine Ranum, and Sarah Bostic, for their help with sundry projects along its way to completion.

Introduction | COVID's First Wave in Ohio

National Trends and Local Realities

Vanessa Carbonell, Katherine Sorrels, Danielle Bessett, Lora Arduser, Edward V. Wallace, and Michelle L. McGowan

> We have been attacked. We've been attacked by this virus, and we're asking our fellow citizens to do extraordinary acts. We're asking them—each one—to do something, each one to do the distancing, where we're pulling apart, we are asking people to make the sacrifice, don't go on that spring break, don't get on that airplane, don't do all the things we normally do, don't go to the pub, don't go to the bar, don't go to the restaurant, and each one of us is making those sacrifices. And just as in a time of war, where we have been hit by a foreign country, we have been attacked by this virus, we have to pull together [...] We have it within ourselves in making small decisions, seemingly small decisions, to impact human life. We have it within ourselves to stop it from spreading from one human being to another.
>
> —Ohio Governor Mike DeWine, Coronavirus News Conference, March 19, 2020 (DeWine 2020, 3:10)

In early March of 2020, Americans watched with uncertain terror as the "novel coronavirus" pandemic unfolded in the coastal cities of Seattle and Boston as well as around the world. No one in the heartland state of Ohio had been infected—as far as we knew, given the scarcity of tests. One week later, on March 9, Ohio announced its first confirmed cases of the disease we now call "COVID-19" or just "COVID." Only one year later, the state's case count was nearly one million and over 18,000 Ohioans had lost their lives (Ohio Department of Health 2020a). In 2022, as this volume goes to press, the pandemic drags on: vaccines battle variants across the globe while death counts continue to tick up. What happened over the course of that first pandemic year is not only a story of a public health disaster, but also a story of social disparities and moral dilemmas, of lives and livelihoods turned upside down, and of institutions and safety nets stretched to their limits.

This volume tells the human story of COVID in Ohio, America's "bellwether" state. The volume was conceived in our Health Humanities Research Group, a project of the Taft Research Center at the University of Cincinnati. We are six scholars housed in six different academic departments: History, Philosophy, Sociology, English, Africana Studies, and Women's, Gender, and Sexuality Studies. Individually, we study issues of human health and well-being using the tools of our respective disciplines. Together, we collaborate across our disciplines to shed new light on complex problems. There is much discipline-based research on COVID that advances the state of knowledge in particular fields. While this is valuable, it is not our aim. Although our group happily includes empirical social scientists along with humanists, we see this project as falling within the interdisciplinary field known as *Health Humanities*. The book, like the field of Health Humanities itself, takes an approach to human health and well-being that is "inclusive, outward-facing, and applied" (Crawford et al. 2010).

Reflecting on our roles as researchers at a public university in the middle of a catastrophic public health event, we see this volume as an opportunity to bring together diverse voices and make their perspectives accessible, at no financial cost, to a wide audience within and beyond Ohio. The book is therefore not only an example of Health Humanities but also *Public Humanities*. It features work that is "collaborative and relational, political and personal, happening in public and producing new understandings for the humanities" (Smulyan 2020: 1). To this end, we issued a call for proposals that encouraged a wide range of responses from within and outside academia. Our contributors all lived or worked in Ohio when COVID-19 hit, but they are not all professional scholars or researchers. They include activists, educators, health-care workers, and students. Among them are an intensive care unit (ICU) physician on the front lines (Ginsberg, this volume), a high school math teacher leading a school for newly arrived immigrants (Richter, this volume), a young poet facing an uptick in anti-Asian racism (Jasina, this volume), a woman whose parents were both dying in the same hospital during the worst of COVID (Fitzpatrick, this volume), and a man who faced the first wave of the virus while incarcerated in an Ohio prison (Lanphier and Behne, this volume).

This book is an attempt to *record* and to *make sense of* what happened in Ohio during the first year or so of the pandemic. Our contributors do not write with a single unified voice, nor argue for a single unified thesis. Likewise, our chapters do not all take one form: some present original scholarly research or analysis, some take the form of shorter personal reflections, and a few take a hybrid approach; we have marked chapters as *research* or *reflection* (or both) to help readers navigate the volume. Several of the research chapters also incorporate interviews or focus groups, allowing us to capture the experiences of Ohioans in their own words. These include people seeking abortion care (Gyuras et al., this volume), high school students recently arrived from Central America (Richter, this volume), and physicians confronting local health disparities (Wallace, this volume). The volume's Afterword is an interview with the state's former health director, Dr. Amy Acton, who played a central role in Ohio's early pandemic response.

Despite its wide scope and diversity of perspectives, two related themes tie this volume together: how the pandemic exacerbated social inequalities, and how it revealed a deep tension between individual autonomy and the collective good. Or, put another way, our contributors focus our attention on the friction between freedom and compassion. This friction is intimately connected to social inequality, in the sense that the harms of this pandemic fell disproportionately on people of color, people with disabilities, people living in poverty, and essential workers. Therefore, every choice—whether personal or political—to strike a particular balance between individual autonomy and the collective good is also a choice to place more or less of a burden on already marginalized groups. When we lean more toward freedom than toward compassion, we add burdens for some groups, even as we may relieve burdens for others. In this way, the pandemic forced policy makers, leaders, and even families to balance public health protections against dearly held ways of life. Ohio proved to be an early laboratory for testing out those balances, and an important case study for understanding trends that later played out nationally.

Tensions over individual autonomy and collective good unfolded simultaneously on two levels: the general (statewide, political, abstract) and the particular (local, personal, concrete). At the general level, Ohio initially stood out as a leader in its pandemic response, but soon became embroiled in conflicts over values and became a site of backlash and backtracking. But as much as we can learn from this general arc, we also have much to learn from the particular experiences of individuals and communities living through this turmoil. As Mary Fissell et al. point out, "pandemics are global phenomena, but they are lived locally" (Fissell et al. 2020, 546). The story of Ohio during COVID is really the sum of many smaller stories—teachers adjusting lesson plans on the fly, families struggling to support loved ones from afar, physicians battling to keep patients alive, health-care leaders facing unprecedented strains on institutions, policy makers trying to balance competing interests, and more.

We have tried to capture this contrast of scale—between the general and the particular—by dividing the book into two parts. Part 1, Values in Conflict: Policy, Politics, and Ethics, consists of chapters that zoom out to address high-level questions about how to balance individual and collective interests, showing how this balance is reflected in policy choices. In Part 2, Left Behind: Communities and Individuals under Stress, our contributors zoom in to address the particular challenges, conflicts, and experiences that arose in different corners of Ohio or affected specific groups. The line dividing the sections is of course blurry, as many of our chapters reveal how moral and policy-related questions and the individual experiences of the people and groups affected by those policies shape and are shaped by each other. Nevertheless, the division offers a useful framework, grouping together the main threads of debate on big policy questions without losing sight of their consequences on the ground.

What all our contributions have in common is a focus on the pandemic's toll *in Ohio* during the first and middle phases of the pandemic, roughly March 2020 through summer of 2021. Readers might naturally ask, why a book about *Ohio,* of all places? In what follows we dig deeper into why we think the state presents such an important opportunity for understanding the pandemic. We then offer additional background about public health, conflicting values, and moral principles that we think will help readers contextualize the volume's chapters.

Why Ohio?

As the virus quickly moved across the United States in 2020, state leaders made difficult decisions about how to respond without coordinated federal guidance. States were, in fact, effectively *abandoned* by the federal government, despite its responsibility for nationwide disaster response (Willison et al. 2021). The need to maintain balanced budgets without federal assistance meant that state governments were thrown into a fiscal crisis on top of a health crisis (Singer et al. 2021). All this unfolded while the virus was still an unseen, lurking menace in the Midwest, and when state leaders were still in a position to reassure citizens that they might actually be able to control it. In Ohio, Governor Mike DeWine reported the state's first three cases of COVID-19 in the Cleveland area: a couple who had returned from a Nile River cruise and a man who had returned from a conference in Washington, DC, a now-infamous super-spreader event (Enquirer 2020). Acting on advice from Dr. Amy Acton, the state's director of health, Governor DeWine declared a state of emergency that same day. Dr. Acton issued one of the strictest stay-at-home orders in the nation, and Governor DeWine rallied Ohioans to make wartime sacrifices to beat this "foreign" enemy.

As mentioned above, Ohio was seen as an early leader in its proactive efforts to curb the spread of COVID-19, with "flattening the curve" becoming a recurring theme in Governor DeWine and Dr. Acton's daily televised briefings. The stay-at-home order, social distancing guidelines, K–12 school closings, and statewide mask mandate ushered in debates that dominated expert and popular discourse in the state. One year later, those debates circled around the relaxation of that guidance and the reopening of the state. Vaccines became widely available in 2021 but were also fiercely resisted by many in Ohio and around the United States, even as their scarcity in other parts of the globe left room for new mutant strains to develop. Patience with public health protections wore thin.

By 2022, any lingering solidarity from the pandemic's early stages—any sense that together, we would ride this out—had given way to dizzying waves of optimism and pessimism as cases ebbed and flowed and scientists tracked and assessed new subvariants in the Omicron era. The goalposts shifted from eliminating COVID-19 to finding ways to live with it as an endemic disease. Yet progress toward this goal has not been linear, especially as apathy took root. Vaccines and boosters clearly save lives, but new highly contagious strains still threaten to overwhelm communities. The sheer number of cases has caused unprecedented crises within hospitals and long-term care facilities (Diamond 2021). In Ohio, as in other states, the National Guard was mobilized, with soldiers asked to drive ambulances, clean hospital rooms, and even bathe nursing home residents (Bornancin 2021; Jacobs

2021). This apocalyptic scene played out even as many aspects of life that were disrupted earlier in the pandemic, such as K–12 schooling, were returning to something approaching normalcy.

The pandemic continues to reshape Ohioans' daily lives and experience with health-care delivery. COVID itself is not over, and will be with us indefinitely. Those suffering from "long COVID" and those grieving losses will be forever changed. The health-care system will need to accommodate patients with post-viral illnesses and new disabilities, as well as those who deferred care for chronic conditions that worsened during the pandemic. But the pandemic's ripple effects reach much further. It has deepened the state's political divisions and shaped its legal institutions. Dr. Acton, the "white-coated emblem of the state's forceful coronavirus response," received death threats as armed protesters descended on her family's home in May 2020 (Witte 2021; see also Skinner and Poe, this volume). Political pressures mounted, and Dr. Acton ultimately resigned in July 2020. In 2021, the state legislature limited the executive branch's ability to exercise emergency powers to manage this and future pandemics (Pepper 2021). DeWine and Acton were far from alone in receiving such pushback—that spring, "practically every state [had] at least one measure targeting a governor, either in a legislative committee or in the lawbooks" (Wines 2021). The pandemic also exacerbated anti-Asian racism in Ohio and across the country and brought long-standing health disparities into sharp relief at a time of heightened racial tensions (Richardson 2021). Anti-Chinese racism, in particular, was hardly new, but as Tyler Reny and Matt Barreto have shown, from the pandemic's earliest days, President Donald Trump and influential conservatives intentionally *activated* this prejudice in a distressingly successful effort to link COVID with ostensibly threatening "foreigners" in the public imagination (Reny and Barretto 2022; see also Jardina 2019).

Ohio is not only a fitting point of comparison for other regions but a natural microcosm for the country writ large, especially given its long-standing reputation as a bellwether, a swing state, and, let's face it, a rather *generic* place. Ohio represents a geographic gray zone between neighboring states more easily identifiable as "Eastern" (Pennsylvania), "Southern" (Kentucky), "Appalachian" (West Virginia), and "Midwestern" (Indiana and Michigan). Readers may dispute these classifications, but no one can dispute that Ohio represents the merging of these different regions. Historically, Ohio represented a boundary state between North and South, with its southern boundary defined by the Ohio River. The river demarcated free states from slave states prior to the Civil War and can be considered a westward extension of the original Mason–Dixon line. Like all such boundaries, though, it was a porous one. Major institutions in the southern border city of Cincinnati, for example—including our employer, the University of Cincinnati—were founded or shaped by slaveholders.

Ohio and Ohioans are not famous for any specific, *distinctively Ohioan* characteristics so much as for the lack of such characteristics, which can make the state seem like an especially good model of Midwestern and even American culture more broadly. Politically, it is solidly purple, resembling neither the coastal "blue states" nor the southern "red states." While no longer considered a swing state or a reliable predictor of presidential elections (Fahey 2021; Rothenberg 2022), the state's voters have swung between parties in national elections in recent decades, voting for George W. Bush in 2000 and 2004, for Barack Obama in 2008 and 2012, then for Donald Trump in 2016 and 2020. Constrained by gerrymandering, the recent trend is clearly rightward, with Republicans holding all state-level elected offices and maintaining strong majorities in the state Senate and House of Representatives.

Ohio is neither predominantly rural nor especially urban, but displays a mix of both extremes (and everything in between). It has three major metropolitan areas with over two million residents each: Cleveland, Columbus, and Cincinnati. It says something about Ohio's generic nature that many Americans probably have little sense for what differentiates these three "C" cities, and likely could not point to them on a map. This underscores our point that Ohio is a worthy case study—not because it is distinctive, but because it is representative. It has much in common with a variety of other states, and it tends to exhibit trends that are playing out on a national scale, including, for example, the recent move toward populism and extremism (Adolph et al. 2021; Gray 2021), the influence of Trumpism on local Republican politics (Berman 2022), and the movement to use state legislatures and local politics to restrict abortion rights (Pepper 2021). Ohio got its reputation as a bellwether when it was a swing state in an America where the prevailing force in the political economy was centripetal; it remains a bellwether today, as a purple state, in a political economy pulled by ever strengthening centrifugal forces. As Jacob Grumbach et al. succinctly put it, "there are not just fewer swing-voters; there are fewer swing places" (Grumbach et al. 2022: 210). At the same time, though—and this is relevant to our volume's special focus on social disparities—Ohio is becoming less and less representative of the country's demographics as a whole as the nation becomes more racially and ethnically diverse. Ohio is most certainly *not* a front-runner when it comes to social progress; it represents, instead, a somewhat retrograde or regressive idea of American normalcy, the mythical "real America" so often contrasted with coastal cities in political discourse. Ohioan normalcy, personified in Governor Mike DeWine, has been tested by the political trends of the Trump era, and by the pandemic itself.

DeWine has been described as "the last of the establishment Republicans" (Berman 2022). At age 75, he is amiable and courteous, a throwback to an era where politicians heeded norms of decorum and progressed along linear career paths of increasing responsibility. Before being elected governor, he was a county prosecutor, state senator, lieutenant governor, US senator, and state attorney general. His policy positions are unequivocally conservative but also strategic: "going as far right as necessary—but no further—to win and stay in office" (Berman 2022). At least until recently, his reputation as a reasonable person made him someone both Republicans and Democrats could trust, even when they disagreed with him. And so when the pandemic hit, Ohioans turned to DeWine for guidance and comfort, and he responded with public health protections that—while they may seem progressive in retrospect—he framed at the time as simply a matter of common sense. For a window of time in 2020, before COVID protections had become irreparably politicized, DeWine was the perfect messenger for the quaint notion that commonsense public health measures are something we can all agree on. "We are all in this together" was the comforting motto of the moment, and Ohio was the perfect setting in which to test out Midwestern ideals of neighborly care and caution. (For more on this, see Ayers, this volume; Spelman, this volume; and Skinner and Poe, this volume.)

But the atmosphere of neighborly care and caution did not last long. As alluded to above, DeWine would face pushback from both his constituents and his party, and his proactive response to the early phase of the pandemic would ultimately fizzle out. He backtracked, but not quickly enough to prevent all political damage. In the 2022 gubernatorial race, he faced primary challengers from the right who tried to get voters to "punish DeWine for the sin of believing in science" (Berman 2022). He prevailed, but "establishment Republicans" like DeWine must contend with the far-right forces within their party that are moving aggressively to take over offices and manipulate voting maps (Levine 2022). If it seemed initially like Ohio would be a leader in pandemic management, ultimately the state regressed to the mean: "Ohio now sits in the middle of the pack on metrics such as cases, deaths, and vaccinations" (Berman 2022).

Once again Ohio reflects, and is influenced by, broader social and economic currents in the United States. It is, in many ways, a state divided, just as the nation is divided. Hit hard by deindustrialization and the erosion of unionized jobs, urban and suburban counties continue to draw Ohioans as populations in rural counties decline (Associated Press 2021). Ohio's rural counties also suffer from the kind of disinvestment that characterizes too many other states: lower educational attainment, more limited job opportunities, and underinvestment in social services and health-care infrastructure (Ohio Department of Higher Education 2019). Ohio's political landscape displays the increased polarization seen across the country and particularly the Midwest: although Ohioans count themselves as Republicans and Democrats in almost equal numbers, more conservative Republican lawmakers have come to dominate the state legislature through gerrymandered voting maps (Pew Research Center 2015; Exner 2019; Levine 2022).

Some of the worst inequities in the United States also show up in Ohio, such as growing income inequality: an analysis of tax filings found that the top 1 percent of Ohio households earned 18.6 times as much as the remaining 99 percent in 2015 (McNichol et al. 2012; Sommeiller and Price 2018). Thirteen percent of Ohio households were living in poverty as of 2019 (US Census Bureau n.d.). Thus, when COVID-19 landed in Ohio, it found a state with marked inequalities and contradictions with respect to health care and public health. Ohio, like other states, has serious problems with health disparities across social groups. Poverty, discrimination, pollution, food deserts, and inadequate safety net programs mean that many Ohioans either lack access to adequate health care or are more likely to have poor outcomes despite the care they do receive. Measures of population health for Ohioans, such as life expectancy, infant mortality, and rates of chronic illness, tend to be worse than the national average (Kaiser Family Foundation 2014). Ohio was—and is—one of the states most severely affected by the opioid epidemic (Skinner and Franz 2019).

As in other Midwestern states, Black residents of Ohio have a considerably lower median wage than whites (Gordon 2019). As the Health Policy Institute of Ohio concluded in 2021, "Racist and discriminatory policies, systems and beliefs unfairly limit Black Ohioans' access to resources, representation and opportunity and result in, for example: disproportionate incarceration; residential segregation; and discrimination within the healthcare system" (Aly, Stevens, and Reat 2021, 15). These inequities result in jarring health outcomes: just as Ohioans in general do worse than the national average on these measures, Black Ohioans in particular experience higher rates of premature death, infant mortality, and chronic health conditions such as diabetes and prostate cancer (Aly, Stevens, and Reat 2021; Ohio Department of Health 2020b).

And yet at the same time, Ohio is home to the Cleveland Clinic, one of the most renowned health-care institutions in the world, destination for patients and clinicians alike, and the state's largest employer. Indeed, health-care institutions in the northeast corner of Ohio banded together during the first year of the pandemic to form public–private partnerships for responding to the emergency, and later collaborated to seek federal grants for research on COVID-19 and "long COVID." Such collaborations included eminent private institutions like the Cleveland Clinic and Case Western Reserve University alongside the public safety net system, MetroHealth, and the Louis Stokes Cleveland VA Medical Center (University Hospitals 2021; Boggs 2021).

Ohio is also home to many governmental and nongovernmental organizations working to improve public health. In 2019, Governor DeWine appointed a Democrat and ardent public health advocate, Dr. Amy Acton, to be the state's health director, a bold choice for a politicized position that had most recently been held by officials without medical or public health training. When the COVID crisis arrived in 2020, Ohio was unlike many other Republican-controlled states insofar as its governor was so willing to lean into the expertise of a strong health department director. Appearing together on television almost every day, DeWine and Acton received national press coverage for their calm, competent leadership (Witte 2020; Dosani and Westbrook 2020; Skinner and Poe, this volume). But what at first appeared to be a success story soon morphed into a cautionary tale. Ohio was not only a proving ground for public health emergency orders, but a harbinger for the backlash they would ultimately engender elsewhere (Witte 2020; Goldstein 2021). To understand how what happened in Ohio fits into the national context, we need to step back and look at the broader landscape of health care and public health in the United States.

Where Did Health Care and Public Health Stand in the United States When COVID-19 Hit?

As American readers will be aware, both health care and public health are decentralized in the United States. With a few exceptions, notably care for Native Americans, active military, veterans, and the elderly, the federal government does not provide, pay for, or manage health care or public health. Even the federal safety net health insurance program, Medicaid, is administered by states, often via private companies, leaving wide variation in eligibility and services from one state to another. While the health-care system itself is not the focus of this volume, the injustice and dysfunction that existed in the system prior to COVID-19 foreshadowed and worsened the challenges that would emerge when the pandemic arrived. Getting access to adequate health care, and paying for it, were already very challenging for many Americans in the "Before Times." Well-documented health disparities already existed along every axis of social inequality and disadvantage. With a deadly, highly contagious disease bringing the health-care system to its knees, and with no nationally centralized response or infrastructure, we should not be surprised that problems arose with the availability of testing and treatment, with communication of vital public health information to the public, with downstream effects on routine care, and eventually with hospital staff burnout and turnover resulting in the loss of clinical expertise (Yong 2021c).

While the clinical health-care system struggled, the *public health* system—a largely separate and underfunded web of public services—fared even worse. Within this broad arena, pandemic prevention or management alone involves more than twenty-one agencies and more than one hundred offices at the federal level (Wallace and Sharfstein 2022). Chief among them are the Centers for Disease Control and Prevention (CDC), the agency responsible for public health, and the Food and Drug Administration (FDA), the agency responsible for regulating diagnostic tests, drugs, and devices. The CDC, while often considered a leader among national public health agencies, is famously slow-moving and bureaucratic. Oriented toward producing research based on gold standard evidence, it was not resourced or prepared to act quickly and decisively in the complicated political environment of the year 2020 (Lewis 2021; Banco 2021).

And while the CDC can make recommendations and communicate knowledge, it has little legal authority to regulate what happens in state and local jurisdictions. Each state's department of health was left to follow—or not follow—the CDC's recommendations in setting statewide policies. Each local jurisdiction—county or city—was left to implement and enforce those policies—or not (Wallace and Sharfstein 2022). Governors and state health directors, often responsible for populations the size of entire nations, found themselves not only without adequate assistance from the federal government, but sometimes in active competition with it for supplies, or undermined by contradictory messaging coming from the White House. Failures of leadership at the federal level all but ensured failures at the state level (Singer et al. 2021).

Well before the COVID-19 pandemic, public health in the United States was chronically underresourced. Journalist Ed Yong, whose dogged chronicling of the pandemic won the Pulitzer Prize for explanatory reporting, put it this way: the public health system, "with its overstretched staff, meager budgets, crumbling buildings, and archaic equipment, could barely cope with sickness as usual, let alone with a new, fast-spreading virus" (Yong 2021b). As mentioned earlier, this crisis was exacerbated by the federal government's abandonment of states and the need for states to limit their services to only what could be provided without running a deficit. But in Yong's telling, the problems trace back more than a century. Advancements in the scientific understanding of infectious disease in the early twentieth century led the field of public health to turn away from social reform and toward individualistic models of responsibility for disease. Resistance to social reforms and to public health as activism was strengthened by anti-communist sentiment in the wake of World War II. The field of public health became overshadowed by medicine and turned away from ambitious reform projects. The public health workforce was most recently decimated by the 2008 recession, and it initially got smaller, not bigger, when the pandemic hit. "When COVID-19 arrived, the economic downturn forced overstretched departments to furlough more employees. When states needed battalions of public-health workers to find infected people and trace their contacts, they had to hire and train people from scratch" (Yong 2020a).

The federal government eventually increased aid to states for public health in response to the pandemic. However, because the aid is temporary, states are using it for one-time needs like equipment, rather than to hire the long-term staff who were already needed before the pandemic began, are sorely needed now, and will be needed when the next pandemic hits. According to a detailed report in *The New York*

Times, the pandemic forced more than 220 local health departments to stop providing some of their bread-and-butter services related to ongoing public health crises, such as the opioid epidemic or sexually transmitted diseases (Baker and Ivory 2021). After more than two years of making the pandemic our most urgent priority, we are accumulating a backlog of unmet needs that bode ill for public health in the future. And alongside these long-term health casualties caused by COVID-19 is the "long-haul" version of COVID-19 itself. Emerging research on the extent and severity of chronic cardiovascular problems and mental health issues is alarming (Nordenberg 2022). Particularly distressing are the casualties among those who suffered and died before doctors took patient complaints seriously and research demonstrated the severity of their condition (Güthe 2022).

How Did COVID Reveal a Conflict of Values?

Public health in the United States is not just fragmented and underfunded. It is also, now more than ever, the site where American values are coming into intense, sometimes even violent, conflict. On one side is the cherished value of individual freedom, along with its economic counterpart, the free market. On the other is the collective good, encompassing individual and community health and welfare, and the associated web of moral and social ties we have to each other, including widely shared imperatives to help, or at least not to harm, our neighbors. Modern welfare states like the United States strive to protect both values—freedom and well-being. When the two conflict, leaders must make policy choices that, by necessity, involve trade-offs between them, and are bound to anger partisans of one or the other value.

Public health policies bring these trade-offs into stark relief. There are few greater threats to individual and collective well-being than death. And there are few greater threats to freedom than mandatory quarantine—the restriction of one's freedom of movement and association, including confinement to one's home or even to a designated facility. Early in the pandemic, Americans watched television footage of draconian measures in Wuhan, China, where businesses were shuttered, highways left empty of all vehicles but ambulances, neighborhoods and villages cordoned off, and residents locked in apartment buildings to prevent the spread of the virus. It seemed that nothing as severe—and effective—as those measures could possibly be implemented in the United States, where individual freedom is sacred and individual states have enormous leeway to govern independently of the federal government.

Nevertheless, it turned out that even measures *far short* of what other countries imposed to curb the spread of COVID-19 proved more than our fragile republic could handle without fracturing. "Stay-at-home" orders were met with vociferous protest—despite exceptions allowing people to go to work in essential jobs, to shop, to visit family, to seek medical care or food, and so on. Next it was mask mandates—variously established and enforced by states, cities, businesses, and schools—that generated intense controversy (see Spelman, this volume). Then came vaccine mandates, first in health-care organizations, then universities, then public and private workplaces. As each public health initiative became politicized, resentment and backlash grew, and social fractures widened. What we owe to each other and who should (or could) decide eluded a uniform organizing logic, making the job of public health officials all the more difficult.

Resistance to public health protections is not new (more on this below). Nor can it be isolated from broader political currents and social fractures. We have argued that a central thread in the narrative of the pandemic, in the Midwest and across the United States more broadly, was a tension between the individual and the collective, between freedom and safety. This tension manifests itself in disagreements over the proper role of government in our private lives. As states have moved toward Republican control, support for government provision of services has predictably waned, and public health measures are no exception to this trend (Adolph et al. 2021). Indeed, we are now seeing a wave of legislation aimed at limiting the authority of state and local public health officials. More than one hundred new laws have been passed around the country, including in Ohio, that allow elected officials to limit or overrule health orders put in place by public health authorities (Baker and Ivory 2021). The cruel irony is that despite all the lessons learned from this pandemic, state and local officials will emerge *less* well prepared to address the next pandemic. This fact is hard to deny in 2022 as a new monkeypox outbreak spreads exponentially. Already, problems with the availability of tests, vaccines, and treatments for this pathogen bring forth an eerie déjà vu of the shambolic early COVID days (Mazer 2022). And since COVID isn't over, strained public health officials must now bear the burden of monkeypox response *on top of* a raging respiratory pandemic.

A further unintended consequence of this wave of legislation is that health departments may face challenges in controlling other communicable diseases that were long managed with public health measures that drew little notice. In Ohio, routine childhood vaccine mandates may be the next casualty: the state legislature is considering a bill that would ban schools and employers from requiring any vaccine. Governor DeWine has said he plans to veto it—not because of the threat to public health, but on the grounds that it would be a governmental overreach into private business (Hancock 2021).

The pandemic has also revealed how our sense of collective good is challenged by deep social schisms including racism and xenophobia. From the earliest days of the pandemic, those harboring long-simmering anti-Asian sentiments latched onto the virus's "foreignness" and made Asian Americans scapegoats and targets of violent attacks. Xenophobic rhetoric was stoked by some in the media, and by government leaders including President Trump himself (Reny and Barreto 2022). By May 2020, protests against discriminatory (and specifically anti-Black) law enforcement and police violence, first in Minneapolis and then across the country, revealed that many Americans were willing to risk contagion in order to register their dissent against structural violence that was taking Black lives. But subsequent violence—more victims' names added to memorial lists ("say their names!") and even an attempted insurrection with ties to white nationalist groups—made evident white supremacy's resistance to demands for racial justice.

Racialized violence—and the terror it causes—is itself a public health problem. That such violence called forth massive protests and crowded public gatherings during a respiratory pandemic also raised obvious public health concerns. But the violence and response to it also shape public health in more subtle ways (Pirtle 2020). As sociologist Harvey Molotch (2006) observed of Hurricane Katrina, anti-Black racism stunted rescue efforts by limiting bureaucrats' empathy with those who were suffering. Crucially, he argues that even frontline workers prompted to empathy felt constrained from acting on that impulse because they could not trust that others would see any improvisations on policy as justified: "Anything that inhibits empathy for the victims or weakens the assumption that others share it, undermines the likelihood of effective rescue." Racism threatens our social solidarity and our sense of collective good.

Again, what happens in Ohio mirrors and responds to national trends. We have highlighted some features of that broader context: systemic racism; a decentralized, dysfunctional, and largely for-profit health-care system; a fragmented and underfunded public health infrastructure; a lack of coordination between federal and state and local authorities; clashes over racial justice; and a highly politicized resistance movement borne of deep conflicts between freedom and other public goods. But while the political, legal, and social context is crucial, we think it is also important to recognize that the pandemic presented our society—and its leaders—with a series of *moral* tests.

What Makes COVID a *Moral* Issue?

Decisions about how best to balance freedom and health, or about how to balance an individual's well-being against the greater good, or about how to reconcile the harms prevented by a policy with the harms caused by it, are fundamentally moral decisions. Several of our contributors examine these moral decisions as they manifested in statewide policy debates (Spelman; Ayers; Lanphier and Behne; Gyuras et al., all in this volume), in health-care institutions (Ahmad et al.; Ginsberg; Aultman et al.; and Fitzpatrick, this volume), and in schools (Richter, this volume). To better contextualize these ethical analyses, we take a moment here to dive a little deeper into the moral principles at work. Although the United States is a pluralistic society where citizens often disagree about values, health-care ethicists have proposed a core set of moral guidelines around which there is reasonable consensus. One classical account presents four principles: protection of the patient's rights and choices (autonomy); prohibition on causing unnecessary harm (non-maleficence); promotion of the patient's well-being (beneficence); and fairness in the distribution of resources, risks, costs, and benefits (justice) (Beauchamp and Childress 2019).

The principles serve to guide deliberation, but often conflict with another. There is no algorithmic method for applying these principles to a difficult moral dilemma; some dilemmas require fine-grained contextual analysis, and some conflicts of values simply cannot be reconciled. It is easy to see from these principles alone why the pandemic presented us with so many moral questions. Protecting autonomy means honoring a competent patient's right to refuse medical treatment and to decide for herself what preventive measures to take. But if enough patients refuse a recommended vaccine, thereby spreading the disease and overcrowding hospitals, then health-care providers will struggle to uphold their duty to keep other people safe and well (beneficence). Likewise, the principle of non-maleficence would normally prohibit any intentional departure from the (pre-pandemic) standard of care, if that change would harm the patient—for example, we must give patients on ventilators adequate doses of sedatives to keep them free of pain or discomfort.

But when resources—such as sedatives—become scarce, the principle of justice requires that we distribute them fairly, which may mean depriving some patients of drugs in order to help others. In the first year of the pandemic, shortages were common: initially of masks, gowns, gloves, hand sanitizer, testing supplies, ventilators, and convalescent plasma; later, of oxygen, vaccines, monoclonal antibodies, sedatives, and antiviral drugs. Even dialysis machines, ECMO machines, and the well-trained staff to operate them were in short supply. These shortages presented very real tests for the principles of justice and non-maleficence. Fortunately, in many states the rationing rules hastily drawn up by officials to determine who would get a ventilator never needed to be implemented. But clinicians did have to find ways to do more with less, and many were faced with impossible choices (Kisner 2021).

These moral conflicts are thorny in the case of medicine (see Ahmad et al.; Aultman, Birnbaum, and Garchar; Ayers; and Ginsberg, all in this volume). Matters are even more complicated in the context of public health (Bayer and Fairchild 2004). Traditionally, public health has developed as a separate discipline from medicine. Its goal is not the treatment or cure of an individual's disease but the prevention of disease and promotion of health in the community at large. Since public health happens in the community, where health is just one aspect of people's messy, busy lives, it must reckon more directly with the social, political, and economic background conditions that bear on illness and wellness. This is especially true in the case of a highly contagious respiratory disease, as we must all share the same air in our housing, in our workplaces, on public transportation, in grocery stores and airports, and in schools.

Dr. Anthony Fauci put it this way: "you, as an individual, are more than somebody that's just in a vacuum. You are part of a community" (Barbaro 2021). Fauci is now well known as the long-serving director of the National Institute of Allergy and Infectious Disease, chief medical advisor to President Biden, and former member of President Trump's

Coronavirus Task Force. Like Ohio's Dr. Amy Acton, Dr. Fauci became both an icon and a target of vicious attacks during the height of the COVID crisis. But his insight here came not from his expertise in infectious diseases or public health, nor from any ideological commitment to a particular balance between freedom and safety. It is a simple, obvious human insight that has been remarkably underappreciated in this ordeal: *our behavior affects others.* We may think that our individual autonomy permits us to make our own risk-versus-benefit calculations—wearing a mask or not, getting a vaccine or not—but if the only risks and benefits we weigh are our own, we are not only being selfish but we are also being downright irrational, because we are all connected in a complex web of cause and effect.

There is a limit, though, to what we can do as individuals to fight the pandemic. As Governor DeWine observed, triumphing over the virus requires us to "pull together," even as we "pull apart." Early public health campaigns reminded us that we are "all in this together," and the State of Ohio even used celebrity messages to rally Ohioans around the hashtag #InThisTogetherOhio (Campbell 2020). The pandemic is a collective action problem, and we need central authorities, or at least trusted guides, to help us coordinate our behavior for the benefit of all. This is a tall order in a time and place where the populace is already deeply divided and mistrustful of authorities. Americans, after all, are famous for rugged individualism. And yet, protests over public health restrictions have been prevalent in many democratic countries during the pandemic, including even Scandinavian countries where collectivist values and robust social welfare programs are broadly accepted. And such protests are neither new nor unique to this moment in time. Indeed, such resistance to public health measures has been a feature of pandemics throughout history (Loomis 2018).

Why Do People Resist Public Health Protections?

A century ago, these same conflicts played out across the world during the 1918 influenza pandemic. In her book *Pale Rider,* Laura Spinney writes,

> Quarantine and other disease-containment strategies place the interests of the collective over those of the individual. When the collective is very large [...] those strategies have to be imposed in a top-down fashion. [...] The competing interests of the collective

> are the reason that historian Alfred Crosby, who told the story of the flu in America, argued that democracy was unhelpful in a pandemic. The demands of national security, a thriving economy and public health are rarely aligned, and elected representatives defending the first two undermine the third, simply by doing their job. In France, for example, powerful bodies including the Ministry of the Interior and the Academy of Medicine ordered the closure of theaters, cinemas, churches and markets, but this rarely happened, because prefects in the French departments didn't enforce the measures "for fear of annoying the public." (Spinney 2017, 98–99)

To say that the public will be "annoyed" surely understates the problem, as we have now seen public health officials receiving death threats and harassment at their homes, armed protests in state capitals, and even a plot to kidnap the governor of Michigan (Gray 2021). These acts of violence are part of larger trends toward far-right, anti-government, and antidemocratic extremism playing out across the Midwest and the nation more broadly, culminating most dramatically in the attempted coup on January 6, 2021. Such protests, therefore, should not be taken entirely at face value: they are more akin to domestic terrorism than to the mere expressions of "annoyance" Spinney refers to. And with powerful interests providing financial backing, they are not necessarily even sincere expressions of the people's attitudes toward public health measures (Stanley-Becker and Romm 2020).

That said, setting aside the cases of violent extremism, some who chafed at public health measures or declared themselves "over COVID" had legitimate grievances against rules that seemed hastily thrown together, inconsistently enforced, or inadequately explained. Others were simply victims of the fundamental trade-off we have discussed: some measures will necessarily make certain individuals worse off even as they protect other individuals and make the collective better off as a whole. Some people lost their livelihoods when industries shuttered. Families were separated. Surgeries were postponed. Many parents were stretched to their breaking points trying to balance their children's remote schooling and childcare closures with their own jobs. Adults and children alike experienced extraordinary stress, and mental health suffered (Yong 2021a).

As Spinney mentions, Alfred Crosby claimed that democracy is a hindrance to managing a public health crisis. This is a tempting diagnosis, as is the more specific claim that federalism—in which individual states are largely self-governing—is a hindrance. To be sure, the ability of states to make their own rules about public health, while people move between states carrying a contagious virus, has been a source of frustration and confusion throughout the pandemic. Disaster response is one area where the federal government is supposed to take charge (Willison et al. 2022). During the first wave, the Trump administration instead took a hard federalist line, abandoning states for several months (Singer et al. 2021), and giving the impression that the administration's failures were therefore traceable to states' actions (or inaction). Ohio was praised for its public health response early in the pandemic, but later criticized for abandoning or even tying the hands of local authorities (Goldstein 2021; Calcaterra 2021).

In her book *Democracy in the Time of Coronavirus,* political theorist Danielle Allen argues that, properly understood and implemented, federalism can be an asset in a crisis (Allen 2021). Contagious diseases are easier to control in smaller, bounded geographic areas, such as counties and states, as long as we have good understanding of the networks that bring people together and generate transmission. In a well-functioning democracy, a good federalist response would require that we focus not on the separateness of states but on harmonizing the ties that bind states together, and on mustering the resources of the federal government to coordinate action among them. Germany and Australia are examples of countries that did this well.

In Allen's telling, one reason the United States has been unable to muster a successful coordinated response to the pandemic is that fractures in our democracy have left us without a crucial civic virtue—solidarity. "Solidarity is the resource that enables people to make small sacrifices of liberty so as to avoid harm to others with whom they have a social bond" (Allen 2021, xii). Without solidarity, people succumb to fear in the face of existential threats, and the social contract breaks down. (Ginsberg, in this volume, discusses how this breakdown of the social contract manifests in the life and death drama of an ICU.) Instead of asking how we can act cooperatively to care for our fellow citizens, and trusting our governmental institutions to coordinate our actions, we find ourselves focused on our individual risks and needs.

Allen traces our inability to pull together in this crisis to a "dark truth" that predates the pandemic: "We don't know, in conditions of emergency, that we will be OK together" (2021, 89). She lists the people who were abandoned in the early stages of the pandemic: the elderly, essential workers, the young, African American and Hispanic/Latinx Americans, rural Americans, and, we would add, disabled Americans. Patterns of abandonment mirror long-standing social, economic, and racial inequities, as we discussed earlier in this introduction. In other words, social bonds of solidarity, necessary for a successful crisis response in a democracy, had long been severed.

To be fair, coordinated action requires a shared factual understanding of what is happening, and public health authorities did not always do a good job communicating evolving scientific information, leaving the public to seek information through anecdote or social media. Restrictions that are hard to bear will be even harder if one doesn't understand or accept the justification for them, or if one doesn't trust the people charged with disseminating the information about them. And both history and current events offer ample cases that explain why trust can be hard to win. Public health authorities have been complicit in enabling unchecked state power both in instances when governments have chosen to censor news vital to public health during pandemics (Sivaramakrishnan 2020) and, conversely, when they have used pandemics as a pretext for pursuing unrelated political ends (Serhan 2020). The well of shared understanding has been further poisoned in our own moment by bad actors spreading misinformation, either for profit or to serve political ends. Vaccine scientist Dr. Peter Hotez has argued that the (pre-COVID-era) anti-vaccine movement and the resistance to public health measures during the pandemic are all part of a broader "anti-science" agenda that is organized, well funded, and aggressively predatory (Hotez 2021, 119–124). We ignore this resistance movement at our peril.

Of course, not everyone who grumbled at public health measures did so out of libertarian ideology, anti-science aggression, or broader skepticism of government overreach. Some people simply felt that the risk of catching or spreading the virus was being overestimated while the social and economic costs of shutdowns were underestimated. To be sure, the costs of shutdowns for Americans' mental health and students' learning may not be fully known for years. And it is true that in some phases of the pandemic, risks were lower in small towns and counties, because the virus did not disperse evenly throughout the whole country at the same time. Even as the CDC was trying to make recommendations that would apply everywhere, different regions, states, and even cities experienced very different situations over time.

Moreover, even within a geographic area, the virus has not spread evenly but in random spurts, with some cases fizzling out while others become "super-spreaders." As sociologist Zeynep Tufecki argued in *The Atlantic*, the virus (or at least early variants of it) was "overdispersed [...] meaning that it tends to spread in clusters" (Tufecki 2020). Because of this, some people may have heard on the news that the virus was out of control while they went about their lives without encountering anyone who had become ill or died, leading them to wonder if the threat was exaggerated. Some even succumbed to conspiracy theories that the virus was a hoax. Meanwhile, health-care workers lived dissonant double lives, moving between somber overcrowded ICUs and carefree public spaces where mask-less crowds went about their business as usual (Yong 2020b).

Epidemiologists measure contagiousness via the construct "R0" (R-naught), the *average* number of people infected by each host, and the related construct "R", which is the average contagiousness at a particular time given real-world conditions and mitigation efforts. If the average person infects two or three other people, an outbreak will grow exponentially. But as Tufecki has argued, the average contagiousness is a misleading measure if there is high variability in contagiousness from one case or one gathering to another. "There are COVID-19 incidents in which a single person likely infected 80 percent or more of the people in the room in just a few hours. But, at other times, COVID-19 can be surprisingly less contagious. Overdispersion and super-spreading of this virus are found in research across the globe. A growing number of studies estimate that a majority of infected people may not infect a single other person" (Tufecki 2020). While more contagious variants continue to complicate the picture, it remains true that case rates vary widely across our large nation, and that some lines of transmission end abruptly after an effective isolation period, while others run rampant.

This variability—and the fact that travelers and super-spreaders seeded different outbreaks around the country at different times—means that Americans experienced the pandemic in myriad ways. While some *felt* that their lives were being figuratively shut down by government restrictions, others' lives *were* being literally shut down as they or their loved ones fell ill, ended up in the ICU, or even died, a story told with tragic vividness in Angie Fitzpatrick's contribution to this volume. Collectively, the volume's authors capture a broad spectrum of personal experiences and scholarly insights. The theme threaded throughout, the problem underlying so many of the issues that the volume addresses, is social disparities. And little wonder: as Ed Yong wrote, "The coronavirus found, exploited, and widened every inequality that the U.S. had to offer" (Yong 2020a). We know, for example, that Black, Hispanic, and Asian patients have had worse COVID-19 outcomes than white patients (Lopez et al. 2021). We also know that poverty has greatly exacerbated people's vulnerability to the virus, due to factors including crowded housing environments, inability to work from home, and lack of access to affordable health care (Perry, Aronson, and Pescosolido 2021). Throughout the book, our contributors show how inequities and injustices that predated COVID shaped an uneven landscape of suffering. This uneven landscape, as it is lived here, locally, in Ohio, demands to be documented.

A Tragedy and a Teacher

In "How the Pandemic Defeated America," Yong writes, "the pandemic has been both a tragedy and a teacher" (Yong 2020a). But what has it taught us? It is tempting to seek easy lessons, ways we can be more prepared for next time, ways we can improve funding structures, communication strategies, clinical care practices, and so on. Scholar of science and technology studies Sheila Jasanoff warns against such an approach. She has argued that the apt lesson is not that we need to be more prepared, but that we need to be more humble. Preparedness and prediction-centered approaches presume a clear goal and focus on technological knowledge and logistics, such as the efficient mobilization of resources. In so doing, they encourage us to adopt a posture of confidence and control. As Jasanoff (2021) puts it, in the preparedness paradigm, "pandemics are primarily biological and actions fail mainly because science didn't try to know soon enough what we all know we should have known."

Yet such models are not good at accounting for "intangible and volatile" concepts and variables—precisely the problems of political polarization, social disparities, poverty, and distrust of science and organized medicine that have undermined Americans' political will to cooperate with public health guidelines and mitigate COVID's consequences for the most vulnerable among us. And these are factors that, though hard to factor in military-style predictive models, were hardly difficult to anticipate as serious obstacles to a successful pandemic response. Jasanoff (2021) says we ought to focus on precaution, with special attention to the "unknown unknowns" and the communities that might be most affected by unforeseen events.

Humility, Jasanoff (2021) writes, "demands that we ask in advance what new vulnerabilities might be produced by our bravest acts of preparedness, in theaters of public health, economy, environment, or war. The technologies of humility would have us reflect longer and harder on the obligations we incur when acting on imperfect knowledge, by adopting the perspectives of those who are acted upon or are themselves not able to intervene." We would extend Jasanoff's argument to suggest that in addition to existing experts shifting their focus and listening to members of marginalized communities, humility requires a kind of deep reflection that draws on a broader and less technocratic body of informed perspectives. As the chapters in this book make clear, the pandemic capitalized on tears and weak spots in our social fabric; we must repair that social fabric, or even the best-laid pandemic preparedness plans will fail us in future plagues. Likewise, we must bolster our democratic institutions so that they can serve us better.

This Volume's Organization

As noted above, this book is organized into two sections: Values in Conflict: Policy, Politics, and Ethics, and Left Behind: Communities and Individuals under Stress. The authors in Part 1 directly examine some of the state-level policy decisions and the political winds shaping the decision makers; the authors in Part 2 focus more on individuals and groups who bore the downstream consequences of those decisions. Each section begins with an introductory synopsis that explains how it tackles the book's main focus and offers a brief overview of its chapters. Both sections include a mix of original research contributions, short reflective pieces written from the first-person perspective, and at least one article that blends the two forms. For example, Part 1 includes a research article on women's reproductive health that features excerpts from interviews with women seeking abortion care during the pandemic, a personal reflection by an ICU doctor, and a blended research and reflection article by an educator who surveys the impact of COVID on students with limited or interrupted formal education and shares her personal perspective on working as a K–12 teacher with newly arrived immigrants. Part 2 contains research on Ohio's rural-versus-urban divide in COVID preparedness, a personal refection by a woman who lost both parents, and a blended research and reflection article about ableism in Ohio's COVID response authored by a disabled scholar of disability studies.

Some themes cut across both sections as we see different perspectives on the same issue. For example, in Part 1 we hear from health-care workers grappling with institutional and clinical decisions about how best to care for the influx of patients in the hospital (Ahmad et al., Ginsberg); in Part 2 we hear from someone whose family members were on the receiving end of that care (Fitzpatrick). Likewise, in Part 1 we learn about the leaders deciding who must work and who must stay home, who would get the first vaccines and who would have to wait (Skinner and Poe, Spelman); in Part 2 we learn about what it was like to be incarcerated during the pandemic, to be both extra vulnerable and perpetually "locked down" (Lanphier and Behne). Each section of the book offers a distinct window into the volume's central themes: tension between individual freedom and the collective good, and the social inequalities that are implicated in every attempt to strike a balance between those values. Together, the two parts illustrate how the topics of health, education, political cultures, disability, poverty, women's rights, and racial justice cannot be isolated from each other in our reckoning with the implications of COVID.

The volume closes with an Afterword in which editors Michelle L. McGowan and Danielle Bessett interview Dr. Amy Acton, who served as director of health for the State of Ohio at the outset of the pandemic and later as public health advisor to the governor of Ohio. As discussed in several chapters in this volume, Dr. Acton played a central role in both the state's response and the public's understanding of the crisis. She was the public face of the pandemic for Ohioans and the leader responsible for signing historic emergency orders. In the interview, she offers a behind-the-scenes look at the state's early decision-making, reflecting on the conflicts and compromises public health leaders were forced to grapple with, and how the lessons learned from this pandemic ought to inform future pandemic readiness and responsiveness.

REFERENCES

Adolph, Christopher, Kenya Amano, Bree Bang-Jensen, Nancy Fullman, and John Wilkerson. 2021. "Pandemic Politics: Timing State-Level Social Distancing Responses to COVID-19." *Journal of Health Politics, Policy and Law* 46, no. 2: 211–233. https://doi.org/10.1215/03616878-8802162.

Allen, Danielle. 2021. *Democracy in the Time of Coronavirus*. Chicago: University of Chicago Press.

Aly, Reem, Amy Bush Stevens, and Zach Reat. 2021, April. 2021 Health Value Dashboard. Health Policy Institute of Ohio. https://www.healthpolicyohio.org/2021-health-value-dashboard/.

Associated Press. 2021. "Census: Columbus, Cincinnati Grow as Population in Cleveland, Rural Ohio Shrinks." Spectrum News 1, August 13, 2021. https://spectrumnews1.com/oh/columbus/news/2021/08/13/census--columbus-grows-as-population-in-rural-ohio-shrinks.

Baker, Mike, and Danielle Ivory. 2021. "Why Public Health Faces a Crisis across the U.S." *New York Times*, October 18, 2021. www.nytimes.com/2021/10/18/us/coronavirus-public-health.html.

Banco, Erin. 2021. "'It Is Embarrassing': CDC Struggles to Track COVID Cases as Omicron Looms." *Politico*, December 20, 2021. www.politico.com/news/2021/12/20/cdc-covid-omicron-delta-tracking-525621.

Barbaro, Michael. 2021. Interview with Tony Fauci. *The Daily*, November 12, 2021. Transcript: www.nytimes.com/2021/11/12/podcasts/the-daily/anthony-fauci-vaccine-mandates-booster-shots.html?showTranscript=1.

Bayer, Ronald, and Amy L. Fairchild. 2004. "The Genesis of Public Health Ethics." *Bioethics* 18, no. 6: 473–492.

Beauchamp, Tom L., and James F. Childress. 2019. *The Principles of Biomedical Ethics*, 8th ed. Oxford: Oxford University Press.

Berman, Russell. 2022. "The Last of the Establishment Republicans." *The Atlantic*, April 3, 2022. www.theatlantic.com/politics/archive/2022/04/how-ohio-governor-mike-dewine-survived-trump/629450/.

Boggs, Justin. 2021. "Cleveland's University Hospitals to Research Long-Haul COVID." SpectrumNews1, November 10, 2021. https://spectrumnews1.com/oh/columbus/news/2021/11/09/cwru--university-hospitals-to-research-long-haul-covid.

Bornancin, Ashley. 2021. "Nurses Walk Out at Fox Run of Findlay, National Guard Comes to Aid." 13abc.com, December 29, 2021. www.13abc.com/2021/12/29/nurses-walk-out-fox-run-findlay-national-guard-comes-aid/.

Calcaterra, Craig. 2021. "Ohio Leading the Way in Pandemic Dysfunction." ColumbusAlive.com, December 28, 2021. www.columbusalive.com/story/entertainment/human-interest/2021/12/28/local-politics-ohio-leading-way-pandemic-dysfunction/9032226002/.

Campbell, Falycia. 2020. "#InThisTogetherOhio: Famous Ohioans Share Positive Messages During Coronavirus Pandemic." abc6onyourside.com, March 24, 2020. https://abc6onyourside.com/news/local/inthistogetherohio-famous-ohioans-share-positive-messages-during-coronavirus-pandemic.

Cincinnati Enquirer. 2020. "Three Cases of Coronavirus Confirmed in Cuyahoga County; DeWine Declares State of Emergency. *Cincinnati Enquirer*, March 9, 2020. www.cincinnati.com/story/news/2020/03/09/coronavirus-covid-19-ohio-positive-case/5003009002/.

Crawford, Paul, Brian Brown, Victoria Tischler, and Charley Baker. 2010. "Health Humanities: The Future of Medical Humanities?" *Mental Health Review Journal* 15, no. 3: 4–10. https://doi.org/10.5042/mhrj.2010.0654.

DeWine, Mike 2020. Ohio Governor DeWine Coronavirus News Conference, C-SPAN, March 19, 2020. www.c-span.org/video/?470509-1/ohio-governor-dewine-coronavirus-news-conference.

Diamond, Dan. 2021. "First They Ran Short of PPE, Then Ventilators. Now, the Shortage Is Hospital Staff." *Washington Post*, December 30, 2021. www.washingtonpost.com/health/2021/12/30/hospitals-staffing-shortages-omicron/.

Dosani, Sanya, and Adam Westbook. 2020. "The Leader We Wish We All Had." *New York Times*, May 5, 2020. www.nytimes.com/video/opinion/100000007111965/coronavirus-ohio-amy-acton.html.

Exner, Rich. 2019. "Ohio Democrats Nearly Match Republicans in Statehouse Votes, But Will Remain in the Deep Minority; What's Ahead for Gerrymandering." *Cleveland.com*, September 19, 2019. www.cleveland.com/news/erry-2018/11/0f32e762411182/ohio-democrats-outpolled-repub.html.

Fahey, Kevin. 2021. "What Happened? The 2020 Election Confirmed That Ohio Is No Longer a Swing State." London School of Economics Phelan Center USAPP Blog, September 2, 2021. https://blogs.lse.ac.uk/usappblog/2021/09/02/what-happened-the-2020-election-confirmed-that-ohio-is-no-longer-a-swing-state/.

Fissell, Mary E., Jeremy A. Greene, Randall M. Packard, and James A. Shafer Jr. 2020. "Introduction: Reimagining Epidemics." *Bulletin of the History of Medicine* 94, no. 4(Winter): 543–561.

Goldstein, Amy. 2021. "Anger over Mask Mandates, Other Covid Rules, Spurs States to Curb Power of Public Health Officials." *Washington Post*, December 25, 2021. www.washingtonpost.com/health/2021/12/25/covid-public-health-laws-restricted.

Gordon, Colin. 2019. *Race in the Heartland: Equity, Opportunity, and Public Policy in the Midwest.* Iowa Policy Project, Policy Matters Ohio, COWS, and the Economic Analysis and Research Network (EARN). Accessed January 4, 2022. www.policymattersohio.org/files/research/raceinthemidwest-final-interactive1.pdf.

Gray, Kathleen. 2021. "In Michigan, a Dress Rehearsal for the Chaos at the Capitol on Wednesday." *New York Times*, January 9, 2021. www.nytimes.com/2021/01/09/us/politics/michigan-state-capitol.html

Grumbach, Jacob M., Jacob S. Hacker, and Paul Pierson. 2022. "The Political Economies of Red States." In *The American Political Economy: Politics, Markets, and Power*, edited by Jacob S. Hacker, Alexander Hertzel-Fernandez, Paul Pierson, and Kathleen Thelen, 209–244. Cambridge: Cambridge University Press.

Güthe, Nick. 2022. "My Wife Had Long Covid and Killed Herself. We Must Help Others Who Are Suffering." *The Guardian*, January 12, 2022. www.theguardian.com/commentisfree/2022/jan/12/long-covid-wife-suicide-give-others-hope.

Hancock, Laura. 2021. "Gov. Mike DeWine Said He'll Veto an Ohio Bill That Prohibits Employers, Schools from Mandating Vaccines." *Cleveland.com*, December 14, 2021. www.cleveland.com/news/2021/12/gov-mike-dewine-said-hell-veto-an-ohio-bill-that-prohibits-employers-schools-from-mandating-vaccines.html.

Hotez, Peter J. 2021. *Preventing the Next Pandemic.* Baltimore: Johns Hopkins University Press.

Jacobs, Andrew. 2021. "National Guard Empties Bedpans and Clips Toenails at Nursing Homes." *New York Times,* December 22, 2021. www.nytimes.com/2021/12/22/health/covid-national-guard-nursing-homes.html.

Jardina, Ashley. 2019. *White Identity Politics.* Cambridge: Cambridge University Press.

Jasanoff, Sheila. 2021. "'Preparedness' Won't Stop the Next Pandemic." *Boston Review,* December 8, 2021. https://bostonreview.net/forum/preparedness-wont-stop-the-next-pandemic/.

Kaiser Family Foundation. 2014. "The Ohio Health Care Landscape." August 1, 2014. www.kff.org/medicaid/fact-sheet/the-ohio-health-care-landscape/.

Kisner, Jordan. 2021. "What the Chaos in Hospitals Is Doing to Doctors." *The Atlantic,* January/February 2021. www.theatlantic.com/magazine/archive/2021/01/covid-ethics-committee/617261/.

Levine, Sam. 2022. "The Republican Judge Blocking Her Party from Rigging Electoral Districts." *The Guardian,* April 12, 2022. www.theguardian.com/us-news/2022/apr/12/ohio-republican-judge-blocking-party-from-distorting-electoral-districts.

Lewis, Michael. 2021. *The Premonition: A Pandemic Story.* New York: W.W. Norton.

Loomis, Joshua. 2018. *Epidemics: The Impact of Germs and Their Power over Humanity.* Nashville: Turner Publishing Company.

Lopez, L., L.H. Hart, and M.H. Katz. 2021. "Racial and Ethnic Health Disparities Related to COVID-19." *JAMA* 325, no. 8: 719–720. https://doi.org/10.1001/jama.2020.26443.

Mazer, Benjamin. 2022. "We're Testing for Monkeypox the Wrong Way." *The Atlantic,* July 21, 2022. www.theatlantic.com/health/archive/2022/07/monkeypox-outbreak-fda-testing/670594/.

McNichol, Elizabeth, Douglas Hall, David Cooper, and Vincent Palacios. 2012. "Pulling Apart: A State-by-State Analysis of Income Trends." Center on Budget and Policy Priorities. Accessed January 4, 2022. www.cbpp.org/research/poverty-and-inequality/pulling-apart-a-state-by-state-analysis-of-income-trends.

Molotch, Harvey. 2006. "Death on the Roof: Race and Bureaucratic Failure." New York: Social Science Research Council. Accessed January 4, 2022. https://items.ssrc.org/understanding-katrina/death-on-the-roof-race-and-bureaucratic-failure/.

Nordenberg, Tamar. 2022. "VA Research Spells Out COVID's Down-the-Road Risks for Cardiovascular and Mental Health." US Department of Veterans Affairs. VA Research Currents. February 16, 2022. www.research.va.gov/currents/0222-VA-research-spells-out-COVIDs-down-the-road-risks-for-cardiovascular-and-mental-health.cfm.

Ohio Department of Health. 2020a. COVID-19 Dashboard. Accessed January 4, 2022. https://coronavirus.ohio.gov/wps/portal/gov/covid-19/dashboards.

Ohio Department of Health. 2020b. *Ohio Annual Cancer Report 2020.* Ohio Department of Health, Bureau of Health Improvement and Wellness, Columbus, Ohio. Accessed January 4, 2022. https://odh.ohio.gov/wps/wcm/connect/gov/afa96bf8-6285-42cc-829e-7f404c924263/Ohio+Annual+Cancer+Report+2020.pdf.

Ohio Department of Higher Education. 2019. *Ohio Attainment 2019 Annual Report.* Accessed January 4, 2022. www.ohiohighered.org/sites/default/files/uploads/attainment/Attainment-Report-2019_FINAL_012220.pdf.

Pepper, David. 2021. *Laboratories of Autocracy: A Wake-Up Call from Behind the Lines.* Cincinnati, OH: St. Helena Press.

Perry, Brea L., Brian Aronson, and Bernice A. Pescosolido. 2021. "Pandemic Precarity: COVID-19 Is Exposing and Exacerbating Inequalities in the American Heartland." *Proceedings of the National Academy of Sciences* 118, no. 8. https://doi.org/10.1073/pnas.2020685118.

Pew Research Center. 2015. "Party Affiliation among Adults in Ohio." Religious Landscape Study. Accessed January 4, 2022. www.pewforum.org/religious-landscape-study/state/ohio/party-affiliation/.

Pirtle, Whitney N.L. 2020. "Racial Capitalism: A Fundamental Cause of Novel Coronavirus (COVID-19) Pandemic Inequities in the United States." *Health Education & Behavior* 47, no. 4: 504–508. https://doi.org/10.1177/1090198120922942.

Reny, Tyler T., and Matt A. Barreto. 2022. "Xenophobia in the Time of Pandemic: Othering, Anti-Asian Attitudes, and COVID-19." *Politics, Groups, and Identities* 10, no. 2: 209–232.

Richardson, Seth. 2021. "Lt. Gov. Jon Husted's Coronavirus Tweet Left Asian Americans Feeling Disappointed in Ohio Leadership." *Cleveland.com,* April 3, 2021. www.cleveland.com/open/2021/04/lt-gov-jon-husteds-coronavirus-tweet-left-asian-americans-feeling-disappointed-in-ohio-leadership.html.

Rothenberg, Stuart. 2022. "As Ohio Became Reliably Red, the Republican Party Was Changing." *Roll Call,* February 24, 2022. https://rollcall.com/2022/02/24/as-ohio-became-reliably-red-the-republican-party-was-changing/.

Serhan, Yasmeen. 2020. "The EU Watches as Hungary Kills Democracy." *The Atlantic,* April 2, 2020. www.theatlantic.com/international/archive/2020/04/europe-hungary-viktor-orban-coronavirus-covid19-democracy/609313/.

Singer, Phillip M., Charley E. Willison, N'dea Moore-Petinak, and Scott L. Greer. 2021. "Anatomy of a Failure: COVID-19 in the United States." In *Coronavirus Politics: The Comparative Politics and Policy of COVID-19,* edited by Scott L. Greer, Elizabeth J. King, Elize Massard da Fonseca, and André Peralta-Santos, 478–493. Ann Arbor: University of Michigan Press. https://doi.org/10.3998/mpub.11927713.

Sivaramakrishnan, Kavita. 2020. "Looking Sideways: Locating Epidemics and Erasures in South Asia." *Bulletin of the History of Medicine* 94, no. 4(Winter): 637–657.

Skinner, Daniel and Berkeley Franz, eds. 2019. *Not Far from Me: Stories of Opioids and Ohio.* Columbus, OH: Trillium.

Smulyan, Susan. 2020. "Introduction." In *Doing Public Humanities,* 1–4. New York: Routledge.

Sommeiller, Estelle, and Mark Price. 2018. *The New Gilded Age: Income Inequality in the U.S. by State, Metropolitan Area, and County.* Economic Policy Institute. July 19, 2018. www.epi.org/publication/the-new-gilded-age-income-inequality-in-the-u-s-by-state-metropolitan-area-and-county/#epi-toc-11.

Spinney, Laura. 2017. *Pale Rider: The Spanish Flu of 1918 and How It Changed the World.* New York: Public Affairs Press.

Stanley-Becker, Isaac, and Tony Romm. 2020. "The Anti-Quarantine Protests Seem Spontaneous. But Behind the Scenes, a Powerful Network is Helping." *Washington Post,* April 22, 2020. www.washingtonpost.com/politics/inside-the-conservative-networks-backing-anti-quarantine-protests/2020/04/22/da75c81e-83fe-11ea-a3eb-e9fc93160703_story.html.

Tufecki, Zeynep. 2020. "This Overlooked Variable Is the Key to the Pandemic." *The Atlantic,* September 30, 2020. www.theatlantic.com/health/archive/2020/09/k-overlooked-variable-driving-pandemic/616548/.

United States Census Bureau. n.d. QuickFacts Ohio. Accessed January 4, 2022. www.census.gov/quickfacts/fact/dashboard/OH/INC110219.

University Hospitals. 2021. "SARS-COV-2 Task Force Accelerates Study of Impact of COVID-19." Innovations in Cardiovascular Medicine and Surgery, February 1, 2021. www.uhhospitals.org/for-clinicians/articles-and-news/articles/2021/01/sars-c0v-2-task-force-accelerates-study-of-impact-of-covid-19.

Wallace, Megan, and Joshua M. Sharfstein. 2022. "The Patchwork U.S. Public Health System." *New England Journal of Medicine* 386, no. 1: 1–4. https://doi.org/10.1056/NEJMp2104881.

Willison, Charley E., Phillip M. Singer, Melissa S. Creary, Soha Vaziri, Jerry Stott, and Scott L. Greer. 2022. "How Do You Solve a Problem Like Maria? The Politics of Disaster Response in Puerto Rico, Florida and Texas." *World Medical & Health Policy,* 14, no. 3: 490–506. https://doi.org/10.1002/wmh3.476.

Wines, Michael. 2021. "State Lawmakers Take Aim at the Emergency Powers Governors have Relied on in the Pandemic." *New York Times,* March 27, 2021. www.nytimes.com/2021/03/26/world/covid-governors-emergency-powers.html.

Witte, Griff. 2020. "Ohio's Amy Acton Inspires Admiration, and a Backlash, with Tough Coronavirus Response." *Washington Post,* May 18, 2020. www.washingtonpost.com/national/a-white-coated-hero-or-a-medical-dictator-ohios-amy-acton-inspires-admiration-and-a-backlash-with-tough-coronavirus-response/2020/05/17/fa00cd1c-96d4-11ea-82b4-c8db161ff6e5_story.html.

Yong, Ed. 2020a. "How the Pandemic Defeated America." *The Atlantic,* August 4, 2020. www.theatlantic.com/magazine/archive/2020/09/coronavirus-american-failure/614191/.

Yong, Ed. 2020b. "'No One Is Listening to Us'." *The Atlantic,* November 13, 2020. www.theatlantic.com/health/archive/2020/11/third-surge-breaking-healthcare-workers/617091/.

Yong, Ed. 2021a. "What Happens When Americans Can Finally Exhale." *The Atlantic,* May 20, 2021. www.theatlantic.com/health/archive/2021/05/pandemic-trauma-summer/618934/

Yong, Ed. 2021b. "How Public Health Took Part in Its Own Downfall." *The Atlantic,* October 23, 2021. www.theatlantic.com/health/archive/2021/10/how-public-health-took-part-its-own-downfall/620457/

Yong, Ed. 2021c. "Why Health-Care Workers Are Quitting in Droves." *The Atlantic,* November 16, 2021. www.theatlantic.com/health/archive/2021/11/the-mass-exodus-of-americas-health-care-workers/620713/

PART ONE

Values in Conflict: Policy, Politics, and Ethics

The first wave of the pandemic saw policy makers and public health officials scrambling to put in place COVID response policies. While every public health crisis is mediated by its social context, COVID seemed, almost immediately, to be especially fraught with political and moral conflict. In fact, such conflict about abstractions often took center stage, overshadowing the very real health crisis that was unfolding. This section of the book analyzes the tensions over policy, politics, and ethics that policy makers and public health officials confronted as they tried to put COVID measures into place.

The section begins with an analysis of Dr. Amy Acton's role in shaping pandemic policy as the first woman physician to head the Ohio Department of Health. Rarely, authors Daniel Skinner and Kathryn Poe note, have state health directors become household names in the history of American public health, but in the case of Ohio and COVID, Dr. Acton became a visible public presence, attracting both hero worship and death threats. They examine how the havoc Acton confronted compromised public health and safety in Ohio. In Chapter 2, Jonathan Spelman digs deeper into the politics Acton navigated through a close analysis of Governor Mike DeWine's shifting position on masks. Drawing a parallel between mask mandates and public health regulations against smoking indoors, the chapter evaluates the fairness of mandates that prevent employees from infecting customers but do nothing to protect them from customers. Intensive care unit physician Zac Ginsberg reflects in Chapter 3 on his time in the eye of the political storm around COVID in southwest Ohio. He grapples with the emotional toll of fighting a politicized pandemic, and uses Jean-Jacques Rousseau's concept of the social contract to contemplate the public's failure to take seriously their roles in contributing to the death and suffering of their most vulnerable fellow Ohioans.

In Chapter 4, Hillary J. Gyuras and her collaborators address the effect of the pandemic on abortion care as so-called nonessential medical procedures were delayed or canceled, showing how the pandemic's politicization has threatened reproductive health care accessibility for people in vulnerable positions. They argue for the implementation of an ethic and politics of care that would prioritize the health and wellness of the population of people who may need abortion over the politicization of this issue. Chapter 5 zooms out from the level of individual rights and responsibilities highlighted in the previous two chapters to decision-making at the level of a large hospital system in northeast Ohio. This research piece by Mahwish U. Ahmad, Joshua S. Crites, and Prabalini Rajendram analyzes logistical challenges, discrepancies in care provision, and the use of novel or "off label" treatments for COVID-19 in this complex setting. Together the cases they analyze deal with the ethical aspects of critical care that were overshadowed by other efforts relevant to the pandemic response, as well as lessons learned about how health-care institutions must collaborate, rather than compete, in a crisis.

Julie Aultman, Deborah Barnbaum, and Kimberly K. Garchar then take a closer look at discrepancies in care provision in northeast Ohio in Chapter 6. They reflect on how COVID-19 exacerbated existing inequalities by, for example, raising the stakes of disparities in health literacy, and unsettling assumptions regarding risk and benefit. In Chapter 7, Sarah K. Richter examines the impact of COVID-19 on another vulnerable population: students with limited or interrupted formal education. Such students—who already have distressingly high drop-out rates—have had their education detrimentally affected by the pandemic possibly more than any other group of learners. The chapter examines this problem through a case study of the effects that COVID-19 had on recently immigrated students to Ohio from Central America in one suburban Cincinnati school district.

The section closes by turning to the past. In Chapter 8, John A. Lynch and his coauthors examine how Ohio's journalists looked to the 1918 flu to make sense of what was happening as COVID-19 appeared in Ohio. Papers from across the state leveraged 1918 to issue warnings and to draw lessons. In the process, they retold stories of that pandemic's politicization and revealed, sometimes unwittingly, how the racism of a century ago is echoed in the racism wrapped into the politics of COVID-19. Taken together, the chapters in Part 1 illustrate how tension between individual liberty and collective responsibility set the terms of debate about appropriate pandemic response and the parameters for feasible COVID measures.

1 | "The Leader We Wish We All Had"

Ohio, Gender, and What the Pandemic Taught Us about the Politics of Public Health

Research Article

Daniel Skinner and Kathryn Poe

In this research piece, a health policy scholar and a public policy professional analyze Dr. Amy Acton's role in shaping pandemic policy as head of the Ohio Department of Health.

Ohio is a place of paradoxes. The state holds bragging rights as the home of renowned health-care institutions. For example, Ohio's children's hospitals are regularly ranked among the best in the nation, and the Cleveland Clinic is known globally as a destination medical facility that provides care to world leaders, celebrities, and tycoons. Yet, for all this achievement, according to the Health Policy Institute of Ohio's 2021 "Health Value Dashboard," Ohio ranks 47 out of the 50 states and Washington, DC, in health value. The report concludes: "Ohioans are living less healthy lives and spending more on health care than people in most other states" (Health Policy Institute of Ohio 2021).

Among public health experts, there is consensus that the key variable in Ohio is not health care as such, but public health—and especially *preventive* public health. After all, just beyond the doors of many of Ohio's elite health-care institutions, one often finds entrenched poverty, food deserts, poor housing, and, as a result, gaping health disparities (Thomas 2020). In a February 2021 press conference, almost a year after the outbreak of COVID-19, Ohio Governor Mike DeWine acknowledged what public health experts in the state already knew: "We've ignored public health in this country for too long" (Buchanan 2021). DeWine said "country," but really, he was talking about Ohio.

In this chapter, we explain why COVID-19 revealed a great deal about the politics of public health in Ohio, and, specifically, the consequences of what the state's relationship to public health revealed about gender dynamics. During the early months of Ohio's response to the COVID-19 pandemic, this politics was exposed in dramatic fashion by reactions to Dr. Amy Acton, director of the Ohio Department of Health (ODH). While Acton's leadership set a tone and built a degree of public confidence in the state's nationally recognized response to COVID-19, it also provoked public and eventually legislative backlash, with the latter aimed at stripping the governor and his health officials of their powers.

Enter COVID-19 ... and Acton

It is rare for a public health director to become a household name. Accordingly, it is unlikely that many Ohioans knew of Acton before March 2020, just as they were likely unaware of ODH, its work, or the scope of its authority. While there were a few important public health mobilizations in previous years, most notably during an Ebola scare in 2014, ODH mostly operated below the level of public consciousness before 2020. But there Acton was, standing alongside DeWine for their first series of daily COVID press conferences in the second week of March, when the first Ohio COVID-19 case was confirmed in Cuyahoga County. For several months, these briefings would become daily spectacles, which fans eventually dubbed "Wine with DeWine" and "Snackin' with Acton." Many Ohioans who were working from home or unemployed would tune in to hear the latest from DeWine, Acton, and a host of other voices.

Each day, DeWine would include a range of administration officials in the sessions, as well as experts from around Ohio. But it was Acton, distinguished by her physician's white coat, who would rise to prominence. Although Acton's role was to oversee public health systems for the state rather than to practice medicine, DeWine would often call her to the podium to explain what was happening as a relatable family doctor might explain a diagnosis to a patient. Acton brought a physician's authority to the proceedings. On March 19, Medicaid director Maureen Corcoran, who is a nurse, appeared to offer a slight correction on this score: "You've heard the Governor and Dr. Acton say in recent weeks that Dr. Acton is the doctor for Ohio. She takes care of the *public* health of all Ohioans" (Acton, March 19, 2020, 16:00, emphasis added).[1] It made sense that the key metaphor of Ohio's public health response was direct patient care, both because public health and its functions were barely known to the public and because physicians remain among the most trusted groups in the United States (Funk and Gramlich 2021). Corcoran was alluding to the little understood reality that, in public health, the key focus is on larger populations. This general lay confusion around how physicians' work differed from that of public health experts, and officials provided opportunities for misunderstanding and even distrust throughout the pandemic.

At the outset of the pandemic, Acton was praised not only for her expertise but also her leadership skills. In the beginning, she received an effusive outpouring of support, including a "Dr. Amy Acton Fan Club" on Facebook, which produced yard signs that were posted throughout the state. *Time* magazine characterized her "calm amid calamity" (Vesoulis 2020). This praise centered on her willingness to talk straight to Ohioans, which felt like an implicit critique of the absence of effective leadership at other levels of government. While President Donald Trump promised, contrary to all available evidence, that Americans would be back in church by Easter, Acton refused to overpromise. And while President Trump and some of his advisers were criticized for offering obfuscatory rhetoric that neither took responsibility for the situation nor proposed serious measures for responding to the pandemic, Acton was praised for her "brutal honesty" (Dosani and Westbrook 2020) and fidelity to available data. Acton delivered bad news as a physician is trained to do. When she was uncertain, she admitted it.

Acton's seemingly intuitive grasp of the politics of public health in Ohio, supplemented by her formal master's-level public health studies at The Ohio State University, positioned her to help Ohioans understand how their individual actions were key to improving outcomes within their communities, counties, and beyond. These actions, Acton promised, were critical to the larger aims of reopening schools, restaurants, and sporting events. To convey this, Acton heroized individual actions at a time when many were feeling helpless in the face of a large-scale public health crisis. At a briefing on March 19 (39:07), Acton noted, "There are everyday heroes everywhere. We know that

1. Unless otherwise specified, this and all Amy Acton quotations are from State of Ohio COVID daily press conferences as transcribed on Rev.com.

not all heroes wear capes." Acton then asked Ohioans to do their part: "I need you to wear both the cape and the mask [...] to help protect each other. It's beautiful weather and I need you to understand we're fighting for lives now trying to cure stuff like this" (WKYC Staff 2020).

In another moment of skillful health communication, Acton called up a well-known model—the so-called "Swiss cheese model," used since the 1990s in aviation and other industries concerned with layered safety (Reason 1990)—to describe why the imperfection of any single public health measure required layering to yield comprehensiveness. Acton explained on April 7,

> Those were the Swiss cheese efforts, from limiting mass gatherings to closing schools to all the measures on social distancing we've taken. We said that none of them are perfect alone. That it really is like slices of Swiss cheese. When you layer them slightly over the holes with each layer, collectively that makes a difference. And what we now know here in Ohio and around the world is it truly works. (April 7, 2020, 22:41)

In addition to helping Ohioans understand the relationship between individual actions and a collective response, Acton's use of the metaphor of Swiss cheese addressed something that, even by April, had undercut the state's response: confusion about and the misrepresentation of science. In acknowledging that no one solution was likely to slow COVID-19's spread, Acton called up an established public health metaphor for characterizing the aggregate effects of individual measures (Roberts 2020). This point was an important supplement to Acton's daily emphasis on the fluid nature of public health officials' understanding of COVID-19 itself.

In offering transparency instead of certainty, Acton portrayed herself and other state leaders as humble, imperfect, but nonetheless well-intended public servants. On March 19, Acton (2020; 39:48) pleaded:

> I constantly say that we're going to get this 80% right. This is a moving train that's moving very quickly. We cannot linger on things like "do we have enough tests or don't we?" [now] is the time for action and I need everyone to focus on following what the Governor says and staying home and taking these actions as we go up on this curve. Asking for grace, even me, I know people are saying, I'm so nice. I have a little fierceness in me. We should just admit it. I even lose my temper, as my kids and family will

> tell you, when pushed far enough, and we're all asking for grace with each other in this time.

Here Acton was not only setting expectations, but taking a humanistic, understanding approach to family life that many Ohioans undoubtedly could relate to.

For Acton, effective public health promotion requires encouraging people to take actions that they might not fully understand, and that they might not see the fruits of for some time. As Acton noted in mid-March, "On the front end of a pandemic, you look a little bit like an alarmist. You look a little bit like a Chicken Little—the sky is falling. On the back end of the pandemic, you didn't do enough" (Balmert and Borchardt 2020). Leadership sometimes requires making hard and often unpopular decisions. The question for DeWine (the politician) and Acton (the public health official) was how their unpopular decisions would be received, and what it would mean for the Ohio pandemic response.

Style and Leadership

Ohio's public health response was praised and profiled in national media. Acton garnered national attention as the key force within the Ohio COVID response. The first national spotlight came with a multimedia profile published in the opinion section of the *New York Times* entitled "The Leader We Wish We All Had" (Dosani and Westbrook 2020). While the goal of the piece was to explore Acton's competence and public health savvy, the *Times* feature's subheading—"A Look at the Style of Dr. Amy Acton"—made clear that the focus was not on Acton's clinical or public health expertise, or even her strategizing about messaging during a public health crisis. The aim was to analyze Acton's leadership "style." Dosani and Westbrook praised Acton for talking openly in her daily presentations about such difficult themes as vulnerability, forgiveness, apology, anxiety, and pain. They noted how Acton "empowers us" by confronting fear, counseling Ohioans, "I don't want you to be afraid. I am not afraid. I am determined." While admitting that "All of us are going to have to sacrifice," she cast the COVID challenge as a willingness to "do hard things." Above all, according to the *Times* feature, Acton's rhetorical approach aimed to cultivate relationships. For example, Acton's "repeated use of 'I' tells us she's in it with us" and her use of the accusative 'you' is intended to help viewers "feel a connection with her." But Acton's key skill is her ability to move from "I" and "you" to a collective voice: "She's in charge, yet she's made us feel like the heroes."

Another skill of Acton's, according to Dosani and Westbrook, was her ability to prepare Ohioans for bad news ("I know that's a hard truth for people, because we want there to be a right answer and a right way") and adeptness at synthesizing complicated topics so that people with minimal medical knowledge can understand them—as in the Swiss cheese metaphor discussed above. In so doing, Acton not only promotes understanding but skillfully navigates important gendered expectations as well (Palmary 2014). Acton's translational work "cares" for the community while serving as a contrast to the "cure," a masculinist trope with which medicine has long been associated (Poole and Isaacs 1997; Jecker and Self 1991; Treiber and Jones 2015). Though Acton is a physician, her role as a public health official also casts her as a caregiver of a different sort, a motivator and coach in addition to a physician and public health expert.

Additional spotlights on Acton's leadership, each with a particular emphasis on her presence and style, appeared in the *Washington Post* and even *Glamour* magazine. As a helpful contrast to the gender politics at work in these features, consider how Dr. Anthony Fauci was portrayed in a widely discussed *InStyle* feature (Stone 2020), containing not only glamour shots of Fauci but also content that was wholly focused on Fauci's expertise and professional trajectory. The opening line made clear that Fauci was "well-respected by the scientific community" (O'Donnell 2020). In contrast to Acton, Fauci's long record of distinguished service to the nation, and his role as a top infectious disease expert tended to frame Fauci's appearances in public forums.

While Acton's communicative style illustrates one part of the gender politics of Ohio's COVID response, there was also a good deal of attention to Acton's role vis-à-vis the Republican governor in whose administration she (a Democrat) served. The *Glamour* profile noted,

> Observers have marveled over DeWine's readiness to defer to Acton. Some have expressed shock that the same man who signed legislation to ban abortions after six weeks has been willing to listen to not just a woman with medical expertise, but a former organizer for President Barack Obama. (Stankorb 2020)

The word choices are important. DeWine does not "depend" on Acton, but he "defers." Observers "marvel" at DeWine's "readiness to defer" because they did not expect it. While DeWine, as we have noted, made health care for women and children a hallmark of his administration early on, the broader gender politics of Republican and Democratic priorities was never far from the public's lived experience of COVID-19. For example, almost without exception, as we now know, COVID workplace policies disproportionately impacted Ohio women, and women of color in particular. And while these policies, such as those in the restaurant industry, may not have been avoidable, little direct support was made available from the state to soften the blow. Women, of course, were disproportionately impacted by COVID-19 in large part because they tended to be overrepresented in industries considered essential (Kaiser Family Foundation 2021).

To understand the DeWine–Acton dynamic, consider a contrast from Washington, DC, where President Trump routinely recast the words of his coronavirus coordinator, Dr. Deborah Birx, so that they would align with his message, undermining her authority and confusing the science (Howard and Kelly 2021). The DeWine-Acton relationship is different. As the author of a profile in the Midwestern *Belt* magazine explained, "I have no idea what percentage of the praise goes to [DeWine], his decision to step aside from the microphone and let Acton speak, and to adopt her suggestions, or to Acton herself" (Trubek 2020). In this telling, it is noteworthy that the governor "let" Acton speak at all.

Not only did Acton wear her white coat in an important signposting of fidelity to science, but the dynamic with her male superiors was arranged to amplify and legitimize her voice. Just as DeWine "let" Acton speak, and actually listened to her, so, too, can we assume that DeWine "let" Acton wear her white coat. Can we imagine Trump "letting" Birx do so? Instead, Birx was subjected to a sexist public fixation on her extensive collection of decorative scarves. *Elle* magazine reported, "When Dr. Deborah Birx delivers indispensable information on the federal government's response to the pandemic, she does it in Hermès" (Minutaglio 2020).

At key points as well, with Acton's public approval high, she went out of her way to encourage Ohioans to listen to the governor, assuring them that his advice received her stamp of approval. For example, on March 24, she said, "Thank you for following the governor's sage guidance. Honestly, I couldn't explain our situation better than he is explaining it today. So, please continue to follow his guidance and his lead" (Acton various dates, 24:56). Some of DeWine's critics appeared to regard his deferral to Acton, not on medical judgment but public policy, as tantamount to an emasculating move at a time when a masculinist culture is driving resistance to public health expertise. This is especially true with regard to the question of masks, where refusal to wear a mask reminds us that "ignoring the risks of coronavirus is the tough or strong thing to do" (North 2020). One of the more high-profile instances of a prominent Ohioan refusing to wear a mask was Representative Jim Jordan. In publicly excoriating Jordan for refusing to take this well-established public health measure, Representative Jamie Raskin challenged Jordan: "It's obviously not a sign of bravery not to wear a mask [...] It's a sign of irresponsibility towards other people" (Eaton 2020).

Public Health Orders and Advisories

Beyond Acton's leadership qualities, it is important to acknowledge the centrality of the politics of gender to the challenges of the public health response itself. Ohio was the first in the nation to close its schools, but also the first to shutter large segments of its economy, most notably restaurants and bars. Acton assured Ohioans that it wasn't DeWine and her order that lead to economic devastation, but the other way around:

> And I really want Ohioans to understand this, because it is the virus. Our economy was already being disrupted, and there's already data showing that before there ever was an order, because this is a global pandemic that's having global effects on supply chains, and people are out sick for a week at a time and then can't work. And so it's bigger than all of us here. (Acton, May 5, 1:01:14)

The idea that policies put in place by DeWine and Acton were not the cause of economic collapse in the state was central to their messaging. But it seemed increasingly unlikely that a certain segment of Ohioans, including many in the legislature, would accept their reasoning. What many Ohioans, and many others in the nation, saw as the early adoption of best practices and impressive leadership, was cast as alarmism and recklessness by the DeWine administration's Republican critics.

One such mechanism, the state "stay-at-home" order, provides an important illustration of the complexities of the politics of public health at the time. While it is assumed that COVID-19 fundamentally altered aspects of American society, gender is an underrecognized aspect of this social change. For example, Acton specifically identified childcare—at that time already a major policy topic in the United States—as heroic, noting, "You're heroic when you stay at home and watch your neighbor who is a nurse's child." Though the message was delivered as a universal, one senses that in addition to nurses and other health professionals, who are mostly women, Acton was also speaking to fathers, who were being asked during the pandemic to reconfigure their own relationships to professional advancement and become part of a familial and community response. This appeal was made, of course, despite the fact that women—and women of color in particular—were the hardest hit, economically, by the pandemic (Boesch and Phadke 2021). Acton's appeal makes sense; however, as Acton and DeWine learned, the public health plea to "stay home" had a distinct gender politics to it. Staying home during workdays, including working from home, has a long and gendered history, especially given the political economy and cultural politics associated with "stay-at-home moms" (Galley 2014). For her part, Acton was at this time, but also in general, the opposite of a stay-at-home mother, and it is worth considering the possibility that Acton's strong leadership position, implicated in affecting radical changes in Ohioans domestic relations, was at least a partial cause of the pervasive resentment evoked by the administration she served and the policies they put in place. She reminded Ohioans of this fact on March 19 when she asked them to "Put that flag out everyone," adding that "I thought that was the most wonderful suggestion by Fran DeWine, our first lady. I asked my husband to put ours out, and it'll be a little symbol to all of us of what we're doing" (Acton, March 19, 40:29).

This political moment led *Forbes* magazine to ask whether the pandemic might be "good for gender equality" (Kramer 2020), and CNBC to ask whether COVID-19 might accelerate a trend in stay-at-home fathering (Connley 2021). Underpinning anxieties concerned with professional attainment during the pandemic, particularly for those with children who were now learning remotely from home, was the fact that stay-at-home fathering had been experiencing a steady climb prior to the pandemic (Lee and Lee 2018). Despite the intense anger from men about DeWine and Acton's strategy—especially men in the legislature attempting to strip them of their powers to respond to the pandemic—the burden of caregiving disproportionately increased for women (Power 2020). And while economic considerations often trumped public health concerns in popular opinion, we also know that it was women, and women of color in particular, who paid the highest price for pandemic-related disruptions in their professional lives (Cahn 2020). Layered on these disproportionate effects were concerns about the intensification of domestic violence while stay-at-home orders were in place. As Acton explained, "People were hunkered down in the second half of March, all of April and into May," which meant that "Domestic violence survivors have been trapped at home with abusers and weren't able to reach out for resources. Then, as life opened back up, they were able to get help" (Futty 2020).

Acton's Departure and the Challenges of Replacing Her

For all of the positive reactions and praise Acton elicited, Ohio's rancorous and deeply gerrymandered state-level politics were also revealing a larger critique about public health itself, which would apply constant pressure on Ohio's health and political leaders. Though, in the early months of the pandemic, DeWine received high marks for Ohio's overall response to COVID-19, it was Acton who was the target of much of the most visceral public anger for the economic fallout. These criticisms included gendered and anti-Semitic attacks from protesters and some state legislators amid a general narrative of government overreach (Buchanan 2020a). DeWine consistently came to Acton's defense, calling those taking their protests to Acton's home "obnoxious" and hailing Acton as a dedicated public servant. He reminded them, as well, that "the buck stopped with him," explaining, "members of my cabinet, Dr. Acton included, work exceedingly, exceedingly hard, but I set the policy." DeWine, it should be remembered, was an early adopter of some of the more aggressive early public health responses. For example, he was the first US governor to close bars and restaurants for dine-in service, and also the first to close schools (Houser 2020).

Much to the surprise of many Ohioans, Acton made the decision to leave her post at ODH in June 2020, though she would stay on for some months as an adviser to DeWine. Soon after Acton left the post, COVID-19 case numbers began to climb, intensifying in the fall and peaking at 10,330 newly reported cases in December. Two months after a CDC recommendation on mask usage was issued in April 2020, DeWine instituted a statewide mask mandate in late July (Dwyer and

Aubrey 2020). By mid-January 2021, cases started to fall as part of a five-month decline that led DeWine to rescind his mask mandates and loosen other restrictions on June 2, 2021. As cases increased again throughout the summer of 2021 with the appearance of the so-called Delta variant, DeWine issued no new statewide mask mandate.

Given the high-profile role Acton played in Ohio’s COVID response, it is somewhat dizzying to remember that she led ODH for only about the first three months of the pandemic, which was also the period during which Ohio had the fewest number of cases it would see during the year. Acton’s legacy is likely to be, in part, her willingness to take seriously what she knew from available epidemiological evidence, namely, that testing only provided a snapshot of much wider community spread. Ohio’s public health recommendations in the spring of 2020 were met with a level of resistance that drew national attention. While managing the backlash was only a small part of the state’s pandemic response, that work has been ongoing. In fact, Acton and other Ohio officials would spend most of the pandemic managing the backlash created by the state’s proactive early response.

In particular, with palpable “COVID fatigue” setting in, industries began to assert themselves, and the Republican supermajority in the Ohio legislature moved to strip the state of the powers the governor and the director had used to address the pandemic. One couldn’t help but notice that Acton’s absence from ODH coincided with a shift in the way DeWine spoke. As case numbers began to rise again in the fall and winter of 2020, DeWine, under increasingly intense pressure from his party, did not issue new mandates until November, when cases had surged into the thousands (Ryan 2020). And while he did eventually institute curfews (Putrich and Forbes 2020), shutdowns and stay-at-home orders seemed to have become politically unpalatable policy options. DeWine’s press conferences now centered on encouraging Ohioans to wear masks and social distance—an appeal to individual responsibility instead of a more collective response. As the number of confirmed cases swelled, Ohio’s public health community waited anxiously for announcements of newly aggressive policies, but they never came. Instead, in a highly anticipated primetime November television address, DeWine “threatened” action, admonishing Ohioans that “If the current trend continues and cases keep increasing, we will be forced to make these closures” (Planalp and Schupp 2020). By this point, it was assumed that DeWine would face stiff legal challenges in Ohio’s courts if he made good on his threat (Tobias 2020). The “We” that was such a hallmark of Acton's rhetorical approach had been mostly eclipsed by an individualistic appeal.

Ohio got a clear sense of the lasting effects of the backlash when, in September of 2020, DeWine's nominee to head up ODH, Dr. Joan Duwve, withdrew her name from consideration. According to Duwve, "In conversations preparing for the transition to the Ohio Department of Health, I was informed that the former director's family had faced harassment from the public." She added: "While I have dedicated my life to improving public health, my first commitment is to my family. I am a public figure. My family is off-limits. I withdrew my name from consideration to protect my family from similar treatment." In the background of the formal reasons for the withdrawal, however, it was also apparent that Duwve's past work in 1984, as a volunteer for Planned Parenthood, would likely become an obstacle to her confirmation, despite her already having been confirmed by the very conservative South Carolina legislature for a similar post (Borchardt and Balmert 2020). Though Acton was easily confirmed by the Ohio Senate in 2019, there were fears that Duwve would not be. A great deal had changed in the state legislature's thinking about public health between 2019 and 2020.

Eventually, DeWine was able to appoint Stephanie McCloud, a lawyer who served as the administrator of the Bureau of Workers Compensation, to head up ODH in November of 2020. Though McCloud was regarded as an accomplished public servant with considerable administrative experience, which DeWine suggested qualified McCloud to oversee the state's vaccine distribution efforts, some critics noted that she lacked formal public health experience. *The Dispatch* reported that, though Governor DeWine had "stressed public health experience when he appointed former health director Dr. Amy Acton in 2019," a records request showed that several medical and public health experts had applied but not been chosen to replace her. Critics noted that Ohio law required that the director either be a physician or have "significant experience in the public health profession." As evidence of McCloud's public health experience, DeWine pointed to her service on the board of a behavioral health and treatment center (Ludlow 2020).

In the wake of Duwve's withdrawal, it appeared to many that McCloud's strong antiabortion stance was among the reasons why she was appointed and ultimately confirmed. By November of 2020, Ohio had come full circle, with the legislature affirming conservative resistance to many of the positions historically associated with public health—from social responses to public health crises to family planning.

With the ODH facing unusually intense political pressures, Ohio stumbled through the next few months.

Not only had the experience with COVID-19 failed to bring this particular group of Ohio legislators to appreciate the importance of public health preparations and action, but they also took substantial steps toward ensuring that the legislature would have the power to resist future efforts by the ODH director to aggressively address future crises. In early 2021, two Republican Ohio senators (one of whom was a physician) introduced Senate Bill 22, establishing an advisory committee over the executive branch's current and future health orders. Though DeWine vetoed the bill, the legislature was easily able to override the veto. The bill's long-term effect on future pandemics and health crises is unknown at this time, but one could guess that it will make it difficult for Ohio to be cast as a leader when the next public health crisis arrives, since the state's public health experts will lack some of the tools that they were able to use in the early months of the COVID-19 pandemic. Specifically, future governors may have to wait for the legislature to act on measures such as stay-at-home orders and mask mandates. As the 2020–2021 school year came to a close and summer arrived, COVID-19 cases remained manageable and, in many parts of Ohio, nonexistent. Yet, the question of what lessons were learned from the experience was—and remains—an open question.

Months after her departure from ODH, Acton briefly entered the spotlight again when rumors started circulating that she might run for US Senate. When she announced, in April of 2021, that she would not seek the seat, her words reprised her recognizable civic-minded approach. "While I am not entering the race for U.S. Senate, I recognize there is a genuine longing for a fresh approach to leadership that is honest, collaborative and empowering." Somewhat prophetically, she added what appeared to be a lesson from her time as director: "Ohioans—do not accept anything less from your elected officials. Our leaders' words and actions matter. We must set the bar higher" (Spicker 2021).

Postscript: Ohio's Politics of Public Health Come Full Circle

Though Acton is the focus of this chapter, it is important to end not with Acton, but with what the early months of Ohio's COVID response—as well as the many months of the pandemic after Acton stepped down—tell us about public health both in Ohio and in the United States more generally. Part of what made Acton's pandemic leadership unique was how she was able to navigate the political moment, which consisted at first of a simmering resistance that soon gave way to an open and often ugly political turn against public health thinking itself. Acton endured the early formulation of this politics at a time when the state was desperate to gain a foothold in a crisis it could see coming. As that crisis continued to worsen throughout 2020, Ohio discovered the depth of its citizens' ideological resistance to key public health tools—especially mandates—and just how much influence gender had on the policy-making process itself.

Throughout the summer of 2020 and into the fall, with COVID-19 cases rising steadily, the DeWine administration found itself under attack by the Republican leadership in a state legislature increasingly committed not only to disassembling the state's public health response, but also to defanging the state's public health institutions for future public health crises. As we have argued, the fact that this legislature was predominantly (73 percent) composed of men (Buchanan 2020b) whose masculinity bristled at many evidence-based public health measures instituted by Acton and DeWine was central, and not a mere adjunct, to the politics of public health that set in during the first few months of Ohio's COVID-19 response. The centrality of gender in the politics of these early months is underscored by the fact that COVID policies (such as those mandating face coverings) were placed in a partisan blender with reproductive policies as Ohio passed newly restrictive antiabortion laws (Chappell 2020). The fact that the anti-public health campaign was led by Republican men is particularly revealing in light of the fact that, as we have already noted, working-class women—and women of color, in particular—bore the brunt of the pandemic's economic devastation (Bateman and Ross 2020). At various moments in spring 2020, Acton had been falsely accused on social media and elsewhere of being an abortion-rights activist, an accusation the *Columbus Dispatch* debunked (Rowland 2020). In the wake of Duwve's withdrawal from consideration as Acton's replacement, Lance Himes, a man with antiabortion bona fides, became the ODH's interim director.

The partisan divide over public health in many ways mirrored the state's overall situation. Women were not only more likely to wear masks but also moved faster and in larger numbers to get vaccinated, no doubt to some degree a function of their majority presence in professions being prioritized within the vaccine distribution order. For example, 75 percent of Ohio's K–12 teachers identify as women

(Fordham Institute 2020), and Ohio's nurses are disproportionately women at a ratio of 11.3 to 1 (Rappleye 2017). In a Gallup poll from July 2020, for example, only 34 percent of American men stated that they always wore a mask outside of the house (Brenan 2020). This gender gap was lodged within a glaring geographic divide that is, in one sense, a rural/urban distinction, but also mapped onto partisan allegiances (Ivory, Leatherby, and Gebeloff 2021). This resistance found support from the White House itself as President Trump mocked then-candidate Biden for his mask wearing during a presidential debate ("Trump Mocks Biden for Wearing a Mask" 2020). To be clear, however, these figures are hardly surprising since the gender disparity in mask and vaccine uptake is what would be expected based on what we know about gender disparities in preventive health measures and health care-seeking behaviors more generally (Galdas, Cheater, and Marshall 2005).

Meanwhile, the undermining of public health had larger sociocultural effects as well. At a time when many Ohioans watched their livelihoods crumble, Acton brought an air of competence and calm, but the policies that she and DeWine instituted were sometimes cast as the cause of economic strife instead of responses to an economically devastating virus (Shear et al. 2020). Scholars have begun to study whether or not gender played a role in public compliance with public health orders and have found that a leader's gender is a significant factor with regard to a public's willingness to comply with contact tracing efforts during the first year of the pandemic (though the same study found little difference with regard to policies pertaining to face coverings and social distancing) (Bauer, Kim, and Kweon 2020). An established need to better understand the gendering of public health compliance will be one of COVID-19's scholarly legacies.

Acton's role also raised questions about the role of women in positions of public health leadership, a point that was driven home by the failed appointment of Duwve to ODH. It is well known that double standards pervade the contexts within which women leaders find themselves. Scholars have long discussed the "double bind" in which, compared to men, women in leadership roles have limited space in which they can maneuver (Jamieson 1995; Eagly 2007). The "bind" itself, as gender and feminist theorists have argued, comes from the simultaneous presence of two seemingly irreconcilable, but nonetheless important, demands being made on women. A common illustration of such a bind concerns a call for women to be more assertive to put themselves on equal footing with men, alongside the tendency for women who show assertiveness to be met with critiques that they are overly aggressive, calculating, and "unlikable" (Rankin 2020). This bind is doubly precarious within public health, where so many contentious gender issues are located. But the politics of public health also raises questions about where and to what extent promoting and preserving health should guide policy making and when economic and other social considerations should take priority.

Acton's role in Ohio's COVID reminds us that women are differently situated within this politics. Acton was subject to many of the traditional instantiations of this double bind, as well as some new ones that appear to be unique to Ohio's moment. Ohio's COVID response exposed many fault lines that had been present in Ohio politics, and reminded us that political actors often exploit those fault lines during times of crisis. As Ohioans process their experience with the COVID-19 pandemic, they must decide whether they are willing to learn from their state's policy successes and failures. If policy makers are interested in preparing the state to respond effectively to future public health crises, they will need to take a hard look at what Amy Acton and the response to her leadership tells us. These lessons will undoubtedly concern not only policy but also how an entrenched cultural politics—especially the gendering of that politics—can undermine our state's ability to let professionals do what citizens hired them to do.

REFERENCES

Acton, Amy. Various dates. "Ohio Governor Mike DeWine Transcripts." Rev.com. www.rev.com/blog/transcript-tag/ohio-governor-mike-dewine-transcripts.

Balmert, Jessie, and Jackie Borchardt. 2020. "Why Ohio Is Leading U.S. Coronavirus Response." *The Dispatch*, March 14, 2020. www.dispatch.com/news/20200314/why-ohio-is-leading-us-coronavirus-response.

Bateman, Nicole, and Martha Ross. 2020. "Why Has COVID-19 Been Especially Harmful for Working Women?" The Brookings Institution. www.brookings.edu/essay/why-has-covid-19-been-especially-harmful-for-working-women.

Bauer, N., J. Kim, and Y. Kweon. 2020. "Women Leaders and Policy Compliance during a Public Health Crisis." *Politics & Gender*, 16, no. 4: 975–982.

Boesch, Diana, and Shilpa Phadke. 2021. "When Women Lose All the Jobs: Essential Actions for a Gender-Equitable Recovery." Center for American Progress, February 21, 2021. www.americanprogress.org/issues/women/reports/2021/02/01/495209/women-lose-jobs-essential-actions-gender-equitable-recovery/.

Borchardt, Jackie, and Jessie Balmert. 2020. "Why It's So Hard Now to Find an Ohio Health Director." *The Dispatch*, September 14, 2020. www.dispatch.com/story/news/politics/2020/09/14/why-its-so-hard-now-to-find-ohio-health-director/42617043/.

Brenan, Megan. 2020. "Americans' Face Mask Usage Varies Greatly by Demographics." Gallup, July 30, 2020. https://news.gallup.com/poll/315590/americans-face-mask-usage-varies-greatly-demographics.aspx.

Buchanan, Tyler. 2020a. "Dr. Acton Resignation Follows Months in the Spotlight, Crosshairs." *Ohio Capital Journal,* June 11, 2020. https://ohiocapitaljournal.com/2020/06/11/dr-acton-resignation-follows-months-in-the-spotlight-crosshairs/

Buchanan, Tyler. 2020b. "Most Ohio Legislators Are Men. Will That Change in 2021?" *Ohio Capital Journal,* October 7, 2020. https://ohiocapitaljournal.com/2020/10/07/most-ohio-legislators-are-men-will-that-change-in-2021/

Buchanan, Tyler. 2021. "DeWine Seeks More State Spending for Public Health Causes in Ohio." *Ohio Capital Journal,* February 3, 2021. https://ohiocapitaljournal.com/2021/02/03/dewine-wants-more-state-spending-for-public-health-causes-in-ohio/

Cahn, Naomi. 2020. "COVID-19's Impact on Women of Color." *Forbes,* May 10, 2020. www.forbes.com/sites/naomicahn/2020/05/10/mothers-day-and-covid-19s-impact-on-women-of-color.

Chappell, Bill. 2020. "Ohio House Passes Bill Requiring Fetal Abortion Remains to Be Buried Or Cremated." NPR, December 4, 2020. www.npr.org/2020/12/04/943249413/ohio-passes-bill-requiring-fetal-abortion-remains-to-be-buried-or-cremated.

Connley, Courtney. 2021. "More Dads Are Choosing to Stay at Home with Their Kids. Will Covid-19 Accelerate This Trend?" CNBC, May 7, 2021. www.cnbc.com/2021/05/07/stay-at-home-dads-were-on-the-rise-pre-pandemic-will-covid-accelerate-the-trend.html.

Dosani, Sanya, and Adam Westbrook. 2020. "The Leader We Wish We All Had." *New York Times,* May 5, 2020. www.nytimes.com/video/opinion/100000007111965/coronavirus-ohio-amy-acton.html

Dwyer, Colin, and Allison Aubrey. 2020. "CDC Now Recommends Americans Consider Wearing Cloth Face Coverings In Public." NPR, April 3, 2020. www.npr.org/sections/coronavirus-live-updates/2020/04/03/826219824/president-trump-says-cdc-now-recommends-americans-wear-cloth-masks-in-public

Eagly, Alice H. 2007. "Female Leadership Advantage and Disadvantage: Resolving the Contradictions." *Psychology of Women Quarterly* 31: 1–12.

Eaton, Sabrina. 2020. "Rep. Jim Jordan, Refusing to Wear Mask at Contentious Hearing, Calls Proposed Coronavirus Oversight Subcommittee a Democratic Plot to Attack Trump." Cleveland.com, April 23, 2020. www.cleveland.com/open/2020/04/rep-jim-jordan-refusing-to-wear-mask-at-contentious-hearing-calls-proposed-coronavirus-oversight-subcommittee-a-democratic-plot-to-attack-trump.html

Fordham Institute. 2020. "Characteristics of Ohio Teachers." Ohio Education by the Numbers, 4th edition. March 2020. www.ohiobythenumbers.com.

Funk, Cary, and John Gramlich. 2021. "Amid Coronavirus Threat, Americans Generally Have a High Level of Trust in Medical Doctors." Pew Research Center, March 13, 2021. www.pewresearch.org/fact-tank/2020/03/13/amid-coronavirus-threat-americans-generally-have-a-high-level-of-trust-in-medical-doctors.

Futty, John. 2020. "Reports of Domestic Violence Spike in Central Ohio." *The Dispatch*, July 21, 2020. www.dispatch.com/story/news/local/2020/07/21/reports-of-domestic-violence-spike-in-central-ohio/112805994/.

Galdas, P.M., F. Cheater, and P. Marshall. 2005. "Men and Health Help-Seeking Behaviour: Literature Review." *Journal of Advanced Nursing* 49: 616–623.

Galley, Jacob. 2014. "Stay-at-Home Mothers through the Years." US Bureau of Labor Statistics. www.bls.gov/opub/mlr/2014/beyond-bls/stay-at-home-mothers-through-the-years.htm#:~:text=In%201967%2C%2049%20percent%20of,to%2029%20percent%20in%202012.

Health Policy Institute of Ohio. 2021. "2021 Health Value Dashboard." www.healthpolicyohio.org/2021-health-value-dashboard.

Houser, Nick. 2020. "DeWine Closes Restaurants and Bars in Ohio." Ideastream, March 15, 2020. www.ideastream.org/news/dewine-closes-restaurants-and-bars-in-ohio.

Howard, Jacqueline, and Caroline Kelly. 2021. "Birx Recalls 'Very Difficult' Phone Call from Trump Following Her Covid-19 Warnings." CNN.com, March 28, 2021. https://www.cnn.com/2021/03/28/politics/birx-trump-covid-very-uncomfortable-phone-call/index.html

Ivory, Danielle, Lauren Leatherby, and Robert Gebeloff. 2021. "Least Vaccinated U.S. Counties Have Something in Common: Trump Voters." *New York Times*, April 17, 2021. www.nytimes.com/interactive/2021/04/17/us/vaccine-hesitancy-politics.html

Jamieson, Kathleen Hall. 1995. *Beyond the Double Bind: Women and Leadership*. Oxford University Press on Demand.

Jecker, Nancy, and Donnie Self. 1991. "Separating Care and Cure: An Analysis of Historical and Contemporary Images of Nursing and Medicine." *Journal of Medical Philosophy* 16, no. 3: 285–306.

Kaiser Family Foundation. 2021. "From Accessing Health Care to Work, Childcare, and Caregiving, the COVID-19 Pandemic Continues to Disproportionately Impact Women." KFF.org, March 22, 2021. www.kff.org/womens-health-policy/press-release/from-accessing-health-care-to-work-childcare-and-caregiving-the-covid-19-pandemic-continues-to-disproportionately-impact-women/.

Kramer, Andie. 2020. "Why Stay-At-Home Orders Might Be Good for Gender Equality." *Forbes*, April 1, 2020. www.forbes.com/sites/andiekramer/2020/04/01/why-stay-at-home-orders-might-be-good-for-gender-equality/?sh=4409f7201576.

Lee, Joyce Y., and Shawna J. Lee. 2018. "Caring Is Masculine: Stay-At-Home Fathers and Masculine Identity." *Psychology of Men & Masculinity* 19, no. 1: 47–58.

Ludlow, Randy. 2020. "Several Physicians Applied to Be Ohio's Next Health Director. DeWine Hired a Lawyer," *The Dispatch*, November 20, 2020. www.dispatch.com/story/lifestyle/health-fitness/2020/11/20/physicians-sought-become-ohio-health-director-dewine-hired-lawyer/6353863002/.

Minutaglio, Rose. 2020. "Dr. Deborah Birx Sure Has a Lot of Scarves." *Elle*, April 10, 2020. https://www.elle.com/fashion/trend-reports/a32106845/deborah-birx-scarves-hermes/

North, Anna. 2020. "What Trump's Refusal to Wear a Mask Says about Masculinity in America." Vox.com, May 12, 2020. www.vox.com/2020/5/12/21252476/masks-for-coronavirus-trump-pence-honeywell-covid-19

O'Donnell, Norah. 2020. "Dr. Fauci Says, 'With All Due Modesty, I Think I'm Pretty Effective.'" InStyle, July 15, 2020. www.instyle.com/news/dr-fauci-says-with-all-due-modesty-i-think-im-pretty-effective

Palmary, Ingrid. 2014. "A Politics of Feminist Translation: Using Translation to Understand Gendered Meaning-Making in Research." *Signs: Journal of Women in Culture and Society* 39, no. 3: 576–580.

Planalp, Brian, and Kim Schupp. 2020. "DeWine Announces New Orders, Threatens Shutdowns If Virus Continues to Spread." Fox19 Now, November 11, 2020. www.fox19.com/2020/11/10/gov-dewine-make-primetime-address-ohio-reaches-critical-stage-with-covid-.

Poole, Marilyn, and Dallas Isaacs. 1997. "Caring: A Gendered Concept." *Women's Studies International Forum* 20, no. 4: 529–536.

Power, Kate. 2020. "The COVID-19 Pandemic Has Increased the Care Burden of Women and Families." *Sustainability: Science, Practice and Policy* 16, no. 1: 67–73.

Putrich, Gayle, and Glen Forbes. 2020. "DeWine Institutes 21 Day Curfew to Curb Covid-19 Spread." Ideastream, November 17, 2020. www.ideastream.org/news/dewine-institutes-21-day-curfew-to-curb-covid-19-spread

Rankin, Lauren. 2020. "Elizabeth Warren Couldn't Escape the Double Bind of Misogyny." BitchMedia, March 11, 2020. www.bitchmedia.org/article/elizabeth-warren-double-bind-of-misogyny.

Rappleye, Emily. 2017. "Gender Ratio of Nurses across 50 States." Becker's Hospital Review, February 21, 2017. www.beckershospitalreview.com/hr/gender-ratio-of-nurses-across-50-states.html.

Reason, James. 1990. "The Contribution of Latent Human Failures to the Breakdown of Complex Systems." *Philosophical Transactions of the Royal Society of London. Series B, Biological Sciences* 327, no. 1241: 475–484.

Roberts, Siobhan. 2020. "The Swiss Cheese Model of Pandemic Defense." *New York Times*, December 5, 2020. www.nytimes.com/2020/12/05/health/coronavirus-swiss-cheese-infection-mackay.html

Rowland, Darrel. 2020. "Fact Check: Ex-Ohio Health Director Amy Acton Has No Ties to Abortion Charities, Clinic." *Cincinnati.com*, June 23, 2020. www.cincinnati.com/story/news/factcheck/2020/06/23/fact-check-ohios-amy-acton-has-no-ties-abortion-charities-clinic/3241600001/.

Ryan, Lisa. 2020. "DeWine Issues New Mask Requirements, Limits on Gatherings for Ohioans," Ideastream, November 11, 2020. www.ideastream.org/news/dewine-issues-new-mask-requirements-limits-on-gatherings-for-ohioans

Shear, Michael D., Noah Weiland, Eric Lipton, Maggie Haberman, and David E. Sanger. 2020. "Inside Trump's Failure: The Rush to Abandon Leadership Role on the Virus." *New York Times*, July 18, 2020. www.nytimes.com/2020/07/18/us/politics/trump-coronavirus-response-failure-leadership.html

Spicker, Kristen. 2021 "Acton Not Running for U.S. Senate; Calls on Ohioans to Inspire 'Culture of Commitment' to Each Other." *Dayton Daily News*, April 6, 2021. www.daytondailynews.com/local/acton-not-running-for-senate-calls-on-ohioans-to-inspire-a-culture-of-commitment-to-each-other/ZNIV4UBGF5EJPARE2R6FSJ3I6M/

Stankorb, Sarah. 2020. "Is Amy Acton the Pandemic's Most Midwestern Hero?" *Glamour*, May 18, 2020. www.glamour.com/story/dr-amy-acton-ohio-profile-coronavirus

Stone, Cassandra. 2020. "Dr. Anthony Fauci Goes Full Silver Fox On The Cover Of InStyle Magazine." ScaryMommy, July 17, 2020, https://www.scarymommy.com/dr-fauci-instyle-cover

Thomas, Wendi C. 2020. "Nonprofit Hospital Almost Never Gave Discounts to Poor Patients during Collections, Documents Show." ProPublica, December 4, 2020. www.propublica.org/article/nonprofit-hospital-almost-never-gave-discounts-to-poor-patients-during-collections-documents-show.

Tobias, Andrew J. 2020. "More Legal Battles Likely If Ohio Gov. Mike Dewine Follows Through on Threat to Shut Down Bars, Restaurants and Gyms." Cleveland.com, November 12, 2020. www.cleveland.com/open/2020/11/more-legal-battles-likely-if-ohio-gov-mike-dewine-follows-through-on-threat-to-shut-down-bars-restaurants-and-gyms.html.

Treiber, Linda, and Jackie Jones. 2015. "The Care/Cure Dichotomy: Nursing's Struggle with Dualism." *Health Sociology Review* 24, no. 2: 152–162.

Trubek, Anne. 2020. "Listening to Dr. Amy Acton." *Belt Magazine,* March 25, 2020.

"Trump Mocks Biden for Wearing a Mask." 2020. *Washington Post,* October 2, 2020. www.washingtonpost.com/video/politics/trump-mocks-biden-for-wearing-a-mask/2020/10/02/27db3539-141b-447a-885a-a4e4e69ecb7e_video.html.

Vesoulis, Abby. 2020. "From Homeless to Health Director: Meet the Woman Fighting to Flatten the Coronavirus Curve in Ohio." *Time,* April 8, 2020. https://time.com/collection/coronavirus-heroes/5816890/amy-acton-ohio-coronavirus.

WKYC Staff. 2020. "'Wear the Cape and the Mask': Dr. Amy Acton Warns That Masks Aren't a Substitute for Physical Distancing." April 4, 2021. www.wkyc.com/article/news/health/coronavirus/wear-the-cape-and-the-mask-dr-amy-acton-warns-that-masks-arent-a-substitute-for-physical-distancing/95-17fcdb3e-b020-4bed-985e-ad577c775c5f.

2 | Mike DeWine, Mask Mandates, and the Value of Moral Philosophy

Research Article

Jonathan Spelman

This research piece by a philosopher evaluates Ohio Governor Mike DeWine's DeWine's decision to exempt customers from his initial mask mandate, thereby protecting the health and safety of one group but not another.

Mike DeWine and Mask Mandates

In the early days of the COVID-19 pandemic, the *Washington Post* published an article titled "Ohio Gov. Mike DeWine's Coronavirus Response Has Become a National Guide to the Crisis" (Witte and Zezima 2020). In support of this claim, its authors pointed to the fact that Governor DeWine was one of the first governors in the country to cancel a large-capacity event (on March 3, 2020), to recommend the suspension of in-person college classes (on March 10), to announce the closing of public schools (on March 12), and to order the closing of restaurants and bars to in-person dining (on March 15).

Why was DeWine ahead of the curve? When asked this question by the *Post*, DeWine cited his experience, which included almost forty years of public service.[1] He acknowledged that his biggest mistakes

1. DeWine's career includes four years as a county prosecutor (1977–1981), a brief stint as a member of the Ohio Senate (1981–1982), eight years in the US House of Representatives (1983–1991), several years as lieutenant governor of Ohio (1991–1994), twelve years in the US Senate (1995–2007), and eight years as the attorney general of Ohio (2011–2019).

had stemmed from not "digging deeply enough into the facts" and from not "trusting experts" (Witte and Zezima 2020). To avoid making those same mistakes in his response to the coronavirus, DeWine was in constant contact with experts like Dr. Amy Acton, director of the Ohio Department of Health, from the beginning of the pandemic. In the article by the *Post*, DeWine says, "I have a basic belief that if you have the right facts you're probably going to make the right decision" (Witte and Zezima 2020).

On March 22, 2020, DeWine announced his stay-at-home order, which prohibited nonessential travel. Then, on April 27, as Ohio prepared to reopen, DeWine announced his reopening plan, which would have required both employees and customers of Ohio businesses to wear masks while indoors. That evening, however, DeWine received pushback, and by the next day, he had changed his position. When his "Stay Safe Ohio" order was issued on April 30, only employees were required to wear masks while indoors (Acton 2020). Although DeWine did eventually extend his mask mandate to customers, that was not until July 23, 2020, and at that point, Ohio was the twenty-ninth state to mandate masks in public (Kim, Andrew, and Froio 2020).[2]

DeWine's leadership during the early days of the pandemic was admirable, but, in this chapter, I want to focus on his decision in April to exempt customers from his mask mandate. This, I argue, was a mistake. But it was not just a *public health* mistake; it was also a *moral* mistake. In fact, I contend that it was the sort of moral mistake that those with training in moral philosophy would have almost universally opposed.

In the process, I try to show that, contrary to what DeWine said, having the "right facts" is not sufficient for making the right decision. Making the right decision also requires the ability to sort through the moral dimensions of an issue. If that's correct, then those with training in moral philosophy have a kind of expertise from which leaders throughout our society could benefit.

---

2. By this time, statewide mask mandates had taken effect in a number of "red states" with Republican governors including Texas (July 3), West Virginia (July 6), Alabama (July 15), and Arkansas (July 20). By contrast, there was only one "blue state" with a Democratic governor that did *not* have a similar mandate at the time (viz., Minnesota), and it announced its statewide mask mandate on the same day as DeWine (July 22). That mask mandate went into effect on July 25.

Promoting Public Health and Respecting Autonomy

At the beginning of the COVID-19 pandemic, there was uncertainty about how SARS-CoV-2 spread and about what Americans should do to reduce its transmission. On February 29, 2020, the then-US surgeon general, Dr. Jerome M. Adams, took to Twitter to actively discourage people from purchasing masks because "They are NOT effective at preventing the general public from catching #Coronavirus" and because "if health care providers can't get them to care for sick patients, it puts them and our communities at risk" (cited in Fazio 2021). Similarly, throughout March, the CDC did not encourage healthy people to wear face masks unless they were caring for others who were sick (CDC 2020a).

In retrospect, public health officials seem to have known that masks, at least surgical masks and N95 respirators, were somewhat effective at protecting people from infection. That explains why the then-surgeon general wanted health-care providers to have access to them (Tufekci 2020). So, the primary reason they were discouraging people from purchasing masks was probably that there was a mask shortage. At the same time, however, it seems as though public health officials were working under the false assumption that SARS-CoV-2 was transmitted exclusively, or almost exclusively, by symptomatic individuals. That explains why the CDC was not encouraging healthy people to wear masks unless they were caring for others who were sick.

It also explains why, in early April, in light of new evidence suggesting that asymptomatic and presymptomatic individuals could transmit the virus, the CDC started to encourage everyone, even healthy people, to wear cloth face coverings, especially in situations where social distancing was difficult (CDC 2020c). This new guidance drew a distinction between surgical masks and N95 respirators, which remained in short supply and were to be reserved for health professionals, and cloth face coverings, which people could make for themselves at home. Whether cloth face coverings would protect those who wore them from infection was unclear, and the CDC went out of its way to avoid saying that they would. Instead, it said, "The cloth face cover is meant to protect other people in case you are infected" (CDC 2020b).

Despite the fact that the CDC was recommending that people wear cloth face coverings to prevent asymptomatic and presymptomatic transmission, Governor DeWine decided, on April 28, to exempt customers from the mask mandate he had announced the day before. As indicated above, I believe this decision was a mistake.

One way to argue against DeWine's decision (to exempt customers from his mask mandate) would be to point out that it would have negative health outcomes. Exempting customers from his mask mandate would reduce mask wearing, which would increase SARS-CoV-2 infection rates, that in turn would increase hospitalization and premature death. I'll call this *the simple health-based argument* against DeWine's decision.

The simple health-based argument against DeWine's decision is plausible at first blush, but it seems to presuppose that we should do whatever we can to avoid negative health outcomes. I doubt that anyone would accept this principle on reflection. Consider cigarette smoking. By allowing people to smoke cigarettes, the government increases chronic obstructive pulmonary disease (COPD), lung cancer, and death. But we do not infer from this that we should ban cigarette smoking (at least, not in private) since we also want to respect people's autonomy; that is, we want to give them the freedom to make their own choices. If people enjoy smoking, and they think it is worth the increased risk of COPD, lung cancer, and death, then we let them do so. This tells us is that the simple health-based argument against DeWine's decision is unsound. Sometimes policies that have negative health outcomes are, nevertheless, justified in virtue of the fact that they respect people's autonomy.

When we look carefully at DeWine's press conference announcing his decision to exempt customers from his mask mandate, we see that he emphasized this same idea: that the government should respect people's autonomy. Despite encouraging customers to wear masks, essentially acknowledging that doing so was best for public health, he defended his decision to exempt them from that requirement by saying, "I heard from a lot of different people who felt that, 'I may wear a mask or I may not wear a mask but the government should not be telling me what to do'" (DeWine 2020a). I will call this argument *the simple autonomy-based argument*. According to this argument, DeWine's decision was justified because it respected people's autonomy.

Although the simple autonomy-based argument, like the simple health-based argument, is plausible at first blush, it seems to depend on the principle that the government is never justified in telling people what to do. And while it may be true that there are a wide range of cases in which the government is not justified in telling people what to do, there are also a fair number of cases in which the government is justified in telling people what to do. Although Ohio's government allows people to smoke, for example, it does not allow them to smoke in public places or places of employment. This is because smoking is dangerous not only to the smoker but also to those nearby. So, even though the government may not always be justified in telling people what to do, it does seem to be justified in telling people what to do in cases where their behaviors endanger others. In other words, policies that restrict people's autonomy are at least sometimes justified by the fact that they prevent one group of people from harming those around them.

Mask Mandates and Smoking Bans

The analogy between mask mandates and smoking bans can be instructive.[3] If mask mandates are like laws that would ban smoking *altogether,* then DeWine would be justified in exempting customers from his mask mandate. If, however, mask mandates are like laws that would ban smoking *in public,* then DeWine would not be justified in exempting customers from his mask mandate.

Which is it? If the primary purpose of mask wearing was to protect mask wearers from being infected, then requiring customers to wear masks would have been like banning smoking *altogether,* since the primary purpose of the law would have been to protect people from *themselves.* But the primary purpose of mask wearing, according to the CDC at least, was not to protect mask wearers from being infected. It was to prevent mask wearers from infecting others. Accordingly, requiring customers to wear masks was more like banning smoking *in public,* since the primary purpose of the law was to prevent people from harming those around them.

If this analogy holds, then DeWine's decision was morally equivalent to exempting customers from the law that bans smoking in public. But, of course, no state that bans smoking in public makes an exemption for customers. This includes Ohio. Moreover, it is hard to see how such an exemption could be justified. For not only would such an exemption endanger employees and other customers, but it would

3. The analogy between mask mandates and smoking bans is not original to me. Many others have highlighted the similarities between the two. Two of the earliest to do so, as far as I can tell, were Josh Quinn (2020) and Doug Buchanan (2020), both of whom use the analogy to make an argument that is similar to the one I make here.

also be unfair to employees insofar as it would require them to protect customers without requiring customers to protect employees. This suggests that DeWine's decision was not only a public health mistake; it was also a moral mistake.

DeWine's Decision and Moral Philosophy

In the preceding section, I highlighted an analogy between mask mandates and smoking bans, and I used that analogy to argue that DeWine's decision to exempt customers from his mask mandate was not only a public health mistake but also a moral mistake. In this section, I explain why DeWine's decision was the sort of moral mistake that those with training in moral philosophy would have almost universally opposed. This is not because there is a strong analogy that speaks against it, since not everyone who is trained in moral philosophy would have noticed that analogy. Additionally, it is not because DeWine's justification for his decision was weak, since many leaders have difficulty justifying their decisions.

Instead, the reason why those with training in moral philosophy would have almost universally opposed DeWine's decision is that consequentialism, libertarianism, contractarianism, and virtue ethics would all oppose it. After explaining why this is, I will say more about why it is significant.

Consequentialism is a theory on which actions or policies are justified if and only if they are expected to produce better consequences for society than the alternatives.[4] The simple health-based argument presented above is an example of a consequentialist argument and, as we saw there, it speaks against DeWine's decision. Although it is easy to see why DeWine's decision to exempt customers from his mask mandate would have been expected to have better consequences *for him* than the alternatives (since it would have appeased those on the right wing of his party), it is hard to see why it would have been

4. In order to use consequentialism to evaluate actions or policies, consequentialists need to identify what makes one set of consequences better than another. According to the most popular version of consequentialism, utilitarianism, a set of consequences is better than another if it includes more net pleasure or net happiness than the other. This view traces back to Jeremy Bentham and John Stuart Mill.

expected to have better consequences *for society* than the alternatives.[5] DeWine himself seemed to know this, as evidenced by the fact that, even after exempting customers from his mask mandate, he strongly encouraged them to wear masks to protect employees.

Libertarianism is a theory on which actions or policies are justified if and only if they respect people's rights, where an action or policy respects people's rights as long as it does not unduly restrict people's liberties (or freedoms) without their consent.[6] The autonomy-based argument presented above is an example of a libertarian argument, and as we saw there, it has the potential to provide DeWine with a partial defense. The thought is that mask mandates unduly restrict customers' liberty, and therefore violate their rights. On this view, DeWine was justified in exempting customers from his mask mandate, but his decision didn't go far enough. For just as mask mandates for customers unduly restrict their liberty, mask mandates for employees unduly restrict their liberty. Thus, DeWine's decision may have respected customers' rights, but it did not respect employees' rights.[7]

Contractarianism is a theory on which actions or policies are justified if and only if they are fair, where an action or policy is fair, roughly, if and only if self-interested people who do not know how that action or policy would affect them would consent to it.[8] For example, since I know that I have brown hair, I might happily consent to a policy

5. One scenario in which DeWine's decision would have had better consequences for society than the alternatives is if the opposition to a mask mandate had been so fierce that exempting customers from the mask mandate was necessary to avoid a degree of social unrest that was even more dangerous than COVID-19. Thanks to the editors for pointing this out.

6. This view can be traced back to Immanuel Kant's principle of humanity, but it is more commonly associated with the political philosophies of John Locke and, more recently, Robert Nozick.

7. As one editor pointed out, it is important to note that not all libertarians would endorse the argument just given since not all libertarians would endorse the claim that mask mandates *unduly* restrict people's liberties. This is because they think that governments are justified in restricting certain liberties to protect other ones. For example, some libertarians think that governments are justified in limiting how many fish one can take from a lake to ensure that everyone has a chance to take some fish from that lake. This group of libertarians would not endorse the argument given above, but they would be no less opposed to the position that DeWine ultimately arrived at.

8. This way of understanding fairness comes from John Rawls, but he is drawing on Kant's principle of universalizability, and Kant is drawing on the Golden Rule.

that exempts brown-haired people from paying taxes. However, if I did not know whether I had brown hair, I would not consent to that policy. Thus, this policy is unfair, and since it is unfair, it is unjustified according to contractarianism. A similar argument entails that DeWine's decision was unjustified according to contractarianism. If a person knows that they live and work in a rural area where stores are not particularly crowded and that they are not particularly at risk of being hospitalized or dying from COVID-19, then they might happily consent to a policy that exempts customers from DeWine's mask mandate, especially if they find masks uncomfortable. However, if that person does not know where they live, where they work, or whether they are at risk of being hospitalized or dying from COVID-19, they would not consent to that policy. Thus, DeWine's decision to exempt customers from his mask mandate is unfair, and since it is unfair, it is unjustified according to contractarianism.

Finally, virtue ethics is a theory on which actions or policies are justified if and only if they demonstrate virtue and promote the flourishing of society.[9] DeWine's decision did not do either of these things. Paradigmatic virtues include wisdom, courage, and justice, but DeWine's decision seems to have been foolish, cowardly, and unjust. He ignored the advice of public health experts, which was foolish; he caved to political pressure, which was cowardly; and, in the process, he privileged the interests of customers over those of employees, which was unjust. Additionally, DeWine's decision did not promote the flourishing of society. According to virtue ethicists, a flourishing society is one where people live in harmony and work together for the common good. At times, this means that certain people or groups of people have to face greater dangers than others. For example, a society may have to send some of its citizens into battle to defend it from an invading army. This is justified because something of great value is at stake, namely, the lives of its people or the society's way of life. DeWine's decision, like a society's decision to send some of its citizens into battle, forces a certain group of people (viz., employees) to face greater dangers than others. The problem is that DeWine did so not because something of great value was at stake, but because customers simply did not want to wear masks.[10]

---

9. This view traces back to Socrates, Plato, and Aristotle.

10. As an editor pointed out, a virtue ethicist could try to defend DeWine's decision by arguing that it spared employees the burden of having to police his

In the preceding paragraphs, I have suggested that DeWine's decision was expected to have bad consequences, that it did not respect employees' rights, that it was unfair, and that it did not demonstrate virtue or promote the flourishing of society. Those with training in moral philosophy regularly defend policies that have one or two of these flaws. For example, they might, in their analyses, defend a policy that is unfair to a certain group by appealing to its good consequences, or they might defend a policy that does not demonstrate virtue or promote the flourishing of society by appealing to the fact that it respects people's rights. But rarely do they defend policies that have all four of these flaws. This suggests that few people with training in moral philosophy would have supported it. This does not entail that his decision was wrong, but this does create a strong presumption against it. But maybe that presumption can be overcome.

Just as arriving at good policies requires "digging deeply enough into the facts," it also requires taking a closer look at the moral principles at play. In the next section, then, I want to investigate the arguments both for and against DeWine's decision a bit more carefully. To begin, I highlight two features of DeWine's decision that made it particularly problematic. Then, I consider how DeWine or someone else who supports his decision would respond to my criticisms of his decision.

Digging Deeper

The analogy I presented earlier, between Governor DeWine's decision and a policy that would exempt customers from a law that bans smoking in public, suggested that DeWine's decision was unfair. Libertarianism and contractarianism did as well. These arguments, in addition to the consequentialist and virtue ethical ones, give us good reasons to think that it was a moral mistake. But there are, I contend, two additional features of DeWine's decision that make it particularly problematic.

We can see this by looking at two differences between DeWine's decision and a policy that would exempt customers from a law that

mask mandate. It's worth noting, however, that nothing DeWine said in defense of his decision suggested that he was thinking this way. But even if he was, it is implausible that he would have been justified in thinking that protecting employees from the threat of angry customers was more pressing than protecting them from the threat of unmasked customers.

bans smoking in public. First, smoking is known to be dangerous to one's health, but shopping unmasked was not known to be particularly dangerous to one's health, at least at the time of DeWine's decision. (Remember that, at the time, the CDC was recommending that people wear face coverings to prevent them from infecting others.) This is significant because it means that, whereas people have a strong self-interested reason not to smoke even if it is not banned in public, people did not have a self-interested reason to wear a mask unless it was mandated, or at least they did not have a particularly weighty one.

If mask wearing was not uncomfortable, this might not be significant. But mask wearing often is uncomfortable, not only physically but also psychologically, especially in places where other people are not wearing them. As a bit of autobiography, I feel strong social pressure not to wear masks in places where other people are not wearing them, and I suspect that most other people feel similarly. This means that, at the time of DeWine's decision, even if people had some self-interested reasons *to* wear a mask, people often had stronger self-interested reasons *not* to wear a mask. This creates a collective action problem. Whereas it was in society's collective interest that everyone do a certain thing (viz., that they wear masks to slow the spread of COVID-19), it was simultaneously in each individual's self-interest not to do that thing (viz., that they not wear masks since mask wearing was uncomfortable and was not supposed to provide them with significant protection against COVID-19).

Solving a collective action problem requires finding a way to align each individual's self-interest with the society's collective interest. Governments are well positioned to do this because they can use incentives or the threat of punishment to change people's incentives. And that is what DeWine could have done here, by requiring both customers and employees to wear masks. This not only would have aligned each individual's self-interest with society's collective interest, but it would have also distributed the risk of infection more evenly across the members of society. Instead of doing that, however, DeWine chose sides. By exempting customers from his mask mandate, he forced employees to sacrifice both their comfort and their safety while requiring customers to sacrifice neither their comfort nor their safety.

To return to the analogy, what this suggests is that DeWine's decision was not quite like exempting customers from a ban on smoking in public. It was more like exempting customers from a ban on smoking in public in a world where smoking is not dangerous to smokers. In our world, there's already an incentive for customers not to smoke in public, namely, that it is dangerous. So, even if the government does not ban customers from smoking in public, relatively few people are going to do it. But in a world where there is no incentive not to smoke in public, if the government does not ban customers from smoking in public, then everyone who is self-centered is going to do it. This is one reason to think that DeWine's decision was particularly problematic.

A second reason to think that DeWine's decision was particularly problematic is that, whereas employees who are exposed to secondhand smoke do not pose a danger to others, employees who are exposed to unmasked customers do pose a danger to others. A smoking customer's secondhand smoke may harm an employee, but it cannot give that employee a transmissible disease. An unmasked customer's cough, however, can give an employee a transmissible disease. By analogy, then, DeWine's decision was not quite like exempting customers from a ban on smoking in public. It was more like exempting customers from a ban on smoking in public in a world where the health conditions associated with secondhand smoke are transmissible to one's family and friends. This puts employees at danger not only of falling ill but also of harming their loved ones.

Despite these additional criticisms of DeWine's decision, it is crucial that we consider how someone else who supports it, or DeWine himself, would respond to the arguments I have made against it. So, below, I will consider two such defenses. Each of them grants that DeWine's decision was unfair but tries to justify that unfairness by appealing to some benefit of that decision.

According to the *first defense*, DeWine's decision, despite having been unfair to employees, was justified by virtue of the fact that it was in the employees' best interest. How could that be? The thought here is that employees who were furloughed during Ohio's stay-at-home order needed to get back to work to make money. But to make that happen, DeWine needed to get a sufficiently large number of customers back in stores, and that could not happen unless he exempted customers from his mask mandate.

This defense has the potential to justify DeWine's decision not only to impartial observers but also to those whom DeWine was supposedly treating unfairly. There are a couple problems with it, however. First, while there may have been a fair number of customers who would not go back to stores if they were required to wear masks, it is not obvious that there were so many of them that, had DeWine not exempted customers from his mask mandate, then businesses would have had to close and their employees would have lost their jobs. That assumption is dubious, especially given what we know now, that people were generally willing to comply with DeWine's decision in July to expand his mask mandate to customers. But even back in April, there were reasons to be dubious of this assumption, in light of the analogy with the ban on smoking in public. Given that people who were addicted to nicotine were able to modify their behavior to comply with the ban on smoking in public, DeWine probably should have been confident that people who simply did not want to wear masks would be able to modify their behavior to comply with his mask mandate.

Furthermore, even if DeWine had reasons to think that a mask mandate would discourage one group of customers from returning to stores (viz., customers who did not want to wear masks), he also had reasons to think that a mask mandate would have the opposite effect on another group of customers (viz., customers who were scared of being infected by unmasked customers). Because unmasked customers endanger not only employees but also their fellow customers, it is likely that, even if DeWine's decision to exempt customers from his mask mandate encouraged some people to return to stores, it also kept other people away from stores.

This casts doubt on the first defense's assumption that DeWine needed to exempt customers from his mask mandate in order to get a sufficiently large number of customers back in stores. But even if that was true, it is not clear that employees needed to get back to work in the first place. If a pandemic makes it impossible for businesses to continue operating without endangering employees, then even if those employees need to make money, the solution is not to endanger employees so that they can make money. The solution is to give the employees the financial support they need to get by until they can safely return to work.

But maybe that is not the right way to defend DeWine's decision. According to the *second defense*, DeWine's decision was justified, not in virtue of the fact that it was in the *employees'* best interest, but in virtue of the fact that it was in *society's* best interest. The thought here is that even though DeWine's decision unduly endangered employees, it was necessary to save Ohio's economy. Accordingly, it was analogous to the sort of decision that a government makes when it conscripts soldiers to defend it from a hostile nation. In both cases, the government unduly endangers a particular group of people to save it from disaster. This is a sort of consequentialist or virtue ethical defense of DeWine's decision.

While I am skeptical that DeWine needed to endanger employees to save Ohio's economy for the reasons given above, even if that were true, the second defense would still be unsound. This is because, in cases where the government unduly endangers a group of people to save it from disaster, the government owes that group of people special compensation. If, for example, a government conscripts soldiers to defend it from a hostile nation, it has an obligation not only to pay them for their service, but also to cover any health-care costs they incur as a result of their service and to compensate them for opportunities they lost as a result of being required to serve in the military. A government might meet this obligation by providing its conscripts with various medical, educational, and employment benefits that go over and above their financial compensation.

Analogously, then, because DeWine's decision unduly endangered employees, he owed them special compensation. He could have met that obligation by offering them hazard pay or by providing them with some other benefit.[11] But he did not do that. Alternatively, he could have at least offered unemployment benefits to employees who were unwilling to return to their previous job, at least while they looked for new work. But on June 16, 2020, DeWine issued an executive order expressly *prohibiting* such employees from collecting unemployment benefits unless they met certain conditions (DeWine 2020b). The fact that their previous job would have been more dangerous than it had been prior to the pandemic should have been justification enough.

In this section, I identified two reasons to think that DeWine's decision was worse than a policy that would exempt customers from a ban on smoking in public. Then, I considered two defenses of it. Of those two defenses, the second is stronger, and it gives us some reason to think that DeWine's decision could have been justified if it had been necessary to save Ohio's economy and if DeWine had adequately compensated employees for the additional risk he required them to take on. But since it is implausible that exempting customers from DeWine's mask mandate was necessary to save Ohio's economy and since DeWine did not adequately compensate employees for the

11. In a report from the Brookings Institution, Molly Kinder (2020) argues that essential workers deserve hazard pay for their work during the COVID-19 pandemic. Here, I am arguing that DeWine's decision treats all employees like essential workers (since it unjustifiably endangers them for the sake of the common good) and, therefore, that all of them deserve hazard pay.

additional risk he required them to take on, even the second defense of DeWine's decision fails.

The Value of Moral Philosophy

To this point, I have argued that Governor DeWine's decision to exempt customers from his mask mandate was the sort of moral mistake that those with training in moral philosophy would have almost universally opposed. But as I mentioned at the beginning, DeWine updated his mask mandate a few months later by requiring everyone, even customers, to wear masks in all Ohio businesses. Moreover, as I write this, vaccines are widely available. So, why does this issue still matter?

My primary goal in this chapter has not been to criticize DeWine so much as to demonstrate the value of training in moral philosophy, which provides people with the theoretical frameworks and argumentative skills to sort through the moral dimensions of novel moral issues like this one. I cannot help but think that if DeWine and his staff either had this sort of training themselves or consulted someone who did, DeWine would have made a different decision in this case.

This is speculative, of course. It is possible that DeWine's decision was politically motivated. Maybe it was a concession he felt he needed to make to the right wing of his party in order to have any hope of reelection in 2022. But on the assumption that DeWine was trying to make the right decision, he must have failed to see that his decision was deeply morally problematic. If that is correct, it suggests that he would have benefited from consulting with someone with training in moral philosophy.

This suggestion that DeWine would have benefited from consulting with someone with training in moral philosophy is controversial because it implies that people with training in moral philosophy are moral experts (i.e., are generally better than others at evaluating the morality of actions), and this claim is controversial, even among moral philosophers (see, e.g., Archard 2011 and Cross 2016).

Maybe the most common argument against this claim, that people with training in moral philosophy are moral experts, is that if it were true, then there would be widespread agreement among moral philosophers about how to answer moral questions. But, in fact, there is widespread *disagreement* among moral philosophers about how to answer moral questions (e.g., the morality of abortion and euthanasia). Thus, people with training in moral philosophy are not moral experts.

Although I cannot hope to settle this issue here, I would point out that, just because those with training in a discipline disagree about how to answer *some* of their discipline's questions, that does not entail that they are not experts with respect to those questions. During the pandemic, for example, there was disagreement among public health experts, especially early on, about the primary mode by which SARS-CoV-2 is transmitted, about how deadly it was, and about whether the health-related benefits of long stay-at-home orders outweighed the health-related costs. But despite these disagreements, we should still expect public health experts to be better than others at judging what is best for public health and should still consult them when faced with difficult public health decisions, especially on issues where they generally agree. The same, I submit, is true of those with training in moral philosophy. Despite their disagreements, we should still expect them to be better than others at judging what is morally right and should still consult them when faced with difficult moral decisions, especially on issues where they generally agree. If this is correct, it follows that people with training in moral philosophy were probably underutilized during the pandemic. Not only could politicians have benefited from their expertise, but businesses, churches, hospitals, and schools could have benefited from it as well since they all faced difficult moral decisions throughout the pandemic.

The COVID-19 pandemic has definitely given me a newfound appreciation for the value of epidemiologists and public health experts, but it has also given me a newfound appreciation for the value of my own discipline, moral philosophy. My hope is that others might develop a newfound appreciation for the value of moral philosophy as well.[12]

REFERENCES

Acton, Amy. 2020. "Director's Stay Safe Ohio Order." Ohio Department of Health. March 22, 2020. https://coronavirus.ohio.gov/static/publicorders/Directors-Stay-Safe-Ohio-Order.pdf.

Archard, David. 2011. "Why Moral Philosophers Are Not and Should Not Be Moral Experts." *Bioethics* 25, no. 3: 119–127.

Buchanan, Doug. 2020. "DeWine Should Reverse Himself (Again) on Mask Mandate." *Columbus Business First*, April 30, 2020. www.bizjournals.com/columbus/news/2020/04/30/from-the-editor-dewine-should-reverse-himself.html.

12. Thanks to Darrin Snyder Belousek, Anne Marie Hardy Spelman, Ross Kauffman, and the editors of this collection for their helpful feedback on earlier drafts of this chapter.

Center for Disease Control and Prevention. 2020a. "How to Protect Yourself." March 31, 2020. https://web.archive.org/web/20200331053105/https://www.cdc.gov/coronavirus/2019-ncov/prevent-getting-sick/prevention.html.

Center for Disease Control and Prevention. 2020b. "How to Protect Yourself." April 4, 2020. https://web.archive.org/web/20200404002655/https://www.cdc.gov/coronavirus/2019-ncov/prevent-getting-sick/prevention.html.

Center for Disease Control and Prevention. 2020c. "Recommendation Regarding the Use of Cloth Face Coverings, Especially in Areas of Significant Community-Based Transmission." April 3, 2020. https://web.archive.org/web/20200403221424/https://www.cdc.gov/coronavirus/2019-ncov/prevent-getting-sick/cloth-face-cover.html.

Cross, Ben. 2016. "Moral Philosophy, Moral Expertise, and the Argument from Disagreement." *Bioethics* 30, no. 3: 188–194.

DeWine, Mike. 2020a. "Ohio Governor Mike DeWine—COVID-19 Update | April 28, 2020." The Ohio Channel. Streamed live on April 28, 2020. YouTube video, 1:59:50, www.youtube.com/watch?v=oHVBGlbCL8g.

DeWine, Mike. 2020b. "Executive Order 2020–24D." June 16, 2020. https://governor.ohio.gov/wps/portal/gov/governor/media/executive-orders/executive-order-2020-24d.

Fazio, Marie. 2021. "How Mask Guidelines Have Evolved." *New York Times,* April 27, 2021. Last modified May 13, 2021. www.nytimes.com/2021/04/27/science/face-mask-guidelines-timeline.html.

Kim, Allen, Scottie Andrews, and James Froio. 2020. "These Are the States Requiring People to Wear Masks When Out in Public." CNN, June 19, 2020. Last modified August 17, 2020. www.cnn.com/2020/06/19/us/states-face-mask-coronavirus-trnd/index.html.

Kinder, Molly. 2020. "COVID-19's Essential Workers Deserve Hazard Pay. Here's Why—and How It Should Work." Brookings Institution. April 10, 2020. www.brookings.edu/research/covid-19s-essential-workers-deserve-hazard-pay-heres-why-and-how-it-should-work/.

Quinn, Josh. 2020. "One Retailer's View on Gov. DeWine's Face Mask Flip-Flop." Alive, April 29, 2020. www.columbusalive.com/opinion/20200429/op-ed-one-retailers-view-on-gov-dewines-face-mask-flip-flop.

Tufekci, Zeynep. 2020. "Why Telling People They Don't Need Masks Backfired." *New York Times,* March 17, 2020. www.nytimes.com/2020/03/17/opinion/coronavirus-face-masks.html.

Witte, Griff, and Katie Zezima. 2020. "Ohio Gov. Mike DeWine's Coronavirus Response Has Become a National Guide to the Crisis." *Washington Post,* March 16, 2020. www.washingtonpost.com/national/coronavirus-ohio-dewine-outbreak/2020/03/16/9bde6b1e-67b2-11ea-9923-57073adce27c_story.html.

3 | Lessons in Resiliency during a Pandemic

Did We Do Everything We Could?

Personal Reflection

Zac Ginsberg

In this personal reflection, a physician recounts his experience working in an ICU in southwest Ohio during the first wave of COVID-19 and contemplates how inadequate public health measures and individual noncompliance violated the social contract.

"Doc, do everything you can to get him home. He has a grandchild he has never met." At first, the words caught me off guard, because my patient seemed too young to be a grandfather yet. It was late at night and I was on the phone talking with my patient's family about his course of COVID-19. The patient was on a ventilator and, despite our efforts, was doing poorly. I wanted his family to know my concerns and that he wasn't responding to our treatments. I reassured his son that we were doing everything we could. He thanked me and we both hung up—he to his worry and I to my work. I was in an intensive care unit (ICU) in southwest Ohio, working as an emergency and critical care physician on my ward of COVID patients.

COVID-19 was choking off my patient's lungs' ability to deliver oxygen to the bloodstream. Despite the ventilator delivering maximal support at 100 percent oxygen (normally, we breathe just 21 percent), his oxygen levels were incompatible with life. The severity of lung disease caused by COVID-19 had reached the point where the patient would struggle to breathe while lying on his back due to the inflammatory debris left by the virus. To help, we needed to rotate him onto his belly—"prone" him—so the oxygen could move to less damaged areas of the lung. We willfully made the care situation harder for ourselves by literally doing ICU care upside down, because it was what our patients needed. Rotating him was dangerous. If his breathing tube got dislodged even by a centimeter, it could cause him to die. We secured the endotracheal tube that hooked him up to the ventilator and adhered all the catheters that were inserted into his arteries, veins, and bladder so they wouldn't get dislodged. Sinking him into a chemically induced coma we paralyzed him because, even with the ventilator, his lungs were so frail a cough could tear a hole in them and kill him. He was so ill that just moving side to side caused massive swings in his blood pressure that, if it had dropped low enough, could have caused his heart to stop. Every day, he needed to be rotated again to avoid the breakdown of his skin, and we repeated the rotation in the hopes that the lungs could recover.

It takes five to six people to be able to prone a COVID patient safely. By contrast, typical intensive care unit (ICU) care requires only one or two. So, every member of the ICU team was a part of every COVID patient's care. This level of critical illness left the staff worried that each heartbeat would not be followed by another. Constantly primed for the worst, we all persevered to deliver the best of ourselves. Repeatedly throughout that week, I returned to my patient's bedside, and, in so doing, to the conversation with his son, this imperative, this plea to keep his family whole. In the face of everything we could do, despite maximum life support, the patient died. He never met his grandson and he never returned to his family. My team was devastated. I dissected his case, looking for any flaw in our care to make ourselves better for the next person. But there were no flaws. This was simply a case in which we'd made all the right decisions, yet it still ended with a life lost to COVID-19. This scenario was occurring across our country's ICUs on a daily basis.

It was rare to see the type of severe lung disease that COVID-19 causes; proning a patient used to be uncommon. This scene had become the daily norm. Before the pandemic, deaths in the ED or ICU occurred only a couple of times a week. As a result, the staff at the bedside were able to put aside their own experience and hold space for the families to grieve or express their anger at the outcome. Then, among ourselves, away from the bedside, we supported one another to grieve privately. Those taking care of patients in other areas of the ED or ICU and who were spared the pain that comes from bearing witness firsthand to someone's death, were able to support those who had been at the bedside. A great day felt as if we saved a life. A good day had no deaths. A bad day might have one. The worst kind of day had several deaths, which felt like a freight train hitting the entire department. Thankfully, our hard-earned coping mechanisms were tested infrequently.

The pandemic changed everything. When COVID-19 emerged, it swept across the globe, and when it reached Ohio, we were warned it caused severe lung disease and a host of other complications, which targeted the elderly and chronically infirm. We barely knew anything about COVID-19, but we knew it was airborne, contagious, and dangerous. The early stages of COVID-19 pushed the boundaries and the limits of the ED and ICU care. In the ED, we were working out of tents in the ambulance bay, with our hospitals overflowing. When the ED beds filled and we had more people in the waiting room than there were beds in the entire department, we stepped up. I was proud of my ED and ICU colleagues who picked up extra shifts, slept in trailers or hotels, and willingly put their own safety on the line against this unknown threat. When the storm hit the EDs and ICUs, we stood clad in makeshift personal protective equipment (PPE), which sometimes took the form of trash bags and masks donated from our neighbors' home workshops. These felt like life rafts in a tsunami. Death flooded our days. Before we could grieve the last loss, the next came in as part of an unrelenting wave. We were forced onward to try to save the next patient. We clung to our PPE like our lives depended on it—because they did—and we were grateful for our community's support. We faced the constant fear that any momentary lapse could cause our own death, a thing which happened to too many on the front lines. The toll of caring for COVID patients was measured in blood, sweat, and tears—and we did it because it mattered. The ED and ICU teams brought everything, every time, no matter the obstacle, because that was the job. This was our promise—our social contract (to cite Rousseau)—to fight the odds and reunite as many people as possible with their loved ones, to return them to their lives, to keep our community whole.

On the front lines, we've been struggling for over 28 months now. I've seen the resilience drain from our system. When people ask us what it's like, no one is prepared to hear the truth. How do we talk about the memories of the hundreds or thousands of deaths? How do we describe the people we've spoken to, who shared their fears with us before we watched them die? Or what it has been like to cry with our patients' families as we watch them grieve? The legacy of this pandemic for those on the front lines will be the faces of patients we've lost and their loved ones. Watching someone gasp for air or wither from critical illness is painful. Being yelled at for enforcing visitation restrictions to keep the public safe and having to relegate families to screen-mediated, virtual visits as the only way to be with their loved ones feels exhausting. Stepping into the room to hold the hand of the dying because we can't bear to have them die alone breaks us. Again and again, we experience the pain of watching families lose their loved ones to the degree that they can start to merge in our memories. This makes the experience of those of us on the front lines an unending stream of suffering. Feeling this amount of grief is impossible to sustain. Each of us can only take so much concentrated grief before the only choice left is to become numb or quit. It's not a lack of empathy; rather, it's a self-protective emotional and mental distancing from the suffering. In the first year and a half of the pandemic, our colleagues' emotional wells dried up and no reserve support was coming. Many quit. Working on the front lines of the pandemic has felt simultaneously like the greatest honor to serve our community and like the deepest betrayal by them. Every step of this pandemic has felt like a fight, both for and with the very community we serve.

Having witnessed firsthand the front lines of this pandemic, I no longer say "we did everything we could." The truth is, as a society, we have not. We have turned on one another. We have lost sight of the reality that hundreds of thousands of families were grieving and let our public interactions devolve into vitriol and yelling. We have left those who are grieving alone and isolated, rather than upholding the social contract to support one another. We have left a stain on history for our callousness and the tragedy of the lives lost. The numbers continued to swell even after vaccines and PPE became widely available due in large part to the actions and inactions of the communities we serve. I fear the emotional damage that will haunt those who one day will realize their own complicity and contribution to the death toll. With asymptomatic transmission easily hidden and hard to track, people have disavowed their role in the spread as COVID swept through our communities like a tornado.

When a tornado tears through a community, two houses standing next to one another can have wildly different outcomes: one may remain whole while the other is torn apart. In the critical, early stages of the pandemic, those who gathered together in a pandemic without universal testing and without precautions such as masks—whether to make a political point or because they felt whatever they were doing was important enough "to cheat"—were a major obstacle to containing the spread. Their choices turned the pandemic into a larger tornado. Instead of sheltering in place, everyone ran out to watch and then wondered why the death toll was so high. It felt like my community did not understand—or, worse, did not care—that how we all behaved impacted the waves of illness that were drowning and suffocating so many patients in our hospitals. I wondered if seeing the viral particles depicted as a toxic, red gas, which becomes ever denser as it fills a room, would somehow impress upon people the threat of the virus and promote safer behaviors. Perhaps the invisible nature of an unseen viral particle made the threat that much harder for some to conceptualize. I've wondered, if this infection were as extreme as Ebola, and if we had people bleeding in public rather than coughing, whether people would be more cautious.

While the unending grief from the front lines made me expect widespread national mourning, what I saw instead has felt like callousness. We couldn't have spared everyone, but the toll didn't need to be so high. The tragedy has been buried beneath a political debate that distracted us from the most basic premises of our social contract. Following a tornado, we measure our disaster response by our ability to help those most hurt and to rebuild as a community. We do not measure the response by the condition of those least affected.

This pandemic has illuminated the bravest and basest elements of human nature for all to see. From the start of the pandemic, the reality of the front lines has felt disjointed in relation to community perceptions. With the mask mandates, Ohio's leaders downplayed the harm caused by recklessness. The truth is that someone who is infected (even if asymptomatic) and who walks into a public space unmasked puts the lives of those around them at risk. It doesn't matter whether or not they intended to be a threat to the public.

While I watched people struggle for breath, I heard people use their own breath to argue for their freedom to buck proven safety precautions. Never mind my patient's right to avoid this threat to his life. While doing everything we can on the front lines, it feels insulting to be told that covering the bottom half of one's face is too much, when it could save someone's life. As a society, we have failed to do everything we could to protect ourselves from harm and misinformation.

Over the course of the pandemic, a battery of treatments has been proven and disproven by the rigor of scientific testing, which has always guided medical practice. A historic global collaboration produced a singular therapy—the vaccination—which could push COVID into the history books. When it was announced, it felt like a protective shield against the threat we faced daily. Hope was renewed and then, whether from fear or something more malevolent, the integrity of medical care was called into question by those leveraging a legacy of mistrust among some and fostering it anew in others. I have watched people pass up a proven and approved vaccine, only to opt for the modern version of snake oil. I have watched people so convinced COVID-19 isn't real that they deny any COVID-specific therapy while simultaneously asking medical providers like us to do everything possible—and they have died. Surges have become commonplace. As a society we should not need to ask how many lives lost—and, in the surge of late 2021, how many children's lives lost—is enough to change our behavior. We all should wear masks and get vaccinated out of respect for those lost during the pandemic. On behalf of frontline workers, those we've lost, and their grieving families, we are angry about the callous disregard for all our lives and the pain inflicted on our communities. When we tell a family that their loved one has died, we reassure them that we did everything we could. As the ticker of lives lost increases, I think of all the families and the stream of faces of those I've seen die and wonder what happened to our agreement, our social contract. This pandemic has been the first time the statement "we did everything we could" has felt like a lie.

As this book highlights, so many aspects of our healthcare system are struggling. We must reflect on how we can do better and acknowledge the failures of our response. While the political rhetoric has focused on masks and vaccines, the pandemic exposed fundamental weaknesses in our healthcare infrastructure that we must address. This pandemic overwhelmed our healthcare system quickly and exposed its frailty. Our healthcare system before the pandemic was already a cachectic system on life support, barely able to stand up to the daily deluge of chronic illness, let alone a pandemic. In the United States, your demographics are more likely to predict health outcomes; the pandemic exposed this on a larger scale with the fact that it has been more deadly for the poor and people of color (Abrams and Szefler, 2020; Hostetter et al. 2018; Turner-Musa et al. 2020; Mude et al. 2021). While we extolled advanced technology such as new medications or surgical tools, we ignored that it was unavailable to entire communities and large segments of our population. Our most vulnerable populations fare the worst in our current system and the reasons are myriad: their built environment, lack of access to care, lack of insurance coverage, mistrust on the part of patients, and mistreatment from providers (Newhouse 1993; IOM 2000; Hall et al. 2015; Fiscella et al. 2016; Belmont Report 1978).

The disproportionate number of deaths during this pandemic of the poor and ethnic minorities is the inevitable outcome of a society that ignored how our most vulnerable already bore the burden of the crumbling healthcare infrastructure. The most profound lesson of our pandemic is that structural racism has been operationalized through healthcare as a means of suppression (Bailey et al. 2017). While the damaging rhetoric of a vocal minority must be addressed to help us transition out of the COVID-19 pandemic, we cannot let it distract from our need as a country to uphold our social contract. I hope the legacy of this pandemic will be to rebuild our crumbling health-care system to align with the values of equity and a just distribution of resources for the betterment of us all.

REFERENCES

Abrams, Elissa M. and Stanley J. Szefler. 2020. "COVID-19 and the Impact of Social Determinants of Health." *The Lancet. Respiratory Medicine* 8, no. 7: 659–661.

Bailey, Zinzi D., Nancy Krieger, Madina Agénor, Jasmine Graves, Natalia Linos, and Mary T. Bassett. 2017. "Structural Racism and Health Inequities in the USA: Evidence and Interventions." *Lancet (London, England)* 389, no. 10077: 1453–1463.

The Belmont Report: Ethical Principles and Guidelines for the Protection of Human Subjects of Research. 1978. Bethesda, MD: The Commission.

Fiscella, Kevin, and Mechelle R. Sanders. 2016. "Racial and Ethnic Disparities in the Quality of Health Care." *Annual Review of Public Health* 37: 375–394.

Hall, William J., Mimi V. Chapman, Kent M. Lee, Yesenia M. Merino, Tainayah W. Thomas, B. Keith Payne, Eugenia Eng, Steven H. Day, and Tamera Coyne-Beasley. 2015. "Implicit Racial/Ethnic Bias among Health Care Professionals and Its Influence on Health Care Outcomes: A Systematic Review." *American Journal of Public Health* 105, no. 12: e60–76.

Hostetter, Martha, and S. Klein. 2018. "Reducing Racial Disparities in Health Care by Confronting Racism." The Commonwealth Fund, September 27, 2018. www.commonwealthfund.org/publications/2018/sep/focus-reducing-racial-disparities-health-care-confronting-racism.

Institute of Medicine (US) Committee on Quality of Health Care in America. 2000. *To Err is Human: Building a Safer Health System.* Edited by Linda T. Kohn et. al., 1–15. Washington, DC: National Academies Press.

Mude, William, Victor M. Oguoma, Tafadzwa Nyanhanda, Lillian Mwanri, and Carolyne Njue. 2021. "Racial Disparities in COVID-19 Pandemic Cases, Hospitalisations, and Deaths: A Systematic Review and Meta-Analysis." *Journal of Global Health* 11: 05015.

Newhouse, Joseph P. and the Insurance Experiment Group. 1993. *Free for All? Lessons from the RAND Health Experiment*. Cambridge, MA: Harvard University Press.

Rousseau, Jean-Jacques. 1947. *The Social Contract*. Edited by Charles Frankel. New York: Hafner Publishing.

Turner-Musa, Jocelyn, Oluwatoyin Ajayi, and Layschel Kemp. 2020. "Examining Social Determinants of Health, Stigma, and COVID-19 Disparities." *Healthcare (Basel, Switzerland)* 8, no. 2: E168.

4 | Abortion and the Politics of Care in Ohio during the COVID Pandemic

Research Article

Hillary J. Gyuras, Mikaela H. Smith, Danielle Czarnecki, Alison H. Norris, Michelle L. McGowan, and Danielle Bessett

This research piece by a team of gender and reproductive health scholars analyzes the effect of the pandemic on abortion care in Ohio before the Dobbs *decision, with special attention to the state's struggle over the definition of "essential" health care services.*

Vanessa's[1] voice was tired on the phone. We spoke in early December 2020, while she was preparing to drive to an abortion clinic nearly one hour away from her newly secured housing. This was the second time she had to make this trip to obtain the abortion care she needed, as she had already been to the clinic once for a state-mandated consultation, followed by a 24-hour waiting period. Since her abortion was a two-day procedure that would necessitate a third visit, she was set to return for one final appointment the next day.

The pandemic had been especially tough for Vanessa, a Black woman and single mother of five children living in Ohio. She lost her job when, early in the pandemic, schools closed and day cares regularly shut down due to COVID-19 outbreaks. Without adequate childcare, she could not work, and she shared that this inability to work meant she was, "literally [...] sitting on my last $400." For a time, she and her children lived in a motel.

1. All participants have been given pseudonyms.

Given her financial circumstances, Vanessa had struggled to procure funds for an abortion. When she initially scheduled an appointment with the abortion clinic nearest her in October 2020, she learned she could not be seen unless she paid a consultation fee of several hundred dollars. The weeks had quickly passed while she tried, without success, to secure money for the appointment.

After months of delay, she finally decided to travel to a clinic farther away. That clinic connected Vanessa to an abortion fund, an organization which provides financial support to those in need. Not only did the organization help her cover the consultation and procedure costs, but it also paid for overnight lodging, so she did not have to drive home between her second and third appointments.

Despite the many challenges Vanessa faced, she explained how comfortable she felt with the staff in the clinic, how they took time to hear about her financial situation and find the funds she needed, and how they validated her reason for having an abortion. With their support—with their *care*—she finally got the abortion she sought.

Our research team has interviewed nearly 20 individuals like Vanessa, each with their own unique and multifaceted story. Their stories span a year of struggle. The year 2020 was a difficult one for many people we interviewed, both because of the COVID-19 pandemic and because the pandemic exacerbated the existing struggles of everyday life. We found that those who already experienced structural racism, poverty or financial instability, and who, pre-pandemic, had difficulty accessing culturally responsive or gender-affirming medical care, experienced heightened challenges under pandemic conditions. Likewise, we found that the barriers to abortion care that existed prior to the emergence of COVID-19 were magnified (Carpenter et al. 2022).

Our empirical investigation of how abortion seekers and abortion clinic staff experienced the pandemic reveals that Ohio's abortion regulations caused real physical, mental, emotional, and financial harms. The stories of our participants also demonstrate a dire need to challenge the status quo of abortion politics (and politics, more broadly) in the State of Ohio.

In this chapter, we describe how Ohio's abortion restrictions, both before and during the coronavirus pandemic, have impacted the lives of Ohioans seeking a safe, relatively common medical procedure. We first provide an overview of Ohio's restrictive abortion landscape before the pandemic and examine how the state further increased regulations at the onset of the coronavirus pandemic in early 2020. Next, we explore the impact of these laws and regulations on Ohioans, with special attention to their experiences during the pandemic. Then, to address the unmet needs and harms that result from these policies, we build on prior work, which reframes abortion provision as an act of care. Finally, we argue that, to undo years of overregulation and prevent future harms—in the pandemic and in the post-*Dobbs* era—the state must adopt both an ethic and a politics of care (Boston Review and Verso Books 2020; Tronto 1993; Noddings 1984; Gilligan 1988; Ruddick 1995) that could radically reshape the political environment and legislative landscape to re-center the needs of people in Ohio, including for abortion care.

Decades of Regulation: Abortion in Ohio, 2005–2020

To understand the state's treatment of abortion and abortion patients during the pandemic, we must look back on decades of intense scrutiny and hyperregulation of abortion care. Ohio policy has grown increasingly hostile toward abortion provision in the early twenty-first century (Norris et al. 2020). The state legislature has proposed or passed over 20 pieces of abortion-restrictive legislation, including laws that require abortion clinics to have a transfer agreement with a local hospital (despite hospitals being required to accept patients in an emergency), limit abortion provision in public hospitals, prohibit doctors from performing an abortion if they know the decision to abort is based on a fetal diagnosis of Down syndrome, and prohibit abortion after embryonic cardiac cell activity, around six weeks gestation (initially enjoined in 2019, this law went into effect following the *Dobbs v. Jackson Women's Health Organization* decision that overturned federal protections for abortion in 2022). For the purposes of this chapter, we will detail key pieces of legislation that became particularly limiting during the pandemic: the 24-hour waiting period, the in-person consultation requirement, and the so-called 20-week abortion ban.

Since 2005, the state has required that abortion patients have an in-person consultation appointment at least 24 hours prior to having an abortion. This requires patients to make at least two trips to the clinic, resulting in many having to take time off work or school, arrange for additional childcare, pay more for transportation to and from the clinic, or pay for lodging (Cohen and Joffe 2020).

In 2017, Ohio's 20-week abortion ban went into effect, banning abortions after 21 weeks, six days from a patient's last menstrual period (i.e., 20 weeks postfertilization)—except in select cases. Though most abortions occur before 12 weeks (Guttmacher Institute 2019), some individuals cannot obtain care earlier. This may happen for several reasons, including having difficulty securing sufficient funds, learning of a pregnancy or fetal anomalies at a later stage of gestation, or experiencing medical emergencies later in a pregnancy (Foster 2020).

These types of restrictive bills are common among other conservative state legislatures (Guttmacher Institute 2021) and were part of a larger movement to erode abortion care at the state level and overturn *Roe v. Wade* (Holland 2016; Kaneya 2019; North 2019; O'Connor 2019; Ryman and Wynn 2019; Zelikova, Baran, and Goldman 2019). Despite antiabortion rhetoric framing these laws as protecting pregnant people's health, there is no evidence that they do (Cohen and Joffe 2020; Guttmacher Institute 2020). On the contrary, multiple rigorous scientific studies have confirmed that abortions are extremely safe (Gerdts, Fuentes et al. 2016; National Academies of Sciences, Engineering, and Medicine 2018): 14 times safer than carrying a pregnancy to term (Raymond and Grimes 2012). Furthermore, obstetrician-gynecologists (OB-GYNs) report that abortion laws prevent doctors from acting on their own medical expertise and clinical judgment about the care their patients need (Freedman 2010; Field et al. 2022).

Ohio's policy changes have contributed to the closure of several abortion facilities and uneven access to abortion methods across the state, particularly in rural areas (McGowan, Norris, and Bessett 2020; Norris et al. 2020). In 2010, there were 15 clinics that provided procedural abortions (abortions performed by a licensed physician in a clinical setting to physically extract products of conception from the uterus). By the start of the pandemic in 2020, only six remained, while another seven facilities only provide medication abortion services (wherein physicians prescribe patients two different medications to trigger the discharge of the products of conception, often at home).

In addition to clinic closures, the hurdles that result from restrictive abortion laws lead to additional health-care and economic burdens for patients (Blake and McGowan 2020; Darney and Reid 2020; Foster et al. 2018; Gerdts, Dobkin et al. 2016). Notably, these burdens are not evenly distributed among the population, but instead are felt most strongly by people with low incomes, people of color, those living in rural and Appalachian areas, and others experiencing interlocking systems of oppression (The Combahee River Collective 1979; Joffe and Parker 2012; Krieger et al. 2016b; Luna and Luker 2013; Martins et al. 2016; Roberts 2014, 2017; Ross and Solinger 2017; Solazzo 2019).

As we explain below, these preexisting hurdles were heightened amid a deadly pandemic.

Abortion in Ohio during the COVID-19 Pandemic

In the early stages of the coronavirus pandemic, Ohio took swift action aimed toward containing the virus. As part of its emergency order, the state ordered the cessation of all nonessential surgeries to preserve personal protective equipment (PPE) and limit person-to-person transmission of the virus (Acton 2020). While the American College of Obstetricians and Gynecologists described the essential, time-sensitive nature of abortion care during the pandemic, Governor Mike DeWine and Attorney General (AG) David Yost suggested that abortions were elective procedures that could be delayed without undue harm (American College of Obstetricians and Gynecologists 2020; Da Silva 2020; Richmond 2020). Acting in response to complaints from anti-choice groups, AG Yost sent cease-and-desist letters to three abortion clinics that provide procedural abortions, prompting the clinics to take legal action in order to continue providing care. Simultaneously, the Ohio Department of Health (ODH) conducted surprise inspections of these clinics in March 2020, even though they had already been working with the state to ensure they were operating safely during the pandemic. The state argued that, in accordance with the emergency order limiting nonessential surgeries, beginning in March 2020, clinics would be required to administer medication abortion (as opposed to procedural abortion) to eligible patients under ten weeks' gestation and push back any abortions that could be delayed until a later date (Mello, Smith, Hill, Norris et al. 2021). Ultimately, the clinics fought the state in court to be treated like all other Ohio health-care facilities complying with the order; that is, to make case-by-case determinations about whether to provide procedural abortions based on their own expertise. A judge ultimately ruled in favor of the clinics; as such, their physicians were able to use their clinical judgment about providing procedural abortion care during the pandemic. By May 2020, the initial executive order was lifted and the state no longer had standing to restrict abortion under the guise of pandemic protections (Mello, Smith, Hill, Norris et al. 2021).

Importantly, as the popularity of telemedicine (the practice of remote medical consultations) surged in other health-care fields in order to limit transmission of the virus, the Ohio legislature sought to halt medication abortion distribution via telemedicine that existed at a few sites in the state. While clinics in other states were able to take advantage of relaxed Food and Drug Administration requirements won in federal courts during the pandemic, those in Ohio were not, due to preexisting state law requiring abortion medications be dispensed in clinic (Mello, Smith, Hill, Norris et al. 2021). Furthermore, in December 2020, the Ohio state legislature passed a state telemedicine abortion *ban* that was to go into effect in Spring 2021. Though this ban is temporarily blocked in the courts, it would have stopped the already limited telemedicine practiced in the state. The intent to constrain abortion care is clearer when contrasted with the multiple accommodations made by the state to promote telemedicine in nearly all other aspects of health care.

Despite the state's interference in abortion provision, 12 of the 13 abortion facilities in Ohio remained open throughout the pandemic, though service availability was impacted. For example, some clinics reported increases in wait time, while others described adding additional hours in order to accommodate the shift in patient load (Smith et al. Under review).

While this increased scrutiny and overregulation of abortion facilities is not unique to the pandemic, it posed additional barriers to accessing abortion care. The state's decision to use the emergency orders of the COVID-19 pandemic and the legislative process to further limit access to abortion care is emblematic of the legacy of restricting abortion access in the State of Ohio. We next describe how these restrictions were experienced by the people of Ohio during the pandemic.

Impact of COVID-19 on Ohioans Seeking Reproductive Health Care

Though shifts in health-care practices in medical settings were common during the pandemic, Ohio's abortion-restrictive landscape shaped how pandemic-related constraints on care were experienced by clinics and their patients. The particular combination of preexisting abortion restrictions, pandemic-related protocols, and confusion over the state's executive order led to the delay and cancellation of many abortion appointments and shifts in methods of abortion available to patients. For example, ongoing research has found a stark increase in the proportion of medication abortions relative to procedural abortions in March 2020, as patients were required, under the state emergency order, to receive medication abortions if they were under ten weeks' gestation (Smith et al. Under review). This confluence of factors also led to fluctuations in the gestation at which patients received procedural abortions as the pandemic extended into the year, with the relative number of early abortions dipping dramatically in April 2020, when these shifted to be medication only (Smith et al. Under review).

While most of the participants we interviewed did not directly cite the state's executive order banning procedural abortions as a barrier to care, many were impacted by the fallout from the order, as it contributed to a backlog of appointments and led to delays in care. Appointment cancellations and delays during the pandemic, alongside Ohio's existing abortion restrictions, resulted in decreased opportunities for timely care, which often resulted in higher procedure costs, more travel to find a clinic with capacity, and emotional and physical burdens (Carpenter et al. 2022).

For example, Leila, a young Asian immigrant and mother, was pushed well into her second trimester, despite her desire for an earlier termination. Leila first attempted to schedule her appointment in July when she was nine weeks pregnant, but was delayed until almost 20 weeks—nearly to the state's gestational limit—because the clinic closest to her could not schedule an appointment for her for weeks. This scheduling delay was caused by the clinic's need to decrease the number of patients in the clinic at any one time to ensure proper social distancing, by staffing shortages, and by a backlog of patients who could not be seen earlier in the pandemic.

Because her gestation was nearly 20 weeks by the time she was seen, Leila's abortion required three visits: first, a consultation; then, placement of cervical dilators; and finally, the actual procedure. She shared how difficult it was to make three separate appointments for care while simultaneously highlighting the stigma of seeking an abortion:

> It was annoying because [...] I could have been out in just two appointments [if I had been seen earlier]. And also because like every time I had to go, I had to get a babysitter. I had to [...] [think about] the privacy issues, like, oh my gosh, what if somebody sees me here? What would the protestors do? [...] And I had to go three times. And also [...] in my house, I didn't want anyone to know [...] I had to schedule the earliest appointment, when everyone was sleeping.

In addition, Leila's procedure ended up costing hundreds of dollars more than if she were seen at nine weeks, and it also required that her sister take multiple days off school to help her get to and from the clinic. While the state was only partly responsible for the backlog of patients during the early days of the pandemic, state law mandating counseling and waiting periods directly impacted Leila's experience of seeking her abortion.

Appointment delays and cancellations also led to intense physical symptoms as pregnancies progressed and generated a great mental and emotional toll. For example, Jordan, a Black trans participant, noted that when an Ohio clinic cancelled their abortion appointment, it felt destabilizing. They noted:

> So, I scheduled the initial [abortion] appointment [...] and it felt really good for me [...] it felt secure, because I was like, okay, great, like even though there's a pandemic, I'm still going to be taken care of [...] this is still going to be able to happen [...] I feel really affirmed .... And so [...] when that flooring was just pulled out from underneath me, when I just lost my grounding [...] it just felt like shoot, like, now I really don't know what to do. [...] I started getting paranoid [...] I was like [...] what if like other clinics deal this way? You know, what if this happens again? [...] What if I schedule and it doesn't work? [...] Am I going to have to think about, like, a back-alley abortion?

The appointment cancellation caused so much anxiety for Jordan that they ultimately traveled out of state to access abortion care.

Meanwhile, Cassey, an Asian undergraduate student, became so overwhelmed by anxiety when she could not find an appointment at a clinic in her home city that her boyfriend had to take over the search for clinics farther away. She shared, "I got super stressed out about it. And [...] it just made me honestly want to cry. But luckily [...] because my boyfriend was being so supportive, he kept finding new places. Because after I called all the places in [an Ohio city], I was [...] really upset. I just wanted to sit there and cry, because I was scared that I was going to be forced to have a child." Cassey traveled more than an hour away from home to find care, and said she would have traveled farther if necessary.

Like many interviewees, Maara, a white graduate student, expressed concern after being told that clinics in her region were not scheduling appointments due to state orders limiting abortions. Her abortion was delayed by nearly one month while she struggled with pregnancy-related nausea and fatigue that kept her from working. She explained,

> I just got really concerned [...] I was just concerned about getting an appointment then because I was getting really sick [...] and

> I really couldn't work and stuff like that. So, I was worried about having it delayed even more [...] and maybe not even being able to get an abortion, because it's just not feasible being a student and having a child right now.

Maara also considered traveling out of state for her procedure.

Angela, a Black mother with young children, noted her abortion was delayed until nearly the state's gestational limit, despite her having had pregnancy complications in the past that put her health and life at risk. She worried that she might be forced to carry this pregnancy to term if she were unable to finally secure an appointment. She said, "it's unsafe for me to actually even be pregnant [...] there was just a lot of risk involved [...] if I did not terminate." But when asked what she would have done if she could not find an abortion provider close to home, she replied, "I would have had no choice but to not terminate [...] I wouldn't have had a choice." Together, pandemic conditions and Ohio's abortion restrictions put Angela's life at risk.

These stories illustrate how the state's efforts to restrict access to abortion care both prior to and during the pandemic, adversely impacted those seeking care. Attempts to receive an abortion were particularly burdensome for those needing to raise additional funds, find childcare, or who had other medical comorbidities. In line with previous scholarship, those from structurally disadvantaged groups faced increased burdens (Ross and Solinger 2017; Luna and Luker 2013).

A recent study assessing racial disparities in accessing sexual and reproductive health care in Ohio during the pandemic found that all racial groups reported delays in obtaining care, but groups were impacted differently depending on the period of the pandemic. In addition, Black participants faced greater challenges both in accessing sexual and reproductive health care and securing job stability, reporting higher rates of job loss for themselves, their partners, and their family compared to their white counterparts (Johns-Wolfe et al. 2021). These findings track with the stories of several interviewees. For example, both Angela and Vanessa experienced job loss and difficulty finding abortion care, as did Kiara. Kiara, a Black single mother, suffered so severely from nausea and vomiting due to pregnancy that she could not care for her children and had to send them to stay with relatives until she could get her delayed abortion. She required two visits to the emergency room for IV fluids while she waited for her procedure and recalled feeling like she was "on my deathbed," due to extreme nausea that caused her to lose 11 pounds in one week. Prior to sending her children to stay with family, she decreased her work hours by more than half in order to care for her children, who were home due to school and day care closures. A babysitter looked after them overnight, while Kiara worked night shifts to make ends meet. Work during the pandemic was difficult, as was managing the stress of potentially bringing the virus home to her family. Kiara described the relief she felt when she finally was able to visit the clinic: "it saved my life." The persistence of racial disparities in accessing care and maintaining stable employment during the pandemic profoundly shaped experiences of obtaining abortion care.

Pandemic conditions and the new executive orders compounded the barriers posed by Ohio's existing abortion laws for those seeking abortion care. Participants were met with challenges at every turn. Already, they faced many obligations and challenges in their daily lives, including caring for other children and family members with little or no caregiving support, struggling with substance use or other health issues, juggling schoolwork, and being financially insecure. Angela, Cassey, Kiara, and other Ohioans seeking abortion care during the pandemic might have given up, yet they did not. The fact that everyone we interviewed was ultimately able to access abortion care—sometimes farther away than they felt comfortable traveling, sometimes with a type of care that was not their preference, usually later than they wanted, often at a much greater cost than they could afford—speaks to their faith in the rightness of abortion for them, as well as their persistence and the importance of financial assistance in overcoming the hurdles.

Much like the state's existing abortion legislation, the state's interference in abortion care during the COVID-19 pandemic had serious implications for those seeking care. In the next section, we turn our attention to an alternative: more widespread recognition of abortion as a form of essential care and a political commitment to providing care for all.

Abortion and Care

The designation of procedural abortion as "nonessential" health care by the State of Ohio during the pandemic is one instance of the persistent stigmatization of abortion and its providers, which functions to decouple abortion from essential care. Advocacy organizations, abortion providers, and feminist scholars have challenged such depictions by reframing abortion provision as an essential and legitimate aspect of reproductive health care provided by qualified medical professionals. For example, Abortion Provider Appreciation Day, which occurs annually in March, invokes the language of love, gratitude, and appreciation for abortion providers' essential work, a practice that challenges stigmatizing stereotypes and myths about abortion (Luna 2018). Moreover, the National Abortion Federation (NAF), a professional association for abortion providers, put out the following statement early in the pandemic when states like Ohio were issuing orders to halt abortion provision: "Today, we want to make it abundantly clear that abortion is not only health care; it is time-sensitive, essential health care—and must remain so during this public health crisis" (National Abortion Federation 2020).

Ohio clinics' legal challenges to pandemic-related abortion restrictions highlight providers' conscientious commitment to provide essential care. At the federal level, conscience-based protections in health care were developed following *Roe v. Wade* and are limited to those who refuse to provide contested services such as abortion (Harris 2012). Harris notes, "opposition to abortion [...] catalyzed the development of law, theory, and practice of conscientious objection in medicine" (2012, 981). Yet, scholars have recently begun to expand notions of conscience to include conscientious *provision*, a moral commitment to providing abortion care (Buchbinder et al. 2016; Czarnecki et al. 2019; Dickens and Cook 2011; Harris 2012, 2018). This shift and wider recognition of abortion provision as compassionate care can also be found circulating on social media posts shared by reproductive advocacy groups and reproductive justice organizations to highlight abortion as care.

Importantly, it is not only those who identify as abortion providers or those without personal opposition to abortion who frame abortion provision in terms of care. A recent study found that some labor and delivery nurses who were personally opposed to abortion drew on a Christian ethic of care to reconcile their religious opposition to abortion with their professional obligation to care for patients in need of abortion, illustrating a radical shift in their understanding of abortion as care (Czarnecki et al. 2019). Feminist bioethicists studying the ethics of care have similarly shown that autonomy is relational, meaning that decision-making does not happen in isolation (Mackenzie and Stoljar 2000; McLeod and Sherwin 2020; Scully, Baldwin-Ragaven, and Fitzpatrick 2010). A decision to end a pregnancy can be an act of care for oneself and for others in one's life. Individuals weigh and consider various obligations and commitments, such as responsibilities to family, friends, patients, and coworkers, when making decisions about obtaining—or providing—abortion care. Political systems and relations of power shape the contours of these obligations and decisions.

We have detailed how Ohioans seeking abortion negotiated various obligations, all while facing numerous challenges in obtaining the care they needed. Health care, including abortion care, should be designed and implemented in ways that are empathic, that respect the autonomy of the pregnant person, and take into consideration the complexity of people's lives and how political systems impact them. We next turn our attention to what this new vision of care would look like and how it can be achieved.

An Ethic and a Politics of Care

Taken together, clinic-reported data and the stories and lived experiences of abortion seekers, reproductive health-care providers, and advocates illuminate that abortion is, in fact, care. Such an understanding of abortion as care, and the impact on those for whom such care has been rendered inaccessible, points to the urgent need to reconsider the values underpinning our political system.

Building on earlier research arguing that care should be included as a critical component of moral and ethical systems (Gilligan 1988; Ruddick 1995; Noddings 1984), political scientist Joan Tronto theorized that one can evaluate systems of power by analyzing how care is distributed in a society (Tronto 1993). Examining who receives adequate care—and who does not—reveals who is enabled to wield political and social power.

In order to build a more equitable society, Tronto suggested adopting an ethic of care. She describes an ethic of care as the incorporation of a duty to care for others into one's sense of what is moral, including practicing care for others in one's daily life. In addition, it requires not only listening to the perspectives of those in need of care and how they describe their needs, but also setting aside both preconceived notions of what others need and one's own agenda in order to provide good care.

Tronto further argues that by ensuring all people have access to competent care, a society can effectively begin to redistribute power. To do so, an ethic of care must be embedded into a political system such that it is woven into the beliefs and values that guide the system.

Tronto's political theory of care offers a way of thinking about nature, humanity, politics, and society that forces us to reimagine human interdependency, revalue care and care work, and meet people's needs more equitably. It would require us to place a higher value on care, on humans, and on the natural world. As such, it may be viewed as a disruption to systems of governance that have, for decades, championed disinvestment in health, education, and social support programs, and promoted individual responsibility in lieu of much-needed structural changes—all to the detriment of the populace.

In the context of abortion access during COVID-19, an ethic of care would mean listening and attending to patients' needs, eliminating barriers to abortion care by expanding access to telemedicine services, and eradicating the requirements for two in-person clinic visits and a 24-hour waiting period between counseling, consent, and inducing the abortion. It would also remove gestational limits and eliminate prohibitions on insurance coverage for abortion. An ethic of care would certainly not use a crisis to introduce new barriers to care.

Politics of care, as a concept, has resurfaced more broadly during the COVID-19 pandemic. In *The Politics of Care*, contributors explore how a dearth of care for people and the planet has led to this particular moment in time (Boston Review and Verso Books 2020). Taylor (2020) argues that lack of care for the natural world led to the proliferation of disease among animals and allowed for the spread of COVID-19 to humans, thereby highlighting the interconnectedness of humans and nature. Waxman (2020) asserts that political rhetoric during the pandemic has deemed some people, such as the elderly and those with disabilities, "disposable," and not worthy of care. This rhetoric, he says, fails to imagine and support a future for all. Meanwhile, in his analysis of the protests in 2020 in support of Black Lives Matter and against state-mandated COVID restrictions, Rogers (2020) explores the sometimes fatal intersection of systemic racism, pandemic conditions, and care for people of color. He notes that long-standing failure to care about health inequities and state violence in the United States has exacerbated the pandemic for Black people and led to a troubling political moment. In fact, some patients whom we interviewed drew connections between abortion restrictions and other contemporary injustices they saw in their communities. For example, Jordan connected abortion laws to other restrictions on bodily autonomy and to systemic injustices that the Black Lives Matter and Water is Life movements protest. Likewise, Vanessa worried about raising a Black son who, she expected, like her brothers and cousins, would be racially profiled by the police in her community. She said she was afraid to raise a son only to lose him to police violence. Carla linked her abortion experience to the struggle to be taken seriously, as a woman of color, by her doctor and to the difficulty accessing her preferred birth control method. The connections made by interviewees draw attention to the complexity of their lives and how some see their experiences as fitting into broader social, political, and historical narratives. These connections also underscore the need for a more comprehensive understanding of care.

Moreover, the work of the contributors to *The Politics of Care* reminds us that lives are not one-dimensional and that there are no one-dimensional solutions to ensuring equitable abortion access. For example, Vanessa's story is about so much more than barriers to abortion access during the COVID-19 pandemic. She was failed, simultaneously, in so many ways. The state did not provide her (and thousands upon thousands of working mothers and parents) with adequate support to care for children while trying to hold onto a job during the pandemic. It did not provide her with sufficient funds to care for her family after experiencing job loss. And, it actively participated in the creation of the structural violence experienced by her family members. Vanessa deserved more accessible abortion care, and she needed (and deserved) so much more than that. In thinking about an ethic and a politics of care, we start to see a more comprehensive vision to meet her needs: widespread and radical political change.

Conclusion

While Ohio's abortion clinics strive to provide care, the state recently reaffirmed—after years of abortion restrictions that fly in the face of scientific evidence and the testimony of patients and health-care professionals—its role as an architect of many of the struggles abortion patients face. Overregulation of abortion providers and care thwarts clinical innovation, constrains patient autonomy, puts people's lives and health at risk, and keeps the focus on restrictive abortion legislation in lieu of lawmaking that would benefit the state's people. As such, the state is a key contributor to the creation and perpetuation of racial, economic, and health-care disparities.

In 2020, the state had the opportunity to expand access to telemedicine services for abortion, and yet it chose to move in the opposite direction. It wielded the pandemic as a political tool to further restrict abortion, increasing the mental, emotional, physical, and financial harm to Ohioans seeking abortion. Moreover, those who were already struggling under systemic racism, poverty, and the other challenges of the pandemic were particularly hard hit by the state's actions against abortion and abortion providers. These harms—especially to those already structurally disadvantaged—are a stark preview of what is to come in the post-*Dobbs* era, wherein abortion care is nearly impossible to access in Ohio.

So long as the state remains hyperfocused on restrictive abortion laws, people suffer. The state's actions demonstrate a lack of care and respect for the people living in the state. As such, we are arguing in favor of an ethic and a politics of care as a way forward, because abortion seekers deserve to be treated with care and dignity, and because we understand the potential these ethical and political frameworks have to make powerful changes within and beyond abortion care.

Implementing an ethic of care will require widespread and collaborative organizing that is inclusive of various social movements. It will need the involvement of civil society and scholars theorizing care, power, and justice across academic disciplines to sustain pressure on the state and demand it make significant and lasting changes. We believe this type of collaborative effort is possible. People are already doing such valuable intersectional work, and have found public support across social movements in Ohio. For example, in 2020, Women Have Options Ohio, an abortion fund (since renamed Abortion Fund of Ohio), helped raise money for the Columbus Freedom Fund, a bail fund for mothers of color struggling within a racist criminal justice system.

We support these cross-cutting initiatives, and yet we are asking for more. We are arguing that social movements must come together in a unified voice to demand that the state change the very values and ethics undergirding its practices and more adequately attune its policies to the priorities of the people living in the state.

Research shows that people in the United States have consistently been supportive of abortion despite federal and state restrictions, and the same is true in Ohio. In a recent survey of 2,356 adult Ohio women of reproductive age, 59 percent agreed that safe, effective, and affordable methods of abortion care should be available to people in their community; only 22 percent disagreed; while 19 percent neither agreed nor disagreed (Smith et al. 2021). The legislative and executive branches in Ohio are prioritizing the minority viewpoint. In order to be responsive to the populace, a more balanced and nuanced approach is necessary, one that would more closely reflect the will of the people. As such, we are arguing that this unified voice must require the state's guiding principles be an ethic of care: care for *all* our people, care for our environment, and care for our future.

Such a unified call benefits a range of social justice causes, because, when adopted as a guiding principle, an ethic of care challenges the state to critically examine its values and priorities, and to revalue, reprioritize, and re-center the people it purportedly serves. Embracing an ethic of care will require that public servants listen to advocates, medical experts, scientific evidence, and those seeking abortions about why abortion access is critical even and especially in a pandemic.

Care for Ohioans and the environment must be demonstrated in each piece of policy, in each initiative, and in every action by the state. In adopting a politics of care more widely, the state will better care for and meet the needs of the people—not just those with privilege and not just those seeking abortion—but all of us.

Acknowledgments

The authors would like to thank those who made this research possible, including Stef Murawsky, Ariel Volk, Morgan Gimblet, Jessie Hill, Kari White, Emma Carpenter, Kristen Burke, and the anonymous foundation that funds our work.

We especially thank our interviewees—for their trust and willingness to share their stories with us.

REFERENCES

Acton, Amy. 2020. "Directors Order for the Management of Non-Essential Surgeries and Procedures throughout Ohio." Ohio Department of Health. https://content.govdelivery.com/attachments/OHOOD/2020/03/17/file_attachments/1403950/Director%27s%20Order%20non-essential%20surgery%203-17-2020.pdf.

American College of Obstetricians and Gynecologists. 2020. "Joint Statement on Abortion Access during the COVID-19 Outbreak." Retrieved January 20, 2021. www.acog.org/news/news-releases/2020/03/joint-statement-on-abortion-access-during-the-covid-19-outbreak.

Baran, Nicole M., Gretchen Goldman, and Zelikova, Jane. 2019. "Abortion Bans Based on So-Called 'Science' Are Fraudulent." *Scientific American* (blog). August 21, 2019. https://blogs.scientificamerican.com/observations/abortion-bans-based-on-so-called-science-are-fraudulent/.

Blake, Valarie K., and Michelle L. McGowan. 2020. "Filling a Federal Void: Promises and Perils of State Law in Addressing Women's Health Disparities." *The Journal of Law, Medicine & Ethics* 48, no. 3: 485–490. https://doi.org/10.1177/1073110520958873.

Boston Review and Verso Books, ed. 2020. *The Politics of Care: From COVID-19 to Black Lives Matter*. New York: Verso and Boston Review.

Buchbinder, Mara, Dragana Lassiter, Rebecca Mercier, Amy Bryant, and Anne Drapkin Lyerly. 2016. "Reframing Conscientious Care: Providing Abortion Care When Law and Conscience Collide," *Hastings Center Report* 46: 22–30.

Carpenter, Emma, Hillary Gyuras, Kristen L. Burke, Danielle Czarnecki, Danielle Bessett, Michele L. McGowan, and Kari White. In press. "Seeking Abortion Care in Ohio and Texas during the COVID-19 Pandemic." *Contraception*. 2022 Oct 11:S0010-7824(22)00381-X. https://doi.org/10.1016/j.contraception.2022.09.134. Epub ahead of print. PMID: 36240904; PMCID: PMC9554324.

The Combahee River Collective. 1979. "A Black Feminist Statement." In *Capitalist Patriarchy and the Case for Socialist Feminism*, edited by Zillah R. Eisenstein, 362–372. New York: Monthly Review Press.

Cohen, D.S., and C. Joffe. 2020. *The Obstacle Course: The Everyday Struggle to Get an Abortion in America*. Berkeley: University of California Press.

Czarnecki, Danielle, Renee R. Anspach, Raymond G. De Vries, Mercedez D. Dunn, Katrina Hauschildt, and Lisa H. Harris. 2019. "Conscience Reconsidered: The Moral Work of Navigating Participation in Abortion Care on Labor and Delivery." *Social Science & Medicine* 232(July): 181–189. https://doi.org/10.1016/j.socscimed.2019.03.034.

Da Silva, Chantal. 2020. "Ohio Attorney General Faces Backlash over 'Non-Essential' Abortion Ban amid Coronavirus Outbreak." *Newsweek*, March 22, 2020, sec. U.S. www.newsweek.com/ohio-attorney-general-abortion-ban-coronavirus-covid-19-outbreak-1493635.

Darney, Blair G., and Jessica Reid. 2020. "What Are the Consequences of Using Restrictions to Decrease Abortions?" *American Journal of Public Health* 110, no. 7: 935–936. https://doi.org/10.2105/AJPH.2020.305727.

Dickens, Bernard M., and Rebecca J. Cook. 2011. "Conscientious Commitment to Women's Health." *International Journal of Gynecology & Obstetrics* 113, no. 2: 163–166. https://doi.org/10.1016/j.ijgo.2011.02.002.

Field, Meredith P., Hillary Gyuras, Danielle Bessett, Meredith J. Pensak, Alison H. Norris, and Michelle L. McGowan. 2022. "Ohio Abortion Regulations and Ethical Dilemmas for Obstetrician–Gynecologists." *Obstetrics & Gynecology* 140, no. 2: 253–261. https://doi.org/10.1097/AOG.0000000000004870.

Foster, Diana Greene. 2020. *The Turnaway Study: Ten Years, a Thousand Women, and the Consequences of having—Or Being Denied—an Abortion*. New York: Scribner.

Foster, Diana Greene, M. Antonia Biggs, Lauren Ralph, Caitlin Gerdts, Sarah Roberts, and M. Maria Glymour. 2018. "Socioeconomic Outcomes of Women Who Receive and Women Who Are Denied Wanted Abortions in the United States." *American Journal of Public Health* 108, no. 3: 407–413. https://doi.org/10.2105/AJPH.2017.304247.

Freedman, Lori. 2010. *Willing and Unable: Doctors' Constraints in Abortion Care*. Nashville: Vanderbilt University Press.

Gerdts, Caitlin, Liza Fuentes, Daniel Grossman, Kari White, Brianna Keefe-Oates, Sarah E. Baum, Kristine Hopkins, Chandler W. Stolp, and Joseph E. Potter. 2016. "Impact of Clinic Closures on Women Obtaining Abortion Services after Implementation of a Restrictive Law in Texas." *American Journal of Public Health* 106, no. 5: 857–864. https://doi.org/10.2105/AJPH.2016.303134.

Gerdts, Caitlin, Loren Dobkin, Diana Greene Foster, and Eleanor Bimla Schwarz. 2016. "Side Effects, Physical Health Consequences, and Mortality Associated with Abortion and Birth after an Unwanted Pregnancy." *Women's Health Issues* 26, no. 1: 55–59. https://doi.org/10.1016/j.whi.2015.10.001.

Gilligan, Carol. 1988. *In a Different Voice: Psychological Theory and Women's Development*. Cambridge, MA: Harvard University Press.

Guttmacher Institute. 2019. "Induced Abortion in the United States." September 2019. www.guttmacher.org/fact-sheet/induced-abortion-united-states.

Guttmacher Institute. 2020. "Targeted Regulation of Abortion Providers (TRAP) Laws." January 2020. https://www.guttmacher.org/evidence-you-can-use/targeted-regulation-abortion-providers-trap-laws.

Guttmacher Institute. 2021. "An Overview of Abortion Laws." August 1, 2021. https://www.guttmacher.org/state-policy/explore/overview-abortion-laws.

Harris, Lisa H. 2012. "Recognizing Conscience in Abortion Provision." *New England Journal of Medicine* 367, no. 11: 981–983. https://doi.org/10.1056/NEJMp1206253.

Harris, Lisa H. 2018. "Divisions, New and Old—Conscience and Religious Freedom at HHS." *New England Journal of Medicine* 0(0):1–3. https://doi.org/10.1056/NEJMp1801154.

Holland, Jennifer L. 2016. "Abolishing Abortion: The History of the Pro-Life Movement in America | The American Historian." *The American Historian* (blog). Organization of American Historians. November 2016. www.oah.org/tah/issues/2016/november/abolishing-abortion-the-history-of-the-pro-life-movement-in-america/.

Joffe, Carole, and Willie J. Parker. 2012. "Race, Reproductive Politics and Reproductive Health Care in the Contemporary United States." *Contraception* 86, no. 1: 1–3. https://doi.org/10.1016/j.contraception.2012.03.009.

Johns-Wolfe, Elaina, Jeremy Brenner-Levoy, Abigail Norris Turner, Zoe Muzyczka, Tamika Odum, and Danielle Bessett. 2021. "Challenges Faced by Black and White Patients Seeking Abortion Care during the COVID-19 Pandemic in Ohio." Society for Family Planning Science All Year Series. Virtual presentation, March 3.

Kaneya, Rui. 2019. "Progressives Borrow Strategy from Anti-Abortion Groups: Use Copycat Legislation." *USA Today*, September 30, 2019. www.usatoday.com/in-depth/news/investigations/2019/06/19/abortion-law-progressives-borrow-winning-strategy-pro-life-groups/1483920001/.

Krieger, Nancy, Sofia Gruskin, Nakul Singh, Mathew V. Kiang, Jarvis T. Chen, Pamela D. Waterman, Jason Beckfield, and Brent A. Coull. 2016. "Reproductive Justice & Preventable Deaths: State Funding, Family Planning, Abortion, and Infant Mortality, US 1980–2010." *SSM—Population Health* 2 (April): 277–293. https://doi.org/10.1016/j.ssmph.2016.03.007.

Luna, Zakiya. 2018. "Feeling Intersectionality: Women of Color and The Emotional Politics of Solidarity." Abortion beyond Bounds Conference, McGill University, Montreal, Canada, October 11–12.

Luna, Zakiya, and Kristin Luker. 2013. "Reproductive Justice." *Annual Review of Law and Social Science* 9, no. 1: 327–352. https://doi.org/10.1146/annurev-lawsocsci-102612-134037.

Mackenzie, Catriona, and Natalie Stoljar. 2000. *Relational Autonomy: Feminist Perspectives on Autonomy, Agency, and the Social Self*. Oxford: Oxford University Press.

Martins, Summer L., Katherine A. Starr, Wendy L. Hellerstedt, and Melissa L. Gilliam. 2016. "Differences in Family Planning Services by Rural–Urban Geography: Survey of Title X–Supported Clinics in Great Plains and Midwestern States." *Perspectives on Sexual and Reproductive Health* 48, no. 1:9–16. https://doi.org/10.1363/48e7116.

McGowan, Michelle L., Alison H. Norris, and Danielle Bessett. 2020. "Care Churn—Why Keeping Clinic Doors Open Isn't Enough to Ensure Access to Abortion." *New England Journal of Medicine* 383, no. 6: 508–510. https://doi.org/10.1056/NEJMp2013466.

McLeod, Carolyn, and Susan Sherwin. 2020. "Relational Autonomy, Self-Trust, and Health Care for Patients Who Are Oppressed." In *Relational Autonomy: Feminist Perspectives on Autonomy, Agency and the Social Self*, edited by C. MacKenzie and N. Stoljar, 259–279. New York: Oxford University Press.

Mello, Kelsey, Mikaela Smith, Jessie Hill, Alison Norris, and Michelle McGowan. 2021. "Federal, State, and Institutional Barriers to the Expansion of Medication and Telemedicine Abortion Services in Ohio, Kentucky, and West Virginia during the COVID-19 Pandemic." *Contraception* 104, no. 1: 111–116. https://doi.org/10.1016/j.contraception.2021.04.020.

National Abortion Federation. 2020. "Reproductive Health Care Providers: Abortion Is Essential." *National Abortion Federation*. Retrieved June 3, 2021. https://prochoice.org/reproductive-health-care-providers-abortion-essential/.

National Academies of Sciences, Engineering, and Medicine. 2018. *The Safety and Quality of Abortion Care in the United States*. Washington, DC: National Academies Press.

Noddings, Nel. 1984. *Caring: A Feminine Approach to Ethics and Moral Education*. Berkeley: University of California Press.

Norris, Alison H., Payal Chakraborty, Kaiting Lang, Robert B. Hood, Sarah R. Hayford, Lisa Keder, Danielle Bessett et al. 2020. "Abortion Access in Ohio's Changing Legislative Context, 2010–2018." *American Journal of Public Health*, May, e1–7. https://doi.org/10.2105/AJPH.2020.305706.

North, Anna. 2019. "The Downfall of Roe v. Wade Started in 2010." *Vox*, December 23, 2019. www.vox.com/2019/12/23/21024312/abortion-laws-2019-ohio-georgia-roe-wade.

O'Connor, Ema. 2019. "All These Six-Week Abortion Bans Are Likely to Get Blocked by the Courts. That's the Point." *BuzzFeed News*, May 16, 2019. www.buzzfeednews.com/article/emaoconnor/state-heartbeat-abortion-ban-national-overturn-roe-v-wade.

Raymond, Elizabeth G., and David A. Grimes. 2012. "The Comparative Safety of Legal Induced Abortion and Childbirth in the United States:" *Obstetrics & Gynecology* 119, no. 2(Part 1): 215–219. https://doi.org/10.1097/AOG.0b013e31823fe923.

Richmond, Matthew. 2020. "Ohio Could See up to 8,000 COVID-19 Cases per Day at Peak; Coronavirus Update, March 26, 2020." Ideastream, March 26, 2020. www.ideastream.org/ohio-could-see-up-to-8000-covid-19-cases-per-day-at-peak-coronavirus-update-march-26-2020.

Roberts, Dorothy. 2014. *Killing the Black Body: Race, Reproduction, and the Meaning of Liberty*. New York: Knopf Doubleday Publishing Group.

Roberts, Dorothy. 2017. *Radical Reproductive Justice: Foundation, Theory, Practice, Critique.*, edited by Loretta Ross, Lynn Roberts, Erika Derkas, Whitney Peoples, and Pamela Bridgewater Toure. New York: The Feminist Press at CUNY.

Rogers, Melvin L. 2020. "We Should Be Afraid, But Not of Protestors." In *The Politics of Care: From COVID-19 to Black Lives Matter*, edited by Boston Review, 180–183. New York: Verso and Boston Review.

Ross, Loretta, and Rickie Solinger. 2017. *Reproductive Justice*. Berkeley: University of California Press. www.ucpress.edu/book.php?isbn=9780520288201.

Ruddick, Sara. 1995. *Maternal Thinking: Toward a Politics of Peace*. Boston: Beacon Press.

Ryman, Anne, and Matt Wynn. 2019. "For Anti-Abortion Activists, Success of 'Heartbeat' Bills Was 10 Years in the Making." *The Arizona Republic*, December 2, 2019. www.azcentral.com/in-depth/news/local/arizona/2019/06/19/abortion-laws-2019-how-heartbeat-bills-passed-ohio-missouri-more/1270870001/.

Scully, Jackie Leach, Laurel E. Baldwin-Ragaven, and Petya Fitzpatrick. 2010. *Feminist Bioethics: At the Center, on the Margins*. Baltimore: Johns Hopkins University Press.

Smith, Mikaela H., Abigail Norris Turner, Payal Chakraborty, Robert B. Hood, Danielle Bessett, Maria F. Gallo, and Alison H. Norris. 2021. "Opinions about Abortion among Reproductive-Age Women in Ohio." *Sexuality Research and Social Policy* 19(October): 909–921. https://doi.org/10.1007/s13178-021-00638-y.

Smith, Mikaela H., Molly Broscoe, Payal Chakraborty, B. Jessie Hill, Robert B. Hood, Michelle L. McGowan, Danielle Bessett, and Alison H. Norris. Under review. "Changes in Abortion Care in the Ohio River Valley during the Early Months of the COVID-19 Pandemic."

Smith, Mikaela H., Molly Broscoe, Payal Chakraborty, Robert B. Hood, and Michelle L. McGowan. 2020. "Impacts of COVID-19 on Ohio Abortion Care." OPEN Annual Conference. Virtual, October 18.

Solazzo, Alexa L. 2019. "Different and Not Equal: The Uneven Association of Race, Poverty, and Abortion Laws on Abortion Timing." *Social Problems* 66, no. 4: 519–547. https://doi.org/10.1093/socpro/spy015.

Taylor, Sunaura. 2020. "What Would Health Security Look Like." In *The Politics of Care: From COVID-19 to Black Lives Matter*, edited by Boston Review, 67–78. New York: Verso and Boston Review.

Tronto, Joan C. 1993. *Moral Boundaries: A Political Argument for an Ethic of Care*. New York and London: Routledge.

Waxman, Simon. 2020. "A Politics of the Future." In *The Politics of Care: From COVID-19 to Black Lives Matter*, edited by Boston Review, 164–177. New York: Verso and Boston Review.

5 | Bioethics and Critical Care in the Time of COVID

Research Article

Mahwish U. Ahmad, Joshua S. Crites, and Prabalini Rajendram

In this research piece, two ethicists and a physician analyze how a large hospital system in Northeast Ohio handled novel ethical decision-making challenges presented by COVID-19 in the context of existing obstacles such as competition between health-care institutions.

As of mid-summer, 2022, Ohio has had just under three million COVID-19 confirmed cases to date, with almost 39,000 Ohioan deaths (Ohio Department of Health 2022a). These sobering statistics have led to roughly 120,000 discrete hospitalizations within Ohio hospitals, with close to 14,000 of those leading to intensive care unit (ICU) admissions in one of our Ohio hospital systems (Ohio Department of Health, 2022b). In this chapter, we will reflect on our experiences within one large academic medical center and in collaboration with other northeast Ohio healthcare systems across three aspects of critical care that emerged over the past year of the COVID-19 pandemic in Ohio: namely, pandemic planning, differences in hospital care provision for COVID-19-positive and -negative patients, and research within a pandemic period. In so doing, we aim to elucidate general bioethical and medical considerations related to the pandemic, increase awareness of how those considerations were applied to specific decisions, and reflect on lessons learned in those applications.

Pandemic Planning

Beginning in early 2020, the Cleveland Clinic healthcare system—along with almost all healthcare systems across the United States—established plans for managing a potential shortage of available medical equipment and other healthcare services in the face of an overwhelming surge of patients needing critical care (i.e., "crisis standards of care" or "allocation of scarce medical resources"). News from Italy described the grim loss of life due to hospitals being overrun with more patients who would benefit from critical care than could receive such care (Horowitz 2020; Di Blasi 2020). Hospitals and healthcare systems were also watching early developments in the United States, and the precipitous rise of the number of individuals testing positive for COVID-19 in New York City (Rothfeld et al. 2020).

Consistent across these early efforts was a primary focus on "spaces" and "supplies," two areas of focus widely accepted in crisis management (Hick et al. 2009). Reports from other areas of the world and within the United States raised concerns about spaces, and some hospitals, including our own, were taking drastic measures to prepare for similar volumes of patients. Our own healthcare system created the "Hope Hospital," by repurposing space previously used for education as a field hospital with up to 1,000 beds for overflow of patients being treated for COVID-19 (Cleveland Clinic 2020). Personal protective equipment (PPE) was, of course, in high demand, and adjustments to previous standards of use were being considered, including multiple-day use of N95 masks, which normally would have been discarded after a single use. Concurrently, there was feverish drafting of proposals for how to determine who should receive a critical-care bed space or a ventilator if there were not enough available to all patients who might benefit from them.

At this point, it may be helpful to review the predominant framework for carrying out the plans made by hospitals during the pandemic. Though not the absolute final word, and not specific for how to operationalize the allocation of scarce medical resources under conditions of extreme shortage caused by a disaster or pandemic, a series of reports sponsored by the Institute of Medicine (IoM) provide guidance for states and individual healthcare organizations creating their own specific plans (IoM 2012, 2013). In general, this framework outlines different aspects of providing care when there are no shortages, when resources are strained, and when there are serious shortages in one or more areas of healthcare. Under normal conditions, or what is known as "conventional" care according to the IoM framework, patients receive care according to usual uses of space, usual staff-to-patient ratios, usual use of supplies, and usual standards of care (Hick et al. 2009; IoM 2012). Ethically, decisions about whether or not an individual patient is offered specific treatments are guided by patient preferences and clinical assessment of whether or not that patient is likely to benefit from the treatment under consideration. Although there is rarely a need to decide between two or more patients, the sickest patients are considered to be highest priority. As demand for resources increases, care moves into a "contingency" phase. Here, spaces may be repurposed for higher levels of care, staff-to-patient ratios may be increased (after calling in additional staff), and efforts may be made to conserve, adapt, substitute, and reuse supplies. These responses to increased demand should have minimal impact on usual standards of care; they are intended to preserve the "functional equivalence" of conventional care. Thus, the ethical framework for making decisions about provision of treatment under contingency situations is largely the same as during conventional situations (i.e., offering treatment likely to benefit an individual patient, according to that patient's preferences).

When demand for medical treatment exceeds resources—even after efforts in contingency situations have been exhausted—use of space, staff, and supplies, and the corresponding standards of care move to "crisis" level (IOM 2013). Under these conditions, areas of the hospital not normally used for critical care (or for any level of care) may become makeshift ICUs. There is insufficient availability of critical care healthcare professionals, which necessitates expanded care models and high staff-to-patient ratios. If there is also a significant and irremediable shortage of supplies, then staff must decide which patients to prioritize for care with the limited supplies. When conditions meet criteria for crisis-level response, the usual standards of care are unsustainable; patient care is guided by crisis standards of care (CSC).

Importantly, this shift to CSC—triggered by an absolute shortage of space, staff, or supplies—is supported by a corresponding shift in the basic ethical justification for provision of medical care. Rather than focusing primarily on the needs of individual patients with the goal of maximally benefiting each patient, provision of healthcare services—particularly critical care—must be guided by a more utilitarian aim: to maximize the number of lives saved. Under this framework, and given that there are not enough resources for all patients who would benefit from receiving such treatment, treatment priority is given to those patients most likely to survive after receiving the intervention under consideration. Practically, this may mean that some "less sick" patients are treated before "sicker" patients, a marked shift from usual standards of care.

Returning now to initial planning in Ohio, it is important to note that the course of the pandemic in other places (again, notably Italy and New York City) emphasized the need to plan for a spike in patients requiring resources (Robertson et al. 2020). This was most stressful on space and supplies—especially ventilators. Moreover, it was expected that this type of sharp rise in infection rates would mean that hospitals would be rapidly overwhelmed, thereby moving quickly through the contingency level of response into the crisis level of response. Thus, planning during the early phases of the pandemic in Ohio also focused primarily on space and supplies, anticipating a similar strain on healthcare systems in the state.

Unlike several other states, Ohio did not have an approved, statewide plan for how hospitals should respond to a pandemic or disaster (Colorado Department of Public Health & Environment 2022; Daugherty-Biddison et al. 2017; Minnesota Department of Health 2020; New York State Department of Health 2015; Pennsylvania Department of Health 2020). Instead, following Governor Mike DeWine's separation of the state into three "Healthcare Zones," a group of healthcare professionals representing different specialties drafted, over approximately a six-week period, a proposed plan for potential application within the Cleveland Clinic Health System. Similar proposed plans were drafted at other hospitals and healthcare systems in Zone 1 (roughly the northern third of the state), and efforts were made to maximize consistency across the region among those hospitals and healthcare systems. In every case, the primary focus was on everyone's greatest fear: not having enough ventilators.

There were two primary ethical considerations driving the construction of these plans. First, the guidelines for making decisions about who should receive treatment when there would not be enough resources to provide treatment to all who would benefit from it should actually lead to outcomes that maximize overall survival. In other words, recognizing that it is ethically supportable under crisis conditions to shift from an individual patient's needs to the needs of the broader society, there needed to be a reliable mechanism for actually maximizing the greatest good. Second, because individual physicians have obligations to make decisions that are in their specific patients' best interest, the plan for how to make decisions under crisis conditions had to place responsibility for making those decisions outside an individual physician's purview. In most cases, this was accomplished by creating an interdisciplinary triage team, which would follow an algorithm for making determinations about who would receive scarce resources.

Over the subsequent five months in 2020, while COVID-19 cases in several other states threatened to overwhelm healthcare systems, positivity rates in Ohio remained relatively steady. With the exception of an uptick and a new plateau in late June, hospitalizations remained manageable, with some contingency responses. Fortunately, this meant that plans for addressing the widespread ventilator shortage did not have to be implemented during this period in Ohio. Still, the focus remained primarily on planning for the possibility of a severe ventilator shortage. The lull in cases at this time also allowed organizations to scrutinize and revise guidelines in light of national conversations about the pandemic's clearly disproportional impact on minorities and patients with disabilities (see Kara B. Ayers chapter in this volume), and this helped them improve their proposed allocation plans. Of course, even before the pandemic, there were significant health disparities in the United States, and while there is intense debate about how to redress those disparities within specific allocation plans, those plans should at least not make disparities worse. In the second half of 2020, the formal guidelines for allocation of scarce medical resources of a number of states were reconsidered, in some cases after intervention by the Office of Civil Rights at the US Department of Health and Human Services (Mello et al. 2020). In Ohio, the Department of Developmental Disabilities (DODD) issued guidance for creating or revising CSC in a manner that it believed would minimize disproportionate treatment of vulnerable populations. The effect of any such guidance (federal or state) was different in Ohio than in other states because Ohio did not have state-level CSC guidelines, but called attention to many of the same considerations for individual hospitals or healthcare systems creating their own guidelines. The DODD guidance primarily: a) criticized any criteria that would exclude patients from receiving critical care resources as determined by disability status, underlying health conditions, race, or ethnicity (emphasizing instead the need for individualized clinical assessment); b) cautioned against using "long-term survivability" as a factor for determining which patients might receive critical care resources; c) called for reconsideration of prevailing indices for helping determine the likelihood of short-term survival; d) condemned any policy that allowed for reallocation of personally owned ventilators or other durable medical equipment; and e) suggested not relying on assessment of resource intensity or duration of need as part of allocation decisions (Ohio Department of Developmental Disabilities 2020; Health and Human Services 2020). These experiences point out that the likelihood of creating effective and fair allocation plans is maximized by working directly with patients, such as patients with disabilities, who are affected by disparate health outcomes due to structural racism and other systemic factors.

As the pandemic wore on in the last quarter of 2020, Ohio began to see a sharp and significant rise in COVID-19 cases, far exceeding numbers from earlier in the year. Hospitals across the state were temporarily canceling or postponing certain types of medical procedures, such as elective surgeries, as part of the effort to preserve space for patients hospitalized for treatment of COVID-19. Two additional factors further complicated planning and response efforts during this phase of the pandemic. First, healthcare professionals in Ohio (and everywhere in the United States) had been caring for patients under contingency conditions for an extended period of time. Examples included increased clinical responsibilities for nursing staff, limited entry into COVID-19-positive patients' bed space so as to conserve PPE, and altered models for the delivery of healthcare services to ensure their functional equivalence to conventional standards of care. Although healthcare professionals remained committed to providing the best care possible, many were expressing strong feelings of fatigue and burnout. The new wave of hospitalizations further demoralized healthcare professionals, who now risked engaging in practices that many viewed as compromising their obligations to patients. These included resterilizing PPE and having to move ventilators outside of COVID-19 isolation bed spaces for easier access. The situation was compounded by a higher-than-usual caregiver-to-patient ratio due to low staffing caused by prolonged high hospital census. The second factor that complicated planning during this phase of the pandemic in Ohio was that, like the general public, healthcare professionals were increasingly becoming ill with COVID-19. With necessary quarantines added to the time required to recover, there were fewer healthcare professionals available at exactly the time they were needed most. This reduction in workforce risked making it untenable to continue to care for more patients—even when hospital leaders were often able to find or create additional bed spaces for patients with COVID-19.

Novel ethical considerations accompanied these challenges. Although Ohio's COVID patients overall seemed to be less critically ill than its COVID patients from earlier in the pandemic, and although, in comparison with other states' experiences, Ohio was facing less demand for certain critical resources such as ventilators, the sheer number of patients requiring care severely threatened overall hospital capacity. Up to this point, the ethical frameworks helping hospital leaders plan during this time had only been applied to proposed guidelines for making allocation decisions about an absolute shortage of ventilators. Now they also had to consider the limits of modifying hospital spaces, delaying care for patients seeking nonessential treatment, and asking healthcare professionals to cross-cover or work under significantly modified care models in which nonessential care personnel might evaluate patients via virtual technology. There simply was no precedent in recent memory for assessing how far such modifications could be pushed before care could no longer be delivered safely or with adequate quality to ensure a minimally acceptable benefit.

At about this same time in the fourth quarter of 2020, the COVID-19 vaccines were close to receiving Emergency Use Authorization from the Food and Drug Administration (FDA). The allocation of vaccines was much better defined by federal and state guidelines, although there was still a need to decide which healthcare professionals should be prioritized for vaccines when they first became available in mid-December. Cases began to fall soon in Ohio after vaccinations began, most likely due to shifting disease patterns of COVID-19 variants and increased adherence to masking and distancing recommendations. The Ohio case count continued its strong downward trend as vaccines became more widely available in early 2021. Moratoriums on elective surgeries were lifted and healthcare systems launched public outreach efforts and television and radio advertisements assuring people that it was again safe to seek care, and encouraging them to schedule or reschedule treatment that had been delayed.

With these developments, the urgency and vigilance associated with Ohio's pandemic response waned. It also allowed reflection on missed opportunities and blind spots during initial and ongoing pandemic responses. Planning had proceeded with the best available information at the time, and, of course, certain missteps are visible only in retrospect. With that in mind, in some cases, obligations created by the duty to plan could have been discharged more thoroughly, and with additional efforts to assess the proposed allocation guidelines both for clinical accuracy and operational practicability. But because of the immense pressure and immediacy of growing numbers of patients with COVID-19, simulations were possible only in a limited number of instances to test those guidelines against a sample set of patients, or to run "table-top exercises" to identify areas where the allocation process could be improved. The takeaway from this observation is that healthcare must examine carefully how best to respond to a widespread pandemic, including assessing response plans in simulated situations, under non-pandemic conditions. Simply stated, the time to plan for a pandemic is not during a pandemic.

Looking back at the initial planning, it also became apparent that, at least in Ohio, the biggest threat to the state's COVID response was not supplies such as PPE and ventilators, but a combination of stresses to space and staffing. Existing CSC helped shape initial plans for how to respond, but were largely intended as guides for a disaster or for extremely rapid spread of a viral disease. Overdependence on existing CSC can create blind spots when a pandemic follows a different pattern, as was the case with COVID-19 in Ohio.

For much of 2020, this "slow-burn" pattern of COVID-19 created extended periods of strain on healthcare professionals. Partly the result of increased work demands, partly the result of discomfort and uncertainty over delivering care in ways that differed from how those healthcare professionals had been trained to care for patients, this strain points to the possibility of educating healthcare professionals on alternative care models and of the ethical justification for different standards of care under different circumstances. Later in 2020, when COVID-19 rates spiked, the primary challenge was finding an ethically supportable and operationally feasible response that not only increased space and extended staff, but also balanced obligations to patients needing care for non-COVID-related reasons against obligations to patients needing treatment for COVID-19. As mentioned, many patients during this time had "elective" or "nonurgent" procedures postponed, including some orthopedic procedures, some dermatological procedures, or certain cancer-related surgeries such as mastectomies. These delays were enacted both to conserve space in hospitals (for inpatient procedures requiring at least an overnight stay) and to preserve healthcare professionals who might be needed to care for more critically ill patients (in the case of outpatient procedures). Ethically, it is extremely difficult to discern when it is acceptable to postpone a beneficial treatment that could be delayed without serious negative consequences—especially as a means to avoid tipping into crisis conditions. Not only are determinations of what can be considered an "elective" or "nonurgent" procedure ill-defined, but also the boundaries between making decisions in the interest of individual patients as opposed to on behalf of larger societal interests become obscured in this context. Although never the intent, and justified on the grounds of minimizing overall negative outcomes of a pandemic, this approach often prioritized the health needs of patients with COVID-19 over those of other patients who might equally benefit from timely care but whose care could be postponed without significant longer-term harm. Coupled with this was patients' reluctance to be in hospital settings so as to avoid COVID-19 exposure, which enhanced the challenges seen in early 2021 resulting from delayed care circumstances.

It is worth underscoring that, despite these very many challenges, not all lessons to be learned stem from missed opportunities. On the positive side, healthcare systems worked together to prepare and establish workflows to save lives, and they managed this in anticipation of the most unimaginable of circumstances: a near complete overwhelming of healthcare resources in the state. Moreover, many healthcare teams developed innovative care-delivery approaches, which not only kept healthcare professionals safer but also resulted in improved patient care. Some innovations were implemented at the bedside, such as moving monitors and machines outside patient rooms to limit the use of PPE and contact points with patients who were COVID-19 positive. Others leveraged the growing use of telemedicine encounters, or "virtual visits," to maintain or increase access for patients receiving primary and specialty care. Other necessary innovations that are likely to have a lasting positive impact include the novel or expanded use of virtual platforms for educating medical students and physician trainees (Woolliscroft 2020).

In the remainder of this chapter, we will go a bit deeper into two aspects of care during the COVID-19 pandemic in mid- to late 2020. Recognizing the important topic of disparities based on race, socioeconomic status (SES), disabilities, and similar factors, we will focus on: a) discrepancies in care of patients with COVID-19 compared to patients without COVID-19; and b) disparities in care of patients with COVID-19 based on hospital location and the available level of care. Next, we will discuss the impact of novel therapies, which continue to influence the treatment of critically ill patients during the COVID-19 pandemic. These therapies challenge traditional ethical justifications for nonstandard, "off-label," or otherwise innovative treatments.

We will examine their implications for standards of care during a pandemic. Our focus here will be on the ethical considerations of both these topics (disparities and novel therapies) and on opportunities to learn from responses to the pandemic.

Shifts in Clinical Practices

In this section, we reflect on differences in provision of critical care to patients who were COVID-19 positive versus COVID-19 negative in the hospital ICU setting. Some of these differences were necessary due to the highly infectious nature of COVID-19 disease (infectivity), while others were due to the multifaceted nature of the symptoms and signs that patients manifest as they get sick enough to warrant ICU-level care (severity of disease).

When cases surged in the last quarter of 2020, hospital officials and clinical leadership turned their attention from general preparedness planning to setting specific protocols for taking care of patients in the intensive care unit (ICU). This conversation and agenda setting, as outlined in the first section, had to establish protocols not only for taking care of COVID-19 cases within the ICU setting, but also for minimizing risk of cross-infection to patients who were sick enough to need ICU-level care but were not infected with COVID-19.

Altered clinical models of care delivery included a change in how COVID-19-positive patients were intubated. It was decided that only senior and experienced members of the Cleveland Clinic critical care team would perform intubations, so as to minimize the time spent on each and thereby reduce chances of infection to clinical staff. Recommended protocols were also put into place for how to do bronchoscopy, which is a procedure that lets doctors look at the patient's lungs and air passages. The optimal timing of bronchoscopy procedures for COVID-19 patients (which was thought to be aerosol generating, and thus having potential for infectiousness) was unknown in early 2020, but more data and recommendations were published toward the end of the year (Wahidi et al. 2020). These new data provided evidence-based guidance, which suggested clinicians consider discretionary use of bronchoscopy for COVID-19-positive patients, given the procedure's limited prognostic value and high risk of transmission.

In spring 2020, to prepare for a first and a potential second deadly surge of the COVID-19 pandemic in northeast Ohio, Cleveland Clinic leadership held an enterprise-wide discussion to consider changes to hospital rules regarding which procedures required different levels of PPE. These efforts focused on rationing and safeguarding PPE for the most risky and lengthy procedures that might lead to COVID-19 transmission from patients to care team members, in hopes that the hospital system could steward their available resources for a longer time if faced with an onslaught of infected patients who needed care. To this end, up until early fall 2020, N95 masks were used in all intubations—a departure from usual practices—as the likelihood that the patient could potentially have COVID-19 went up as the year progressed. While some of these changes represented increased vigilance to reduce transmission, other alterations, such as institutional shifting of PPE to the most necessary areas of clinical care and encouraging reuse of some PPE, were necessary to conserve limited resources. This was all happening against a backdrop of global shortages in face mask availability, which created an atmosphere of fear among healthcare professionals.

As if these hurdles were not enough, Cleveland Clinic hospitals and other Ohio health systems were implementing a number of alterations in care delivery. Under pandemic conditions, they worked on how best to isolate patients who had been potentially exposed to the SARS-CoV-2 virus and how to encourage patients who called in before coming to the hospital to quarantine at home unless they became critically ill, so as not to overwhelm testing capabilities or hospital capacity. To ensure that COVID-19-positive patients got the critical care they needed, while also optimizing the safety of non-COVID-19 patients and all the healthcare professionals caring for them in ICUs, the ICU critical care structure now required separate areas for COVID-19-positive and COVID-19-negative patients. Nursing care also shifted dramatically, with limitations placed on how frequently nurses entered patient rooms and interacted with visitors. As mentioned earlier, ventilators and vital sign monitors were also relocated outside of patients' rooms, for easier access and to minimize movement in and out of the spaces occupied by COVID-19 patients. While these changes were intended to prioritize the safety of the patient and the treating team alike, they were made with only a rudimentary and still-evolving sense of what they would mean for patient outcomes as the pandemic progressed—a fact that cannot be emphasized enough. Healthcare teams were under acute pressure to craft best practices without yet having the benefit of any evidence-based, disease-specific, and bedside-practice data.

An additional alteration in the provision of care that had implications both for healthcare professionals and patients and their families were changes to visitation policies for hospitalized patients, regardless of their COVID-19 status. These alterations, though justified by a superseding obligation to keep patients and caregivers safe, were not ethically neutral, and there was not always a clear ethical priority of safety over family presence. Family members and loved ones are partners in comprehensive patient care, and the absence of these individuals created gaps in the therapeutic benefits of familiar faces during hospitalization. Other aspects of care, such as having conversations about what is most important to patients, were made more difficult by the need to have those conversations only by phone or via videoconferencing technology. Apart from some compassionate exceptions made for patients at the very end of life, visitor restrictions meant that some patients spent most of their last days without family present.

Lessons Learned

1. Power of Collaboration

In the context of rapidly shifting activity across Ohio, a key element to minimizing discrepancies in care between COVID-19-positive and COVID-19-negative patients was remaining nimble with local shifts in best practices and care models. New information, acquired at a rapid pace, constituted a steep learning curve for many northeast Ohio-area hospitals such as Metro Health System, University Hospitals health system, and Cleveland Clinic Health System, which became closely aligned with the governor's office and the state's emerging public health guidance. These neighboring hospital systems banded together to strengthen local ties among hospital facilities, leveraging existing strengths to best serve Cleveland-area patient communities and making plans to divert admissions if one facility reached maximum capacity. These efforts represent the most salient lesson learned: the power of collaboration.

2. Hospital Education and Training

Other lessons learned included how crucial education and training were to providing patients with level-appropriate, hospital-based care while minimizing infection spread, and the importance of maintaining adequate hospital staffing to accommodate surges and bedside care. Education modules on these topics (now being refined for future use) helped our primary COVID-19-designated facility, Cleveland Clinic Marymount Hospital (MMH), become adept at treating acute respiratory distress syndrome (ARDS) patients with COVID-19, and assistance and nursing supplementation from other facilities helped harmonize critical care delivery. With an eye to limiting infection spread and ensuring adequate staffing, the Cleveland Clinic planned to take on specialty care at Main Campus so that MMH and other COVID "hubs" would have added capacity for incoming COVID-19 patients. This plan was justified from an ethics perspective insofar as its intention was to minimize impact on COVID-19-negative patients needing acute and specialty care, while centralizing resources to provide enhanced care for patients who were COVID-19 positive.

In addition to targeted cross-training and specialty care education, it was essential that hospitals and healthcare systems build in supports for the psychological well-being of healthcare professionals. One example of such efforts is the "moral distress reflective debrief" resource created by the Cleveland Clinic's Center for Bioethics in collaboration with its Office of Caregiver Experience. These sessions focus on the moral distress of healthcare professionals to offset some of the emotional- and practice-based trauma experienced by our compassionate clinical team members during the height of the pandemic (Morley and Horsburgh 2021).

COVID-19 Therapy Innovation and Research

As of this writing, the still-evolving pandemic dictates that society as a whole contain the clinical situation by controlling the spread of the virus and ensuring deaths are minimized, and that the medical community evaluate existing treatments while developing further treatments. Furthermore, addressing the needs of the pandemic alongside the need for clinical research to develop treatments represents a necessary balance between ethical obligations associated with research and with providing evidence-based, effective care. Therefore, responsibilities lie with policy makers, clinicians and researchers, and other stakeholders to identify and mobilize time and resources to ensure that research is an integrated part of the pandemic response. In this section, we discuss the impact of novel therapies, clinical uncertainty in the face of a novel disease, the feeling of desperation, and the addressing of logistics of the consenting process for clinical trials in the face of a highly communicable contagion.

COVID-19 Research in Ohio

In Ohio, researchers from local academic hospitals developed networks to promote fair and meaningful community participation in an inclusive shared decision-making process. At the Cleveland Clinic, an interdisciplinary committee, which included clinical research, bioethics, and regulatory personnel, reviewed and prioritized proposed research studies according to their scientific quality and likelihood of impacting local patients. The committee also ensured that the studies could attain necessary recruitment numbers by not selecting too many studies that would be competing for the same patient population. These efforts supplemented streamlined Institutional Review Board (IRB) processes and approved flexible methods for obtaining consent, including via remote platforms.

Underlying these processes is a scientific and ethical urgency to conduct research during a public health emergency. In 2021, several medications and interventions to manage medical conditions associated with COVID-19, such as cytokine storm and ARDS, have been put into the clinical trial pipeline in hopes of finding effective and safe treatments to lower case-fatality rates. Because it is impractical to create new drugs in the compressed time frame necessitated by a novel illness, some of these studies examine how drugs already approved by the FDA for other uses can be used against COVID. This allows investigators to accelerate the research process by foregoing many of the early studies usually required of drugs that have not yet been FDA approved (Senanayake 2020; Fan et al. 2020). Despite the potential need to accelerate research and to increase openness to novel therapies during a pandemic, core ethical standards must still be met. These ethical standards are, at their core, similar to those that apply to research conducted outside of a pandemic. That is, they must have scientific validity, and a reasonable risk-benefit ratio, while including collaborative partnership and fair and voluntary participation. They must provide social value, undergo an independent review, and maintain respect for both participants and affected communities (WHO 2021).

There are a number of examples of how this accelerated process was carried out during the COVID-19 pandemic. One approach involved a mechanism that is also used under non-pandemic conditions to increase the application of a particular drug; namely "expanded access use," through which patients with immediately life-threatening conditions can, without being in a clinical trial, gain access to investigational medical products (drugs, biologics, and medical devices) when no other satisfactory alternative therapy options are available. Early in the pandemic, Remdesivir, an antiviral drug manufactured by Gilead and initially approved for treatment of hepatitis C and respiratory syncytial virus, was being administered to treat severe COVID-19 under expanded access use (Grein et al. 2020). Due to overwhelming requests for Remdesivir, however, and to meet obligations created by the core ethical standards outlined above, Gilead suspended expanded access use and prioritized clinical trials. Gilead initiated two clinical trials, beginning in mid-March, comparing Remdesivir to standard-of-care treatments in moderate to severe COVID-19. These studies are considered "randomized" because research subjects were randomly assigned to receive either Remdesivir or standard of care, and "controlled" because those receiving Remdesivir were compared to those who received the standard of care. This methodological approach represents the best way to be sure that outcomes are the result of the experimental treatment. The results of the Gilead clinical trials and the National Institute Health–initiated Adaptive COVID-19 Treatment Trial revealed that Remdesivir was superior compared to placebo in shortening the time to recovery of patients who required hospitalization due to COVID-19, and that five days of Remdesivir was adequate treatment time to provide benefit (Beigel et al 2020; ClinicalTrials.gov 2020; Eastman et al. 2020; Gilead 2020; Goldman et al. 2020). The ethical significance of these studies is that, through the "gold standard" of scientific research (i.e., randomized controlled trials), there was rapidly evolving data to support an evidence-based change in practice faster than would usually occur.

Another medication that was in question for approximately a year is Tocilizumab. It had successfully been used to treat other diseases that, like COVID-19, involved immune system overreactions. Based on this inference, the Cleveland Clinic administered Tocilizumab "off-label" to patients who had severe COVID-19 symptoms (Salama et al. 2021, Salvarani et al. 2021). Although drugs are approved by the FDA for specific uses, a healthcare provider may prescribe a drug for an unapproved or "off-label" use when they judge that it is medically appropriate for the patient—usually because the medical condition does not have an approved drug or because all approved therapies have failed to help the patient. Early on in the pandemic, there was medical and ethical justification for the use of Tocilizumab in the absence of better treatments and based on the scientific inference that Tocilizumab's effectiveness for similar viral infections meant it would likely work for COVID-19-positive patients. As the pandemic has evolved, however, the medical community has pivoted away from any off-label use of this drug, as there is now more data from clinical trials to guide medical treatment.

Guided by ethical obligations to provide only those treatments with a favorable balance of benefits and risk, and based on developing available data, the Cleveland Clinic accordingly removed Tocilizumab as a possible therapeutic option in the summer of 2020. However, the most recent study of Tocilizumab shows that treatment with Tocilizumab and another similar agent (Sarilumab) improved patient outcomes and promoted survival in critically ill COVID-19 patients receiving organ support in ICUs (Gordon et al. 2021). In light of this study, the Cleveland Clinic again changed its position on using Tocilizumab and is currently providing the medication for patients who meet the guidelines. These shifts highlight the need to remain agile and current with the large influx of new data, while also maintaining alignment with evidence-based medicine during a pandemic.

Informed Consent for Pandemic Research

One of the most central ethical components of clinical research is the process of informed consent, whereby a research subject confirms his/her understanding of and willingness to participate in a study. Two key elements of the process of informed consent entail ensuring that a prospective research subject understands: 1) that the intervention is part of research, and 2) that the research involves some level of risk. In the context of a pandemic involving a novel disease, these aspects are uniquely challenging, especially early on, as there are uncertain risks and a perception that some intervention—even an unproven one—is better than no intervention. These considerations raise concerns about a research subject's ability to distinguish between research (which is intended to provide data that will increase knowledge about a disease or treatment) and treatment (which is intended to directly benefit the patient). Researchers' potential inability to fully describe risks (because a disease or treatment is so new), coupled with situations in which the only available treatment is the intervention that is part of a research study (because there is no other approved standard of care), could make it difficult to provide adequately informed consent.

Further complicating research during a pandemic are situations that would be challenging even outside of a pandemic. For example, any patient who may not be able to provide his/her own informed consent must be managed carefully. Some patients are simply too ill to be able to give consent for themselves, which means either that a legally acceptable representative (LAR), or someone authorized to make decisions for them, such as a family member, would need to provide consent, or that the research project may have to exclude such patients. The latter possibility poses a particular challenge for research during a pandemic, as the success of the research is dependent upon those very patients. During the worst of the pandemic, even the option of engaging in a consent process with LARs was challenged by restrictions on in-person interactions between researchers and potential research subjects. To address this hurdle, on March 18, 2020, the FDA recommended and approved alternative approaches to consent, which took the form of telephone calls, video conferences, direct signature, or witnessed signature sent via electronic methods (FDA 2020; Gaba and Bhatt 2020). Patients and families in the northeast Ohio area who were treated in the Cleveland Clinic System were willing to give informed consent via remote options, which meant that studies could enroll patients.

Conclusion

A crisis that threatens public health—especially a novel viral pandemic such as COVID-19—requires timely and appropriate response and treatment. By focusing on pandemic planning ahead of COVID-19's emergence in Ohio, by explicating differences within critical care provisions for COVID-19-positive and -negative patients, and by expanding upon elements central to research for cures and treatment for an emerging disease, we have attempted to build a context for the ethical and clinical aspects of what Ohio hospital systems and individual health-care workers faced during the COVID-19 pandemic's first year. The invaluable lessons of that year have shown the importance of collaboration among hospital systems and of being preemptively prepared as a hospital for pandemic situations.

REFERENCES

Beigel, John H., Kay M. Tomashek, Lori E. Dodd, Aneesh K. Mehta, Barry S. Zingman, Andre C. Kalil, Elizabeth Hohmann, Helen Y. Chu, Annie Luetkemeyer, Susan Klin et al. 2020. "Remdesivir for the Treatment of COVID-19—Final Report." *New England Journal of Medicine* 383, no. 19: 1813–1826.

Cleveland Clinic. 2020. "How We Created a Hospital for COVID-19 Patients in Less Than a Month; The Story of Cleveland Clinic's Pandemic Surge Facility". Cleveland Clinic Consult QD, April 15, 2020. https://consultqd.clevelandclinic.org/how-we-created-a-hospital-for-covid-19-patients-in-less-than-a-month/.

ClinicalTrials.gov. Adaptive COVID-19 Treatment Trial (ACTT). Accessed April 10, 2020. https://clinicaltrials.gov/ct2/show/NCT04280705.

Colorado Department of Public Health & Environment. 2022. "CDPHE All Hazards Internal Emergency Response and Recovery Plan, Annex B: Colorado Crisis Standards of Care Plan January 4, 2020." Amended May 12, 2022. https://cdphe.colorado.gov/colorado-crisis-standards-care

Daugherty-Biddison, Lee, Howard Gwon, Alan Regenberg, Monica Schoch-Spana, and Eric Toner. 2017. "Maryland Framework for the Allocation of Scarce Life-sustaining Medical Resources in a Catastrophic Public Health Emergency." August 24, 2017. http://bioethicstoday.org/wp-content/uploads/2020/03/Daugherty-Maryland-framework-PH-emergency-2017.pdf?x41592

Di Blasi, Erica. 2020. "Italians Over 80 Will Be Left to Die As Country Overwhelmed by Coronavirus." *The Telegraph,* March 14, 2020. www.telegraph.co.uk/news/2020/03/14/italians-80-will-left-die-country-overwhelmed-coronavirus/.

Eastman, Richard T., Jacob S. Roth, Kyle R. Brimcombe, Anton Simeonov, Min Shen, Samarjit Patnaik, Matthew D. Hall. "Remdesivir: A Review of Its Discovery and Development Leading to Emergency Use Authorization for Treatment of COVID-19." *ACS Central Science* 6, no. 5: 672-683.

Fan, Shiyong, Dian Xiao, Yanming Wang, Lianqi Liu, Xinbo Zhou, and Wu Zhong. 2020. "Research Progress on Repositioning Drugs and Specific Therapeutic Drugs for SARS-CoV-2." *Future Medicinal Chemistry* 12, no. 17: 1565–1578.

Food and Drug Administration (FDA). 2020. "FDA Guidance on Conduct of Clinical Trials of Medical Products during COVID-19 Public Health Emergency." www.fda.gov/media/136238/download.

Gaba, Prakiti, and Deepak Bhatt. 2020. "The COVID-19 Pandemic: A Catalyst to Improve Clinical Trials." *Nature Reviews Cardiology* 17, no. 11: 673–675.

Gilead. 2020. "Gilead Sciences Initiates Two Phase 3 Studies of Investigational Antiviral Remdesivir for the Treatment of COVID-19." www.gilead.com/news-and-press/press-room/press-releases/2020/2/gilead-sciences-initiates-two-phase-3-studies-of-investigational-antiviral-remdesivir-for-the-treatment-of-covid-19.

Goldman, Jason D., David C. B. Lye, David S. Hui, Kristen M. Marks, Raffaele Bruno, Rocio Montejano, Cristopher D. Spinner, Massimo Galli, Mi-Young Ahn, Ronald G. Nahass, et al. 2020. "Remdesivir for 5 or 10 Days in Patients with Severe Covid-19." *New England Journal of Medicine* 383, no. 19: 1827-1837.

Grein, Jonathan, Norio Ohmagari, Daniel Shin, George Diaz, Erika Asperges, Antonella Castagna, Torsten Feldt, Gary Green, Margaret L Green,

Francois-Xavier Lescure et al. 2020. "Compassionate Use of Remdesivir for Patients with Severe COVID-19." *New England Journal of Medicine* 382, no. 24: 2327–2336.

Hick, John L., Joseph A. Barbera, and Gabor D. Kelen. 2009. "Refining Surge Capacity: Conventional, Contingency, and Crisis Capacity." *Disaster Medicine and Public Health Preparedness 3* (Supplement 1): S59–S67.

Horowitz, Jason. 2020. "Italy's Health Care System Groans under Coronavirus—a Warning to the World." *New York Times,* March 12, 2020. www.nytimes.com/2020/03/12/world/europe/12italy-coronavirus-health-care.html.

Institute of Medicine. 2012. *Crisis Standards of Care: A Systems Framework for Catastrophic Disaster Response.* Vol. 1: *Introduction and CSC Framework.* Washington, DC: National Academies Press. https://doi.org/10.17226/13351.

Institute of Medicine. 2013. *Crisis Standards of Care: A Toolkit for Indicators and Triggers.* Washington, DC: National Academies Press. https://doi.org/10.17226/18338.

Mello, Michelle M., Govind Persad, and Douglas B. White. 2020. "Respecting Disability Rights—toward Improved Crisis Standards of Care." *New England Journal of Medicine* 383: e26.

Minnesota Department of Health. 2020. "Minnesota Crisis Standards of Care Framework: Ethical Guidance." January 10, 2020. https://health.minnesota.gov/communities/ep/surge/crisis/framework.pdf

Morley, Georgina, and Cristie Cole Horsburgh. 2021. "Reflective Debriefs as a Response to Moral Distress: Two Case Study Examples." *HEC Forum,* January 26, 2021. https://doi.org/10.1007/s10730-021-09441-z.

New York State Department of Health. 2015. "Ventilator Allocation Guidelines." November 2015. www.health.ny.gov/regulations/task_force/reports_publications/docs/ventilator_guidelines.pdf

Ohio Department of Developmental Disabilities. 2020. "Updated Guidance—June 29, 2020: COVID-19 Standards of Care for Vulnerable Populations." https://dodd.ohio.gov/about-us/communication/news/news-guidance-covid-19-standards-of-care

Ohio Department of Health. 2022a "COVID-19 Dashboard." Last updated Oct. 27, 2022. https://coronavirus.ohio.gov/wps/portal/gov/covid-19/dashboards.

Ohio Department of Health. 2022b. "COVID-19 Dashboard: Current Trends." Last updated Oct. 27, 2022. https://coronavirus.ohio.gov/wps/portal/gov/covid-19/dashboards/current-trends.

Pennsylvania Department of Health. 2020. "Interim Pennsylvania Crisis Standards of Care for Pandemic Guidelines." Version 2, April 10, 2020. www.health.pa.gov/topics/Documents/Diseases%20and%20Conditions/COVID-19%20Interim%20Crisis%20Standards%20of%20Care.pdf.

REMAP-CAP Investigators (Anthony C. Gordon, Paul R. Mouncey, Farah Al-Beidh, Kathryn M. Rowan, Alistair D. Nichol, Yaseen M. Arabi, Djillali Annane, Abi Beane, Wilma van Bentum-Puijk et al.). 2021. "Interleukin-6 Receptor Antagonists in Critically Ill Patients with COVID-19." *New England Journal of Medicine* 384, no. 16: 1491–1502.

Robertson, Campbell, Edgar Sandoval, Lucy Tompkins, and Simon Romero. 2020. "U.S. Sets Coronavirus Case Record amid New Surge." *New York Times,* October 23, 2020. www.nytimes.com/2020/10/23/us/covid-worst-day.html.

Rothfeld, Michael, Somini Sengupta, Joseph Goldstein, and Brian M. Rosenthal. 2020. "13 Deaths in a Day: An 'Apocalyptic' Coronavirus Surge at an N.Y.C. Hospital." *New York Times*, March 25, 2020. www.nytimes.com/2020/03/25/nyregion/nyc-coronavirus-hospitals.html.

Salama, Carlos, Jian Han, Linda Yau, William G. Reiss, Benjamin Kramer, Jeffrey D. Neidhart, Gerard J. Criner, Emma Kaplan-Lewis, Rachel Baden, Lavannya Pandit et al. 2021. "Tocilizumab in Patients Hospitalized with COVID-19 Pneumonia." *New England Journal of Medicine* 384, no. 1: 20–30.

Salvarani, Carlo, Giovanni Dolci, Marco Massari, Domenico Franco Merlo, Silvio Cavuto, Luisa Savoldi, Paolo Bruzzi et al. 2021. "Effect of Tocilizumab vs Standard Care on Clinical Worsening in Patients Hospitalized with COVID-19 Pneumonia: A Randomized Clinical Trial." *JAMA Internal Medicine* 181, no. 1: 24–31.

Senanayake, Suranga. 2020. "Drug Repurposing Strategies for COVID-19." *Future Drug Discovery* 2, no. 2: FDD40.

US Department of Health and Human Services Office for Civil Rights in Action. 2020. "Bulletin: Civil Rights Protections Prohibiting Race, Color and National Origin Discrimination during COVID-19." July 20, 2020. www.hhs.gov/guidance/document/bulletin-civil-rights-protections-prohibiting-race-color-and-national-origin.

Wahidi, Momen M., Samira Shojaee, Carla R. Lamb, David Ost, Fabien Maldonado, George Eapen, Daniel A. Caroff, Michael P. Stevens, Daniel R. Oulette, Craig Lilly et al. 2020. "The Use of Bronchoscopy during the Coronavirus Disease 2019 Pandemic: CHEST/AABIP Guideline and Expert Panel Report." *Chest* 158, no. 3:1268–1281.

Woolliscroft, James O. 2020. "Innovation in Response to the COVID-19 Pandemic Crisis." *Academic Medicine* 95, no. 8: 1140–1142.

World Health Organization (WHO). 2021. "Ethical Standards for Research during Public Health Emergencies; Distilling Existing Guidance to Support COVID-19 R&D." Last updated May 10, 2021. www.who.int/publications/i/item/WHO-RFH-20.1

6 | Bioethical Considerations in the Age of COVID

The Intersections of Medicine, Science, and Public Health in Ohio

Personal Reflection

Julie Aultman, Deborah Barnbaum, and Kimberly K. Garchar

In this reflection, three philosophers who specialize in health care ethics, and who provide ethical guidance in clinical, research, and public health contexts, grapple with the ethical issues that arose during the early stages of the pandemic in northeast Ohio.

We are three Ohio-based bioethicists with experience addressing medical, scientific, and public health ethical issues and dilemmas in rural and urban Ohio. In this chapter, we reflect together on the ethical impact of COVID in the varied contexts in which we work: at the patient's bedside, within health-promoting and biomedical research organizations, and within the community at large.

As bioethicists we work within public spheres to promote human flourishing through education, clinical consultation, research, advocacy, and public health. However, such efforts have been significantly impacted by the pandemic. In what follows, we offer a brief background section that explains the context in which we work and the methods we use, and then we examine that impact in the form of a roundtable discussion organized around several themes. For each theme, we offer our individual perspectives on this challenging time in US history while also remaining in dialogue with one another. Throughout, we draw on our varied professional observations and practices in health care, research, and community settings, respectively.

The authors are Julie M. Aultman, PhD, a bioethicist who works with nonprofit community-based organizations and at a medical university, promoting ethical decision-making to improve health equity; Deborah Barnbaum, PhD, who serves on several national data safety monitoring boards (DSMBs) and contributes to ethical review of locally designed and executed research as well as national multisite clinical trials; and Kimberly K. Garchar, PhD, an ethicist who serves on regional hospital ethics committees and contributes to policy development and ethics consultation at the bedside. All three authors are bioethics educators of undergraduates, graduate students, and medical professionals in northeast Ohio.

Background

The Profession of Bioethics: Diverse Experiences, Guiding Principles, and Methodologies

The purpose of this chapter is to promote a deeper understanding of the diverse roles and responsibilities of bioethicists who have guided ethical decision-making central to health-care delivery and research in the age of COVID. Bioethics is a vast field, covering the theory and practice of ethical health care, the treatment of animals, our relationship to the environment, and the bioscientific research that guides decision-making in each. As you can see from our backgrounds, our specializations focus on ethical issues in clinical care, public health, and medical research. Bioethicists working in academia uniquely combine theory and practice in their research and scholarship. In our capacity as academic bioethicists, we don't exclusively research bioethical issues, we also work in the field to promote the implementation of ethical practices. COVID brought significant challenges to the way that clinical care, public health, and research were conducted in Ohio. As the health-care landscape changed, so did ethical practices.

Although there are several different methods and frameworks in bioethics, one of the more accessible and well-known approaches is through principlism (Beauchamp and Childress 1979, most recently revised in 2019), which commonly focuses on four basic principles: autonomy, beneficence, non-maleficence, and justice.

In brief, autonomy emphasizes the dignity of persons and the value of self-direction. The principle of beneficence represents our ethical obligation to attempt to promote good by helping others, while non-maleficence represents the well-known dictum of "do no harm." Justice, at base, involves the application of fairness and equality to individuals, systems (e.g., of health), and clinical and research practices.

These principles serve as a framework for a methodology of reflective equilibrium, which incorporates already established ethical theories, such as consequentialism, deontology, virtue ethics, and care ethics, as well as specific contextual aspects of given cases. The term "principlism" may evoke thoughts of singular approaches or straightforward formulas, but this is not the case. Ethical deliberation, analysis, and decision-making are complex, multilayered, and nuanced processes aimed at promoting good and making ethically right actions that take into account the values of persons and communities.

The Roles and Responsibilities of Bioethicists in the Field during COVID

Prior to the pandemic, there were well-documented systemic inequities negatively impacting residents' basic human capabilities to achieve their full health potential, defined as human flourishing, or those valuable functions that give us the freedom to live a life with dignity, such as control over one's environment. In the age of COVID, many of our Ohio residents have experienced heightened injustices, particularly linked to race and ethnicity, health status, disability, gender identity, and socioeconomic status. These injustices have contributed to unhealthy and unsafe environments and have served as barriers to health decision-making and access to care.

Clinical bioethicists address ethical conflicts as they arise in clinical care, which means we assess ethical challenges and dilemmas as they affect the patient, the patient's friends and family, and healthcare practitioners themselves. This charge thus includes ethical consultation, education, and critical review of policy and procedure. Part of the role is to help identify values conflicts and work toward ethical recommendations and practices in medicine.

Another important role of the bioethicist is to collaborate with clinical researchers, including biostatisticians, to ensure the bioethical principles of autonomy, beneficence, non-maleficence, and justice are upheld in clinical research. The disruptions of the pandemic affected both researchers and research participants. There has been a lot of discussion of COVID's impact on researchers, especially women, whose research was in many cases derailed by the twin demands of their profession and family care. This subject shouldn't be shortchanged, but the professional focus of a bioethicist is on the well-being of research participants in clinical trials, such as those impacted by COVID.

Ethical Tensions Caused by COVID in Ohio: Three Perspectives

To better understand how bioethicists may be called upon to examine and address core ethical issues or tensions caused by such events as a pandemic, the following section presents our perspectives and experiences in the settings in which we commonly practice.

Dr. Garchar: Bioethicist in the Clinical Setting

Early in the pandemic, protecting the health of frontline workers was paramount since we needed healthy practitioners to help sick patients. Health-care professionals were not only working longer and more stressful hours with a dramatic increase in highly distressing patient cases, but they also faced a very real, very lethal, contagious disease to which they were themselves susceptible. The shortage of personal protective equipment (PPE) caused what was arguably the largest national rationing project since World War II. Additionally, COVID placed nearly crushing expectations on many practitioners and the anxiety they experienced had measurable, detrimental effects on their moral, mental, and physical well-being. This tension could be framed as a tension between beneficence—the obligation to promote good for patients—and non-maleficence—the obligation not to harm practitioners. It was also a crisis in terms of justice, as we saw hoarding and ineffective (or a complete lack of) distribution plans by the government for distribution of PPE.

Of course, further rationing and distribution crises arose as COVID-19 surged, causing a shortage in critical care resources and intensive care unit (ICU) facilities. These crises trickled down from the macro level of PPE distribution and institutional decision-making to individual decisions about what treatments each specific patient should receive. These micro decisions, often made by practitioners themselves, created additional anxieties that contributed to the threats to their own well-being.

Dr. Barnbaum: Bioethicist in Research

The tension between the duties of beneficence, or promoting good by collecting accurate data, and non-maleficence, or not harming research participants by putting them at increased risk, played out in the research setting also. One concern was protecting the interests of participants whose enrollment predated the shutdown. Once the shutdown happened, it was important to maintain a positive risk/benefit ratio in each study by continuing to collect reliable data. Otherwise, the benefits of the research would be lost, even as participants endured the risks of participation. In some cases, it made sense to alter data-collection strategies, because the risk profile of data collection had changed. For example, a six-minute walk test would typically be "minimal risk"—a measure whose risks do not exceed those of everyday life, including routine physical and psychological tests. However, during the pandemic the associated risk of *simply entering* a pulmonologist's office for a six-minute walk test increased significantly. The result was that the risk/benefit profiles of much research changed overnight; tension between beneficence and non-maleficence required real-time recalibration by DSMBs.

Researchers employed novel strategies, including video, telephone, or computerized data collection, when possible. This worked in some cases, such as collecting pill counts, or administering low-risk surveys that evaluate lung function and activities of daily living, such as the St. George's Respiratory Questionnaire, which measures lung function and daily life activities, or asking about certain types of adverse events. The transformative nature of telemedicine is often discussed in the clinical setting, but in research it was also a game changer. In some cases, however, it is impossible to replicate in-person data-collection strategies via telemedicine. There are no remote substitutes for an accurate count in a six-minute walk test, or an optical coherence tomography reading at an ophthalmologist's office. Researchers found themselves rethinking which data was essential. Secondary endpoints, or additional outcomes typically monitored to help interpret the primary results of research, were modified, and, in some cases, jettisoned completely.

Dr. Aultman: Bioethicist in the Community

Health literacy projects emerged in Ohio through academic institutions and nonprofit organizations in the effort to provide informational resources to English and non-English speakers about COVID-19 and health inequity, but, unfortunately, this was not enough. In working with our underserved communities, and deliberately investigating gaps of care experienced by resettled refugee populations living in northeast Ohio, I witnessed early in the pandemic the inability of several families and pockets of community members to find masks, COVID-19 testing, and eventually vaccines due to a lack of transportation, language barriers, and a general lack of clearly translated and accessible informational materials. Our community members, who feared everything from getting ill to job loss and becoming unhomed, were relying on their leaders, understaffed local agencies (many of which had to close during the pandemic), and each other to acquire the information and resources to protect themselves and their families. Further social justice tensions grew with heightened discrimination and racism in our Ohio communities, triggered by political unrest and the deaths of George Floyd, Breonna Taylor, and countless others by the hands of police who took an oath to serve and protect.

From a community bioethicist perspective, the trust among our most vulnerable, marginalized, and underserved populations and community leaders and health-care authorities was disintegrating and had to be repaired through cultural humility, open and honest communication, and better efforts toward fair resource acquisition and allocation. Social justice efforts included such activities as helping the elderly navigate a computer to find a COVID-19 vaccine, putting up fliers about nearby COVID-19 testing site locations in the community's primary language, and problem-solving with local stakeholders and public health agencies to better empower these populations.

How COVID Compromised Communication in Research, Clinical, and Community Settings

Acknowledging ethical and pragmatic issues during a pandemic ranges from the development and implementation of preparedness plans and safety measures to fair allocation of critical resources (e.g., PPE). However, one of the most basic ways to address challenging ethical and pragmatic issues is by respecting persons and communities through clear and honest communication and engaged moral deliberation. In research, clinical, and community settings, we observed and experienced how COVID significantly compromised communication, but, at the same time, how communication was strengthened in response to initial barriers or breakdowns of communication, and the negative impact experienced by research participants, patients, and others.

Dr. Barnbaum: Bioethicist in Research

For better or worse, one of the primary ways in which research risks are communicated to research participants is via consent forms, which are designed to protect the autonomy of research participants. Revised consent forms needed to reflect the COVID protections afforded research participants who required in-person interventions. These included assurances that researchers would wear masks, socially distance when possible, and adhere to stricter sterilization procedures. It was definitely a change from the usual lists of research risks, or scope of confidentiality protections. In my opinion, most informed consent documents are already too long—participants who get too much information are at risk of getting no information at all. The additional COVID protections only added to the seemingly interminable informed consent documents. Sometimes the attempt to protect autonomy has the paradoxical effect of undermining autonomy.

Dr. Garchar: Bioethicist in the Clinical Setting

Communicating information to patients—and potential patients—while fostering autonomous decision-making was a challenge in the clinical setting as well. Media coverage of the pandemic, and the scientific accuracy of that coverage, varied. Further, we witnessed a political polarization in our state and country that resulted in a spectrum of moral convictions and a vast divergence in the trust placed in science and the government. In Ohio, we benefited from Governor Mike DeWine's early, dramatic intervention and shutdown orders, even as we reeled from the disastrous economic implications. We further benefited from Dr. Amy Acton's "flatten the curve" campaign, although she received death threats while serving as director of the Ohio Department of Health.

In the clinical setting, the importance of clear communication doesn't end with the patient. The friends and family members of patients—whether the patient was hospitalized for COVID-19 or nonrelated reasons—were distraught when they could not visit their loved ones, some of whom were dying. Potential patients, especially the elderly and racial minorities, became fearful and even more distrustful of health care and the new restrictions, fearing they or their loved ones would be isolated and die, as one woman put it anecdotally, "alone and surrounded by masks." The balance between fostering autonomy, promoting beneficence, and exercising non-maleficence became even more fraught. For many, health care became a double-edged sword, both necessary and terrifying.

In the intensive care unit, physicians and nurses rely on communication with family members, which was severely limited, if not absent. Technology can only accomplish so much. Subtle cues gained from facial expressions are lost in telephone conversations, and body language is lost in video conferencing. This leads, unsurprisingly, to depression and anxiety in patients and family members, and has also been found to contribute to provider burnout. Absent family members could not communicate with either the patient or practitioners, which complicated what is often a decision-making process attended by grief and guilt. This compromised communication challenged patient autonomy as well as the participation of surrogate decision-makers when patients were unable to make their own decisions.

Dr. Aultman: Bioethicist in the Community

When examining some of the more positive developments that began early in the pandemic, it was clear how health literacy and therapeutic communication, both means of protecting autonomy and promoting agency, improved with telehealth and community outreach. Telehealth and telemedicine, specifically, allowed many individuals in the community to connect with their providers safely while being quarantined at home. Community outreach became a valuable tool to educate, advocate, and connect community members to essential resources.

However, access to telemedicine was a challenge for those who did not have computer or smartphone access and reliable Wi-Fi. Furthermore, even today there remains a paucity of translators and clear COVID health literacy materials for both English and non-English speakers. Our non-English-speaking residents often rely on bilingual family and friends to relay critical information, since translated health information takes too long or is not readily updated. Insufficiently translated COVID health information shortchanges autonomy and undermines the acquisition of direct, accurate information. Even English-speaking communities have found some COVID information inaccurate or difficult to understand, particularly among older adults. Information about how the different COVID-19 vaccines work and their risks and benefits is especially unreliable.

For individuals to exercise autonomous decision-making, and for the community to participate in public health measures, health literacy and fulfillment of basic human needs are essential. I am prepared to guide community leaders and public health and primary care providers to recognize the unique needs of persons and communities by developing health literature through a human capabilities approach. Accessible, available, and accurate information, and expert support have been scarce during the pandemic in northeast Ohio.

While local community leaders worked closely with our public health departments in securing and distributing resources strategically and quickly (e.g., delivering vaccines to our nursing homes), additional state and federal economic support was needed to reach the pockets of underserved populations. Finally, due to politically charged, unreliable, and uncorrected media sources, our community members were unable to make well-informed health decisions. Without advocacy and leadership within our communities, public safety and well-being remain at risk as the pandemic continues to evolve.

Revealing Injustice, Exacerbating Injustice in the Age of COVID

As communication barriers were examined among bioethicists and others, so too were the numerous barriers leading to health disparities and social injustices in the contexts of research, medicine, and community engagement. While it takes a variety of stakeholders to make a direct, positive impact to reduce such injustices, bioethicists are apt to thoroughly examine contributing factors, present ethical guidance in shaping public policy, and engage stakeholders in strategic deliberation and consensus-building approaches toward viable, sustainable resolutions.

Dr. Barnbaum: Bioethicist in Research

Justice was, and continues to remain, an issue in the research setting. Local researchers have seen COVID as a once-in-a-lifetime opportunity to learn about stress, anxiety, relationships, and even eating patterns, during the lockdown. I certainly worried about the injustice of already vulnerable research populations, such as those with preexisting conditions, racial and ethnic minorities, or persons of lower socioeconomic status—in other words, those who were most at risk from COVID-19—being asked yet again to contribute even more. On the other hand, if research wasn't being done on the individuals most at risk from COVID-19, then we would not have been able to learn the best strategies for fighting COVID-19. This, too, is a justice question. I might sound like I'm saying you cannot win: research on vulnerable communities during COVID is an injustice, but the failure to do research on those communities is similarly an injustice. That isn't correct. Rather, COVID has required researchers, and those whose job it is to help protect research participants, like ethicists, to be more vigilant in protecting participants. It's become a cliché to say that COVID has exposed weaknesses in the system that were already there, such as structural racism, inequalities in health-care delivery, and a patchwork health-care system. But COVID has also exposed the need for professionals whose job it is to address those weaknesses to work harder to root out the inequities in our system, and to do more to counter them.

Dr. Garchar: Bioethicist in the Clinical Setting

I think we can all agree that COVID has both revealed and exacerbated ongoing, systemic inequalities in health care. For example, in Summit County, Asian people, especially Asian immigrants and refugees, such as the Nepali-speaking Bhutanese resettled refugee community, were disproportionately hit by the virus. We can identify several factors that led to this disparity, including language barriers and culturally differing beliefs about health care. Nonetheless, the North Hill neighborhood of Akron is an area in which many Asian refugees live; this small immigrant community has consistently comprised 20–30 percent of COVID-19 patients in Summit County.

Dr. Aultman: Bioethicist in the Community

Surviving a pandemic when one is already a victim of poverty, hunger, and violence is a challenge when having to be quarantined and separated from supportive services. Our young children who live in poverty were expected to thrive isolated from their peers and teachers, with hopefully a computer, a desk, and a safe, quiet space to learn at home. And while many groups came together to provide needed educational resources (e.g., computers or tablets), children still lived impoverished. They were hungry, without reliable Internet, and in some cases compelled to comfort a parent who was working multiple jobs, was sick from COVID-19, and/or was being abused by a domestic partner. COVID-19 health literacy and prevention, along with its relationship to mental health (e.g., depression), gun violence, and domestic abuse, among other social determinants, was and remains essential. For bioethicists, it is critical to call attention to these social justice issues while also providing sound recommendations to shape public policies, laws, and ethical guidelines toward effective change. For example, determining through an ethical lens how federal funding for COVID relief ought to be spent at state and local levels can have a more positive impact on those communities with the greatest needs. Additionally, in working with community leaders, bioethicists can address the growing gaps, which prevent the delivery of essential resources to communities greatly in need (e.g., mental health care), and how to narrow or close the gaps (e.g., expansion of mental health care workforce through incentive programs).

COVID's Long-Term Impact

While respect for the dignity of persons and communities can emerge through the closing of communication gaps, antidiscrimination policies and practices, and the promotion of essential public health resources to improve research, patient care, and the overall health of communities, there remain concerns among bioethicists about COVID's long-term impact and how we ought to prepare ourselves for what is to come. From telehealth to the delivery of testing kits, PPE, and therapeutics through federal initiatives, some progress has been made. Nevertheless such "progress" has been reactionary. Thus, our future roles and responsibilities as bioethicists include reflecting on the past several years, asking the difficult questions to prepare for future public health atrocities, and learning how to be better advocates, stewards of patient care, and enforcers of *ethical* regulations, laws, and policies. From our own perspectives we have seen growth and change, but at what cost?

Dr. Garchar, Bioethicist in the Clinical Setting

Certain aspects of health care became "nonessential" so very quickly. As personnel and resources were rerouted to emergency departments and ICUs, wellness checks and non-acute surgical procedures fell by the wayside in the initial months of the pandemic. As the health-care system restabilized, we saw virtual appointments begin to fill the gap for primary care, and increased safety protocols allowed voluntary outpatient procedures to resume to a certain extent.

Dr. Barnbaum: Bioethicist in Research

I often think about permanent changes that may result from COVID. I anticipate less in-person interaction with research participants, more telehealth interaction, more remote monitoring of participants' adherence to experimental treatments. This will result in less participant burden. Beneficence is not merely about promoting good but also preventing harm. Less onus on research participants will contribute to beneficence, and to a better risk/benefit ratio. At the same time, I hope that the in-person interactions don't go away completely. From a data-collection perspective, there are side effects or adverse events that may be missed if we give up on in-person appointments. From an informed consent perspective, each in-person interaction is another opportunity to remind participants of the risks, benefits, and procedures they'll undergo. Informed consent as an ongoing process suffers when participants don't interact in person with researchers. In the same vein, another dreaded change is a permanent move to virtual data safety monitoring committee meetings. I rely on subtle clues from clinicians and statisticians when reviewing data. My role is to take what the medical experts tell me and interpret it through an ethical and regulatory lens. I'm not able to do that as well when I'm not in the same room, and fear that participants' lives and health will suffer as a consequence.

Dr. Aultman: Bioethicist in the Community

Given our collective experiences as bioethicists, and as trite as it sounds, COVID has changed everything and nothing at the same time. However, as we continue to advocate and care for patients and their families, health-care providers, research participants, and the greater community, the work we do as bioethicists can lead to future, positive changes in northeast Ohio and beyond.

REFERENCE

Beauchamp, Tom L., and James F. Childress. 2019. *Principles of Biomedical Ethics*. 8th ed. New York: Oxford University Press.

7 | The Effects of the COVID Pandemic on Students with Limited or Interrupted Formal Education

Research and Reflection Article

Sarah K. Richter

In this hybrid research and reflection essay, an educator analyzes the adverse pedagogical impact of COVID on students with limited and interrupted formal education and recounts her experience with a group of such learners from Central America in one suburban Cincinnati school district.

As politicians at both the national and state levels have distributed recommendation after recommendation for schools during the pandemic, school staff have coped with almost daily changes to their teaching practices. Ohio schools have relentlessly navigated both student and staff needs while engaging in remote, socially distanced, and hybrid learning that has had a tremendous, and sometimes damaging, impact on the mental health and well-being of everyone involved. Though no single group has remained untouched by COVID's effects, possibly none has been more detrimentally affected in their education than the SLIFE population.

SLIFE, or students with limited or interrupted formal education, can be defined as immigrant students who come from a home in which a language other than English is spoken and enroll in a school in the United States with limited or interrupted formal education. This, consequently, coincides with low literacy skills and large academic gaps in knowledge (DeCapua 2016). SLIFE students are a subpopulation of English language learners (ELLs), but are at an even greater disadvantage than their ELL peers. ELLs often perform poorly when compared to other students of the same age or grade due to language deficiencies, but SLIFE students often take even longer than typical ELLs to become proficient in the English language due to their limited formal education (Sheng et al. 2011). Since many school programs provide ELL services, but these services do not include specific programs for SLIFE students, most SLIFE students make very little progress and eventually drop out of school, with even higher probabilities of dropping out as the incoming age of the student increases (DeCapua et al. 2015).

As a growing subpopulation of ELLs, SLIFE have astronomically high dropout rates (DeCapua et al. 2015) with specific needs that must be met to overcome their obstacles. Not only have they had to navigate the dangers existing within their own countries, but they must then wade through the ever-changing policies and politics of immigration in the United States, making this already traumatized population even more vulnerable. I was employed as a teacher and sometimes acting administrator for one district in Cincinnati, Ohio, that was making progress with this at-risk population. With a staff of seven, a school was opened separate from the main campus that would house high school-aged SLIFE students. With a promising first year, the school was well on its way to finishing strong for a second year, but on March 13, 2020, the district closed its doors due to Ohio's statewide stay-at-home orders, and students were sent home indefinitely. As a result, students whose health and well-being are tenuous at best—but who also have little English language development, are often two or more years behind their peers in their education, and possess very few technology skills—began learning remotely.

This chapter will discuss the SLIFE school and the effects that political policies enacted at the state level, such as Governor Mike DeWine's pandemic education policies, and the national level, such as President Donald Trump's anti-immigration policies, have had on a newly immigrated SLIFE population at a SLIFE school in an urban district in southwest Ohio. This will then lead to an understanding of the astounding impact that remote learning due to the COVID-19 pandemic has had on a population that requires teaching and learning strategies that are most effective in an in-person learning environment. As a teacher and acting administrator in the school, I will use attendance data from my own classes and students' recounting of various stories I heard during my time at the SLIFE school. Included are some of the more memorable details of the traumatizing backgrounds that many

SLIFE students from Guatemala and Honduras endure, as well as retention rates, changes in educational methodology, and most importantly, the cultural, communal, and socioemotional implications for SLIFE students that COVID and the resulting politics have inflicted upon an already overburdened population of students.

Building the Plane

It was in August of 2018 that a small SLIFE school in Cincinnati, Ohio, opened its doors for the first time. The first year we grew to have 40 SLIFE students in regular attendance, and it was very much an experience of building the plane and attempting to fly it at the same time. It was at this time that the United States was in the middle of the Trump presidency, which had become known for its anti-immigration policies (Smuskiewicz 2021). Latinos faced an increase in bullying and racial discrimination not only due to the vilification of immigrants by Trump and others with a similar view, but also due to the negative images in the media of the migrant caravans that regularly march to the US–Mexico border attempting to gain entry into the United States.

At the time of the school's opening, multiple executive orders relating to immigration had been signed into law by Trump (Smuskiewicz 2021). Reports of backlogs at the border were rampant, and children separated from family members and immigrants kept in cages were a common theme in the news. "Build the wall!" was chanted regularly even as some of the new anti-immigration policies such as the rescinded Deferred Action for Childhood Arrivals (DACA) program were challenged and denied in court (Smuskiewicz 2021). In June of 2018, the practice of separating families at the border was blocked by a federal judge and families began to be reunited, sometimes requiring DNA testing, but it was still too late for 545 parents who could not be found and reunited with their lost children (Smuskiewicz 2021). Some of the students at the school shared their experiences. In many of the students' stories, they traveled with a group of people led by a coyote.[1]

> **Maria:** Maria and her older brother arranged travel to the US. When she arrived at the border in June 2019, Maria was sent to a detention center for immigrants and asylum seekers while her brother was deported back to Guatemala. She has not seen him since.

1. Stories journaled were shared among students and staff at the school. Names are fictional and used for journaling purposes only.

Jose: Jose was abandoned by his parents as a small child in Guatemala. At 16, he traveled in a group with two of his friends to the United States. Upon arrival at the border, he was sent to an immigration shelter in Texas and was later transferred to another shelter, but only after being separated from his companions. Jose has no idea what happened to his two friends.

Ana: Ana traveled with her father to meet her mother and sister already living in Cincinnati. She and her father were separated at the border where her father was then deported. Ana eventually ended up with her mother and sister but has not seen her father since.

Carlos: Carlos left his immediate family in Guatemala to travel to the United States with his sister. The siblings were separated, and Carlos spend 68 days in a Texas immigration shelter before being released. He and his sister were eventually reunited and now live together in Cincinnati.

I did not understand the implications of the newly instituted immigration policies for our students until I came to work at the SLIFE school. This was more than just a little turbulence. I had had one encounter with a Mexican-American student at the district's main high school who told me of his worries about his dad disappearing one day. Because his father was not a citizen, the family lived in fear that he would be deported at any time—from an Immigration and Customs Enforcement (ICE) raid at work, a routine traffic stop, or any instance that might put him in contact with legal authorities. He had been worried the previous evening because his father was late getting home from work and the family feared that he was not going to return home at all. While I tried to empathize, the realization of that fear did not really take hold until I saw an entire group of students enter the SLIFE building who were new to the country, could not speak any English, and who were so terrified of doing something wrong that they rarely spoke or made eye contact with the adults in the school. This made a resounding impact on me and the rest of the staff.

Meet the Passengers

To fully understand the effect the COVID-19 pandemic would have, one must understand the students involved, their motivations, and their needs. In educating SLIFE students from Central America, one must understand that while students want to learn, they are primarily concerned with their physiological and safety needs. Immigrants from Central America often leave their former countries due high poverty, gang violence, physical or sexual abuse, war, natural disasters, or as victims of or witnesses to a crime (Torres et al. 2018). In a study by Miao Li (2016), it was found that more than half of the immigrants from Central America experienced trauma in their home country before emigrating.

Juan: Juan was sent by his parents to the US to escape gang violence in the city where they lived in Guatemala. One of the gangs had been trying to get Juan to join but he had resisted. Eventually the gang began to threaten Juan's individual family members.

Pedro: Pedro left both of his parents and three younger brothers in a rural area of Guatemala. When asked what he wanted me to know about him, Pedro replied "I came to US to work hard to help my family get out of poverty."

Once the decision is made to travel to the United States, some immigrants rely on human smugglers, or coyotes, to move them to the Mexican-American border (Torres et al. 2018). Those who travel with a coyote are often extorted for money, which may result in their murder if they cannot pay, and up to 60 percent of Latinas traveling with a coyote report sexual assault and kidnapping (Torres et al. 2018). Others may choose *La Bestia*, a well-known cargo train, to travel through Mexico, in which assaults, robberies, falls, and mutilations frequently happen (Torres et al. 2018). The option of traveling with a walking caravan may be the safest mode of transportation, though immigrants must walk the entire way, are subject to nature's elements, and may face death due to lack of food or water. In the case of the students at the SLIFE school in Cincinnati, most spoke of traveling with a coyote and a group of people.

Once a SLIFE student, often traveling as an unaccompanied minor, reaches the Mexican-American border, they enter the United States in one of two ways: seeking asylum at an official border crossing, where they will be detained by US officials until sponsorship is determined, or coming in as an "undocumented immigrant," continuously avoiding detainment, questioning, and deportment by the US government (Galli 2020). Youth attempting to enter the United States illegally may be placed in shelters or detention centers and deported if apprehended (Perez 2014). For those seeking asylum, they often spend their time waiting in immigration shelters, separated from family members and friends they may have traveled with until they appear before a judge. From there, most unaccompanied minors are released to their parents and family members, where they will then go through the many steps for remaining legally in the United States. However, since so many of these family members are considered undocumented, the unaccompanied youth are often exposed to constant fear of deportation of the adult sponsor (Galli 2020) as well as harassment and bullying due to a political climate that can frequently be hostile to immigrants, which has also been, and continues to be, exacerbated due to Trump's anti-immigration policies and rhetoric. For those without family members or friends to sponsor them, they may be placed in long-term foster care (Galli 2020). All of this creates feelings of distrust that educators must overcome to make strides in a SLIFE students' education.

When SLIFE students enroll in public school in the United States, they have already had to face leaving family and friends, contending with social isolation, having difficulty with communication, encountering legal stressors, and facing racial or language-based discrimination. SLIFE students then may face social and academic embarrassment due to receiving little or interrupted formal education in their previous countries (DeCapua 2016). The Central American countries of Guatemala and Honduras, where the SLIFE school students were from, have some of the highest poverty rates combined with the lowest educational attainment rates in all of Latin America (Posner, Martin, and Elvir 2017; Murphy-Graham et al. 2021). In Guatemala, free education is provided through sixth grade but is often unavailable in rural regions (Posner, Martin, and Elvir 2017). Honduras is slightly better, with free education provided through ninth grade, but again with significantly less access to education in rural regions (Murphy-Graham et al. 2021). In both cases, to send a child to school places significant strain on already impoverished families in rural regions of both countries in the form of transportation and finances, resulting in low participation in formal education.

SLIFE students often experience what is called "cultural dissonance," or the feeling of confusion, alienation, and bewilderment caused by the sudden shift to formalized education (DeCapua 2016). Additionally, educators are unlikely to have the training necessary to meet and understand the needs of this unique category of ELL student (Hos 2020).

The consequence is that many SLIFE students, especially those entering the secondary grades, drop out of school. Albert Bandura, a social cognitive psychologist, believed that most learning occurs within "a social context with a dynamic and reciprocal interaction of the person, environment, and behavior" (LaMorte 2019, 1). This means that people observe others and, in this process, acquire knowledge, rules, beliefs, and attitudes (Schunk 2016). This becomes particularly important for SLIFE students entering the atmosphere of formal education with language and learning deficits. For these students, consideration of social context becomes imperative for meeting their specific language acquisition skills as well as their learning processes for other subject areas.

Newcomer SLIFE schools are beginning to emerge in urban areas with high immigrant populations, including the SLIFE school in Cincinnati. These schools are specifically designed to educate immigrants and refugees, are often located on a campus separate from the main schools, and can be enrolled anywhere from six months to two years (Hos 2020). This creates an ideal atmosphere for SLIFE students: they can have the social context they need to acquire new knowledge while also having the opportunity to join the mainstream students later. The goals of these programs usually include providing English language and content instruction, an introduction to American culture, and a chance to acclimate to formal education while catching up with peers of their own age (Hos 2020). This is all in addition to the teachers, administrators, and paraprofessionals. Within the classroom, teachers are encouraged to use differentiated materials that enhance language and content, bilingual support from teaching assistants, small-group work, scaffolding techniques with videos and graphics, and, perhaps most importantly, to value students' previous knowledge. To provide all of these supports remotely would be next to impossible, but the COVID-19 pandemic would test just how well the plane in Cincinnati had been built.

Take Off ...

While building and flying the plane simultaneously, the staff of the SLIFE school in Ohio were able to meet the significant needs of the students. With only a principal, four core teachers, an intervention specialist, and a Spanish-speaking paraprofessional, the school opened in August of 2018. That year, 40 SLIFE students ranging from 14 to 18 years old began their formal education in the United States. The schedule was built to accommodate the work responsibilities of the students, whose most commonly stated goals were to "learn English, use a computer, and get a diploma." Students were bused to the school four times a week for their choice of a morning or afternoon session in which they rotated to their various classes. Since they only attended half a day, lunch was not served, but the necessity to send food home quickly became apparent. A local food charity agreed to make deliveries to the school so that nonperishables could be sent home with each student. Staff also reached out to a local charity organization and the Council of Unaccompanied Minors that were recommended by an ELL teacher at the main campus. This formed a partnership that allowed the staff to send SLIFE students and their families to these organizations when in need of family and legal services that the school could not provide. A bilingual therapist also began sessions with students at the SLIFE school once a week. To say the least, the therapist's schedule filled very quickly.

As the year progressed, the SLIFE students attended English, math, social studies, and science classes and together ended up building a small community that flew our plane collectively. Each teacher made the effort to incorporate English language acquisition and computer technology skills into their classes. Differentiated learning was the word of the year. With so many students at different skill levels, it was imperative for teachers to not only identify and teach skills considered to be remedial and necessary, but also to teach high school-level content so that the students could earn high school credits toward their diploma. All courses ended up as an amalgamation of remedial and higher-level content. Those students who could not read or write in their own language were identified and put into an intensive language class to build their skills.

By the end of the year, several students were identified as being ready to transfer to the main high school campus to continue working toward their diploma. A field trip was arranged with the high school's ELL teachers to have the students meet their future teachers, receive a tour of the building, and play a game of "locate the classroom or locker" to help them get acclimated to the new, very large school that they would attend the next school year. This was very successful in alleviating some of the anxiety and stress the students were feeling with the impending change to a much larger school. Several of these same students did very well at the main campus, kept earning credit through the pandemic, and graduated with their hard-earned diplomas in the spring of 2021. Those who were not ready to transfer to the high school for various reasons—enrolling late in the school year, having poor attendance, or still needing time to acclimate to their current school setting—returned to the SLIFE school for the 2019–20 school year.

Maximum Altitude

The 2019–20 school year saw an increase in SLIFE students from a roster of 40 to a roster of 75 students. This year, the SLIFE school staff was not so much building the plane as much as letting it fly with some occasional maintenance checks. Outside of the school walls, President Trump had amped up his anti-immigrant rhetoric yet again as the presidential election grew nearer. Chants of "Build the wall!" were as popular in 2019 as they had been in 2016, and the campaign promise had been met as some of the US–Mexico border wall had been built. Both the mental and physical health of many Central American immigrants, and of the SLIFE students, had declined due to the high priority the Trump administration had placed on mass deportations, more restrictive paths to citizenship, ICE raids on places of work, and an end to birthright citizenship (Nichols et al. 2018). However, though Latinos in the United States nationwide were feeling the stress from the intensification of anti-immigrant rhetoric and policies, the students and staff of the SLIFE school continued teaching and learning. Then came COVID-19.

The Plane Is Grounded

On March 11, 2020, the director-general of the World Health Organization (WHO) stated that the "WHO has been assessing this outbreak [...] and we are deeply concerned both by the alarming levels of spread and severity, and by the alarming levels of inaction" (Shannon 2020, 1). This would quickly lead to entire cities and countries employing mass quarantine and social distancing measures to quell the spread of COVID-19 (Lakhani et al. 2020). Only a day later, Governor DeWine announced several measures in Ohio to prevent the spread of COVID-19. The measures included closing K–12 schools for three weeks (Ideastream 2021). As a result of the directive, I, as the acting principal at that time, sent the following message to the staff: Team, if you haven't already heard, we will not be having school for the next 3 weeks. However, teachers are expected to report as normal on Friday. Please plan on meeting at 8:00 in my room so I can give you an update of what is expected of us for the 3 week period.

By the next day, packets were prepared to send home to the SLIFE students. They did not have enough experience with technology or home Wi-Fi connectivity to work online. The staff were then sent home and told not to return to the building. By March 22, stay-at-home orders were issued by Governor DeWine for the State of Ohio, which were later extended through May 1, 2020, with hints that schools might stay closed for the remaining days of the academic year (Ideastream 2021). This would be the beginning of months of changing directives from the governor and local and national health organizations that would affect learning in Ohio. The SLIFE school would remain closed through the remainder of the school year with teachers sending home packets a second time. Due to the sometimes transient nature of SLIFE students, the packets did not reach all learners. In other cases, students did the work but had no transportation to return it on account of a lack of transportation. In yet other circumstances, students simply could not do the work because they were not adept enough in the literacy or the content. Problems abounded and students were left wondering how their education would continue.

During this time, the acting secretary for the Department of Homeland Security issued the following statement:

> The US, Mexico, and Canada have each agreed to extend restrictions on non-essential travel across their shared borders for 30 additional days. As President Trump stated last week, border control, travel restrictions and other limitations remain critical to slowing the spread and allowing the phased opening of the country.

This effectively closed the US–Mexico border to immigrants and the possibility that the SLIFE students would see family members outside of the country for the foreseeable future.

Modifying the Plane

Staff at the SLIFE school were told that students would remain in a remote learning environment as a new school year began, though this time students would be taught online. No time line was given. As such, there was a scramble to ensure that students had access to a computer and the Internet in their homes. The SLIFE students had been using computers in the classroom while still in attendance pre-pandemic, but had never been taught to use Google Meets or Zoom, submit assignments online, or post their attendance remotely. The staff spent the first two weeks of school teaching remotely how to use the programs teachers would be utilizing, often taking even longer than the initial two weeks.

During the 2020–21 school year, 49 SLIFE students were in attendance, with only five of them being new students. The decrease in new students can be attributed to the continued closing of the United States borders due to the COVID-19 pandemic. Though schools addressed the pandemic-related social distancing measures differently, the SLIFE school would remain closed due to the close quarters, danger to several staff members with comorbidities attributed to a higher risk of severe COVID-19, and a lack of appropriate ventilation. Students met with a different teacher each day for class during a morning or afternoon session to accommodate their work schedules. Additionally, time was provided twice a day for "office hours" in which students could get help from their teachers with support from the Spanish-speaking paraprofessional. Teachers were instructed to post two or three assignments per week using Google Classroom. However, many students' attendance and subsequent work were sporadic for various reasons during this time.

Marta: Marta would show up to her online classes late, log off early, and sometimes log on and off in the middle of class multiple times. She rarely did homework assignments. Since remote school began, Marta had been babysitting her four younger siblings while her parents went to work. Two of the children were very young and required almost constant attention, resulting in Marta not being able to stay in class or even pay much attention to instruction. Marta eventually stopped attending or doing any work.

Manuel: Manuel's main goal for his education was to learn English. He did not feel he was making enough progress with the online learning and so began to attend the staff's office hours. Often, he did not ask questions about assignments and was doing very well in general. However, when finally asked why he was attending the office hours so often he replied that he just wanted to practice his English and missed talking to everyone.

Francisco: Francisco was attending his online classes but not doing any of his work. When asked about the situation, Francisco was working a full-time job to support his family and had arranged his break times to coincide with his online class times. He was watching on his phone while sitting in his car in the work parking lot and participating as much as he could. Francisco said he did not have enough time to do his homework or go to office hours for help, though. Francisco eventually stopped attending. He had been one of my best students the previous year.

Juana: Juana was working 10-hour shifts every day of the week since her family thought that online school was the same as not attending school. Subsequently, Juana never attended the live teaching sessions and would instead log on every evening around 10 p.m. It was at this time that she would watch the necessary videos and do her homework. While her work was occasionally late, she would always contact her instructors to let them know what had happened and that she would turn it in the next day. Juana stayed with the online learning even after the school opened back up and ended up with the highest grades in all her classes.

It is no secret that the COVID-19 pandemic, and its subsequent public health measures, has had global ramifications for education, both in terms of methodology and in terms of the individuals teaching and learning during the pandemic. Educational leaders agree that the effects of schools shutting down will have long-term impacts within education, including learning gaps between advantaged and vulnerable students, school funding, standardized testing, state graduation requirements, and a shift to social-service coordination like food distribution and mental wellness, not to mention the scramble to get necessary technologies to all students (Sawchuck 2020).

Shifting to fully remote learning was not just a technical issue at the SLIFE school but also a "pedagogical and instructional challenge" (Ali 2020, 22). At the most basic levels, students did not have access to computers and the Internet in their homes, or there were multiple students using the same equipment in the same household, raising concerns about student equity. Teachers needed training for structuring curriculum and instruction to an online system that was simultaneously motivating and engaging (Ali 2020). Both students and teachers required instruction for the use of the multitude of available technologies that were suddenly added into the online learning environment.

As students were learning remotely and isolated for longer periods of time, concern developed for the mental and physical health of students due to inflating levels of stress and a plummeting in emotional well-being (Cowie and Myers 2020). Feelings of anxiety and uncertainty increased. Vulnerable students were trapped in abusive, neglectful, and exploitative homes. Additionally, children from low-income families saw an increase in unhappiness, worry, and clinginess due to escalating emotional difficulties (Cowie and Myers 2020). Considering that a "suitable study and work environment is crucial for improved academic [...] performance" (Silva et al. 2020, 8), it is unsurprising that so many students felt a reduced quality of life while utilizing remote learning during this time of forced isolation. This was especially true for the students of the SLIFE school, seeing that so many lived with multiple extended family members in small, often communal, living spaces.

Old Plane, Lower Altitude

In March of 2021, students were welcomed back to the SLIFE school, though they were given the option to continue working remotely. Only two chose to continue their education with this method. Those who came back to the building only had the option of morning classes this time, instead of morning or afternoon as provided before the pandemic. When in the building, students would attend two of their four classes each day, rotating between teachers. There was no sharing, masks were required, and social distancing measures were in place. The SLIFE plane was nowhere near to being back to normal, but the passengers were happy to be in flight again.

To give a tangible, quantitative grasp of the impact that the COVID-19 pandemic has had on the SLIFE school population, here is some of the data collected from my own classroom, comparing years:

- Upon its opening in 2018, the school gained 40 new SLIFE students. In 2019, the school gained 64 new SLIFE students. However, in 2020 there were 5 new students.
- In the 2018–19 school year, 30 percent of the enrolled SLIFE students stopped attending, which is disappointing but not entirely unexpected considering the high dropout rates within this population. In the 2019–20 school year, 40 percent of students stopped attending. However, in 2020–21, during the COVID-19 pandemic, 57 percent of students stopped attending class.
- Of the 57 percent of students who stopped attending class during the pandemic, exactly half of them returned when the building reopened in March 2021.
- No students transferred to the main campus for the 2021–22 school year.

Conclusion

By the end of the school year, vaccinations for COVID-19 were available and the nation and the majority of schools were reopened. We may never fully know the effects that the pandemic has had on education, on students' mental health after being forced into long-term isolation, or on the SLIFE students at the school in Cincinnati, Ohio. Students with limited or interrupted formal education were experiencing the effects of trauma before the pandemic shut down schools; however, there were support systems in place within the SLIFE program. When schools closed in March 2020 due to the COVID-19 pandemic, SLIFE students not only lost their modes of education, but they also lost their most accessible support systems including teachers, bilingual support staff, trauma counselors, and psychologists. Additionally, many students did not have access to a computer or the Internet to continue working remotely and were left feeling inadequate, wondering what would happen with their already limited schooling.

As the pandemic raged, SLIFE students were more susceptible to additional traumas, not only from the pandemic but also the political climate. Already distanced from peers, the Hispanic community experienced a disproportionate death rate from COVID-19 when compared to others, with 33 percent of the community becoming infected (Falicov et al. 2020). Compounding the problem, the Hispanic community in the United States has the lowest rate of medical health coverage when compared to all other ethnic groups (Gil et al. 2020). Due to the high poverty rates that many SLIFE students experience at home, family members continued working in essential services, living conditions were cramped, and language and insurance barriers prevented testing and treatment for the virus when it was needed (Gil et al. 2020).

As the COVID-19 pandemic and online learning have continued, teachers have adjusted their methodology, and counselors and psychologists have begun to meet with students through video or teleconferencing. SLIFE students' technology skills have improved, which will provide opportunities when real-life issues may occur outside of the school setting. However, the main problem remains, and was exacerbated the longer remote learning continued, that of keeping SLIFE students from dropping out of school. The student-centeredness, engagement, and interactivity that were present in the classroom, were much harder to replicate in a remote classroom. Simply stated, with the lack of social interaction and learning found in in-person learning environments that were prohibited by the COVID-19 pandemic, many SLIFE students turned to more pressing personal needs and wants instead of staying in school.

REFERENCES

Ali, W. (2020). Online and Remote Learning in Higher Education Institutes: A Necessity in Light of COVID-19 Pandemic. *Higher Education Studies,* 10, no. 3: 16–25. https://doi.org/10.5539/hes.v10n3p16.

Cowie, Helen, and Carrie-Anne Myers. 2020. "The Impact of the COVID-19 Pandemic on the Mental Health and Well-Being of Children and Young People." *Children & Society* 35, no. 1: 62–74. https://pubmed.ncbi.nlm.nih.gov/33362362/.

DeCapua, Andrea. 2016. "Reaching Students with Limited or Interrupted Formal Education through Culturally Responsive Teaching." *Language and Linguistics Compass* 10, no. 5: 225–237. https://onlinelibrary-wiley-com.ezproxy.liberty.edu/doi/full/10.1111/lnc3.12183.

DeCapua, Andrea, and Helaine W. Marshal. 2015. "Reframing the Conversation about Students with Limited or Interrupted Formal Education: From Achievement Gap to Cultural Dissonance." *NASSP Bulletin* 99, no. 4: 356–370. https://journals.sagepub.com/doi/abs/10.1177/0192636515620662?journalCode=buld

Falicov, Celia, Alba Nino, and Sol D'Urso. 2020. "Expanding Possibilities: Flexibility and Solidarity with Under-Resourced Immigrant Families during the COVID-19 Pandemic." *Family Process* 59, no. 1: 865–882. https://onlinelibrary-wiley-com.ezproxy.liberty.edu/doi/10.1111/famp.12578.

Galli, Chiara. 2020. "The Ambivalent U.S. Context of Reception and the Dichotomous Legal Consciousness of Unaccompanied Minors." *Social Problems* 67, no. 4: 763–781. https://doi-org.ezproxy.liberty.edu/10.1093/socpro/spz041

Gil, Raul M., Jasmine R. Marcelin, Brenda Zuniga-Blanco, Carina Marquez, Trini Mathew, and Damani A. Piggott. 2020. "COVID-19 Pandemic: Disparate Health Impact on the Hispanic/Latinx Population in the United States." *The Journal of Infectious Diseases* 222, no. 10: 1592–1595. https://doi-org.ezproxy.liberty.edu/10.1093/infdis/jiaa474

Hos, Rabia. 2020. "The Lives, Aspirations, and Needs of Refugee and Immigrant Students with Interrupted Formal Education (SIFE) in a Secondary Newcomer Program." *Urban Education* 55, no. 7: 1021–1044. https://doi-org.ezproxy.liberty.edu/10.1177%2F0042085916666932

Ideastream Public Media. 2021. "Ohio's Coronavirus Pandemic: A Timeline." Accessed June 24, 2021. www.ideastream.org/ohios-coronavirus-pandemic-a-timeline.

LaMorte, Wayne W. 2019. *The Social Cognitive Theory.* Boston University School of Public Health. https://sphweb.bumc.bu.edu/otlt/MPH-Modules/SB/BehavioralChangeTheories/BehavioralChangeTheories5.html

Lakhani, Hari V., Sneha S. Pillai, Mishghan Zehra, Ishita Sharma, and Komal Soldhi. 2020. "Systematic Review of Clinical Insights into Novel Coronavirus (CoVID-19) Pandemic: Persisting Challenges in U.S. Rural Population." *International Journal of Environmental Research and Public Health* 17, no. 12: 4279–4293. https://pubmed.ncbi.nlm.nih.gov/32549334/.

Li, Miao. (2016). Pre-migration Trauma and Post-migration Stressors for Asian and Latino American Immigrants: Transnational Stress Proliferation. *Social Indicators Research* 129, no. 1: 47–59. https://doi.org/10.1007/s11205-015-1090-7.

Murphy-Graham, Erin, Diana P. Montoya, Alison K. Cohen, and Enrique V. Lopez. 2021. "Examining School Dropout among Rural Youth in Honduras: Evidence from a Mixed-Methods Longitudinal Study." *International Journal of Educational Development* 82, no. 1: 1–11. https://doi.org/10.1016/j.ijedudev.2020.102329.

Nichols, Vanessa C., Alana M. W. LeBron, and Francisco I. Pedraza. 2018. "Policing Us Sick: The Health of Latinos in an Era of Heightened Deportations and Racialized Policing." *Political Science & Politics* 51, no. 2: 293–297. www-proquest-com.ezproxy.liberty.edu/docview/2021486474/fulltextPDF/83985879A94B4834PQ/1?accountid=12085

Perez, Ramona L. 2014. "Crossing the Border from Boyhood to Manhood: Male Youth Experiences of Crossing, Loss, and Structural Violence as Unaccompanied Minors." *International Journal of Adolescence and Youth* 19, no. 1: 67–83. https://doi.org/10.1080/02673843.2012.708350.

Posner, C.M. 2017. "Guatemala: A Failing System." In *Education in Mexico, Central America, and the Latin Caribbean,* edited by C. M. Posner, Christopher Martin, and Ana Patricia Elvir. New York: Bloomsbury.

Posner, C. M., Christopher Martin, and Ana Patricia Elvir. 2017. *Education in Mexico, Central America, and the Latin Caribbean.* London and New York: Bloomsbury.

Sawchuck, Stephen. 2020. "When Schools Shut Down, We All Lose." *Education Week,* March 20, 2020. www.edweek.org/leadership/when-schools-shut-down-we-all-lose/2020/03.

Schunk, Dale. (2016). *Learning Theories: An Educational Perspective*. 7th ed. Boston: Pearson Education.

Shannon, Joel. 2020. “Coronavirus Has Been Declared a Pandemic: What Does That Mean, and What Took So Long?” *USA Today*, March 11, 2020. www.usatoday.com/story/news/nation/2020/03/11/coronavirus-pandemic-world-health-organization/5011903002/.

Sheng, Zhaohui, Yanyan Sheng, and Christine J. Anderson. 2011. “Dropping Out of School among ELL Students: Implications to Schools and Teacher Education.” *The Clearing House* 84, no.1: 98–103. www.tandfonline.com/doi/abs/10.1080/00098655.2010.538755.

Smuskiewicz, A. J. 2021. “Trump Administration: Immigration Policy.” *The American Mosaic: The Latino American Experience*. https://latinoamerican2-abc-clio-com.ezproxy.liberty.edu/Search/Display/2169231?webSiteCode=SLN_LAE_AC&returnToPage=%2fSearch%2fDisplay%2f2169231&token=A73D6120CE02028C8450940ADE53A3E2&casError=False.

Silva, Paulo G., Carlos A.L. de Oliveira, Marcela M.F. Borges, Danna M. Moreira, Phillipe N.B. Alencar, Rafael L. Avelar, Renata M.R. Bitu Sousa, and Fabricio Bitu Sousa. 2020. “Distance Learning during Social Seclusion by COVID-19: Improving the Quality of Life of Undergraduate Dentistry Students.” *European Journal of Dental Education* 25, no. 1: 124– 134. https://onlinelibrary-wiley-com.ezproxy.liberty.edu/doi/10.1111/eje.12583

Torres, Stephanie A., Catherine D. Santiago, Katherine K. Walts, and Maryse H. Richards. 2018. “Immigration Policy, Practices, and Procedures: The Impact on the Mental Health of Mexican and Central American Youth and Families.” *American Psychologist* 73, no. 7: 843–854. http://dx.doi.org.ezproxy.liberty.edu/10.1037/amp0000184

8 | Remembering Past Pandemics

COVID News Coverage and Remembrance of the 1918 Flu Pandemic

Research Article

John A. Lynch, Rachel V. Tucker, Haley Fite, Jordyn Adams, Blair Kramer, Chris Laycock, Shelby Singh, and Dirichi Umunna

This research piece by a team of communication scholars analyzes how Ohio journalists used the 1918 flu as a point of reference for understanding COIVD and for advancing positions on public health measures.

How do we make sense of COVID-19 in Ohio? Its infiltration of hospitals, nursing homes, prisons, and schools impacted the state as it did the nation. Ohio moved early to shutter businesses and schools in hopes of "flattening the curve" and slowing the disease's spread. Yet those actions brought backlash in Ohio as they did elsewhere. Ohioans, like the rest of the nation and the world, tried to make sense of what was happening with the disease and what they were being asked to do as COVID-19 spread. In the face of what felt unprecedented, people looked for precedents and found one they then used with stunning regularity—the 1918 flu pandemic. COVID-19 and the 1918 flu are different viruses, but they both presented first as respiratory illnesses accompanied by fever. They both took life in ways that initially baffled experts. They both led public health officials to propose masks and social distancing—policies that were resisted by a sizable minority of the population and political leaders.

These stories and references to the 1918 flu pandemic are what scholars call "public memory." They are a shared understanding of the past that is used to help explain the issues and anxieties of the present (Blair, Dickinson, and Ott 2010, 6). Thomas Dunn explains it this way: "The past operates not as historical *fact* but as historical *interpretation*" (2011, 429; italics in original). We turn to events from the past to help us interpret and make sense of our experiences in the present, even as those experiences and the historical interpretations we use differ and occasionally conflict (Bodnar 1992, 15; Zelizer 1995, 224). According to Nathan Stormer (2015), all discourses have a *mnestic*, or memory-bearing, capacity, which is why scholars have identified public memory work in countless genres and media. Journalistic discourse is no exception. Journalism has a "central role as a primary repository of collective memory in every society in which it finds itself" (Zelizer and Tenenboim-Weinblatt 2014, 2; see also Kitch 2008; Zelizer 2008). While commemorative journalism—stories recognizing anniversaries like the twentieth anniversary of 9/11 or the seventy-fifth anniversary of the end of World War II—are obvious types of public memory in journalism, Michael Schudson (2014) has argued that the bulk of memory work in journalism is noncommemorative. Journalists use public memory to give audiences context for an event, as the 1918 flu pandemic does for COVID-19. Repeating the stories of the 1918 flu over and over not only helps us make sense of the present, but also primes understandings of our experiences so that the present can become the raw material for public memory that may guide a future generation through a new pandemic crisis.

Here, we focus on public memory of the 1918 flu as it appeared in major Ohio newspapers.[1] Journalism is still a major part of "adult education in America," reinforcing cultural values and beliefs (Burke 1961, 332), and the turn to memory in journalism provides a temporal anchor for the beliefs journalism reinforces. While newspapers still

1. Papers from major metropolitan areas were chosen. A state-wide African American newspaper was also included in the analysis to identify Black perspectives on COVID-19 and the 1918 flu pandemic. Papers included are the *Akron Beacon-Journal, Cincinnati Enquirer, Cleveland Plain-Dealer, Columbus Dispatch, Dayton Daily News, Toledo Blade,* and *Call & Post*. Articles were accessed from Access World News and ProQuest databases, and because of database restrictions, the *Akron Beacon Journal* was accessed from their website (www.beaconjournal.com/). All articles identified from searches for "1918 flu" and "Spanish flu" were included, and articles that included that search term more than once in an article were identified for further close analysis.

have print editions, modern newspapers are "transmediated" (Jenkins 2006). This means that newspaper articles are printed and reprinted in multiple newspapers, and they also appear on newspaper websites from which they are further shared to Facebook and Twitter. Those tweeted and shared articles receive comments, likes, and retweets as they move across the digital landscape. We look at these articles to see the lessons they offer about the 1918 flu pandemic. Journalistic invocations of the 1918 flu pandemic highlight four themes: the compelling power of public memory, the use of the 1918 flu as a warning or a lesson, the political lessons of 1918, and the racial and racist components of pandemic experience and memory.

The Power of Public Memory

Edward Casey describes public memory as "an encircling horizon [...] as an active resource on which current discussion and action draw" (Casey 2004, 25). Just as the physical horizon delineates land and sky, public memory as horizon delineates events and helps us understand them. Public memory is also "animated by affect" (Blair, Dickinson, and Ott 2010, 7). This means that events that have been imbued with public feeling or emotion are more readily called to mind. It also means contemporary traumas and emotion will drive us to recall events and stories that help us cope with those feelings (see Blair, Dickinson, and Ott 2010, 13–18; Olick 2007; Schwartz and Schuman 2005). Because public memories become the horizon or frame that helps us make sense of new experiences, we become compelled to reference them often. This compulsion increases as the memory's narrative is animated by our collective feelings and anxieties: the more anxiety we have, the more likely we are to keep turning to stories that help make sense of that anxiety.

Because of the power of public memory, dozens of stories in Ohio newspapers turned to the 1918 pandemic to make sense of the world of 2020. The turn to 1918 was not caused by a lack of choices: Black Death, cholera, AIDs, SARS, and the 2009 bird flu are all pandemics that have marked humanity. Several articles did provide histories of multiple pandemics (Blundo 2020; Filby 2020; Hussain 2020; Wan 2020), but the similarities between COVID-19 and the 1918 flu noted above made the 1918 flu the more powerful historical touchstone.

The 1918 flu pandemic was such a powerful horizon for framing life in 2020 that journalists would even reference it for topics unrelated to COVID-19. In a story about the Cincinnati Opera canceling its 2020 season, the *Cincinnati Enquirer* observes that the Opera "was born in the wake of the 1918–1919 Spanish flu pandemic" (Lyman 2020). While the story is grounded in COVID's impact on the arts, the Cincinnati Opera has no direct connection to the 1918 flu. Yet because the 1918 pandemic helps us understand COVID-19, the article references it. The *Toledo Blade*'s suggestions for last-minute Christmas presents introduces a local steakhouse by noting, "By now, you've no doubt heard about the killer flu pandemic of 1918. Consider that the original Mancy's Steakhouse took root only three years later, in 1921" ("4 Shopping Days Left" 2020). Even when a topic only has a tangential relationship to the 1918 flu pandemic, as with organizations established *after* 1918, journalists still felt the need to tie the 1918 pandemic their reports. It offered such a powerful horizon of intelligibility for 2020 that journalists used it for a range of topics that arose that year.

1918 as Warning or Lesson

The urgency of the COVID-19 pandemic led most journalists to describe the 1918 flu pandemic as a warning or lesson that the past offers for us to navigate the present day. Stories that treat the 1918 flu as a "warning" frame the disease as an exemplar or baseline to establish the threat COVID-19 *could* pose. For example, Jeffrey Alan John (2020) described how Ohio prisoners were sickened by the 1918 flu, a pattern that we now know was repeated with COVID-19. Most articles that present the 1918 flu pandemic as a warning turn to the brute power of statistics to emphasize the danger. Cameron Knight (2020) writes, "In the United States, it's estimated that 675,000 were killed." Mark Price (2020) recounts, "The Spanish influenza sickened more than 7,000 people in Akron, claiming at least 630 lives in 1918 and 1919." Similarly, Barry D. Wood (2020) writes, "Cincinnati suffered greatly from the flu. A quarter of the city's population became infected, and 1,700 people died. In Columbus, 49 miles from the army camp, 1,236 citizens succumbed to flu." The warning was amplified by additional details, like the observation that "hospitals were overwhelmed with patients" as the disease spread (Garrett 2020; Price 2020). These articles come from the early months of the pandemic, when uncertainty about COVID-19 was at its highest. They offered a worst-case scenario to prepare readers for the potential dangers Ohioans might face.

Many articles were less emotionally laden in their recounting of the 1918 flu pandemic and instead describe their observations of the 1918 flu as "lessons." Amanda Garrett's (2020) March 28 article explicitly uses the phrase "lessons from the past." These lessons are often assurances that social distancing and mask use, first proposed to manage the 1918 flu, would work against COVID-19. Sheridan Hendrix (2020) draws from historians who inform him that "decades of research have confirmed that the practices touted by health officials back then [...] are beneficial in stopping the spread of the disease." Mary Kilpatrick tells readers,

> Cleveland has lived through a pandemic before—102 years ago during the 1918 Spanish flu. The city got through it using the very same social distancing precautions public health officials are ordering today. These measures were unpopular at the time, but they worked. (2020)

Peter Krouse (2020) warns that people in 1918 got tired of wearing masks, and an editorial in the *Columbus Dispatch* warns, "Another lesson from 1918 is to not ease social distancing measures too soon" ("Social Distancing Worked..." 2020). Jarvis DeBerry's (2020) column warns, "Instead of learning from the 1918 flu, we're repeating some past mistakes." Over a dozen articles, as well as public announcements by former director of the Ohio Health Department Dr. Amy Acton and Governor Mike DeWine compare the course of the 1918 flu in Philadelphia to its course in St. Louis. Philadelphia did not institute social distancing and let a World War I victory parade proceed, leading to an uncontrolled outbreak of the flu, while St. Louis instituted a variety of social distancing and other public health measures, thus limiting the disease's spread. The comparison of the two cities in 1918 encourages Ohioans to be cautious like St. Louis and not rush to crowded events as the people of Philadelphia did.

Yet even as many articles used the 1918 flu pandemic as a warning or lesson, there was an additional interpretation of these events that emphasized the need to be concerned about COVID-19, but also to avoid panic. Wood employs the same statistics offered in many articles that use the 1918 flu as a warning, but he uses those numbers to minimize a sense of panic. In the last third of his column, Wood (2020) observes, "We think we've got it bad from the coronavirus, and we do. But the Spanish flu was much worse. More than 600,000 Americans died, and

25% of the entire population were [*sic*] infected. Ten times more people died from the flu than perished in World War I. By contrast, on June 1, 2020, U.S. deaths from the corona virus totaled 105,000." For Wood, the COVID-19 pandemic is concerning, but it does not rise to the level of the 1918 flu. A column in the *Akron Beacon Journal* describes the whole range of challenges that those who lived through the 1918 flu would have also experienced, including World War I, World War II, and the Great Depression, before telling readers,

> Perspective is an amazing and valuable gift. Refined and enlightening as time goes on. Let us try to keep things in perspective. Your parents and/or grandparents were called upon to endure all of the above—today we are being called upon to stay home and sit on the couch. ("Tessie's Tidbits" 2020)

When considering the haphazard response of collegiate and professional sports to the COVID-19 pandemic, Tom Archdeacon (2020) tells readers that the 1918 flu pandemic was worse than COVID-19, but that it still provides valuable warnings: "Looking back isn't meant as some kind of scare tactic. We can learn about our current circumstance by taking a good look at a century past." For Archdeacon, the past should not cause panic, as some of the "warning"-style articles might have implied. Rather, contemplating past events should encourage sports teams and universities to be cautious about big sporting events and the possible spread of COVID-19. Whether considering statistics about mortality, the sweep of twentieth-century history, or concerns about sports and disease mitigation, journalists turn to the same details about the 1918 flu pandemic in order to place the demands made by public health officials on Ohioans during COVID-19 in historical context. Some journalists used those details from 1918 to assure readers that mitigation practices would work, and to assuage their potential panic.

Political Lessons of 1918

Some journalists and opinion columnists found political lessons in Ohio's and the nation's experience of both the 1918 flu pandemic and COVID-19. One concern was for voting during the pandemic. In April and October, Representative Marcia Fudge wrote in her "Congresswoman's Corner" column about the importance of planning how to vote in the primary and general elections, respectively. In April, she (2020b) noted, "Even during the current health crisis, our nation must tend in [*sic*] one of the pillars of our democracy: the electoral process. Neither the Spanish Flu epidemic in 1918, nor World War II kept voters from their civic duty." In October, Fudge (2020a) wrote,

> In 1918, America held a mid-term election during the Spanish flu pandemic. [...] That mid-term managed to go forward amid a pandemic and the November 2020 election will too. Still, we must carefully plan to safely have our voices heard, since failing to participate in the electoral process is not an option. Particularly for African Americans.

In addition to voting, political leadership, or its absence, appears prominently in news reports that use the 1918 flu pandemic to make sense of COVID-19. Writing in the *Call & Post*, Rodger Caldwell (2020) notes that in 1918, "lack of leadership from the federal government helped the flu spread like wildfire." For Caldwell, President Woodrow Wilson failed the nation. He compares Wilson with Donald Trump, warning, "The entire country must be shut down in every state and the president must place largescale orders for masks, protective equipment, critical hospital equipment, ventilators and community leaders educating their constituents" (see also DeBerry 2020; Republic Editorial Staff 2020). Knight (2020) claims that, though history showed the federal government's COVID response was a little better than its response to the 1918 pandemic, changes to federal powers and to the interplay of state and city governments made an effective nationwide policy unlikely: in 1918, "cities were largely in charge of their own response, whereas in 2020, governments at the state level are taking a more active role" (see also Wood 2020). As the pandemic progressed, more hopeful assessments of the federal response to the 1918 flu and to COVID-19 gave way to increased cynicism. Doyle (2020) writes, "A century ago, the flu killed roughly 50 million people worldwide, negatively shaped the global order for years afterward and was spectacularly mishandled by political leaders trying mightily to ignore it." Discussions of COVID-19 that included remembrance of the 1918 flu produced a notable consensus in their negative evaluation of Donald Trump and the national COVID response. While the majority of these newspapers had political biases ranging from left-center to right-center ("Media Bias/Fact Check" 2021), even *The Toledo Blade*—the most conservative source in our selection and the one least likely to discuss Trump—noted that Trump's recommendation "Don't be afraid of COVID," left families of COVID-19 victims "upset by the President's words" (Durbin 2020). Most likely, reflections on the political lessons of the 1918 pandemic tended to portray Trump negatively because the historical raw materials for public memory do not allow for favorable or ambivalent remembrance. The available historical narratives—or, perhaps more accurately, the historians cited by journalists—offered unflattering portrayals of Woodrow Wilson and his administration's handling of the pandemic. This limited journalists' ability to create a positive narrative that linked the national political climate of 1918 to the present day. Without the ability to create a clear contrast with President Wilson, the best that newspapers sympathetic to Trump could do was ignore the obvious political comparisons contained in public memory of the 1918 flu pandemic.

James M. Cox, Ohio's governor during the 1918 pandemic, is often invoked in Ohio's public memory as well. In a July speech, Governor DeWine referenced Cox, noting, "Governor Cox and I are both from the Miami Valley, but the reason I keep his figure here is to remind me of the resilience and the strength of all the Ohioans who went through that [1918] tragedy" (Rowland 2020). For DeWine, Cox is a figure of strength, as are all survivors of the 1918 flu pandemic. Hendrix (2020) tells readers, "Then-Ohio Gov. John [*sic*] Cox worked with state and local health officials to determine how to fight the disease and figure out the balance of closing things like schools and businesses for the public good." Yet other reports are critical of Cox and his leadership. Bischoff and Powell lay responsibility for the wildly different approaches to the 1918 flu in Ohio's cities at Cox's door. Cox, they note, "decided to allow local jurisdictions to determine what closures would work best," and permitted outdoor sporting events to continue (Bischoff and Powell 2020). Price (2020) implies that Cox's decisions contributed to the challenges faced by Akron residents during the 1918 pandemic:

> Hospitals were overwhelmed with wheezing patients. The Akron Armory was converted into a ward. Funeral homes could not keep up with demand as 200 died in the first month.
>
> Instead of a centralized approach to the crisis, Ohio Gov. James M. Cox left health decisions up to local governments, producing a patchwork of restrictions across the state.

Cox becomes an ambivalent figure in Ohio's public memory. For some, he wisely balanced the closure and the opening of schools and businesses. This vision is the one that Governor DeWine recalled in his speech. Yet others observe that Cox's flu management strategy looked more like the inadequate national responses to both the 1918 flu and COVID-19. From the same historical record, disparate memories and lessons could be drawn. Cox earned both praise *and* blame from journalists and other critics in their assessments of the lessons offered by the 1918 flu pandemic.

"Spanish" Flu: The Disease as Other

The ultimate source of the 1918 flu pandemic is not known with certainty (Taubenberger and Morens 2006), but evidence suggests it first appeared in American military camps located in Kansas (Hays 2009, 275). Because the influenza appeared during the waning days of World War I, government censors in the countries involved suppressed news of the illness. As a result, journalists in Spain, which had remained neutral in the war, were the first to report the disease's existence. This caused many to assume the disease had originated in Spain (Hays 2009, 277). However, the "Spanish Flu" label was more than the result of mere historical accident. It also reaffirms visions of nationality, race, and health that situate disease as foreign and non-white (Bass 1998). While Spain exists within the "color line" drawn around Europe, marking it as a white continent separated from the rest of the globe (Omi and Winant 2014), that line has historically shifted and been drawn in ways that implied that residents of the southern parts of Europe—Greece, Spain, southern Italy, and others—were less white than the residents of northern European countries (Jacobson 1998). Thus, the "Spanish" moniker for the 1918 pandemic helped reinforce borders around the putatively white nation.

Ohio newspapers in 2020 used both "Spanish flu" and the "1918 flu" or "1918 flu pandemic" as labels for the disease, but the overwhelming majority of articles from Ohio newspapers in 2020 used "Spanish flu" to describe the 1918 pandemic. Only a handful of articles noted the history of the 1918 flu pandemic, much less the history of the labels used to describe it. Theodore Decker (2020) noted, "Researchers believe the first flu cases in 1918 manifested that spring at a U.S. Army camp in Kansas and spread largely through troop movements." Bischoff and Powell's (2020) article made a similar observation: "The Spanish flu likely started in March 1918 at an Army base in Kansas where 500 soldiers were hospitalized." Yet even as they noted the disease was likely American in origin, they continued with the language of "Spanish flu" in their writing. Other articles are more explicit in describing the misnomer of "Spanish flu" and being consistent in their own language. Kate Mitchell's (2020) July 20 column described reading about the 1918 flu to make sense of COVID-19, which led to her discovery that "while commonly called the Spanish Flu, it [the 1918 flu] didn't originate in Spain!" An editorial in the *Cleveland Plain Dealer* began, "The 1918 'Spanish flu' pandemic surged in the military training camps and foxholes of a brutal world war—the perfect incubation conditions for an influenza that historians now believe got its start not in Spain, but in U.S. military camps" ("Remembering the World War I Soldiers..." 2020). Another article in the *Plain Dealer* provided the same story in greater detail: namely, that Spain reported cases while nations actively fighting in World War I censored stories about the flu within their borders. These reports, along with the fact that Spain's king was also taken ill with the flu, "left a permanent mark, tying the country to the deadly outbreak" (Amenabar 2020). In each of these three examples, the misnomer appeared just once, only to be refuted immediately, and the writers consistently used the label "1918 flu" instead.

Lessons about the ethnocentrism and xenophobia of past ages appeared in only the four articles noted above. The remainder of the articles examined in our sample proceeded as if there were nothing problematic happening in naming practices around the 1918 pandemic. Furthermore, newspapers did not consider how calling the 1918 pandemic the "Spanish flu" might reflect a racist and ethnocentric dynamic that was also driving the anti-Asian racism in labels like "Chinese virus," "Wuhan virus," and "Kung flu." Ohio newspapers did report on Trump's use of anti-Asian labels for the disease ("COVID-19 Pandemic Making World More Dangerous" 2020; Scheeser 2021). Some Ohioans, including an adjunct professor of engineering at the University of Cincinnati and Ohio's Lt. Governor Jon Husted, were happy to follow Trump's lead (Borchardt 2021; M. Mitchell 2021; Winter 2020). Yet any connection between the racist and ethnocentric names in the past and in the present is absent from journalistic uses of the public memory of the 1918 flu. Journalists treat the two eras and their naming strategies as isolated episodes, which helps maintain white innocence and white ignorance about the historical conditions that have maintained the racial privileges created by the color line when it comes to health, disease, and national belonging (DiAngelo 2018; Griffin 1998; Kelly 2020; Lipsitz 1995; Ore 2019).

Looking Ahead to Future Public Memory

To help make sense of the experience of COVID-19, many people, including journalists, turned to the historical example of the 1918 flu pandemic. The power of that example was so great that many referenced the earlier pandemic even when they were not talking about COVID-19. The 1918 pandemic provided powerful warnings and lessons for those in Ohio, and it provided a cast of ambivalent political figures and xenophobic labels that resonated with the political dysfunction and racism of the present day. In these public recollections of the 1918 flu pandemic, we can see a template for the memory work that might appear during a future pandemic as people remember COVID-19. In recalling the 1918 flu pandemic, journalists wrote about how the public health strategies of that era were the same ones being used against COVID-19. Masks, social distancing, and the closure of schools and businesses were strategies employed both then and now. And, just as it was in the present, those past orders met with resistance and were not consistently applied across the nation. The public health strategies of 2020 and the trenchant resistance to them will likely become the raw material for remembrance during a future pandemic.

How will Ohio fare in those future retellings of the COVID-19 pandemic? The state instituted social distancing, masks, and closure of businesses and schools early, but Ohio also had politicized protests against public health orders. Like Governor Cox, Governor DeWine also cuts an ambivalent figure during this pandemic. While imposing strong initial public health measures, the governor's policies and political rhetoric became increasingly timid as right-wing protest against COVID-19 restrictions spread across the state and the nation. The protests against DeWine's proposals led to the resignation of Dr. Amy Acton after she endured anti-Semitic slurs from Ohio politicians and protests outside her home (Kaufman 2020; Zelman 2020). These attacks dovetail with the anti-Asian racism many Ohioans used, following the example of Trump. These examples reinforced the boundaries of white privilege and its ties to national identity (Lipsitz 1995; Ore 2019).

Like the public memory of the 1918 flu pandemic, the story of COVID-19 in Ohio provides ambivalent lessons, useful either for praising the state and its leaders or condemning them. The state acted early to mitigate COVID-19's spread, but support for those efforts flagged rapidly. DeWine's leadership during the pandemic can therefore be assessed both positively and negatively. Thus, the story of the pandemic in Ohio provides resources for future stories that will make the state look like both a cautious St. Louis *and* a foolish Philadelphia in 1918. Like Cox, DeWine can be both a model to follow and an object lesson in what not to do. The trend to call COVID-19 the "China" or "Wuhan" virus—as well as the tendency to ignore the increased harms from COVID-19 experienced by Black and Latinx communities (e.g., Paskett 2020)—perpetuates the same type of racism and xenophobia that in 1918 led many to treat the flu as a foreign, "Spanish" invader threatening the purity and health of the white nation. The actions of the world, the nation, and the state in 2020 will be a rich source of invention for future recollections. How we will be remembered? That is in the hands of future generations who will decide how to use these memory-making resources. When future generations write stories about a future pandemic and turn to 2020 as a public memory touchstone, we can only hope their stories treat us kindly.

REFERENCES

"4 Shopping Days Left; What to Buy-Fine Dining." 2020. *Toledo Blade*, December 21, 2020. https://uc.idm.oclc.org/login?qurl=https%3A%2F%2Fwww.proquest.com%2Fnewspapers%2F4-shopping-days-left-what-buy-fine-dining%2Fdocview%2F2476068595%2Fse-2%3Faccountid%3D2909.

Amenabar, Teddy. 2020. "The Deadliest Pandemic in History Is Still Causing Problems." *Cleveland Plain Dealer*, September 6, 2020. https://infoweb.newsbank.com/apps/news/document-view?p=AWNB&docref=image/v2%3A16A7AFEBE94E66E0%40AWNB-17D5265CA3F0E840%402459099-17D52681EB6E224B%4024-17D52681EB6E224B%40.

Archdeacon, Tom. 2020. "Some History We Don't Want to Repeat." *Dayton Daily News*, August 15, 2020. https://infoweb.newsbank.com/apps/news/document-view?p=AWNB&docref=news/17CDF6C1C806CB58.

Bass, Jeff D. 1998. "Hearts of Darkness and Hot Zones: The Ideologeme of Imperial Contagion in Recent Accounts of Viral Outbreaks." *Quarterly Journal of Speech* 84, no. 4: 430–447. https://doi.org/10.1080/00335639809384231.

Bischoff, Laura A., and Lisa Powell. 2020. "Social Distancing a Lesson Learned from Spanish Flu Pandemic." *Dayton Daily News*, March 29, 2020. Accessed 2021/05/28. https://infoweb.newsbank.com/apps/news/document-view?p=AWNB&docref=news/17A0654FF9D46D98.

Blair, Carole, Greg Dickinson, and Brian L. Ott. 2010. "Introduction: Rhetoric/Memory/Place." In *Places of Public Memory: The Rhetoric of Museums and Memorials*, edited by Greg Dickinson, Carole Blair and Brian L. Ott, 1–54. Tuscaloosa: University of Alabama Press.

Blundo, Joe. 2020. "This Isn't the First Time That an Epidemic Has Hit Columbus." *Columbus Dispatch*, March 23, 2020. https://infoweb.newsbank.com/apps/news/document-view?p=AWNB&docref=news/179EE760BABAE1B0.

Bodnar, John. 1992. *Remaking America: Public memory, commemoration, and patriotism in the Twentieth Century.* Princeton, NJ: Princeton University Press.

Borchardt, Jackie. 2021. "Lt. Gov. Husted Defends Tweet Viewed as Insensitive." *Cincinnati Enquirer,* March 30, 2021. https://uc.idm.oclc.org/login?qurl=https%3A%2F%2Fwww.proquest.com%2Fnewspapers%2Flt-gov-husted-defends-tweet-viewed-as-insensitive%2Fdocview%2F2506701354%2Fse-2%3Faccountid%3D2909.

Burke, Kenneth. 1961. *Attitudes toward History.* Boston: Beacon Press.

Caldwell, Roger. 2020. "The Political and Healthcare System Is Broken and Corrupt in America." *Call & Post,* April 29–May 5, 2020. https://uc-idm-oclc-org.proxy.libraries.uc.edu/login?qurl=https%3A%2F%2Fwww.proquest.com%2Fnewspapers%2Fcommentary-political-healthcare-system-is-broken%2Fdocview%2F2440684162%2Fse-2%3Faccountid%3D2909.

Casey, Edward S. 2004. "Public Memory in Place and Time." In *Framing Public Memory,* edited by Kendall R. Phillips, 17–44. Tuscaloosa: University of Alabama Press.

"COVID-19 Pandemic Making World More Dangerous." 2020. *Akron Beacon Journal (OH),* April 28, 2020. https://infoweb.newsbank.com/apps/news/document-view?p=AWNB&docref=news/17AA20498AE7CF20.

DeBerry, Jarvis. 2020. "Instead of Learning from the 1918 Flu Pandemic, We're Repeating Some Past Mistakes." *Cleveland Plain Dealer,* April 16, 2020. https://infoweb.newsbank.com/apps/news/document-view?p=AWNB&docref=news/17A628A90ED370D0.

Decker, Theodore. 2020. "History Only a Rough Guide to Future." *Columbus Dispatch,* May 19, 2020. https://infoweb.newsbank.com/apps/news/document-view?p=AWNB&docref=news/17B152353639B6C0.

DiAngelo, Robin. 2018. *White Fragility: Why It's So Hard for White People to talk about Racism.* Boston: Beacon Press.

Doyle, Chris. 2020. "How We 'Recovered' from Spanish Flu Should Be a Warning." *Akron Beacon Journal,* May 13, 2020. www.beaconjournal.com/opinion/20200513/commentary-how-we-recovered-from-spanish-flu-should-be-warning.

Dunn, Thomas R. 2011. "Remembering 'A Great Fag': Visualizing Public Memory and the Construction of Queer Space." *Quarterly Journal of Speech* 97, no. 4: 435–460. https://doi.org/10.1080/00335630.2011.585168.

Durbin, Kaitlin. 2020. "Trump's Advice Rattles Families of Virus Victims." *Toledo Blade,* October 8, 2020. https://uc.idm.oclc.org/login?qurl=https%3A%2F%2Fwww.proquest.com%2Fnewspapers%2Ftrumps-advice-rattles-families-virus-victims%2Fdocview%2F2457185208%2Fse-2%3Faccountid%3D2909.

"Editorial: Social Distancing Worked against 1918 Flu." 2020. *Columbus Dispatch,* April 8, 2020. https://infoweb.newsbank.com/apps/news/document-view?p=AWNB&docref=news/17A3DBBFA5BCF320.

Filby, Max. 2020. "Doubts on Coronavirus Danger Emerge as Ohio's Outlook Improves." *Columbus Dispatch,* April 19, 2020. https://infoweb.newsbank.com/apps/news/document-view?p=AWNB&docref=news/17A778B47184E528.

Fudge, Marcia L. 2020a. "Congresswoman's Corner." *Call & Post* (All-Ohio edition), October 7–October 13, 2020. https://uc.idm.oclc.org/login?qurl=https%3A%2F%2Fwww.proquest.com%2Fnewspapers%2Fcongresswomans-corner%2Fdocview%2F2460110083%2Fse-2%3Faccountid%3D2909.

Fudge, Marcia L. 2020b. "Congresswoman's Corner " *Call & Post* (All-Ohio edition), April 8–April 14, 2020. https://uc.idm.oclc.org/login?qurl=https%3A%2F%2Fwww.proquest.com%2Fnewspapers%2Fcongresswomans-corner-marcia-l-fudge%2Fdocview%2F2444107392%2Fse-2%3Faccountid%3D2909.

Garrett, Amanda. 2020. "How an Invisible Monster Is Changing Our Lives Indefinitely." *Akron Beacon Journal*, March 28, 2020. www.beaconjournal.com/news/20200328/coronavirus-how-invisible-monster-is-changing-our-lives-indefinitely.

Griffin, Gail B. 1998. "Speaking of Whiteness: Disrupting White Innocence." *The Journal of the Midwest Modern Language Association* 31, no. 3: 3–14. https://doi.org/10.2307/1315355. http://www.jstor.org/stable/1315355.

Hays, J. N. 2009. *The Burdens of Disease: Epidemics and Human Response in Western History*. New Brunswick, NJ: Rutgers University Press.

Hendrix, Sheridan. 2020. "What Can We Learn from the 1918 Spanish Flu?" *Columbus Dispatch*, July 17, 2020. https://infoweb.newsbank.com/apps/news/document-view?p=AWNB&docref=news/17C511AE5D4DB198.

Hussain, S. Amjad. 2020. "Looking at History to Understand Importance of Vaccine." *Toledo Blade*, December 23, 2020. https://uc.idm.oclc.org/login?qurl=https%3A%2F%2Fwww.proquest.com%2Fnewspapers%2Flooking-at-history-understand-importance-vaccine%2Fdocview%2F2476063381%2Fse-2%3Faccountid%3D2909.

Jacobson, Matthew Frye. 1998. *Whiteness of a Different Color*. Cambridge, MA: Harvard University Press.

Jenkins, Henry. 2006. *Convergence Culture: Where Old and New Media Collide*. New York: New York University Press.

John, Jeffrey Alan. 2020. "Prison History Repeats Itself When It Comes to Coronavirus." *Dayton Daily News*, August 8, 2020. https://infoweb.newsbank.com/apps/news/document-view?p=AWNB&docref=news/17CBA7AD895897E8.

Kaufman, Jane. 2020. "Protesters Picket Dr. Amy Acton's Home for Third Time." *Cleveland Jewish News*, May 9, 2020. www.clevelandjewishnews.com/news/local_news/protesters-picket-dr-amy-actons-home-for-third-time/article_d2025d20-925c-11ea-9e10-732d28564173.html.

Kelly, Casey Ryan. 2020. "Donald J. Trump and the Rhetoric of White Ambivalence." *Rhetoric and Public Affairs* 23, no. 2: 195–223.

Kilpatrick, Mary. 2020. "We've Been Here Before: How Cleveland Survived the 1918 Spanish Flu, Compared to Coronavirus." *Cleveland Plain Dealer*, March 24, 2020. https://infoweb.newsbank.com/apps/news/document-view?p=AWNB&docref=news/179E94C6B90EB080.

Kitch, Carolyn. 2008. "Placing Journalism inside Memory—and Memory Studies." *Memory Studies* 1, no. 3: 311–320. https://doi.org/10.1177/1750698008093796.

Knight, Cameron. 2020. "Did Cincinnati's Tactic during the 1918 Spanish Flu Work?: Physical Distancing Helped Stop Deadly Virus." *Cincinnati Enquirer*, April 26, 2020. https://uc.idm.oclc.org/login?qurl=https%3A%2F%2Fwww.proquest.com%2Fnewspapers%2Fdid-cincinnatis-tactic-during-1918-spanish-flu%2Fdocview%2F2394648576%2Fse-2%3Faccountid%3D2909.

Krouse, Peter. 2020. "With No Vaccine, 1918 Flu Pandemic Took Deadly Toll before Widespread Immunity Could Be Achieved." *Cleveland Plain Dealer,* September 14, 2020. https://infoweb.newsbank.com/apps/news/document-view?p=AWNB&docref=news/17D7E764F5D19E50.

Lipsitz, George. 1995. "The Possessive Investment in Whiteness: Racialized Social Democracy and the "White" Problem in American Studies." *American Quarterly* 47, no. 3: 369–387.

Lyman, David. 2020. "History and Future: With 100 Years of Proof, the Opera Will Be Back." *Cincinnati Enquirer,* July 12, 2020. https://uc.idm.oclc.org/login?qurl=https%3A%2F%2Fwww.proquest.com%2Fnewspapers%2Fhistory-future%2Fdocview%2F2422637103%2Fse-2%3Faccountid%3D2909.

"Media Bias/Fact Check." 2021. Accessed August 12. https://mediabiasfactcheck.com/.

Mitchell, Kate. 2020. "Finding the Good in the Bad of 2020." *Toledo Blade,* July 20, 2020. https://uc.idm.oclc.org/login?qurl=https%3A%2F%2Fwww.proquest.com%2Fnewspapers%2Ffinding-good-bad-2020%2Fdocview%2F2430016798%2Fse-2%3Faccountid%3D2909.

Mitchell, Madeline. 2021. "UC Professor Who Called COVID-19 'the Chinese Virus' Asked Not to Return." *FOX 19,* March 22, 2021. https://www.fox19.com/2021/03/22/uc-professor-who-called-covid-chinese-virus-not-asked-return/.

Olick, Jeffrey K. 2007. *The Politics of Regret: On Collective Memory and Historical Responsibility.* New York: Routledge.

Omi, Michael, and Howard Winant. 2014. *Racial Formation in the United States.* Milton Park, Abingdon-on-Thames, Oxfordshire: Taylor & Francis.

Ore, Ersula. 2019. *Lynching: Violence, Rhetoric and American identity.* Oxford: University Press of Mississippi.

Paskett, Electra D. 2020. "African Americans Pay a Higher Price with COVID-19." *Columbus Dispatch,* May 27, 2020. https://infoweb.newsbank.com/apps/news/document-view?p=AWNB&docref=news/17B70CD9A6AA9710.

Price, Mark. 2020. "Local History: Killer Flu Revisited." *Akron Beacon Journal,* May 24, 2020. www.beaconjournal.com/news/20200524/local-history-killer-flu-revisited.

"Remembering the World War I Soldiers Who Succumbed to the 1918 Flu." 2020. *Cleveland Plain Dealer,* May 24, 2020. https://infoweb.newsbank.com/apps/news/document-view?p=AWNB&docref=news/17B290B3C569BA18.

Republic Editorial Staff. 2020. "Other Viewpoints: Trump's First Job Is to Protect the Nation." *Columbus Dispatch,* March 28, 2020. https://infoweb.newsbank.com/apps/news/document-view?p=AWNB&docref=news/17A03E3CA5A43B00.

Rowland, Darrel. 2020. "Read Gov. Mike DeWine's Coronavirus Address to the Residents of Ohio." *Columbus Dispatch,* July 15, 2020. https://infoweb.newsbank.com/apps/news/document-view?p=AWNB&docref=news/17C47CE29BCD3FA0.

Scheeser, Abby. 2021. "Anti-Asian Hate Needs To Be Taken More Seriously." *Cincinnati Enquirer,* May 24, 2021. https://uc.idm.oclc.org/login?qurl=https%3A%2F%2Fwww.proquest.com%2Fnewspapers%2Fanti-asian-hate-needs-be-taken-more-seriously%2Fdocview%2F2530897092%2Fse-2%3Faccountid%3D2909.

Schudson, Michael. 2014. "Journalism as a Vehicle of Non-Commemorative Cultural Memory." In *Journalism and Memory*, edited by Barbie Zelizer and Keren Tenenboim-Weinblatt, 85–96. London: Palgrave Macmillan UK.

Schwartz, Barry, and Howard Schuman. 2005. "History, Commemoration, and Belief: Abraham Lincoln in American Memory, 1945–2001." *American Sociological Review* 70: 183–203. https://doi.org/10.1177/000312240507000201.

Stormer, Nathan. 2015. *Sign of Pathology: U.S. Medical Rhetoric on Abortion, 1800s–1960s*. University Park: Pennsylvania State University Press.

Taubenberger, Jeffrey K., and David M. Morens. 2006. "1918 Influenza: The Mother of All Pandemics." *Emerging Infectious Diseases* 12, no. 1: 15–22. https://doi.org/10.3201/eid1201.050979.

"Tessie's Tidbits: A Look Back, Imagining Being Born in 1900." 2020. *Akron Beacon Journal*, May 18, 2020. www.beaconjournal.com/news/20200518/tessies-tidbits-look-back-imagining-being-born-in-1900.

Wan, William. 2020. "How Will This Coronavirus Saga End? Here's How Similar Epidemics and Pandemics Played Out over the Past Century." *Cleveland Plain Dealer*, March 4, 2020. https://infoweb.newsbank.com/apps/news/document-view?p=AWNB&docref=image/v2%3A16A7AFEBE94E66E0%40AWNB-1797D7AA2CB694E9%402458913-1797D7BDE7D23C9F%409.

Winter, David. 2020. "UC Professor on Administrative Leave after Student Says He Called COVID-19 'Chinese Virus'." WKRC, September 18, 2020. https://local12.com/news/local/uc-professor-on-administrative-leave-after-student-says-he-called-covid-19-chinese-virus-cincinnati.

Wood, Barry D. 2020. "1918 Flu Pandemic Terrorized Ohio Towns." *Columbus Dispatch*, June 27, 2020. https://infoweb.newsbank.com/apps/news/document-view?p=AWNB&docref=news/17BE26B6463602F8.

Zelizer, Barbie. 1995. "Reading the Past against the Grain: The Shape of Memory Studies." *Critical Studies in Mass Communication* 12: 214–239.

Zelizer, Barbie. 2008. "Why Memory's Work on Journalism Does Not Reflect Journalism's Work on Memory." *Memory Studies* 1, no. 1: 79–87. https://doi.org/10.1177/1750698007083891.

Zelizer, Barbie, and Keren Tenenboim-Weinblatt. 2014. "Journalism's Memory Work." In *Journalism and Memory*, edited by Barbie Zelizer and Keren Tenenboim-Weinblatt, 1–14. London: Palgrave Macmillan UK.

Zelman, Brett. 2020. "Ohio State Rep. Nino Vitale Calls Dr. Amy Acton a Globalist—an Anti-Semitic Epithet - The Comments Were in Response to Dr. Acton, Who Is Jewish, Extending the Ohio Stay-at-Home Order to May 29." *CityBeat (Cincinnati, OH)*, May 1, 2020. https://infoweb.newsbank.com/apps/news/document-view?p=AWNB&docref=news/17AB5408AF753B20.

PART TWO

Left Behind: Communities and Individuals under Stress

Part 2 offers an in-depth look at the community struggles and personal health tragedies that were rendered abstract as policy makers and members of the public debated the moral and political issues raised by COVID measures. While Part 1 examined the decisions leaders made early in the pandemic, Part 2 sheds light on the people who bore the consequences of those decisions. This section focuses especially on the way the pandemic—the virus itself as well as the mitigation efforts—increased burdens on already marginalized groups. It draws together discussions of inequality in the contexts of demographic and regional variation, incarceration, food insecurity, mental health, higher education, racial disparity, and disability.

Chapter 9 starts off the section with a broad geospatial analysis of Ohio's uneven critical health-care capacity. In the chapter, Diego F. Cuadros, Chayanika Devi, and Neil J. MacKinnon note that national trends in COVID tracking are not necessarily reflected at the local level, where targeted intervention is critical. They show how Ohio's rural versus urban trends differ from national ones, and discuss the implications for the state's vaccination and treatment plans. Chapter 10 is a blended research chapter and personal reflection in which Elizabeth Lanphier and M. Forrest Behne address COVID-19 in Ohio's Marion prison, which saw one of the first cluster outbreaks in the United States and offered an early indication of things to come for COVID-19 outbreaks in prisons and jails. Behne's reflections as a formerly incarcerated person underscore the urgency of the moral and political challenges involved in protecting incarcerated people during a pandemic.

In Chapter 11, Edward V. Wallace looks more closely at COVID in an urban setting. He addresses the way the pandemic exacerbated racial and ethnic inequalities in health with a particular focus on the consequences of the underrepresentation of African Americans among doctors treating (and preventing) COVID-19. In Chapter 12, Kara B. Ayers offers an overview of how COVID policies have affected people with disabilities. She highlights the ableist consequences of COVID-19's politicization in the way politicians instrumentalized disability while advancing paternalistic and utilitarian policies that denied care to disabled people. Ayers' chapter makes an important contribution to our understanding of COVID-19 in Ohio by analyzing the particular brand of Midwestern ableism that informed state policy and by tying her analysis to her personal experience as a disabled Ohioan during the pandemic. Chapter 13 turns the spotlight onto food insecurity, another problem that COVID has both exacerbated and exposed as a persistent problem. In this chapter, Monica M. Adams examines how the pandemic has impacted the political, social, and health dimensions of food insecurity in Ohio in comparison to other Midwestern states and, in particular, how those experiencing food insecurity have faced greater risk for COVID-related health complications.

In Chapter 14, Kim E. Nielsen reflects on teaching disability history and disability studies while students and faculty lived the realities of health-care inequalities, fears of physical vulnerability and preexisting conditions, economic devastation, ever-expanding family responsibilities, and many profound and sometimes traumatic personal losses generated by the COVID-19 pandemic. She advocates collecting and telling stories of the inequalities experienced in the pandemic as one strategy to interrupt a return to a pre-pandemic normal in which those inequalities on campus are invisible. Finally, in Chapter 15, Angie Fitzpatrick tells the story of both of her parents dying, one from COVID-19, in the same hospital at the same time. She offers a window into the way the moral and political tensions highlighted in this volume not only mediated the way COVID impacted swaths of the population differently, but determined the way it was experienced by individuals and within families. Fitzpatrick's story illustrates in a deeply moving way what this group of chapters shows collectively, which is how the tension between individual liberty and collective responsibility played out for those most immediately and adversely impacted by the pandemic.

9 | Using Spatial Epidemiology to Better Understand COVID in Ohio

Research Article

Diego F. Cuadros, Chayanika Devi, and Neil J. MacKinnon

In this research piece, scholars of health geography, bioinformatics, and population health analyze COVID trends in Ohio, with a particular focus on how the state's rural versus urban divide bucks national trends and demands its own targeted interventions.

Introduction

Throughout history, humans have faced uncountable epidemics; at the time of writing, COVID-19 is simply the latest among them. The COVID-19 crisis has not only challenged the healthcare response of nations but is also having long-term and far-reaching impacts on states, societies, and on international cooperation. Certainly, the COVID-19 pandemic represents a global public health emergency unparalleled in recent history. Since the initial World Health Organization (WHO) report of the COVID-19 outbreak in Wuhan, China, the number of confirmed cases globally rose sharply from 282 to almost 560,000,000 confirmed cases, including close to 6,400,000 related deaths by mid-July of 2022. After the virus's initial emergence in China, cases started appearing in other parts of the world with strong travel links to Wuhan (Lai et al. 2020). The first confirmed case in the United States was a travel-related case in Snohomish County, Washington, screened on January 19, 2020. In late February, a second presumptive case was identified roughly ten miles away from where the first case was treated. As of mid-summer 2022, the United States has reported over eight million confirmed COVID-19 cases and over one million confirmed COVID-19 deaths (Johns Hopkins University n.d.).

Acute respiratory infections (ARI) are responsible for substantial morbidity and mortality worldwide, both as the result of seasonal epidemics and pandemics, such as COVID-19 (Shi et al. 2017). Respiratory viruses spread from person to person through various modes of transmission, including direct and indirect contacts, droplet spray, and aerosols, which are affected by a number of factors including environment determinants, host behavior, and virus infectivity (Izadnegahdar et al. 2013). Infectious diseases, including ARI, have substantial geographic variation in intensity and range of transmission, on account of the uneven distribution of vulnerable populations and risk factors that facilitate (or hamper) the spatial diffusion of the pathogen (Green et al. 2015; Caini et al. 2018; Park et al. 2020; Real and Biek 2007; Sloan, Moore, and Hartert 2011). COVID-19 has been no exception. One of the most notorious characteristics of the COVID-19 pandemic has been the uneven intensity of its transmission in the different regions of the globe, with North America, Latin America, and several countries in Europe suffering the highest burden of COVID-19 cases to date (Figure 9.1, map on top). This spatially heterogeneous dispersion of the infection has been also observed within countries. For example, regions across the United States have not been equally affected by the COVID-19 pandemic, with areas in the Northeast, Midwest, and Southeast experiencing high burden of the cumulative number of infections per 100,000 people as of July 2022 (Figure 9.1, map in bottom left). Likewise, marked local geographic variations are driving the epidemic within states like Ohio (Figure 9.1, map on bottom right).

Spatial epidemiology can help elucidate the spatial distribution of health challenges. Moreover, we can identify locally specific causes and areas to intervene in order to prevent disease. This is particularly important in the COVID-19 pandemic, as global public health measures to contain the disease need to be combined with locally targeted health interventions. Therefore, spatial epidemiology approaches will continue to play a crucial role within the current pandemic and beyond this global health crisis.

The rapid escalation of the epidemic in the United States offers a compelling case study in tracking the dynamics of the disease. Since the beginning of the COVID-19 pandemic, geographic information

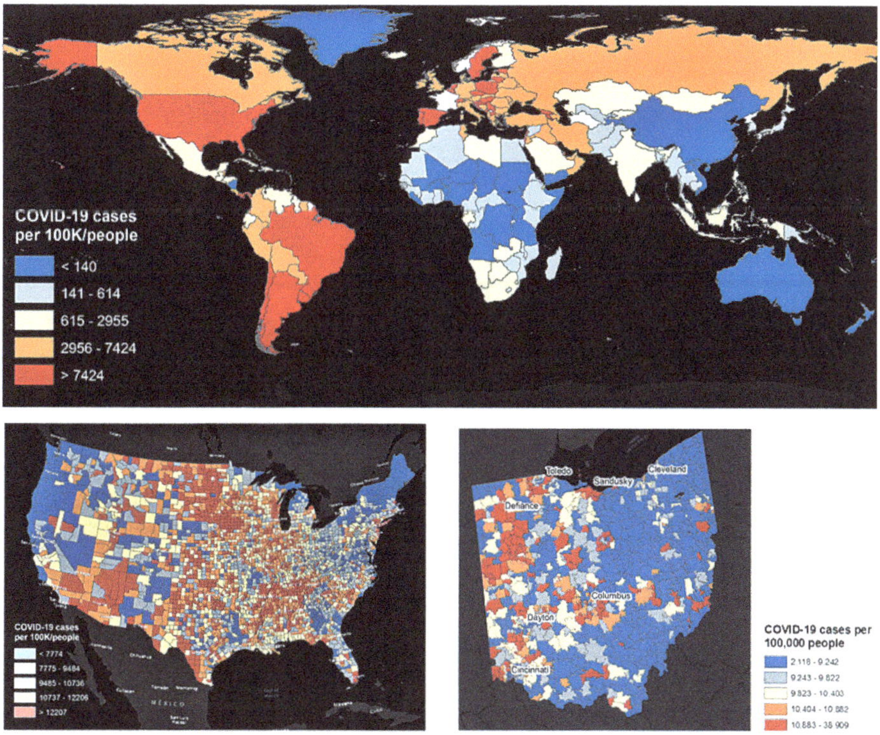

Fig. 9.1. Spatial distribution of COVID-19 in the world (map on top), in the United States (map on bottom left), and in Ohio (map on bottom right) as of July 2022.

systems (GIS) has been used to map the spread of COVID-19 across space and over time, identify hot spots and vulnerable populations. The Johns Hopkins University Coronavirus Resource Center website is one of the most representative examples of the implementation of this technology for tackling the pandemic. Its COVID-19 Dashboard Project, hosted by the Center for Systems Science and Engineering at Johns Hopkins University, has provided a leading reference dashboard for daily updates on cases, deaths, and recoveries recorded worldwide (Ahasan and Hossain 2021). Normally, just offering a map and dashboard would not be an effective way to communicate information to nonspecialists. But the Dashboard Project offers easy search tools, graphics, and daily videos to engage specialists and nonspecialists, alike.

Despite the successful implementation of GIS technologies to track the spread of the disease, the underlying causes of the regional differences in COVID-19's dispersion and intensity have not been completely understood. Understanding the local variation in disease transmission dynamics under heterogeneous geospatial attributes is a crucial step in developing more effective strategies for mitigating risk of infection in vulnerable communities, particularly during the early stages of an epidemic. To this end, this chapter illustrates how GIS techniques and spatial epidemiological approaches were implemented to assess the early stages of the COVID-19 pandemic in Ohio, and how these have been used to inform public health decisions. Our research team not only tracked the changes in, and intensity of, COVID-19 spatial patterns, but also analyzed relationships with various potential influencing factors, including factors that are socio-economic (occupation, income, transportation, population mobility, household density, government response), demographic (age, sex, ethnicity, nationality), environmental (temperature, topographic and built environment), and epidemiological and healthcare-related (comorbidities, social distancing, testing facilities, availability of hospital beds, health inequalities). This information can help us better understand and manage COVID-19, and formulate control strategies and appropriate healthcare measures to contain the spread of potential future pandemics.

The chapter begins by briefly introducing the definition of spatial epidemiology, explaining the role of techniques such as GIS in this field, and discussing how this framework informs the study of important public health challenges like malaria and HIV. Then we assess the spatial structure of the COVID-19 pandemic in Ohio during the early stages of the epidemic and evaluate the impact of non-pharmaceutical interventions in the dynamic transmission and healthcare capacity of the state. We also evaluate the sociodemographic and environmental drivers of COVID-19-related deaths, and spatially identify vulnerable areas in Ohio, which, in the early stage of the pandemic, were both at higher risk of COVID-19 mortality and had low healthcare capacity. Finally, we assess the spatial and temporal changes of the pandemic, focusing on rural communities. This comprehensive study of the spatial characteristics of the early stages of the COVID-19 pandemic in Ohio provides significant information regarding the dynamics of the disease, and how the state initially responded to this public health emergency. It also elucidates gaps in Ohio's healthcare system and what is needed to respond to potential future epidemics.

Spatial Epidemiology and GIS

Epidemiology involves the study of the distribution and determinants of diseases in populations, particularly in human populations (Krieger 2011). Epidemiologists examine the interactions that emerge among the host, agent, and environment (or "the epidemiologic triangle") to identify the underlying causes of a disease and generate interventions for prevention and control (McAnally 2017). Epidemiological studies aim to explain the amount and distribution of disease within a particular population by identifying the persons at risk, the time of disease onset, and the places where they are located (Rothman, Greenland, and Lash 2008; Moore and Carpenter 1999). Epidemiological research focusing on place or location historically has received considerably less attention, but modern epidemiology increasingly incorporates this spatial perspective into research designs and models. As a result, the interconnected fields of *spatial epidemiology* and *health geography* can now explain the spatial heterogeneity of diseases (i.e., how illness is transmitted differently in different locations) by examining spatially explicit health outcomes and predictors (i.e., patterns that are influenced by location). These are novel approaches for understanding and seeking to control current epidemics. In the field of spatial epidemiology, place is a very broad concept that refers to the 'lived space' in which individuals within a given community interact. The lived space includes the natural and built environment, as well as human social networks and interactions. It exists in different scales, from global and regional spaces to spaces used exclusively or nearly exclusively by an individual (Kearns and Joseph 1993).

Policy makers, public health practitioners, community planners, and researchers are increasingly interested in understanding the social, environmental, and structural features of neighborhoods, which have been linked to a wide array of health outcomes. Identifying neighborhood-level assets and deficits provides a baseline for targeting resources and interventions appropriate to the unique needs of the underlying population. As mentioned above, spatial epidemiology's analyses go beyond individual characteristics to consider the social and environmental contexts and interactions that affect individuals' health. In the past several decades, the capacity to explore the role of place in disease dynamics has substantially increased, thanks to advances in quantitative methods and geospatial technologies.

Of equal importance are new understandings about the social elements that characterize a particular setting (i.e., crime rates, poverty, school quality, and educational attainment) and people's interactions with these social and environmental elements, and, ultimately, how these interactions ultimately affect their individual health (Rushton 2003).

Alongside the rapid development of geographic tools, GIS methods, and spatial analysis, massive amounts of geocoded environmental and social data are now available (Nykiforuk and Flaman 2011; Thomas, Richardson, and Cheung 2008). These data and the methodological tools available for analyzing spatial data make possible innovative, spatially explicit approaches to epidemiological research that can shed light on causes linked to health outcomes; they also provide a geographic foundation for health policy making (McLafferty 2003). Spatial analysis methods can be used to understand mapped information by identifying patterns and drivers of disease distribution. These tools also make it possible to detect unusual geographic distributions of health events and follow their evolution in space over time.

Epidemiological research is fundamental to understanding health disparities and preventing an increasing number of new cases of major diseases. Spatial analysis in epidemiological research and disease surveillance has become critical to decision-making processes (Rytkönen 2004). Detection of significant geographic clusters of disease, estimations of disease prevalence, predictive risk mapping, and geographic associations between the intensity of the epidemic and the health factors linked to the disease together enable more effective resource planning for disease prevention resource planning (Odoi et al. 2004). A prerequisite to an overall understanding of the dynamics of diseases is a comprehensive geographic view of a current or emerging epidemic, as well as the factors associated with the spatial dynamics of the disease (Pfieffer et al. 2008). Therefore, epidemiologists are concerned not only with deaths, illness, and disability, but also with the means to improve health (Bonita, Beaglehole, and Kjellström 2006).

Previous studies show that the geographic differences in the distribution of infectious diseases can result from either the spatial aggregation of infected individuals and their social interactions, or from environmental influences that impact multiple locations. Public health researchers have therefore called attention not only to the role of place-based characteristics in the spread of diseases, but also to the spatial relationships or interconnections between places.

Doing so allows a comprehensive understanding of the potential determinants of a novel disease. In the case of the COVID-19 pandemic, the disease is characterized by a high contagious rate, long incubation period, and difficulty in detection, which contribute to its rapid spread. This situation has led to calls for big data technology and GIS to generate rapid analysis of the dynamics of the epidemic to provide timely support for interventions.

In descriptive epidemiology, thematic or color-shaded maps produced with GIS are useful for identifying areas at high risk for epidemics, highlighting population health disparities, examining resource needs, and ultimately, formulating hypotheses that lead to explanatory models. These maps are essential for understanding the spatial spread of infection and its association with the community and environment, especially in the early stages of an outbreak. In analytic epidemiology, spatial epidemiology has mostly been used for studying communicable diseases. It has also been used, relatively indirectly, to study noncommunicable diseases.

The quantitative methods for estimating the net contribution of geographic hot spots (areas experiencing a disproportionately large number of disease cases) and determinants to the ecological and individual-level transmission may facilitate control measures. The identification of these areas can uncover the locations of high-risk populations, while revealing the factors that facilitate the persistence and spread of epidemics. In this context, health geography and spatial epidemiology have become essential tools in the fight against devastating epidemics such as malaria and HIV (Hay and Snow 2006; Wilson and Halperin 2008). For example, the Malaria Atlas Project (MAP) has focused on understanding the spatial distribution of malaria, particularly in sub-Saharan Africa (SSA) (Hay and Snow 2006). Using spatial epidemiology and disease mapping techniques, MAP has uncovered the spatial distribution of malaria transmission with a high level of detail (Figure 9.2A). It also has helped determine the geographic locations where control efforts should be implemented. Similar approaches such as the "Know your epidemic, know your response" framework, for counteracting global HIV epidemics (Wilson and Halperin 2008), have centered on the development of targeted prevention strategies based on detailed knowledge of the epidemic's geographic distribution (Figure 9.2B). High-resolution maps of the HIV distribution in SSA have been used to design cost-effective interventions, which are geographically targeted (Dwyer-Lindgren et al. 2019; Cuadros et al. 2017).

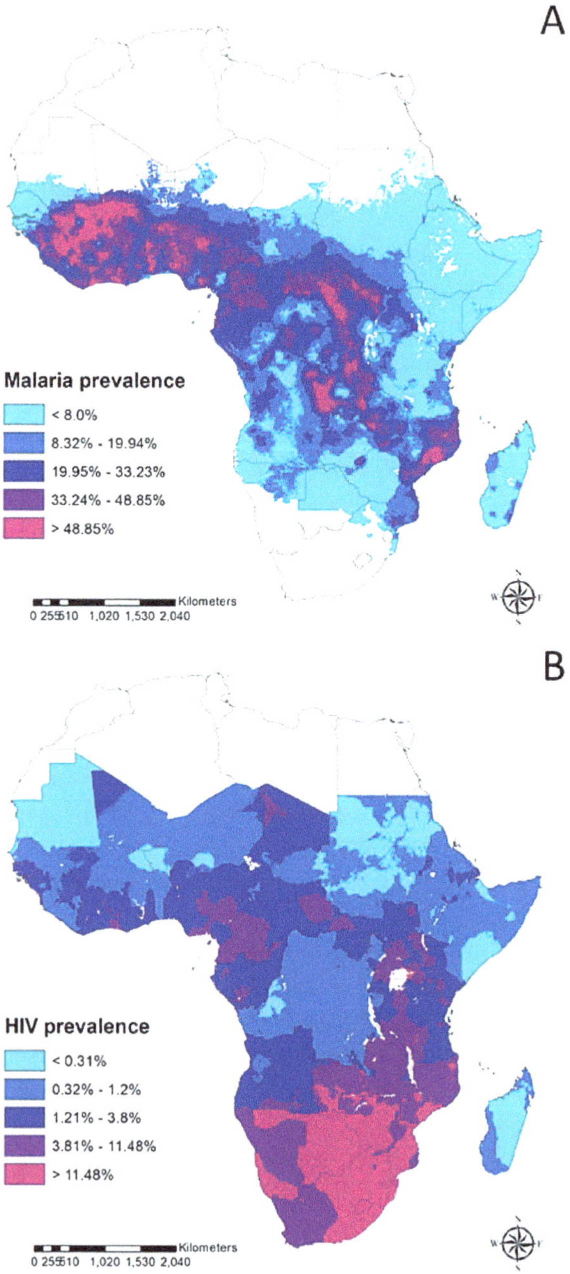

Fig. 9.2. Disease mapping of malaria and HIV. A) Spatial distribution of malaria prevalence in Africa (Hay and Snow 2006). B) Spatial distribution of HIV in Africa (Dwyer-Lindgren et al. 2019).

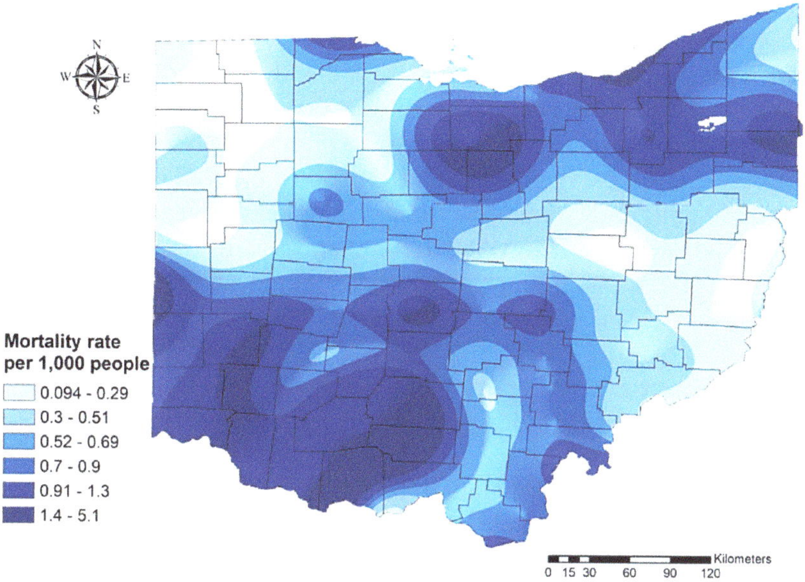

Fig. 9.3. Spatial distribution of the opioid overdose mortality rate in Ohio, 2010–2017.

Disease mapping has also been used to study other health challenges, such as the opioid overdose crisis in the United States, particularly in Ohio. A detailed description of the spatial distribution of this health issue helps identify areas where most of the state's cases are concentrated, and where control interventions should be implemented (Figure 9.3).

These approaches have centered on the development of targeted prevention strategies based on detailed knowledge of an epidemic's spatial dynamics. High-resolution distribution maps enable the design of cost-effective, geographically targeted interventions (Dwyer-Lindgren et al. 2019; Cuadros et al. 2017).

The Geography of the COVID-19 Pandemic and Control Measures Implemented during the Early Stage of the Pandemic in Ohio

In the early stages of a new infectious disease outbreak, it is crucial to understand the spread of an infection (Kucharski et al. 2020). Recognizing the temporal and spatial dynamics of the infection can provide insights into the epidemiological characteristics of the disease and identify geographic hot spots. One of the early goals during the pandemic was to delay and flatten the outbreak. The motivation for this approach was to keep the health system operating below maximum capacity and avoid the saturation of the healthcare system with acutely ill COVID-19 patients while others still needed non-COVID-19-related healthcare. Social distancing measures were critical to slow the progression of the COVID-19 pandemic. Still, there was a great deal of uncertainty about the scale of the epidemic and the effect of these social distancing policies.

In this section, we will discuss the impact of early, non-pharmaceutical interventions in the spread of the COVID-19 and in Ohio's capacity to provide healthcare. In March 2020, it was clear that the COVID-19 pandemic would strike Ohio and would very likely affect some of the state's populations more than others. Ohio is a state with marked demographic and geographic variation and there are substantial differences among its counties' healthcare capacities. For example, Ohio as a whole currently has 3,743 intensive care unit (ICU) beds, of which about 53 percent are usually occupied by non-COVID-19-related patients. Fifty-eight counties each have fewer than ten ICU beds available and only ten counties have more than 25 ICU beds available (Figure 9.4, map in the left).

To understand the spatial structure, we built a mathematical model to predict the county-level spatial dynamics of the COVID-19 epidemic. The model was calibrated using data from the State of Ohio, which was one of the few states producing detailed daily reports of COVID-19 confirmed cases, COVID-19-related cumulative hospitalizations, ICU admissions, and deaths per county. We used data from March 1 to March 23, 2020 (before the implementation of Ohio's stay-at-home order), to model the state's COVID-19 cases and COVID-19-related hospitalizations and deaths in the state. (For further details of this methodology, see Cuadros et al. 2020.) The aim of this modeling exercise was to assess the geographic and temporal dynamics of the COVID-19 pandemic in relation to the distribution of Ohio's healthcare capacity. Specifically, we wanted to: 1) estimate the impact of public health interventions such as social distancing and the stay-at-home order upon the spread of the disease in mid-March, and 2) evaluate whether the relaxation of these interventions impacted healthcare capacity in the state.

The model stratified the population into four different spatial groups, depending on the spatial risk characteristics of the county. The spatial risk groups were defined as following, Group 1: counties

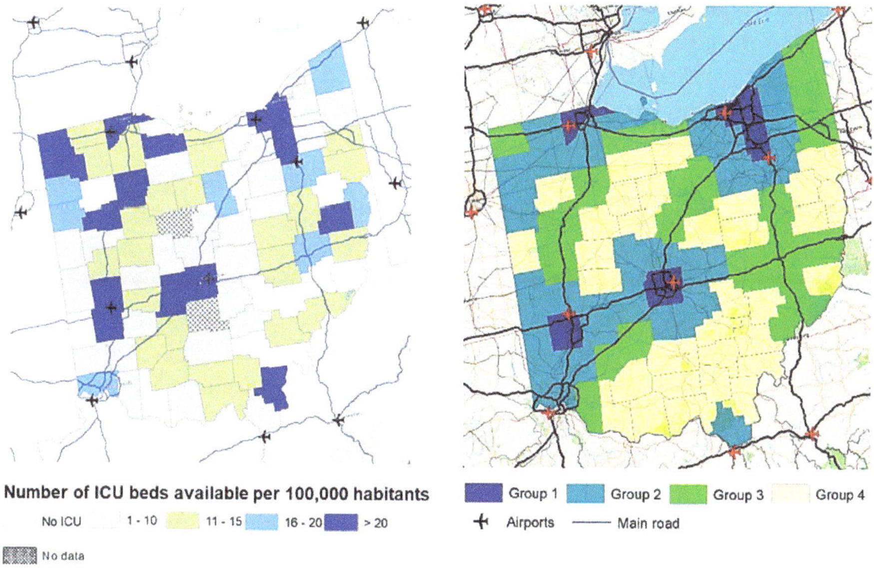

Fig. 9.4. County-level distribution of intensive care unit (ICU) beds (map on the left), and the distribution of the counties in the different spatial risk groups (map on the right) in Ohio. Group 1: counties with airports; Group 2: counties surrounding the counties with airports; Group 3: counties with main highways crossing the county; and Group 4: counties not surrounding counties with airports or being crossed by main highways.

with airports; Group 2: counties surrounding the counties with airports; Group 3: counties with main highways crossing the county; and Group 4: counties not surrounding counties with airports or being crossed by main highways (Figure 9.4, map on the right). Each group had its own dynamic of the disease, and the relationships between groups were assumed to be by flow of infections between the different groups at specific rates.

The analysis suggested substantial geographic variation in the dynamics of the disease during the early growing phase of the pandemic, with some areas experiencing much faster and more intensive spread of the infection compared to other areas. Ohio counties with connectivity enhanced by air transportation had faster spread of infection compared to nearby counties with high road connectivity, and more isolated rural counties in Ohio. More than 47 percent of the confirmed COVID-19 cases in Ohio were concentrated in only five counties from Group 1 (Cuyahoga, Franklin, Lucas, Montgomery, and Summit), with an average infection rate of 274 cases per 100,000 people. These five counties, which are home to 35 percent of Ohio's the total population, were characterized by high population density; they also contain airport hubs that receive more than 10,000,000 passengers every year. The number of air travelers passing through these counties likely produced a high influx of imported infections that boosted local transmission of the virus and, consequently, accelerated the spread of the infection in these areas (World Health Organization 2020; Warren, Bell, and Budd 2010). In contrast, the spread of the infection was substantially lower in the 31 counties from Group 4, in Ohio's rural and less connected areas in Ohio. These less densely populated counties are home to only 11 percent of the total population in Ohio, and their infection rate was more than three times lower than the infection rate in the counties with airport hubs.

We also identified marked differences in the geographic distribution of the critical healthcare capacity of the state. More than 50 percent of the total number of ICU beds available statewide are in the five counties included in Group 1, with a rate of 22 ICU beds per 100,000 people. In contrast, the 31 counties in the rural and less connected areas of the state have only 7 percent of the total number of ICU beds available in the state, with a rate of ten ICU beds per 100,000 people (Figure 9.4, map on the left). Despite these local differences in the state's critical healthcare capacity, our modeling results suggested that the local dynamics of the disease, which showed substantially less transmission in rural and less connected counties, avoided saturating the critical care capacity of those areas.

Using the model, we evaluated the impact of the social interventions implemented early during the pandemic in Ohio and also assessed the effects of relaxing those social interventions in the dynamics of the COVID-19 epidemic in the state. Assuming that interventions implemented in late March 2020, such as social distancing and stay-at-home orders, were relaxed on May 1, 2020, we generated four scenarios with different intensities in the relaxation of the intervention: no change (0 percent), 20 percent, 50 percent, and 70 percent reduction in the intensity of the intervention. Using the mathematical model, we estimated that the interventions implemented in Ohio early during the pandemic reduced the dispersion of the infection in the entire state by 40 percent. The model also showed that, if these interventions had been reduced by 50 percent, the number of COVID-related hospitalizations might increase by 60 percent compared to the likely number of COVID-19 hospitalizations if the interventions were not changed. And if interventions were reduced by 70 percent, hospitalizations might increase by 125 percent. (Figure 9.5, top). Likewise, the model indicated that COVID-related deaths would increase 27 percent if the interventions were reduced by 50 percent,

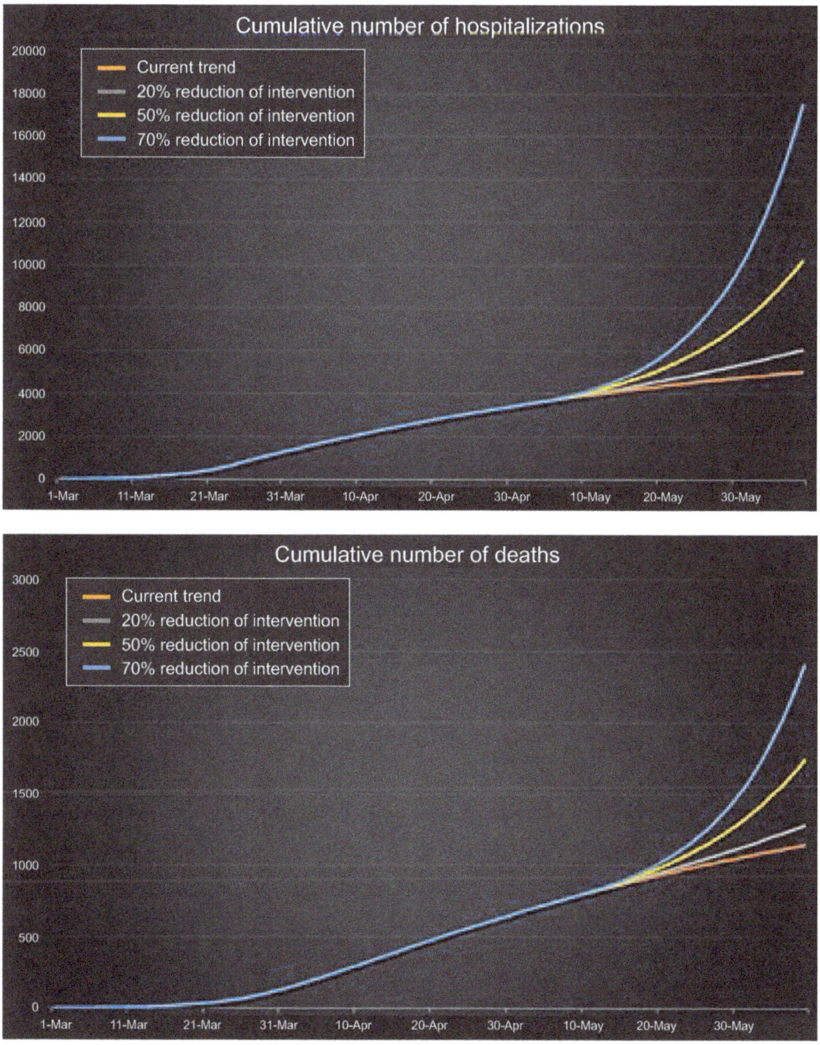

Fig. 9.5. Projected number of cumulative numbers of COVID-related hospitalizations (top) and deaths (bottom) in Ohio assuming no change in the intensity of the March 2020 social distancing intervention (orange line), 20 percent reduction (grey line), 50 percent reduction (yellow line), and 70 percent reduction of the intervention (blue line).

and that deaths would increase by 52 percent if interventions were reduced by 70 percent. (Figure 9.5, bottom).

Although counties such as Franklin, Cuyahoga, and Hamilton had the highest burden of COVID-19 cases, they were also the counties with the highest healthcare capacity. Thus, the critical care capacity threshold for these counties is reached more slowly compared to other counties, such as Trumbull, Delaware, Lake, Butler, Mahoning, and Clermont, which have low critical care capacity, but also a lower burden of cases. It would therefore be strategic to strengthen the healthcare capacity of these counties to have an effective healthcare response across the entire state during health emergencies like the COVID-19 pandemic. Our model showed that, if early intervention were relaxed by 20 percent, the number of ICU beds occupied by COVID-19 patients would remain fairly stable over the next two weeks, and 200 ICU beds would be occupied by COVID-19 patients 30 days after the interventions were relaxed. By contrast, if the early interventions were relaxed by 50 percent, then the number of ICU beds occupied by COVID-19 patients would start increasing more dramatically just 15 days after the interventions were relaxed, and 67 countries would reach full ICU bed capacity in a month's time (Figure 9.6, left panel).

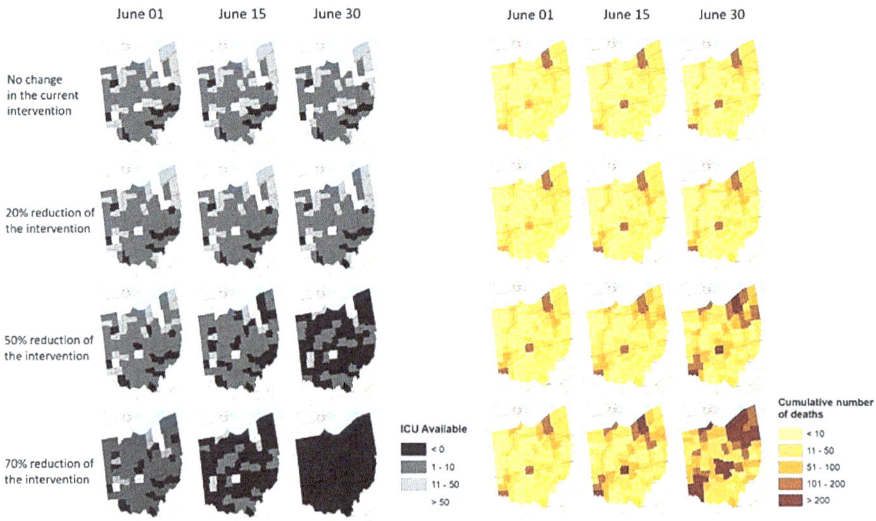

Fig. 9.6. Projection of the spatiotemporal dynamics of the intensive care unit (ICU) beds available (panel maps on the left) and cumulative number of COVID-related deaths (panel maps on the right) under different scenarios of relaxation of the March 2020 social distancing interventions in Ohio.

Using this same mathematical model, we found substantial spatial variation in the potential spread of the disease in Ohio, with the model set to predict how various social and environmental factors would influence transmission. These geographic differences in the spread of the disease might be generated not only by the uneven distribution of the population, but also by geographic factors such as the level of air and road connectivity. As a result, not all local areas in the state could reach their maximum critical care capacity at the same time, and so the inclusion, in the mathematical model, of geographic information is essential to understanding local disease dynamics, especially considering the uneven spatial distribution of the critical healthcare capacity in the state. The higher rates of transmission evident in some highly connected and urbanized areas could substantially impact their critical care response, no matter the relative strength of their healthcare capacity compared to that of their more rural and less connected counterparts (Hall, Kaufman, and Ricketts 2006; Hartley 2004).

Identification of Counties with High COVID-19-Related Mortality Risk in Ohio

Early COVID-19 data from Europe and Asia suggested the pandemic's unprecedented contagion and death rates. In late April 2020, the United States exhibited the fastest growing curve in terms of COVID-19-related deaths across developed countries, with 93,806 deaths as of May 20, 2020. Several countries, including the United States, reported higher mortality rates for older individuals with concomitant comorbidities, including chronic lower respiratory diseases, diabetes, hypertension, and ischemic diseases. Likewise, health-related disparities including sociodemographic and environmental factors were identified as important drivers of deaths caused by COVID-19. To make it possible for policy makers to address the pandemic, the logical next step was identifying which groups and areas of the state were at higher risk of mortality due to COVID-19-related complications.

We therefore conducted a county-level characterization of the COVID-19-related mortality risk, which took into account sociodemographic and socioenvironmental factors across Ohio. Our analysis also assessed the spatial link between COVID-19-related mortality risk and the state's existing critical healthcare capacity. Specifically, we aimed to: a) assess the sociodemographic and environmental drivers of COVID-19-related deaths, and b) spatially identify vulnerable areas of the state that had both a higher risk of COVID-19 mortality and low healthcare capacity.

Using COVID-19 data obtained from the Johns Hopkins University data set (34) from March 1 to May 5, 2020, we conducted a statistical analysis to assess the risk of COVID-19-related deaths per county, adjusting for sociodemographic, health, and environmental factors. Our analysis focused on the State of Ohio, but we used data from the entire country to conduct state comparisons between Ohio and the rest of the country and to derive reliable estimations for the state. (For further details on our methodology, see Correa-Agudelo 2021.) We found that eight states (Colorado, Connecticut, Indiana, Massachusetts, Michigan, Louisiana, New Jersey, and Washington) had higher-than-expected COVID-19-related mortality risk during the early stage of the pandemic in the country. According to our results, Ohio did not have a higher COVID-19-related mortality risk than expected, and its COVID-19-related mortality risk was consistent with the expected mortality risk according to the number of residents in Ohio. For the Midwest region, Indiana and Michigan had the highest mortality risk.

Although Ohio did not have a higher COVID-19-related mortality risk than the country average, we found substantial differences in the COVID-19-related mortality risk between counties within the state.

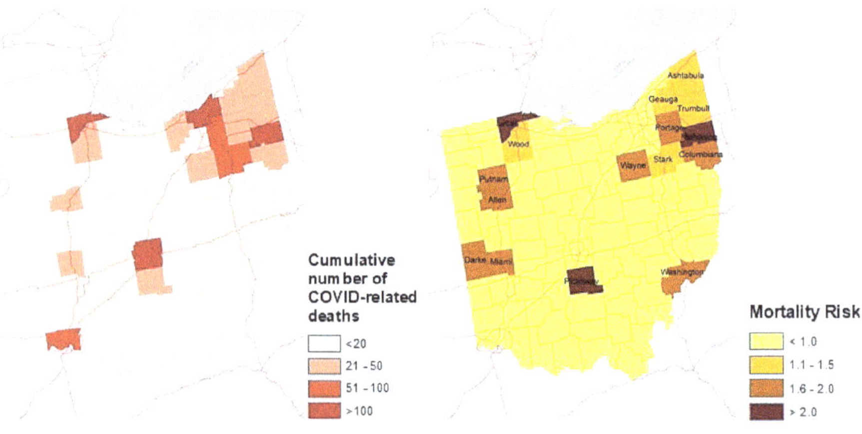

Fig. 9.7. Spatial distribution of the cumulative number of COVID-19-related deaths (left) and COVID-19-related mortality risk (right) in Ohio from March 1 to May 5, 2020. A mortality risk > 1 indicates a higher risk of COVID-19-related death than expected based on the state average.

The map on the left in Figure 9.7 illustrates the cumulative number of COVID-19-related deaths by county in Ohio as of May 5, 2020. The map on the right illustrates the estimated COVID-19-related mortality risk. Even though Cuyahoga, Franklin, and Hamilton counties have the highest cumulative number of COVID-19-related deaths, their COVID-19-related mortality risk is lower than expected based on the total population of these counties. Conversely, counties like Allen, Ashtabula, Columbiana, Darke, Geauga, Lucas, Mahoning, Miami, Pickaway, Portage, Putnam, Stark, Trumbull, Washington, Wayne, and Wood have a higher-than-average COVID-19-related mortality risk than would be expected from their populations.

We generated a map to visualize the association between COVID-19-related mortality risk and the healthcare capacity of each county in Ohio. For the purpose of our analysis, healthcare capacity was estimated as the number of ICU beds available under normal circumstances. Mortality risk (represented by red palette colors in Figure 9.8) was classified as follows: 0–1 indicates lower risk, 1–1.5

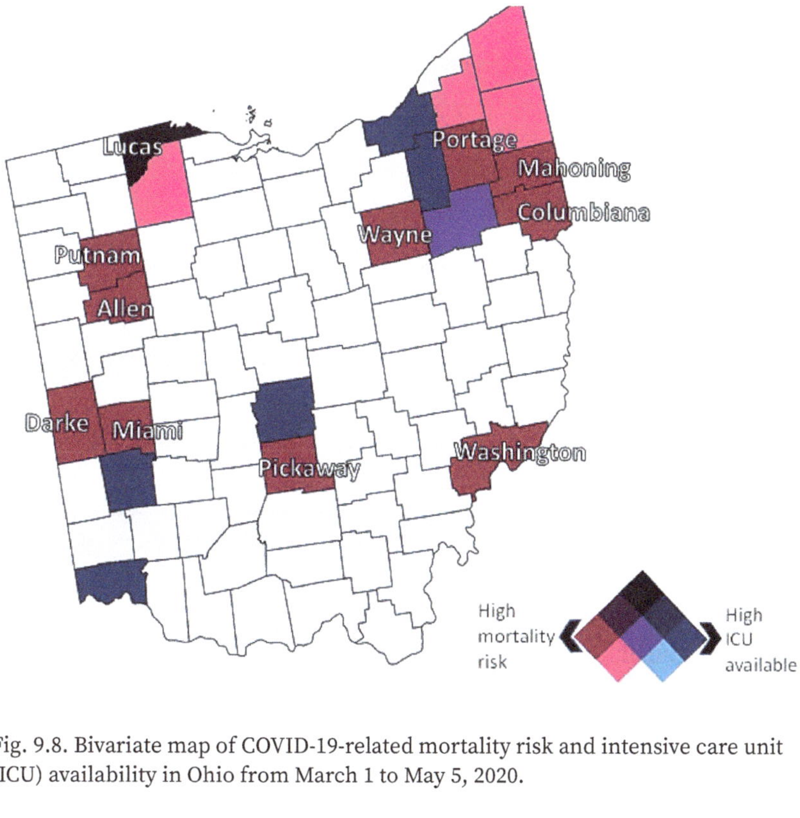

Fig. 9.8. Bivariate map of COVID-19-related mortality risk and intensive care unit (ICU) availability in Ohio from March 1 to May 5, 2020.

indicates medium risk, and >1.5 indicates high risk. ICU beds availability (represented by blue palette colors in Figure 9.8) was classified as follows: < 40 ICU beds indicates low availability, 40–100 ICU beds indicates medium availability, and >100 ICU beds indicates high availability. Counties in dark red indicate high mortality risk and low ICU bed availability, whereas counties in dark blue indicate high ICU bed availability and low mortality risk. Darke, Miami, Pickaway, Washington, Allen, Putnam, Wayne, Portage, Mahoning, and Columbiana are the most vulnerable counties, with a high risk of COVID-19-related death and a low healthcare capacity as estimated as availability of ICU beds.

Collectively, these results suggest that COVID-19-related mortality in Ohio was consistent with the expected deaths based on the total population of the state during the early stage of the pandemic. However, there was a substantial variation in the COVID-19-related risk of mortality among counties in Ohio. Although the population of most of the counties had a low risk of dying due to COVID-19-related complications, we found that in counties like Allen, Columbiana, Darke, Lucas, Mahoning, Miami, Pickaway, Portage, Putnam, Washington, and Wayne, the risk of dying from COVID-19-related complications was almost twice as high compared to the risk in other counties in the state during the early stage of the pandemic. The excess of COVID-19-related deaths in these counties was potentially driven by socioeconomic and environmental factors that were exacerbating residents' risk of COVID-19-related mortality.

Such geographic and social disparities observed during the COVID-19 pandemic aligned along a social gradient of health and environment that produced worse health outcomes for the least advantaged groups (Correa-Agudelo 2021). Moreover, the substantial regional disparities of the healthcare capacity increased the vulnerability of these areas already at higher risk of COVID-19-related mortality. Therefore, the results from this study can be used to guide strategies for identifying and targeting prevention efforts in vulnerable high-risk counties with higher proportions of minority groups, poor air quality, and low healthcare capacity (Correa-Agudelo 2021).

Overview of the COVID-19 Dynamics in Rural and Urban Areas

Rural areas in the United States face many challenges, including reduced access to healthcare resources compared to urban communities. For example, over 4.7 million people live in 460 rural counties across the nation, where there are no general medical or surgical hospital beds. In addition, 16.4 million people live in rural areas with no ICU beds (RUPRI Center for Rural Health Policy Analysis n.d.). Rural US residents have a shorter life expectancy than urban residents, and rural households also report a lower median income (Schroeder 2018). Rural communities also have a larger proportion of residents 65 and older (18.4 percent compared to 14.5 percent) (Schroeder 2018), and thus have a greater need for healthcare services. The proportion of older adults is increasing more quickly in rural communities due to declining birth rates and migration patterns in younger adults (Henning-Smith 2020). Rural nursing homes tend to lag behind in terms of their information technology, and this can adversely affect the safety and efficiency of their care (Henning-Smith 2020). According to the 2016 US Census, the median age in rural areas is 51, whereas the median age in urban areas is 45 (US Census Bureau 2016). Moreover, according to the WHO, older people are at the greatest risk of COVID-19 (Kluge 2020). With rural communities already at a disadvantage in terms of healthcare and population demographics, and with COVID-19 proving to be a greater and deadlier burden in older populations, rural areas were in greater danger compared to better-equipped urban areas during the evolution of the pandemic.

In our research, we evaluated the incidence and mortality rate of COVID-19 in both urban and rural areas in two time periods for the entire country, and then compared these results with the dynamics of the pandemic in rural and urban areas in Ohio. The first time period was from April 1 to May 31, 2020, which encompasses the initial implementation of intervention measures, such as stay-at-home orders and lockdowns. The second time period was from June 1 to July 31, 2020, in which these intervention measures were eased after the first wave of COVID-19. (For further details of our methodology, see Cuadros et al. 2021.)

Our results suggest that the COVID-19 landscape in the United States is dynamic with substantial changes over time and space. Although results at the national level indicated greater COVID-19 incidence rates in urban compared to rural counties in the Northeast and Mid-Atlantic regions of the United States at the beginning of the epidemic, the intensity of the epidemic shifted to a rapid surge in rural areas, particularly in the Southern region in the second period. In the figures below (Figures 9.9 and 9.10), the high incidence rate states are outlined in red, and consist mainly of Southern states. From the first to the second period, the COVID-19 incidence rate in the entire country increased 150 percent in rural counties, whereas the incidence rate increased 82 percent in urban counties.

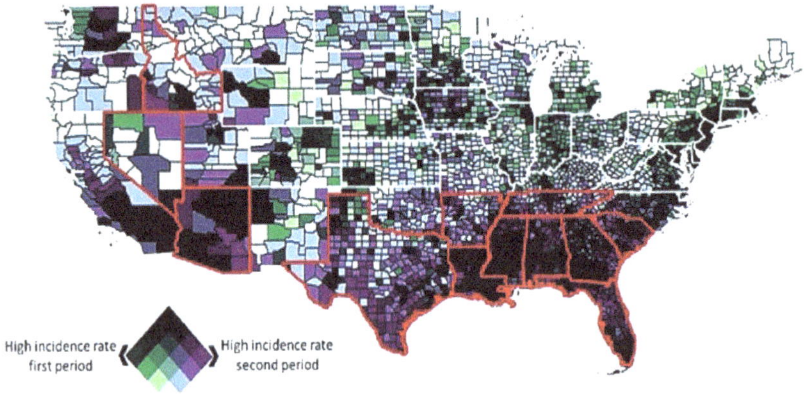

Fig. 9.9. Bivariate map comparing COVID-19 incidence rates in both periods. The first time period was from April 1 to May 31, 2020. The second time period was from June 1 to July 31, 2020. Incidence rates were categorized in quantiles; dark green indicates counties with the highest incidence rate in the first period, whereas dark purple indicates counties with the highest incidence in the second period. Counties in black had high incidence rates in both periods.

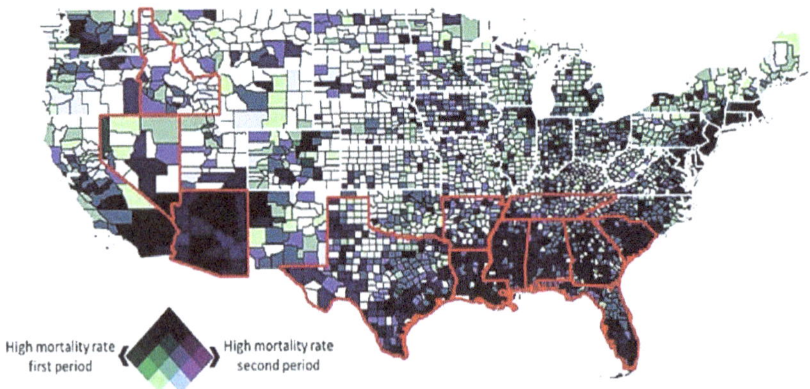

Fig. 9.10. Bivariate map comparing COVID-19 mortality rates in both periods. The first time period was from April 1 to May 31, 2020. The second time period was from June 1 to July 31, 2020. Dark green indicates counties with the highest mortality rate in the first period, whereas dark purple indicates counties with the highest mortality in the second period. Counties in black had high mortality rates in both periods. States outlined in red are in the higher incidence rate group.

There are several reasons for the differential temporal dynamics between urban and rural areas. COVID-19 infection rates were lower, on average, in rural than in urban counties in the early stages of the epidemic. As discussed in a previous section, in large urban areas, the susceptibility driven by high population density and enhanced connectivity forced the implementation of strict non-pharmaceutical interventions such as lockdowns, stay-at-home orders, and social distancing practices, which reduced the community spread of infection in these areas. As a result, the pandemic slowed down in large metropolitan areas, but continued to diffuse from cities to rural communities, which, according to some studies, are communities that probably implemented less intensive interventions during the early stage of the pandemic. For example, effective non-pharmaceutical measures such as face coverings have been met with some resistance among rural communities in the United States (Haischer et al. 2020). Furthermore, health infrastructure in rural areas is a major barrier that public health practitioners, healthcare providers, and local partners need to address to achieve equal health care. Poverty and access to hospitals are most important indicators. In rural counties, health care has mostly focused on preventive and promotive care and does not focus on treatment, which may be another treason that deprived areas are the most adversely affected.

Ohio experienced a higher COVID-19 incidence rate in the second time period compared to the first time period of the study, but, contrary to the national pattern, Ohio suffered the greatest burden of the disease in the urban counties during the early stage of the epidemic, and these areas continued harboring the highest number of COVID-19 cases during the second period of the study. However, there were some rural counties that experienced a surge of the disease during the second period of the study, including Ashland, Athens, Coshocton, Defiance, Holmes, Knox, Preble, Scioto, Seneca, and Shelby counties (Figure 9.11).

A series of recommendations can be derived from these results. Public health policies should take into account county-level interventions and strategies specific to each type of community (urban or rural). When making public health policies, the local government needs to be aware of, and consider, the differences in COVID-19 spread between urban and rural areas, which will allow for more effective disease control. Likewise, with increasing incidence rates in rural areas over time, residents needed to know their increased risk of infection so they can take personal measures to protect themselves, not only for the public health emergency faced during the

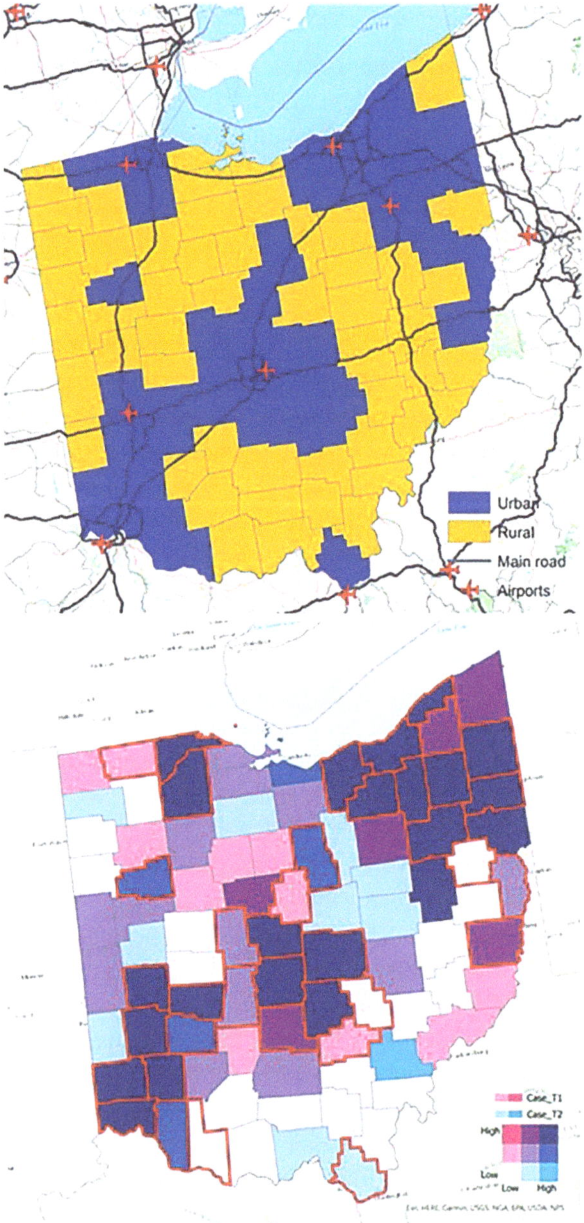

Fig. 9.11. Map on the top illustrates the distribution of the urban (blue) and rural (yellow) counties in Ohio. Map on the bottom illustrates a bivariate map comparing incidence rates of COVID-19 in both periods. The first time period was from April 1 to May 31, 2020. The second time period was from June 1 to July 31, 2020. Dark blue indicates counties with the highest incidence rate in the first period, whereas dark pink indicates counties with the highest mortality in the second period. Counties in dark purple had high incidence rates in both periods. Counties outlined in red are urban counties.

COVID-19 pandemic, but for other future health-related emergencies. Furthermore, critical access hospitals, which are hospitals of 25 beds or less and exist primarily in rural areas, must continue to receive special supplemental federal funding, as they are crucial in treating rural area patients (Schmidt et al. 2020).

Conclusions and Future Challenges

The United States implemented different vaccination plans in different states as the main intervention measure to tackle the pandemic in the country. Initially, COVID-19 vaccine distribution began in mid-December 2020, and all 50 states placed health-care workers and residents and staff of long-term care facilities at the front of the line to receive vaccinations. Despite the differences, most states had vaccinated the highest priority groups by the end of April 2021 and had moved on to inviting everyone over 16 years of age to be vaccinated. By June 2021, 54 percent of the population in the United States received at least one dose, and 45 percent were fully vaccinated. Ohio had a lower vaccination rate compared to the national average, in which 46 percent of the population in Ohio received at least one dose, and 42 percent of the population were fully vaccinated at the end of June 2021. There was a marked difference in vaccination rates between urban and rural counties; 49 percent of the urban population had received at least one dose, whereas 36 percent of the rural population had received at least one dose. Rural counties, like Adams, Highlands, Holmes, Lawrence, and Shelby, are the counties that had the lowest vaccination rates in Ohio; by the end of June 2021, less than 30 percent of their population had received at least one dose. Therefore, vaccination rollout became one of the biggest challenges facing the state, with vaccination rates remaining low, particularly in rural areas (Figure 9.12).

The management of public space in cities will be another of the great challenges that we will continue to face after the pandemic (Honey-Rosés 2020). In addition to the spatial analysis applications summarized in this chapter, the application of GIS methods is a very useful application for post-coronavirus urban planning through the inclusive participation of the population that inhabits these places. Such an application can help identify which spaces are social priorities, as well as context-sensitive, place-based information related to social sustainability and the social, economic, and environmental dynamics that affect a specific community (Samuelsson et al. 2020).

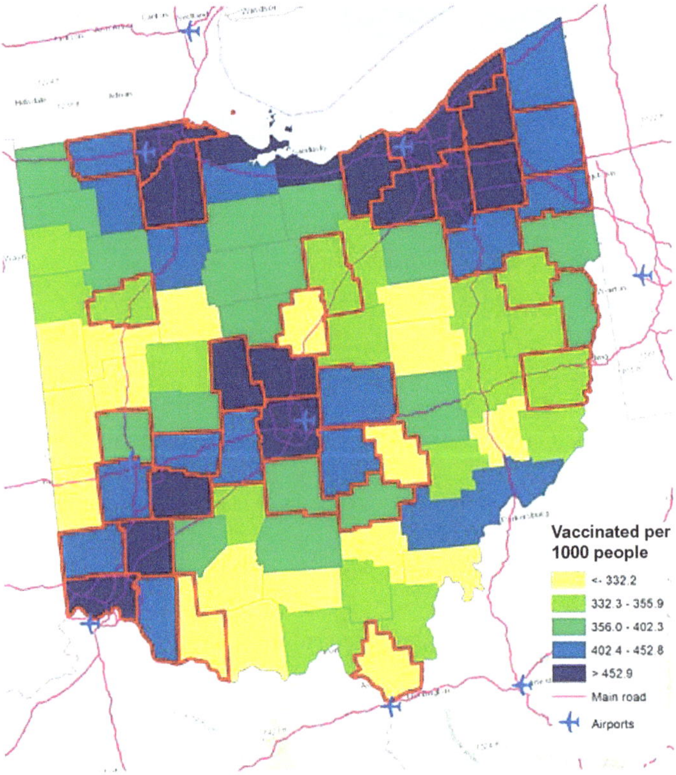

Fig. 9.12. Vaccination rate per county in Ohio as for June 2021. Counties outlined in red are urban counties.

COVID-19 studies with GIS could be valuable tools in decision-making and, more importantly, social mobilization and community responses. Spatial epidemiology has a critical social perspective that is highly relevant, so political decisions can be accountable to all sectors of society, hopefully minimizing the regularity with which marginalized populations are sacrificed or left unprotected. Understanding the spatial-temporal dynamics of COVID-19 is critical to its mitigation, which is why such work is being done in all regions of the world. The COVID-19 pandemic has highlighted the marked variation in patient demographics, access to healthcare, healthcare infrastructure, and preparedness among regions, and these, in turn, have significantly impacted outcomes. These factors are important for health policy, not only for the COVID-19 pandemic but also for future global health challenges.

REFERENCES

Ahasan, Rakibul, and Mahbub Hossain. 2021. "Leveraging GIS and Spatial Analysis for Informed Decision-Making in COVID-19 Pandemic." *Health Policy and Technology* 10, no. 1: 7–9.

Bonita, Ruth, Robert Beaglehole, and Tord Kjellström. 2006. *Basic Epidemiology*. 2nd ed. Geneva, Switzerland: World Health Organization.

Caini, Saverio, Clotilde El-Guerche Séblain, Meral A. Ciblak, and John Paget. 2018. "Epidemiology of Seasonal Influenza in the Middle East and North Africa Regions, 2010–2016: Circulating Influenza A and B Viruses and Spatial Timing of Epidemics." *Influenza and Other Respiratory Viruses* 12, no. 3: 344–352.

Correa-Agudelo, Esteban, Tesfaye B. Mersha, Adam J. Branscum, Neil J. Mackinnon, and Diego F. Cuadros. 2021. "Identification of Vulnerable Populations and Areas at Higher Risk of Covid-19-Related Mortality during the Early Stage of the Epidemic in the United States." *International Journal of Environmental Research and Public Health* 18, no. 8: 4021.

Cuadros, Diego F., Adam J. Branscum, Zindoga Mukandavire, F. DeWolfe Miller, Neil MacKinnon. 2021. "Dynamics of the COVID-19 Epidemic in Urban and Rural Areas in the United States." *Annals of Epidemiology* 59: 16–20.

Cuadros, Diego F., Jingjing Li, Adam J. Branscum, Adam Akullian, Peng Jia, Elizabeth N. Mziray, and Frank Tanser. 2017. "Mapping the Spatial Variability of HIV Infection in sub-Saharan Africa: Effective Information for Localized HIV Prevention and Control." *Scientific Reports* 7: 1–11.

Cuadros, Diego F., Yanyu Xiao, Zindoga Mukandavire, Esteban Correa-Agudelo, Andrés Hernández, Hana Kim, and Neil J. MacKinnon. 2020. "Spatiotemporal Transmission Dynamics of the COVID-19 Pandemic and Its Impact on Critical Healthcare Capacity." *Health & Place* 64: 102404. https://doi.org/10.1016/j.healthplace.2020.102404.

Dwyer-Lindgren, Laura, Michael A. Cork, Amber Sligar, Krista M. Steuben, Kate F. Wilson, Naomi R. Provost, Benjamin K. Mayala et al. 2019. "Mapping HIV Prevalence in sub-Saharan Africa between 2000 and 2017." *Nature* 570: 189–193.

Green, Christopher A., David Yeates, Allie Goldacre, and Charles J. Sande. 2015. "Admission to Hospital for Bronchiolitis in England: Trends over Five Decades, Geographical Variation and Association with Perinatal Characteristics and Subsequent Asthma." *Archives of Disease in Childhood* 101: 140–146.

Haischer, Michael H., Rachel Beilfuss, Meggie Rose Hart, Lauren Opielinski, David Wrucke, Gretchen Zirgaitis, Toni D. Ulrich, Sandra K. Hunter. 2020. "Who Is Wearing a Mask? Gender-, Age-, and Location-Related Differences during the COVID-19 Pandemic." *PLOS One*. https://doi.org/10.1371/journal.pone.0240785

Hall, Susan A., Jay S. Kaufman, and Thomas C. Ricketts. 2006. "Defining Urban and Rural Areas in U.S. Epidemiologic Studies." *Journal of Urban Health* 83: 162–165.

Hartley, David. 2004. "Rural Health Disparities, Population Health, and Rural Culture." *American Journal of Public Health* 94: 1675–1678.

Hay, Simon I., and Robert W. Snow. 2006. The Malaria Atlas Project: Developing Global Maps of Malaria Risk. *PLOS Medicine* 3. https://doi.org/10.1371/journal.pmed.0030473.

Honey-Rosés, Jordi, Isabelle Anguelovki, Vincent K. Chireh, Carolyn Daher, Cecil Konijnendijk, Ulises Sánchez, Maged Senbel et al. 2020. "The Impact of COVID-19 on Public Space: An Early Review of the Emerging Questions—Design, Perceptions and Inequities." *Cities & Health*. 51, supl: S263–S279. https://doi.org/10.1080/23748834.2020.1780074.

Izadnegahdar, Rasa, Adam L. Cohen, Keith P. Klugman, and Shamim A. Qazi. 2013. "Childhood Pneumonia in Developing Countries." *The Lancet Respiratory Medicine* 1: 574–584.

Johns Hopkins University. n.d. "Novel Coronavirus COVID-19 (2019-nCoV) Data Repository. https://systems.jhu.edu/research/public-health/ncov/.

Kearns, Robin A., and Alun E. Joseph. 1993. "Space in Its Place: Developing the Link in Medical Geography." *Social Science & Medicine* 37: 711–717.

Kluge, Hans Henri P. 2020. "Older People Are at Highest Risk from COVID-19, But All Must Act to Prevent Community Spread." April 2. (World Health Organization statement). www.who.int/europe/news/item/03-04-2020-statement-older-people-are-at-highest-risk-from-covid-19-but-all-must-act-to-prevent-community-spread.

Krieger, Nancy. 2011. *Epidemiology and the People's Health: Theory and Context*. Oxford: Oxford University Press.

Kucharski, Adam J., Timothy W. Russell, Charlie Diamond, Yang Liu, John Edmunds, Sebastian Funk, and Rosalind M. Eggo. 2020. *The Lancet Infectious Diseases* 20, no. 5: 553–558.

Lai, Shengjie, Isaac I. Bogoch, Nick W. Ruktanonchai, Alexander Watts, Xin Lu, Weizhong Yang, Hongjie Yu, Kamran Khan, and Andrew J. Tatem. 2020. "Assessing Spread Risk of Wuhan Novel Coronavirus within and beyond China, January–April 2020: A Travel Network-Based Modellings Study." *medRxiv*. https://doi.org/10.1101/2020.02.04.20020479.

McAnally, Heath B. 2017. *Opioid Dependence: A Clinical and Epidemiologic Approach*. New York: Springer.

McLafferty, Sara L. 2003. "GIS and Health Care." *Annual Review of Public Health* 24: 25–42.

Moore, Dale A., and Tim E. Carpenter. 1999. "Spatial Analytical Methods and Geographic Information Systems: Use in Health Research and Epidemiology." *Epidemiologic Reviews* 21: 143–161.

Nykiforuk, Candace I., and Laura M. Flaman. 2011. Geographic Information Systems (GIS) for Health Promotion and Public Health: A Review." *Health Promotion Practice* 12: 63–73.

Odoi, Agricola et al. 2004. "Investigation of Clusters of Giardiasis Using GIS and a Spatial Scan Statistic." *International Journal of Health Geographics* 3, no. 11. https://doi.org/10.1186/1476-072X-3-11.

Park, Minah, Alex R. Cook, Jue Tao Lim, Yinxiaohe Sun, and Borame L. Dickins. 2020. "A Systematic Review of COVID-19 Epidemiology Based on Current Evidence." *Journal of Clinical Medicine* 9, no. 4: 967.

Real, Leslie A., and Roman Biek. 2007. "Spatial Dynamics and Genetics of Infectious Diseases on Heterogeneous Landscapes." *Journal of the Royal Society Interface* 4: 935–948.

Rothman, Kenneth J., Sander Greenland, and Timothy L. Lash. 2008. *Modern Epidemiology.* Philadelphia: Lippincott Williams and Wilkins.

RUPRI Center for Rural Health Policy Analysis. n.d. https://rupri.public-health.uiowa.edu/.

Rushton, Gerard. 2003. "Public Health, GIS, and Spatial Analytic Tools." *Annual Review of Public Health* 24: 43–56.

Rytkönen, Mika J. 2004. "Not All Maps Are Equal: GIS and Spatial Analysis in Epidemiology." *International Journal of Circumpolar Health* 63: 9–24.

Samuelsson, Karl, Stephan Barthel, Johan Colding, Gloria Macassa, and Matteo Giusti. 2020. "Urban Nature as a Source of Resilience during Social Distancing amidst the Coronavirus Pandemic." *OSF Preprints.* https://osf.io/3wx5a/.

Schmidt, Cliff, Gumah Tiah, Lisa Zook, and Erin Inclan. 2020. "COVID-19 Awareness Campaign: Learning from Challenges to Prepare for the Next Public Health Emergency." Gates Open Research. https://gatesopenresearch.org/posters/4-166.

Schroeder, Shawnda. 2018. "Rural Communities: Age, Income, and Health Status." *Rural Health Research RECAP.* November.

Shi, Ting, David A. McAllister, Katherine L. O'Brien, Eric A. F. Simoes, Shabir A. Madhi, Bradford D. Gessner, Fernando P. Polack et al. 2017. "Global, Regional, and National Disease Burden Estimates of Acute Lower Respiratory Infections due to Respiratory Syncytial Virus in Young Children in 2015: a Systematic Review and Modeling Study." *The Lancet* 390: 946–958.

Sloan, Chantel, Martin Moore, and Tina V. Hartert. 2011. "Impact of Pollution, Climate, and Sociodemographic Factors on Spatiotemporal Dynamics of Seasonal Respiratory Viruses." *Clinical and Translational Science* 4: 48–54.

Smith, Carrie. 2020. "The Unique Impact of COVID-19 on Older Adults in Rural Areas." *Journal of Aging & Social Policy* 32: 396–340.

Thomas, Yonette F., Douglas Richardson, and Ivan Cheung, eds. 2008. *Geography and Drug Addiction.* New York: Springer Science & Business Media.

US Census Bureau. 2016. "New Census Data Show Differences between Urban and Rural Populations." www.census.gov/newsroom/press-releases/2016/cb16-210.html.

Warren, Adam, Morag Bell, and Lucy Budd. 2010. "Airports, Localities and Disease: Representations of Global Travel during the H1N1 Pandemic." *Health & Place* 16, no. 4: 727–735.

Wilson, David, and Daniel T. Halperin. 2008. "Know Your Epidemic, Know Your Response": A Useful Approach, If We Get It Right." *The Lancet* 372: 423–426.

World Health Organization (WHO). 2020. "Management of Ill Travelers at Points of Entry—International Airports, Seaports and Ground Crossings—in the Context of COVID-19 Outbreak" (interim guidance). March 19. www.who.int/publications/i/item/10665-331512.

10 | Prisons, Pandemics, and Personal Responsibility

COVID in Ohio's Correctional Facilities

Research and Reflection Article

Elizabeth Lanphier and M. Forrest Behne

This is a hybrid research and reflection essay by a philosopher and a policy analyst who was formerly incarcerated in Ohio. It argues for prison health care reform as a critical element of criminal justice reform, drawing on data related to COVID-19 across Ohio's prisons and jails, and personal experience from a COVID-19 outbreak at Ohio's London Correctional Institution.

Introduction

I was lucky: loved ones visited me regularly. But the week of March 9, I learned from my parents—not the prison—that my scheduled visit with a friend was canceled. Based on what little we knew, temporarily closing prisons to visitors and volunteers seemed a sensible enough decision. Even the most skeptical TV news viewers on my block were beginning to secret away an extra roll of toilet paper. The hoarding of food, water, and TP makes for a reliable measure of unease. But the least they could do was notify us directly ...

In this chapter we analyze Ohio's response to COVID-19 in its prisons and jails from multiple perspectives. One is from Forrest's direct experience being incarcerated in and then decarcerated from the London Correctional Institution in central Ohio. His account is woven throughout in italics. The "we" voice expresses our joint scholarly analysis: Forrest as a researcher on correctional medicine and public health with the Covid Prison Project, and Elizabeth as a philosopher and bioethicist in Ohio.

We explore how Ohio, as the site of the first major COVID-19 outbreaks in corrections facilities in the United States, was a harbinger of things to come in carceral settings across the country. By analyzing available public-facing data about COVID-19 in Ohio's carceral contexts in the early months and year of the COVID-19 pandemic, and assessing these data in conversation with Forrest's first-person experience, we offer a nuanced picture of the practical, logistical, political, and theoretical constraints that hampered Ohio's response to COVID in correctional settings. In centering Forrest's account, we rely on the strength of direct experience as a source of knowledge and evidence, while acknowledging that it does not and cannot speak for the experience of all incarcerated people.

Many features of Forrest's experience are distinctive within mass incarceration in the United States. Forrest was incarcerated due to a rigid application of a law improperly applied to his situation, which was the result of a medical condition. He is a white male, although Black and Hispanic persons are incarcerated at significantly higher rates than white persons in the United States. Forrest was decarcerated during the pandemic. Although decarceration, and once available, vaccination, were two leading strategies identified to reduce COVID-19 transmission among incarcerated populations (Barsky et al. 2021), decarceration was rare in and beyond Ohio. While wrongful incarceration is not uncommon, Forrest was one of relatively few people to eventually be granted clemency after nearly two years of wrongful incarceration.

States failed to prevent COVID-19 cluster outbreaks in their corrections facilities despite Ohio's early warning and the fact that these outbreaks were both predictable and avoidable. The example of Ohio demonstrates how health is inappropriately construed as an individual problem requiring individual solutions in carceral contexts. We argue that this framing aligns with problematic conceptualizations of individual responsibility and rehabilitation within US mass incarceration more broadly and draws attention to the intersection of public health and mass incarceration.

Marion and Pickaway

Word of an outbreak at a neighboring prison started to make its way into the population at my facility. Without any visible leadership from our institution and the Ohio Department of Rehabilitation and Corrections (ODRC), we were left to piece information together from phone calls, staff gossip, and whichever daily press conference we could pick up with our TV antennas. Initially, we were frustrated being "observers" amid a global pandemic. Soon that frustration grew into fear of being participants in the crisis.

Only a month into the declaration of COVID-19 as a global pandemic, 73 percent of incarcerated people at Ohio's Marion prison tested positive for the novel coronavirus—contributing to the 3,500 cases across Ohio's corrections facilities counted in a single week (Chappell 2020). Early on, the ODRC briefly implemented thorough COVID-19 testing and infection rates initially appeared to slow. As of July 2020, Ohio's Marion prison was the single largest cluster of COVID-19 infections in the country.

Marion and Pickaway became household names. These facilities earned the dubious distinction of being the worst outbreaks in the nation, despite the ODRC locking down prisons early. To many on the outside, Columbus' early and sober response to COVID in its prisons seemed sensible. Those of us in state custody were less generous in our assessment, if only because we were the last to know what was happening.

Before the development of vaccines, testing, and contact tracing, along with masking and distancing, were primary public health tools to curb the pandemic. Although the ODRC continued to document new COVID-19 cases throughout the pandemic, it only conducted routine testing in limited facilities during spring 2020, and discontinued mass testing only weeks after implementing it. (Testing in response to screened symptoms did continue.) As of June 2021, when vaccines had become broadly available to the Ohio public, nearly 10,000 COVID infections had already been documented in Ohio's corrections facilities—impacting 20 percent of its total incarcerated population (Marshall Project 2021). The UCLA Law COVID Behind Bars Data Project, which continues to collect and report data on COVID-19 infections, deaths, and vaccines in correctional facilities across the country, "learned in April 2021 that the agency instead removes cases from its data when people are released from custody. This practice obscures the true toll of the coronavirus in Ohio prisons" (UCLA n.d.).

Lack of consistency and transparency is already a feature of correctional systems, but it took on new potency during the COVID-19 pandemic. Given the unreliability of ODRC reporting after mid-2021 and our interest in missed opportunities for an early and effective pandemic response in Ohio's prisons and jails, we focus our data analysis in this chapter on the time between the onset of the pandemic in March 2020 to summer 2021. During this period the data we are analyzing was most reliably reported. It also marks the time by which vaccines were broadly available in Ohio to all adults who chose to become vaccinated (with caveats related to accessibility in the carceral context that we address later in this chapter) and is prior to the introduction of new variables, including additional waves of COVID-19 cases and deaths spurred by novel variants such as Delta and Omicron.

The testing and positivity rates rose so high, so quickly that the state stopped mass testing completely. The outbreaks at Marion and Pickaway were so politically damaging that the ODRC reversed course, and we were never routinely tested at the London Correctional Institution—we were only routinely screened for symptoms. The Ohio National Guard had to run the prisons facing staffing shortages due to illness. Rule changes were announced: some decent, some inane. Some responsible, some punitive. But substantive updates or frank discussion of the crisis before us was noticeably absent. In the absence of information, we speculated. Staff were using up paid time off and quitting to avoid working inside ODRC facilities. We wondered: will the National Guard come here next? Restriction on visitors entering the facility spelled the end for college and rehabilitative programming. Are food service contractors next? Most concerning was the language used to describe the pandemic: "security threat level: red." The same way declaring a state of emergency opens certain policies and funding sources, identifying the pandemic as a security threat meant officers could employ riot-busting strategies as tools of viral mitigation.

Limiting the movement of people between the free world and corrections facilities also limits movement of information—in both directions. The apparent sensibility of "locking down" corrections facilities by limiting insider (incarcerated individual) movements, imposing restrictions to remain in cells, and closing off outsider (non-incarcerated) volunteer and visitor entry to minimize COVID-19 transmission comes with trade-offs. Insiders became further distanced from outsiders and outside information. The ODRC did not have to be accountable to outsiders who would, in normal times, regularly visit corrections facilities (family and friends of insiders, volunteers, or educators), and the conditions of mass incarceration could be kept further hidden from the free world than they already are.

Health Care and Mass Incarceration

COVID has underscored, and exacerbated, problems across the United States related to health-care access, inequities, and disparities predating the pandemic. The same applies to COVID-19 in US prisons and jails. During the initial year of the pandemic, prior to the widespread availability of COVID-19 vaccines, rates of COVID-19 infection in corrections facilities were significantly higher than in the free world. Reports on data collected from 2020 to 2021, for example, showed that in Ohio, infection rates were 2.1 times higher for incarcerated individuals compared to the non-incarcerated population (Marshall Project 2021). US-wide data suggested that confirmed COVID-19 cases were up to four (National Commission 2020), possibly over five (Saloner et al. 2020) times higher in prisons and jails than in the non-incarcerated population. Rates of death in prisons and jails also exceeded those in the free world.

Disparities between incarcerated and free world COVID-19 rates were compounded by both disproportionate rates of incarceration among racial and ethnic minorities (Gramlich 2020), and disproportionate rates of COVID-19 infection among racial and ethnic minorities across the United States. Infection rates for Native American, Black or African American, and Hispanic or Latinx persons in the initial year of the COVID-19 pandemic were reported to be significantly higher than those of white persons in the United States, and hospitalization and death rates even higher among racial minorities. (Lopez, Hart, and Katz 2021).

Incarcerated individuals are the only people in the United States with a constitutionally protected right to health care, rooted in the Eighth Amendment's protection against cruel and unusual punishment, as decided by two Supreme Court cases (*Estelle v. Gamble* 1976 and *Deshaney v. Winnebago County* 1989). Yet this putatively held right could be notoriously difficult to access, even pre-pandemic.

For instance, medical co-pays mandated by most jails and prisons can be 10 to 20 times higher than hourly carceral wages. A five-dollar medical co-pay represents a substantial portion of a base 13-dollar-per-month salary. Most states temporarily paused medical co-pays as a COVID-19 mitigation strategy (12 states did not charge co-pays prior to the pandemic; Ohio did and does charge co-pays). While nine states suspended all medical co-pays during the pandemic, most states limited co-pay waivers for COVID-19 symptom complaints only (Herring 2020). Per an announcement via the ODRC Twitter page, Ohio only waived co-pays for "flu-like symptoms" (@DRCOhio March 12, 2020). Yet COVID-19 symptoms were not limited to respiratory and flu symptoms.

Implementing social distancing and hygiene strategies proved even more complex. Correctional facilities are often cramped environments; in all but the most high-security settings there are multiple people sharing rooms or dorms. There is rarely—if ever—access to personal protective equipment (PPE) and adequate sanitation. Residents (incarcerated individuals) must purchase their own soap at full cost, from wages earned in their institutional job. Hand sanitizer is often banned because of its alcohol content.

Certain COVID policies proved valuable. Free five-minute phone calls facilitated communication between loved ones and residents. The munificence of Global Tel Link would have been an object of scorn under any other circumstances. During the pandemic, though, the ability to communicate was never more appreciated. Walking between parts of the low-to-medium-security facility was restricted, making it more akin to a maximum-security setting. But this facilitated physical distancing between housing units. Noncontact between dorms was strictly enforced. Correctional administrators even had the foresight to house people by occupation, creating units for mask makers, food service workers, and critical infrastructure maintenance. They created redundant dorms for food service in case one population experienced an outbreak.

Each resident is assigned a job that they are required to perform under threat of disciplinary action. Many of these jobs—like laundry, food service, and maintenance—provide for the day-to-day facility operations. Others support facility infrastructure like water treatment systems, the prison's power plant, sanitation, electrical, maintenance, construction, plumbing, and waste management. These jobs are performed for pennies on the hour, if compensated at all. There are no labor and occupational safety protections, though there can be medical exemptions from work requirements. During the pandemic, jobs like barber, law clerk, and tutor were suspended and replaced with new tasks like sewing masks for the prison population.

The most visible COVID-related change was daily symptom monitoring. Every morning we woke to the halogen lights above our beds and a duty officer bellowing "temp check." Row by row, we lined up to wait for staff to apply the pulse oximeter and read our temperature. For some of us this is the first time seeing health-care staff in months—or years—and we were grateful to talk with them. Those with chronic and untreated medical conditions would plead to the medics for help only to be told, "Hey, at least no one in your dorm has caught it yet." One medical worker said to another, loud enough to be heard, "How come they all smell like wet dogs?"

Grouping people in job function cohorts, routine symptom screening, and facilitating telephone communication in the absence of in-person visiting are all logical policy decisions. Other approaches appearing initially reasonable in the setting of mass incarceration had negative, even illogical, consequences.

Solitary confinement became the Swiss Army knife of population management at London Correctional Institution. When anyone transferred between facilities or had been temporarily "out-to-court," they were forced to quarantine in solitary confinement cells. The same happened to those on a "round trip" to an off-site medical facility. Those who had reached the end of their sentence and were awaiting release were placed in "the hole" as well.

Single-occupant cells can facilitate physical distancing and can be more easily disinfected. But solitary confinement cells—disconcertingly ubiquitous in correctional facilities—are also inhumane, often exacerbating mental health crises, and allowing those housed in them to face further marginalization within an already isolated and marginalized environment (Guenther 2013). We also now know that, because COVID-19 is airborne and correctional facility HVACs are often outdated, contaminated air still circulated between solitary cells.

Many who displayed symptoms or tested positive after displaying symptoms were sent to the disciplinary unit to quarantine. Sometimes solitary was a mitigation tool. Other times it was a punishment. Anyone who didn't comply with rules such as mask wearing would end up there too. To self-report symptoms meant risking two weeks of solitary confinement. People were frantically washing their faces with cold water before symptom check to try and beat the thermometer.

Public Health versus Personal Health

Health-care systems in the United States can be costly, difficult to access, bureaucratic, and confusing. Health care in carceral systems is notably different from the free world, yet encounters each of these same challenges, but in distinct ways. Here we describe the process for an incarcerated individual in ODRC custody to be seen by a medical provider, interspersed with vignettes of Forrest's experience of ODRC responses to COVID. These scenes paint a portrait of a system that, paradoxically, expects individual residents to enact health care and prevention at both individual and population levels—measures over which they have little to no control.

Initially, each resident was provided a single-layer cloth mask. Because so little information was shared, many residents viewed this as just another means of control, a belief reinforced by correctional staff punishing those who failed to wear their mask. Only if lying prone on your bed were you permitted to take off your mask. No other exception; not even for brushing your teeth. In the spring heat, our masks quickly became soiled. Additional masks would be weeks and months away, yet we couldn't take the masks off to clean them.

To be treated for flu-like symptoms, a resident must request, complete, and submit proper documentation. These paper medical "kites"—a term originally used between incarcerated individuals for surreptitious communication, but that now refers to any institutional form—are retrieved from correctional staff and deposited in a secure drop box in communal locations, such as a chow hall or infirmary. Individuals cannot simply present to the infirmary or call to schedule an appointment.

People started tearing the sleeves off white cotton T-shirts and wearing these as face coverings, but this was a potential conduct violation. Tearing the shirt was destruction of state property. Makeshift masks were "contraband." Residents were stuck between risking their health or risking a disciplinary report that could be used to deny parole.

The medical "kite" process assumes, or demands, three things of requesters: they can read English and express themselves in writing; they have a working relationship with a correctional officer who will provide a kite; and they can get to the drop box. This system creates barriers for anyone who does not meet these conditions.

We started receiving weekly video messages on CCTV from the warden aiming to be candid and motivational. As time went on, they became pleas to halt the spread of the virus. During one message Warden Robinson offered access to a supposedly brand-new Xbox. We could take turns using it only if we stopped spreading coronavirus. This carrot for our compliance only further alienated those whose cooperation the warden most needed to secure. It made apparent that the onus for health and safety lay with prisoners, and not the prison nor the staff.

The secure drop box is periodically emptied. Requests are routed to the institution's medical services staff, screened, and written responses provided. If your reported symptoms merit an in-person appointment, a time and date for that appointment are attached to the response, which mailroom corrections officers sort and deliver to the original requester. This process may take days or weeks.

Even when routine COVID symptom screening was implemented, it was not always performed by health-care workers and was not designed to increase access to medical care or treatment. All non-COVID medical complaints still went through the medical kite process. Available data, and Forrest's experience, suggest that systematic barriers were not meaningfully removed during the COVID-19 pandemic to better support individual or population health in Ohio's corrections facilities.

Requesting medical care must be weighed against potential repercussions. Given the delay between a medical request and appointment, symptoms might resolve prior to being seen. This creates multiple costs for the requester, who could be accused of (and punished for) malingering and required to pay a co-pay for their visit. Even if one secures an appointment, if the institution goes on lockdown, any pending or scheduled medical appointments are cancelled.

Corrections officers seemed to view themselves as heroes in harm's way of COVID-19 exposure from us, forgetting we were incapable of bringing the virus into the facility ourselves. Visitation was suspended, volunteer-entry prohibited. Any introduction of the virus was singularly attributable to correctional staff. Yet once the virus found its footing in correctional facilities, the narrative framed by local news was of the bravery demonstrated by officers staying the course and not abandoning their posts.

Despite hurdles, people do manage to visit the infirmary, often at great cost of time, money, and well-being to themselves and fellow residents. Delays in identifying and treating those with communicable diseases like flu—or COVID-19—creates opportunities for disease spread. A free person might be able to stay home from work or school to isolate, or might open their medicine cabinet to take a pill to manage cold and flu symptoms. Incarcerated individuals generally cannot. They are unable to self-isolate. And, like other health-related goods in correctional settings, even basic over-the-counter medications remain often inaccessible due to cost.

Residents can purchase limited quantities of medications at full retail price through the institution's commissary, or potentially receive small quantities during a requested medical visit, but either way the cost is exorbitant relative to carceral wages. Charging more than a third of one's salary as a co-pay for a visit it may have taken days or weeks to secure is far from fulfilling a constitutionally protected right to health care.

One day, new benches, exclusively for correctional staff, appeared on the yard facing our chow hall. At this point the facility was on lockdown, but when we were herded between our dorms and meals, officers would point out the wooden plaque affixed to the new bench: "Dedicated to the heroes of the COVID-19 pandemic." Watching these officers' heroism be lauded instead of honoring those who had died within our facility was maddening in ways difficult to express but clearly shared among my fellow residents. Then and now, there were facilities that saw larger, deadlier outbreaks than London, but nearly everyone there had some connection to a now-deceased fellow resident. Many of us also knew those residing in these harder-hit prisons and so such losses were felt deeply. By laying the blame for the pandemic at the feet of prisoners, then claiming heroism in the face of it, the ODRC stoked tensions between staff and residents.

Emergency situations need not rely on the medical kite system. Dorm duty staff can place an emergency call to medical services or dial 911. Yet successfully escalating an emergency is not necessarily straightforward. Wounded or ill individuals still must be able to advocate for themselves. Officers may be skeptical of false claims of urgency and may not be trained to recognize signs of distress. Those with cognitive or speech impairment or non-native English speakers are already at a disadvantage and being seriously sick or injured may further compromise their ability to vocalize a need.

In April 2020, my attorney, Michael Zuckerman of the Ohio Justice and Policy Center, filed for executive clemency, a form of legal relief that if granted by the governor would mean my early release. We cited my medical vulnerability—heightened by the pandemic—as justification for early release. Following my filing, a London Correctional Institution staff member emailed Brigid Kelly, an Ohio House Representative, who could advocate for or against my request, stating I should be denied early release because I was not complying with social distancing rules.

I imagine they were motivated by a mix of personal animus for how I helped other incarcerated individuals navigate the grievance process, and general animus toward all incarcerated individuals that led them to not want to see any of us released—let alone early. Their report, used as a pretext to undermine my chances at early release, was correct, yet disingenuous. I was not complying with social distancing rules. None of us could. Our conditions couldn't allow for it.

Adequate steps were not taken to allow for appropriate social distancing in line with CDC guidance. We were required to stand shoulder to shoulder for head count twice per day. We slept in shared dorms, our beds within arm's reach of each other. The roughly 215 men in my dorm shared one bathroom. In a move ridiculed even by the staff, bunkmates were required to sleep facing opposite directions. No modifications were made to create more space: density on our block remained the same; ventilation was not upgraded. The only time distancing was enforced was outside, waiting in line for food so that any news cameras present would document compliance with departmental policies and federal guidance. Through every announcement, electronic message, and televised press conference, we were told that we, and we alone, were responsible for our health and that of the facility. Yet we were living in a setting that by definition limited our every choice and movement.

Decarceration

Mass incarceration confines a group of people to a fixed space. Facilities are designed to limit occupants' movements and their agency regarding where and around whom to be, or not be. Forrest's narrative makes explicit that residents were held accountable for social distancing and, at the same time, the conditions of incarceration made social distancing impossible.

Without the ability to safely distance, and without vaccines for the first ten months of the pandemic, reducing facility density was the primary public health strategy available after masking and testing. For states to reduce prison density, they had to decarcerate—or expedite the release of their incarcerated population from corrections facilities—though not necessarily from corrections oversight. Decarceration methods can include compassionate release, early release, judicial review, clemency, or pardon.

Judicial review reexamines an incarcerated person's case by a sentencing judge, possibly reducing the sentence. Early release expedites the end of sentences already slated for imminent conclusion, while compassionate release considers a resident's particular vulnerability—usually medical—and continues their supervision through monitoring in the community. Clemency is an executive action taken at the level of the governor (or in the case of federal prison, the president) to reduce a sentence, and may or may not involve a pardon, which is to be absolved of alleged crimes.

The ODRC does not provide exact figures for the total number of people decarcerated during the COVID-19 pandemic. A hodgepodge of data tells part of the story. Notably, the overall incarcerated population in Ohio has been decreasing since 2015. Total releases in 2020 reflect expected releases, not a decarceration strategy. One stopgap measure at the start of the pandemic was the temporary halting of transfers from local jails to ODRC custody after sentencing. As prison sentences ended and individuals were released, this decreased total prison population, but displaced burdens onto lesser-equipped county and municipal facilities throughout Ohio.

By April 2020, Governor Mike DeWine asked that judges consider early release for nonviolent offenders already within 90 days of the end of their prison sentence (Balmert 2020a). This amounted to 141 people, or approximately 0.3 percent of people in ODRC custody. DeWine recommended—but did not require—judicial review of cases for children and pregnant people: only 38 such cases were reviewed (Balmert 2020b). Many decarceration initiatives stopped after spring 2020, as these were not programs defined by clear policy, but ad hoc initiatives taken by the governor. Because data collected by the US Sentencing Commission are not broken out by month, we cannot know the exact timing of the 63 compassionate releases granted in Ohio out of 203 requests through December 2020 (US Sentencing Commission 2021).

More impactful and lasting changes were attainable, though politically unpopular, and thus underutilized. DeWine could have used his clemency powers more broadly. In April 2020, DeWine commuted the sentences of seven individuals (WTOL 2020)—out of 48,927 people incarcerated in Ohio at the time. (According to its own 2015 "strategic capital master plan," the maximum design occupancy for the entire ODRC is 37,004.) Forrest's case was one of the very few in which clemency was eventually granted. The frequency of clemency practices varies widely by state. According to the Restoration of Rights Project (2020), Ohio uses clemency only "sparingly," granting a low percentage of applications. Some states, like Connecticut, already had more robust clemency practices prior to the pandemic, while other states, like New York, saw an 80 percent increase in clemency applications in 2020 due to the pandemic, but not a significant increase in clemencies granted (Segura 2021). The nature of Forrest's case would have warranted his clemency filing regardless of the pandemic, but the pandemic did play a role in its timing.

Before the institutional head count one day in mid-September 2020, six weeks before the end of my sentence, I was quietly pulled into the office of my case manager and given my first COVID nasal swab. They explained that I had been granted clemency and I would be collected for processing an hour later. An hour to call home, pack my belongings, and say goodbye to my friends and neighbors. But I wouldn't be released that day. I would be held in solitary confinement to quarantine until my COVID test returned negative.

My feelings about the COVID test were mixed. I was grateful to finally receive one—it could decide whether I could hug my family. But I wondered about the consequences of a positive result. Would I be denied release because the ODRC had allowed me to fall ill? Was I to be further punished for something out of my control? I was already in solitary confinement, after receiving clemency, while awaiting release.

Days later I was moved from solitary confinement to the ad hoc medical isolation facility in the main building's basement. I didn't have COVID, but I was held by Warden Robinson for nearly a week after Governor DeWine granted my clemency. My paperwork had been misplaced. This was more likely a result of ineptitude rather than malice, though both are plausible. The reason mattered to me less than the fact that I could finally see my family again.

Releases such as Forrest's were also exceedingly rare for the total correctional population in the United States. The Federal Bureau of Prisons (BOP), for instance, houses roughly 150,000 people, of whom 30,969 filed applications for compassionate release beginning in March of 2020. Yet wardens, who provide the initial review of such applications in this system, recommended granting only 374, and the BOP approved only 36 requests according to data collected by Hawai'i Senator Brian Schatz (2021).

Those best equipped to effect population reductions largely failed to do so, likely owing to an unfounded fear of recidivism and violence over a real and imminent deadly virus. Citizens and public officials expressed concerns about what would happen to crime rates following the reintroduction of convicted criminals to their communities. As DeWine remarked, "I'm not just going to open the gates. I think that is an irresponsible thing to do" (Kasler 2020).

Yet keeping people in corrections facilities under existing conditions was also an irresponsible thing to do. Framing the options as a choice between two extremes, continued incarceration or opening the prison doors for everyone to walk out, was a false and reckless dichotomy. Preliminary data does not support a connection between decarceration and increased crime. The ACLU (2020) found that most large US cities saw a decrease in crime despite reductions in jail population. At the time of writing, of 24,000 individuals decarcerated from the Federal Bureau of Prisons, 3 have been arrested for a new offense, only one of which was violent (Kanno-Youngs and Turcotte 2021).

The real danger was not decarcerating individuals but failing to, or decarcerating without proper public health measures in place. The relatively few people released in Ohio early in the pandemic were not tested for COVID, nor provided adequate resources to safely self-quarantine before returning to the community (Bliss 2020). This introduced avoidable health risks to families and communities to which individuals were returning.

We can see from Forrest's experience that Ohio learned over time to perform COVID-19 testing prior to release, though the method of solitary confinement as quarantine introduced new ethical concerns. Despite these missteps, decarceration, when done right, reduces health risks to the individual and community, without introducing new safety risks.

Public health and epidemiology experts have remained unequivocal that decarceration is a necessary component of any successful COVID-19 pandemic response (National Academies 2020a). Researchers found that lower rates of occupancy were associated with lower rates of COVID-19 infection and death inside Texas prisons, for example (Vest et al. 2021). Moreover, decarceration not only protects the health and interests of those who are incarcerated—a population for which the general public frequently has little sympathy. Decarceration is good for the entire population's health.

Prisons and jails may seem to be contained populations that are, in a sense, socially distanced from the free world. Yet corrections staff move between facilities and the community daily. Incarcerated individuals, too, cycle in and out for court appearances or off-site medical appointments, and transfer between corrections facilities. New commitments move residents in, while concluding sentences move residents out. Certain movements slowed during the pandemic, at least temporarily. Yet many continued, often without adequate health precautions.

Eric Reinhart and Daniel L. Chen (2020) showed that in Chicago, the single strongest predictor of COVID rates in a community is the degree of "jail cycling" (individuals being brought into and then released from jail). Not only does this occurrence materially contribute to the length and severity of the pandemic, but it also acts as a driver of health inequalities—as communities of color are disproportionately represented in these jails and consequently experience an outsized impact of COVID-19.

Despite evidence that decarceration improves public health, it was, and continues to be, an underutilized tool (Barsky et al. 2021). The pandemic put on display the institutional reluctance to acknowledge—and listen to—calls for reform. Mass incarceration is a public health issue. Prisons worsen health, shorten life, and exacerbate preexisting health disparities in marginalized communities inside and outside of corrections facilities (Gifford 2019; Daza, Palloni, and Jones 2020; Sundaresh et al. 2021). The answer to correcting these inequities is simple: reduce the total number of incarcerated individuals.

Vaccination

With rehabilitative programming gone, visitation suspended, and most institutional jobs dissolved, most of the residents of London Correctional had little to do during the day. A common misconception is that cable TV is magnanimously given to all who are incarcerated. Not so. Instead, we would pass the time with hobbies such as reading, or conduct days-long card games, or simply talk. In those days, conversation was frequently about the pandemic, and what would come next for us. Many were certain that we would be dead long before a vaccine was available. Others who were more optimistic about the possibility of a vaccine knew implicitly that we would be the last to receive it. Annual flu shots were already rare. Why would a COVID-19 vaccine be any different?

Barksy and colleagues (2021) suggest that "vaccination alone will not be enough to stop carceral outbreaks," and decarceration ought to continue to be part of a twin strategy to reduce carceral transmission of COVID-19. Yet the rapid development and production of multiple safe and effective COVID-19 vaccines further turned attention away from decarceration efforts in prisons and jails, and toward vaccination efforts. One reason vaccination on its own is insufficient is due to the deprioritization of incarcerated populations in many state COVID-19 vaccine allocation plans.

Ohio initially planned to follow the National Academies of Sciences, Engineering, and Medicine (NASEM), which produced comprehensive guidance based on the identification of COVID-19 risk factors, and essential worker roles, as well as contextual realities like the increased vulnerability of those living in congregate settings such as nursing homes, group homes, shelters, and prisons and jails (National Academies 2020b). Although COVID-19 vaccines were developed in record time, they would remain a scarce resource in the United States for months after their initial emergency use authorization by the Food and Drug Administration while production scaled up. The federal government distributed available vaccines to states proportionally, and states developed their own vaccine allocation plans and systems.

The Ohio draft allocation plan identified health care workers, first responders, and older adults and those in congregate settings as most at-risk of contracting or dying from COVID-19 and therefore in the first wave of vaccination priority. Although incarcerated individuals live in congregate settings, they were placed in the second phase in the draft plan, along with those working in corrections facilities. This showed some priority to incarcerated individuals. But given that incarcerated persons contract COVID-19 at four to five times the rate of those in the free world, this planned prioritization was insufficient (Lanphier 2020).

When it came to implementing a COVID-19 vaccination strategy, Ohio never prioritized its incarcerated population (Lanphier 2021). Ohio modified its vaccine strategy multiple times during the rollout period, and corrections workers moved to an earlier allocation phase, while no priority was given to incarcerated individuals before the state made anyone 16 and over eligible for vaccination in April 2021.[1]

Prioritizing correctional staff, who are coming and going between corrections facilities and surrounding communities, might appear to be sufficient for stopping the virus from entering prisons and jails.

1. At the time, no vaccine was authorized for use in persons under age 16, though vaccines have now been authorized for and are being administered in persons under age 16 .

But the slow rate of vaccine acceptance among corrections workers—just like among the general Ohio public—has made it an inadequate approach. Ohio took steps to encourage and publicize its corrections workers' vaccinations (Lao 2021). According to communication directly from the ODRC, as of June 2021, 55.3 percent of corrections staff have received at least one dose of either a single- or two-dose COVID-19 vaccine. This left a significant portion of ODRC workers unvaccinated, moving amid free world communities that remained majority unvaccinated (the official Ohio government COVID dashboard reported that just 46.37 percent of all Ohioans were vaccinated as of August 6, 2021) even though all adults by this time had been eligible for vaccination against COVID-19 for several months, children ages 12 and up had recently become eligible, and concerns about vaccine shortages in the United States had diminished.[2]

By not prioritizing incarcerated individuals and instead making them eligible according to age and comborbidity group, there was no guarantee that vaccine doses would in fact be offered in prisons and jails, even to those qualifying for them. Outsiders in the community faced barriers to vaccine access related to scarcity of appointments, complex online appointment systems, constraints on time and transport to appointments, and general lack of information or misinformation about access, cost, and the vaccines themselves. Nearly all these constraints are exacerbated in corrections contexts when individuals cannot seek out a vaccination appointment for themselves. Vaccines must come to them.

The Franklin Medical Center, an ODRC facility housing medically vulnerable incarcerated individuals, did offer vaccines to its most vulnerable residents for medical reasons (Richmond 2020). Yet when another facility vaccinated incarcerated persons in phase 1 because they live in congregate settings, the Ohio Department of Health indicated this was out of line with its vaccination strategy (Gallek 2021).

Unlike many states, Ohio has no publicly accessible dashboard reflecting rates of vaccines offered or administered in its prisons and jails. The UCLA Covid Behind Bars project gives Ohio an "F" grade on its "Data Reporting & Quality Scorecard," in part because the state fails to make vaccination data available (UCLA n.d.). A selection of journalists and scholars, including the UCLA Law project, are receiving information directly from the ODRC via private email, and it has been used in limited media reporting. Similar to the rates

2. Only those 12 and up were eligible for vaccination as of this date.

of vaccinated ODRC staff as of June 2021, the ODRC reported 24,362 residents, or 53.5 percent, had received at least one dose of vaccine to prevent COVID-19 (UCLA n.d.).

The goal of systematically and transparently reporting ODRC vaccination rates of residents is not to regulate, monitor, or scrutinize vaccine uptake among incarcerated populations, who have the right to accept or refuse vaccination.[3] Instead, it is a way to create public accountability for ensuring equitable access to information and education about vaccines, as well as to the vaccines themselves. State and federal criminal justice systems prosecute, convict, and incarcerate individuals in the name of the people. The people should hold the state accountable for how it acts in their name.

During the pandemic, medical misinformation and distrust of government has been pervasive. Those were already features of incarcerated experience well before the pandemic. As John J. Lennon (2021) writes from state prison in New York:

> Distrust for the American government is almost palpable within the country's prison walls. Many incarcerated people doubt the vaccine's safety. Others question whether other substances will be shot into their arms. Administrators seldom build trusting relationships with prisoners. Now, with Covid-19 raising the stakes, that us-against-them mentality is putting all of us in danger.

Lack of COVID-19 data transparency contributes to distrust, and to the false idea that there is an "us" and a "them" when it comes to public health—an error which, as Lennon says, puts all of us in danger.

The Paradox of Individual Blame

The orthodoxy of corrections—that the individual bears singular responsibility for their situation—became the lens through which the pandemic was viewed in correctional settings. This approach fundamentally shaped Ohio's management of COVID in its prisons and jails. The eyes of the world were watching how Columbus

3. The BOP recommends, but does not require, routine vaccinations within incarcerated populations and issues guidance for recommended vaccinations, schedule, storage, and administration (Federal Bureau of Prisons 2018).

responded to the early, simultaneous crises in Marion and Pickaway Correctional Institutions. These first major outbreaks in correctional facilities could have acted as an early warning system, but Ohio failed to seize this moment, and other states followed suit, with disastrous consequences.

The self-responsibility narrative integral to Ohio's response to the COVID-19 pandemic in its prisons and jails illustrates a deeper paradox of mass incarceration in the United States. Incarcerated individuals are putatively entitled to a constitutional right to health care, yet this care is illusory. Even in a setting that, by definition, restricts individual agency—this restriction being the very punishment that incarceration exerts—incarcerated individuals were expected to, and, in fact, left to, realize their own health care. At the same time, every restriction was placed on their ability to do so. This was true of carceral health care prior COVID-19 and remained true during the pandemic.

One part of this paradoxical imposition of individual responsibility for health reflects a fundamental misunderstanding by policy makers, corrections facilities, and the general public in the free world about the role of punishment within the US carceral system. Another part of this paradox fails to imagine how a system of criminal justice could do justice better.

Regarding what punishment is: it is easy to imagine a lay public that hears of a deadly viral outbreak in a prison and thinks incarcerated persons are simply getting "what they deserve." Or they believe incarcerated folks should not have access to health care, or preventive measures like masks, hand sanitizer, or vaccines, as part of their punishment. The problem is none of these is the punishment to which the incarcerated were sentenced. The prohibition against cruel and unusual punishment ensured by the Eighth Amendment is exactly why incarcerated individuals have, at least on paper, a constitutional right to health care.

This paradox is not only a mistake about what punishment is, but also a misunderstanding about *why* punishment is, and how else it could be. As Elizabeth Lanphier has written with colleagues Takunda Matose and Abu Ali Abdur'Rahman, the notion of "rehabilitation" as a component to mass incarceration incorrectly supposes that individuals were adequately "habilitated" in the first place (Lanphier, Matose, and Abdur'Rahman 2019). A rehabilitation view of incarceration presumes that individuals had sufficient opportunity, education, and access to mental and physical health care (basic goods of "habilitation") and nonetheless individually failed by committing the crime(s) for which they are now incarcerated. According to this approach, the function of incarceration is to restore (*re*habilitate) individuals.

This not true for everyone caught up within the carceral system, however. For many people, this prior habilitated state is more myth than reality. A report from the Health Policy Institution of Ohio (2021) describes how involvement with carceral systems not only negatively impacts health, but how poor health, including mental health and substance abuse, increases the likelihood of involvement with the criminal justice system. Drug dependency, mental illness, and cognitive disability are all significantly overrepresented in US corrections facilities compared to the general population for a variety of reasons we cannot fully explore here. But incarceration does not cause these problems, nor is it designed to address and support them.

Better responses to individual actions that lead to incarceration may be in some, or even many, instances to support an individual to "habilitate," and to take community-oriented and shared-responsibility approaches to criminal justice. This is not to say that individuals cannot or should not be held accountable for their actions. Rather, it is to say that a more productive, healing, and preventive approach to criminal justice would be to target opportunities to habilitate during, but also prior to, one's involvement with the criminal justice system. In a sense, habilitation is a preventive health strategy for criminal justice. And if we have learned anything from the COVID-19 pandemic, it is that prevention is the best way to promote safe, healthy, vibrant communities—inside and outside of corrections facilities.

REFERENCES

American Civil Liberties Union (ACLU). 2020. "Decarceration and Crime during COVID-19." July 27, 2020. www.aclu.org/news/smart-justice/decarceration-and-crime-during-covid-19/.

Balmert, Jesse. 2020a. "Coronavirus in Ohio: DeWine Releases 105 Non-Violent Inmates Near End of Sentences." *Cincinnati Enquirer*, April 14, 2020. www.cincinnati.com/story/news/2020/04/14/coronavirus-ohio-lawmakers-recommend-release-141-non-violent-inmates-near-end-sentences/2990165001/.

Balmert, Jesse. 2020b. "Coronavirus in Ohio: Gov. Mike DeWine Plans to Release Some Prison Inmates Due to COVID-19." *Cincinnati Enquirer*, April 7, 2020. www.cincinnati.com/story/news/2020/04/07/coronavirus-ohio-gov-mike-dewine-give-update-covid-19-response-prison-population/2961390001/.

Barsky, Benjamin, Eric Reinhart, Paul Farmer, and Salmaan Keshavjee. 2021. "Vaccination Plus Decarceration—Stopping Covid-19 in Jails and Prisons." *New England Journal of Medicine* 384, no. 17: 1583–1585. https://doi.org/10.1056/NEJMp2100609.

Bliss, Kevin. 2020. "Ohio Prisoner with Coronavirus Released without Use of Preventative Measures; Cases inside Soaring." *Prison Legal News.* June 1, 2020. www.prisonlegalnews.org/news/2020/jun/1/ohio-prisoner-coronavirus-released-without-use-preventative-measures-cases-inside-soaring/.

Chappell, Bill. 2020. "73% of Inmates at an Ohio Prison Test Positive for Coronavirus." NPR, April 20, 2020. www.npr.org/sections/coronavirus-live-updates/2020/04/20/838943211/73-of-inmates-at-an-ohio-prison-test-positive-for-coronavirus.

Daza, Sebastian, Alberto Palloni, and Jarrett Jones. 2020. "The Consequences of Incarceration for Mortality in the United States." *Demography* 57: 577–598. https://doi.org/10.1007/s13524-020-00869-5.

DeShaney v. Winnebago Cty. DSS, 489 U.S. 189 (1989).

Estelle v. Gamble, 429 U.S. 97 (1976).

Federal Bureau of Prisons. 2018. "Immunization: Federal Bureau of Prisons Clinical Guidance." www.bop.gov › immunization_201808. www.bop.gov/resources/pdfs/immunization_201808.pdf

Gallek, Peggy. 2021. "Some Geuga County Inmates Get COVID-19 Vaccine Ahead of Elderly." Fox 8 News, January 21, 2021. https://fox8.com/news/coronavirus/some-geauga-county-inmates-get-covid-19-ahead-of-elderly/.

Gifford, Elizabeth J. 2019. "How Incarceration Affects the Health of Communities and Families." *North Carolina Medical Journal* 80, no. 6: 372–375.

Gramlich, John. 2020. "Black Imprisonment Rate in the U.S. Has Fallen by a Third since 2006." Pew Research Center. May 6, 2020. www.pewresearch.org/fact-tank/2020/05/06/share-of-black-white-hispanic-americans-in-prison-2018-vs-2006/.

Guenther, Lisa. 2013. *Solitary Confinement: Social Death and its Afterlives.* Minneapolis: University of Minnesota Press.

Health Policy Institute of Ohio. 2021. "Connection between Criminal Justice and Health." June 9, 2021. www.healthpolicyohio.org/connections-between-criminal-justice-and-health/.

Herring, Tia. 2020. "Prisons Shouldn't Be Charging Medical Co-Pays—Especially during a Pandemic." Prison Policy Initiative. December 21, 2020. www.prisonpolicy.org/blog/2020/12/21/copay-survey/.

Kanno-Youngs, Zolan, and Maura Turcotte. 2021. "Thousands of Prisoners Were Sent Home Because of Covid. They Don't Want to Go Back." *New York Times,* June 27, 2021. www.nytimes.com/2021/06/27/us/politics/biden-prison-coronavirus.html.

Kasler, Karen. 2020. "Coronavirus in Ohio: DeWine Won't Ramp Up Release of Prison Inmates." WOSU, July 20, 2020. https://news.wosu.org/news/2020-07-20/coronavirus-in-ohio-dewine-wont-ramp-up-release-of-prison-inmates.

Lanphier, Elizabeth. 2020. "Prisoners, at Great Risk, Should Get Vaccines Early." *Columbus Dispatch,* December 21, 2020. www.dispatch.com/story/opinion/columns/2020/12/21/column-prisoners-great-risk-should-get-vaccine-early/3931465001/.

Lanphier, Elizabeth. 2021. "Ohio's Vaccination Plan Used to Include Incarcerated People. Now It Doesn't." *Cincinnati Enquirer,* March 25, 2021. www.cincinnati.com/story/opinion/2021/03/25/opinion-ohios-vaccination-plan-used-include-incarcerated-people-now-doesnt/6986558002/.

Lanphier, Elizabeth, Takunda Matose, and Abu Ali Abdur'Rahman. 2019. "(Re) Imagining (Re)habilitation: An Argument from Death Row." *Public Philosophy Journal* 2, no. 2. https://doi.org/10.25335/ppj.2.2-04.

Lao, Jennifer. 2021. "Communication of COVID-19 Related Policies in February 2021." Covid Prison Project. April 21, 2021. https://covidprisonproject.com/blog/data/communication-of-covid-19-related-policies-in-february-2021/.

Lennon, John. J. 2021. "How Vaccine Hesitancy Spread in My Prison." *New York Times*, May 24, 2021. www.nytimes.com/2021/05/24/opinion/covid-vaccine-hesitancy-prison.html.

Lopez, L., L. H. Hart, and M. H. Katz. 2021. "Racial and Ethnic Health Disparities Related to COVID-19." *JAMA* 325, no. 8: 719–720. https://doi.org/10.1001/jama.2020.26443.

Marshall Project. 2021. "A State-By-State Look at 15 Months of Coronavirus in Prisons." June 25, 2021. www.themarshallproject.org/2020/05/01/a-state-by-state-look-at-coronavirus-in-prisons#prisoner-state.

National Academies of Sciences, Engineering, and Medicine. 2020a. "Decarcerating Correctional Facilities during COVID-19: Advancing Health, Equity, and Safety." Washington, DC: National Academies Press. https://doi.org/10.17226/25945.

National Academies of Sciences, Engineering, and Medicine. 2020b. *Framework for Equitable Allocation of COVID-19 Vaccine.* Washington, DC: National Academies Press. https://doi.org/10.17226/25917.

National Commission on COVID-19 and Criminal Justice. 2020. "Impact Report: COVID-19 and Prisons." December 6, 2020. https://covid19.councilo ncj.org/2020/12/06/impact-report-covid-19-and-prisons/.

Reinhart Eric, and Daniel L. Chen. 2020. "Incarceration and Its Disseminations: COVID-19 Pandemic Lessons From Chicago's Cook County Jail." *Health Affairs* 39, no. 8: 1412–1418. https://doi.org/10.1377/hlthaff.2020.00652.

Restoration of Rights Project. 2020. "50 State Comparison Pardon Policy & Practice." Collateral Consequences Resource Center. Accessed August 6, 2021. https://ccresourcecenter.org/state-restoration-profiles/50-state-comparison characteristics-of-pardon-authorities-2/.

Richmond, Matthew. 2020. "Ohio Begins Vaccinating Some Prison Inmates and Staff." WOSU Public Media, December 29, 2020. https://news.wosu.org/ideastr eam/2020-12-29/ohio-begins-vaccinating-some-prison-inmates-and-staff.

Saloner, Brendan, Kalind Parish, Julie A. Ward, Grace DiLaura, and Sharon Dolovich. 2020. "COVID-19 Cases and Deaths in Federal and State Prisons." *JAMA* 324, no. 6: 602–603. https://doi.org/10.1001/jama.2020.12528.

Schatz, Brian. 2021. "Following COVID-19 Outbreaks in Prisons Last Year, Schatz Reintroduces Bill to Improve Compassionate Release Process." Press Release. June 17, 2021. www.schatz.senate.gov/news/press-releases/following-covid-19-outbreaks-in-prisons-last-year-schatz-reintroduces-bill-to-improve-compa ssionate-release-process-and-protect-public-health.

Segura, Melissa. 2021. "How Do You Social Distance In Prison? You Don't. You Get COVID." *Buzzfeed News*, January 21, 2021. Accessed August 6, 2021. www.buzz feednews.com/article/melissasegura/prisons-covid-clemency

Sundaresh, Ram, Youngmin Yi, Tyler D. Harvey, Brita Roy, Carley Riley, Hedwig Lee, Christopher Wildeman, and Emily A. Wang. 2021. "Exposure to Family Member

Incarceration and Adult Well-Being in the United States." *JAMA Netw Open* 4, no. 5: e2111821. https://doi.org/10.1001/jamanetworkopen.2021.11821.

UCLA Law COVID Behind Bars Data Project. n.d. Accessed June 17, 2021. https://uclacovidbehindbars.org/states/ohio.

US Sentencing Commission. 2021. *Compassionate Release Data Report, Calendar Year 2020*. www.ussc.gov/sites/default/files/pdf/research-and-publications/federal-sentencing-statistics/compassionate-release/20210609-Compassionate-Release.pdf.

Vest, Noel, Oshea Johnson, Kathryn Nowotny, and Lauren Brinkley-Rubinstein. 2021. "Prison Population Reductions and COVID-19: A Latent Profile Analysis Synthesizing Recent Evidence from the Texas State Prison System." *Journal of Urban Health* 98: 53–58. https://doi.org/10.1007/s11524-020-00504-z.

WTOL Newsroom. 2020. "2 High Profile Prisoners Have Sentence Commuted by DeWine amid Coronavirus Crisis." WTOL, April 17, 2020. www.wtol.com/article/news/health/coronavirus/ohio-prisoners-sentences-commuted/512-3786f7da-1d88-4d6f-b57c-6e18ce89e6c6.

11 | Cincinnati and COVID

The Urgent Need for African American Doctors

Research Article

Edward V. Wallace

In this research piece, a scholar of Africana studies and community health analyzes the underrepresentation of African Americans among physicians as a factor behind racial disparities in COVID-19 infection rates and outcomes.

Introduction

This chapter shows that, before the coronavirus hit, there were inequalities in healthcare and that, during the COVID-19 pandemic, the inequalities in healthcare remained the same or even worsened for people from underserved populations. Specifically, I focus on the consequences of the underrepresentation of African Americans in the medical workforce. I argue that our healthcare system needs to look at the continued lack of trust of the healthcare system, and the connection between education and healthcare professionals. The chapter also includes a face-to-face interview with one of the top African American physicians in Cincinnati, Ohio, regarding the urgent need for more African American physicians. The chapter concludes with why it's important to have diversity in the field of medicine.

The United States spends more on healthcare than any other country and has the worst healthcare outcomes (Tikkanen and Abrams 2020). African Americans in particular are more likely to die of cancer and diabetes than their white counterparts (NAACP 2006). Furthermore, African Americans are approximately 15 percent less likely than white Americans to have access to health insurance (NAACP 2006). When it comes to the coronavirus, it is estimated that the virus has killed over one million people in the United States since the start of the COVID-19 outbreak (Sergio and Wu 2022). Nationwide, everyone has been impacted by COVID-19, but the per capita death rate for African Americans was almost twice as high as the white rate and more than twice as high as the Asian rate (Leonhardt 2022).

In Hamilton County, Ohio, African Americans had a total of 45,000 cases, and a total of 609 deaths from the coronavirus (Ohio Department of Health 2022). During the height of the pandemic, the message was "we are all in this together" despite our race, religion, sexual orientation, ethnicity, socioeconomic status, age, gender, and educational attainment (Kullar et al. 2020).

At the local level, the Cincinnati Health Department traced quite a few COVID-19 cases by zip code. The results (available only through 2020) continued to reveal that communities of color were being hit the hardest. Across Cincinnati's 52 neighborhoods, African Americans were disproportionally being affected by the coronavirus. In Westwood, a predominately African American neighborhood, there were 209 COVID-19 cases in the early months of the pandemic compared to the predominately white neighborhoods of Hyde Park, which had 20 cases, and Oakley which had 29 (Maloney 2020). Similarly, in Evanston, another predominately African American neighborhood where some of the first cases of COVID-19 hit hard and fast, there were 112.2 cases per 100,000. This was higher than the national capital rate for the same time period for all of Ohio, which is 72 cases per 100,000 people (Londberg 2020).

African American Ohioans living in poverty and in overcrowded conditions or who work low-paying service jobs have very little opportunity to "social distance" or work from home (Laurencin and McClinton 2020). This has put African Americans at greater risk of being exposed to COVID-19 especially when they suffer from an array of preexisting health conditions such as heart disease, diabetes, and cancer (Gibson 2020). Under COVID, the high numbers of morbidity and mortality in communities of color unveiled the enduring socioeconomic and racial divide that has plagued Ohio for decades. In cities such as Cincinnati, Cleveland, Akron, and Columbus, African Americans were filling hospital beds and being put on ventilators at an astonishing rate compared to their white counterparts (Francisco 2021; Mills 2021; Zuckerman 2020).

Particularly worth mentioning were the number of under-represented African American doctors in the healthcare profession before the pandemic began to spread. African Americans make up 42 percent of the population of Cincinnati, yet less than 5 percent are physicians (AAMC, 2018). The number of African American medical students rose from 5.6 percent in 1980 to 7.7 percent in 2016, which can be seen as a huge accomplishment, but is still far short of 42 percent. (O'Donnell and Robinson 2019). This disparity hampers efforts to build trust of medical professionals among African American patients and it is an important factor behind the disproportionate impact of COVID in the African American community.

The Continued Lack of Trust among Black Ohioans about the Health-Care System

White professionals dominate the health-care industry (Kennedy, Mathis, and Woods 2007). According to Cort (2004), because of this disparity between white and Black health-care professionals, many African American patients mistrust health-care providers, to the point there is no cultural connection between them. When white health-care providers are dismissive of their patients, or regarded as racist and ignorant of culturally relevant medical issues, this has the potential to cause friction between the patient and the health-care provider. African Americans are justified in not trusting the health-care system. It's a system that systematically denied Blacks from being trained in medicine and becoming members of professional organizations. It's a system that not only justified racial inferiority but also conducted experiments without the consent of Black participants. The Tuskegee experiment, in particular, is one of the oldest deterrents to African Americans trusting the health-care system (Hamilton et al. 2006). LaViest, Nickerson, and Bowie (2000), conducted a study to examine attitudes about racism and mistrust among African American and white cardiac patients, and found a consistent racial disparity in reports of racism and a high incidence of medical mistrust and discrimination on the part of African Americans toward medical providers. Another, similar study conducted nearly two decades later revealed some African American males avoided medical exams and taking prescription medications due to mistrust of health-care providers and the health-care system (Hoffman, Trawaiter, Axt, and Oliver 2016).

The fact that there is still mistrust of medical providers by African Americans is alarming. A study found that African American parents have a growing concern about vaccinations based on faulty scientific information, which has resulted in measles outbreaks (Jaiswal and Halkitis 2019). In addition, the AIDS Foundation found increased speculation and mistrust with regard to pre-exposure prophylaxis (PrEP) to avert HIV infections, again based on misinformation (POZ 2017). In Cincinnati, the early campaign to distribute the COVID-19 vaccine failed to connect with several Black residents, due to their lack of trust in the health system. In an interview with CNBC News, the associate dean of the medical school at the University of Cincinnati talks about trust in the Black community.

> She said, "They want to know and have real reasons to trust. They want to know that the process is going to be fair, that they are not being guinea pigs to a system that is rigged against them." (2020, 1)

During the first six weeks of the vaccine rollout, there were no vaccine sites in four of the ten Hamilton County zip codes (College Hill, Pleasant Ridge, Kennedy Heights, and Avondale). These zip codes have some of the highest percentages of African American residents in the entire city of Cincinnati, but very little has been done to develop trust and get information about the vaccine to Black residents so that they can make informed decisions for themselves and their families (Saker and DeMio 2021).

Despite all the current research and precautions regarding vaccine safety, many Black Ohioans still will not get the vaccine shot. According to a CNBC News report (Lovelace, 2021), a 28-year-old Black attorney shared his thoughts on receiving the Johnson and Johnson vaccine:

> He said, "I see the J&J's vaccine as inferior because its only 72% effective compared to 95% of the other two vaccines. Why go for 72 when you can get 95?" he said. "Just because it is the easiest thing to do because you only have to get one shot does not mean it's the right thing to do." (2021, 2)

This is just one example of how African Americans in Cincinnati are hesitant about the vaccine and have lingering concerns about its effectiveness. The Center For Closing the Health Gap, a nonprofit organization in Cincinnati, conducted a study alongside the Kaiser Family Foundation and found that 35 percent of black adults stated that they would most likely not get the vaccine (Saker and DeMio 2021).

The executive director of the Center For Closing the Health Gap shared this reflection on their hesitancy to get a COVID-19 vaccination:

> She said, "I've read somewhere that we need 70% to 75% of the population to get vaccinated in order to reach herd immunity. We need to meet people where they are, but vaccine hesitancy cannot be erased. I have reservations and questions about the vaccine." (2021, 3)

The city of Cincinnati reflects national attitudes of mistrust by Black Americans toward the health-care system (Hostetter, and Klein, 2021). The mistrust of the health-care system by Black Ohioans can also be attributed to local decisions. For example, as the world became aware of the seriousness of the pandemic, adults taking care of their parents and grandparents had to consider who would look after their parents and grandparents if they were to become ill themselves from COVID-19 (Muttilo, 2020). According to the American Community Survey of the United States,196,000 Black Ohioans provide kinship care to their parents and grandparents (Muttilo 2020). These Black Ohioans could also be considered "essential" frontline workers, and should have been included as a prioritized group to receive the vaccine shot early during the pandemic. Many people of color have multigenerational families living under one roof for socioeconomic and cultural reasons. According to a Pew Research study, 26 percent of Black households reported living in multigenerational family households, compared to 16 percent of white households (Schroeder 2020).

At the height of the pandemic, some Ohioans of color could not avoid in-person shopping for groceries, medical supplies, and other household items, which ultimately put some of their loved ones at the greatest risk of contracting the virus when they returned home. According to Carlisle (2020), for many underrepresented communities, grocery shopping has become one of the most anxiety-producing activities during the pandemic due to the high risk of coming in contact with people who may have COVID-19.

The trauma of being forgotten and pushed to the side by governmental policies and the medical establishment is well etched into Black Ohioans' historical memory.

When it came time to distribute COVID-19 vaccines in 2021, Governor Mike DeWine did not assess Black Ohioans' needs through a health equity lens, which reinforced their mistrust of the health-care system.

Connections between Education and Health-Care Professionals

The proportion of racial/ethnic minorities in the United States is continuing to rise, but the number of minorities receiving a quality education to enter into the health-care profession is not advancing at the same rate (Rao and Flores 2007). It has been estimated that the statistically appropriate ratio of African American physicians to the overall population should be somewhere around 218 per 100,000; however, the ratio presently stands at just 73 per 100,000 (Rao and Flores 2007). African Americans make up only 4.4 percent of all US physicians and surgeons A high-quality education for African Americans is essential for diversifying the health-care workforce and providing access to people from underserved populations (Rao and Flores 2007).

This situation has made Ohio ill-equipped to deal with the coronavirus pandemic and to eliminate health disparities, especially among people of color. The lack of African American physicians not only means fewer patients will be able to be treated by African American physicians, but it also means that very few African American students will be mentored by people who look like them. Rao and Flores (2007) conducted focus-group interviews with 12 African American high-school juniors attending a public school in the Midwest in which 89 percent of the students are African American. The qualitative study showed that, among high school students African Americans were less likely to be mentored by a physician of the same race, compared to white students. The same study showed that, among African American students, there was a lack of emphasis on grades, advanced coursework, and college admissions, all of which are important to becoming a physician or entering into the health-care profession (Rao and Flores 2007). One teenager said,

> "I think as black people we really paying the price. You go to those suburban schools they really focus on grades. Like these classes that we have, they probably have taken them their freshman year. They really focus on education and teach them about college. They be so far ahead of us." (2007, 989)

A lack of rigorous education and exposure to medicine puts many African Americans at a disadvantage when it comes becoming a physician or medical researcher. This ultimately means fewer African American students in the State of Ohio will enter Research 1 institutions to help advance knowledge in the field of medicine about COVID-19 and its impact on people of color.

The Perspective from an African American Physician

One of the leading African American physicians in Cincinnati, Ohio, spoke to the need to increase the number of African American physicians. "Dr. Dawes" (whose real name has been changed to protect his privacy) is a board-certified physician with over 30 years of medical experience. He graduated from the University of Toledo College of Medicine and Life Sciences. Dr. Dawes understands that, despite the marvels of modern medicine and the rapid advances in medical information, chronic and infectious diseases are increasing at an extraordinary rate. He is a firm believer in the philosophy "An ounce of prevention is worth a pound of cure." In keeping with his focus on disease prevention, Dr. Dawes shifted his medical practice from treating illness to promoting health and wellness.

Dr. Dawes is the associate medical director with a national managed care company and he shares his medical knowledge through treating obesity, chairing health and wellness committees, and giving time to at-risk young men. In addition, he is involved in hosting radio programs, presenting keynotes at conferences, and writing health and wellness articles for newspapers and magazines. His number one goal is to improve an individual's quality of life through good health, which Dr. Dawes believes is for everyone.

Interview

Author: How did you know as a child that you wanted to be a physician?

Dr. Dawes: Most kids when they are in elementary school are often asked by their parents or other relatives what do they want to be when they grow up. I like to tell people that I was never asked that question because I did not choose the medical field, the medical field chose me. My grandmother died of a heart attack. My aunt died of a stroke, and my older brother died from an asthma attack. My entire life I had to witness my family and friends get their lives cut short due to some health condition. I guess this is when I realized I wanted to be a doctor to help my family, friends, and people in my community as much as possible. I also was a good student and did well in my science courses in high school.

Author: Is it fair to say that you support STEM and that it's dear to your heart?

Dr. Dawes: I wholeheartedly support STEM and think more Black students should look into STEM careers.

Author: As you know, this book chapter is about the need for more Black doctors and scientists. I'm curious in hearing your thoughts as to whether you think the number of deaths due to COVID in the Black community could have been reduced if we had more Black doctors and scientists?

Dr. Dawes: As you know COVID-19 has caused many Black people in Cincinnati to suffer. Either you had the virus or you knew of someone who had the virus. I believe we would see a decline in the number of deaths in the Black community if we had more Black doctors and scientists. People tend to trust and gravitate towards people who look like them and have shared experiences. If we had more Black doctors and scientists developing PPE equipment, giving out masks, and in leadership roles, while conducting clinical trials for vaccines, then Black people in the community will support these efforts because the Black community would feel as if these Black doctors and scientist are trying to help them.

Author: It's been projected by 2042 people of color will be the majority in the United States. If this is true, why is it important to have more Blacks trained in medicine?

Dr. Dawes: This is an issue that we as a society cannot afford to wait to address. Minorities in our society are becoming the majority and it's happening very quickly. If we just look at the last couple of elections, politicians have won because minorities swayed the outcome with their votes. I will share with you a story. My brother has hypertension. His doctor told him that there are some new medications available that he should consider. It turned out that that this new medication seems to work better than other medications in African Americans. Since my brother had the same Black doctor for years, the same skin color as his doctor, and he trusts his doctor, he decided to take the medication. That's just one example of why we should train more Blacks in medicine. If my brother's doctor was white, I'm not sure if my brother would have complied with taking the medication.

Author: When I first moved to Cincinnati, Ohio, I was told that the demographics in Cincinnati were changing, so much that the number of Blacks almost equals the number of whites in the city. Is that true?

Dr. Dawes: That is true. Depending on which data you look at. It's been said that African Americans in Cincinnati, Ohio, make up almost 50 percent of the city's population.

Author: Ok then. Well, since there are so many Blacks in the city, why haven't we seen more people of color entering and graduating from medical school and STEM programs?

Dr. Dawes: We have gotten better with making sure more people of color get accepted into medical school, but we still have a long way to go, especially if we want to be prepared for the next pandemic. I would say we don't necessarily have to have extremely high numbers of students in medical school to make an impact in the Black community. Having some Black doctors and scientists in the Black community is always better than having none at all.

Author: So even with the small number of Black doctors and scientists we can still have an impact?

Dr. Dawes: We can but it depends on what type of problem we are trying to solve. But for a pandemic of this magnitude, we need more Black doctors and scientists in our Black communities.

Author: As it relates to diversity in our colleges and universities, it seems we cannot get over the hurdle when it comes to diversity of faculty and students. We do a fantastic job talking about the problem, but very little is done in terms of having a solution. So from your years of experience in the medical field as an African American doctor, what would you recommend in terms of adding more diversity when it comes to faculty and students?

Dr. Dawes: Well, from my standpoint, I can tell you that we need to start exposing minorities to medicine and STEM when they are young. We need to see to it that students are learning in elementary and high school. There used to be an old TV commercial that came on television that said, "A mind is a terrible thing to waste." There are a lot of bright Black and Hispanic children in Cincinnati, but we don't see these children in our universities because we are not targeting them early and exposing them to the many possibilities of medicine and STEM. I had an African American student once who struggled in mathematics and science. But I worked with her all the time to sharpen her skills. Later on, she turned out to become a physician and is currently doing well in the discipline. I lived in Cincinnati for a very long time and during my stay here I've gone to poor people's houses and spoken to African American parents because I know that their son or daughter has the potential to become a doctor, but they just need a little help and exposure to the discipline.

Author: So your recommendation is to do what?

Dr. Dawes: That we never assume that because someone is poor or has not had much exposure to certain things in life that they are less intelligent than the next person. I feel as though it's simply a sign that someone has not had the same opportunity as other people in life. There are poor black students in Cincinnati who can perform and, in some cases, outshine those students who live in the rich areas of Cincinnati. The only difference is that they have not had the type of training and opportunities that those students have had living in those [better resourced] communities.

Author: I would like to go back to what you said earlier about children learning in schools from K–12 and getting exposure to medicine and STEM. In Cincinnati, some schools are performing below level. However, there are students in those same schools who are accelerating in their academics and want to go to college. How do we ultimately get these students into medical school and STEM programs? What would be your approach?

Dr. Dawes: When I was going to college we had the Educational Opportunity Program (EOP) that we could rely on as students. The EOP program mainly took inner-city kids who had the academics to excel in college, but did not have the finances to pay for college. This was a program that was designed to have students excel in whatever area of study they were interested in while in college. I'm not sure if this program still exists because this was back in the day, but it sure worked because it kept me on track.

Author: As we begin to wrap up our conversation, do you have any final thoughts that you want to share in terms of why it's important to have more Black doctors and scientists?

Dr. Dawes: The one thing that I want to add to this discussion is what we talked about where African Americans make up 50 percent of the city's population. However, the

> number of Black doctors and scientists in Cincinnati do not reflect the city's population. When I was an undergraduate student in the 1970s, I studied pre-med and there were hardly any Black students taking any science courses. We were talking about diversity, equity, and inclusion back then, but we just called it affirmative action. When I got into medical school, the number of Blacks in my class was even less than my undergraduate experience. What saddens me the most today [is that] I am still talking about the need for more Black doctors and scientists, especially during a pandemic.

Racial Disparities in Medicine and the Need for African American Doctors

According to the larger literature on racism and discrimination, there is no doubt that racism has changed from "Jim Crow laws" to more subtle racism, including in health care. A few studies reveal racial disparities in medicine (Williams and Rucker 2000; Council on Ethical and Judicial Affairs 1990; Nong et al. 2020).

It is unlikely that personal discrimination is the sole reason for disparities in medicine and a lack of African American doctors in the discipline. Institutional racism and the social determinants of health are just as important as individual racism (Williams and Rucker 2000). There are a number of explanations, which include lack of resources for students, medical schools being passive about their recruitment methods of African Americans, lack of diversity among medical school professors and staff, and advisers discouraging minorities from applying to medical school (Lupkin 2016).

Whether it's personal racism or institutional racism, negative attitudes toward people of color do not increase the number of African American doctors and bring about equity, especially when the health-care system and structural conditions are unequal. Focusing on increasing the number of African American doctors in the field of medicine creates a pathway toward health equity that will help everyone beat back the pandemic. The present author proposes a series of ideas that might increase the likelihood of more African Americans entering into the field of medical research.

Address Root Causes of Underrepresented African Americans in Medicine to Prevent the Next Pandemic

Addressing the root cause of why African Americans are underrepresented in medicine requires real-world solutions if we are ever to assuage the COVID-19 health crisis in African American communities. The primary concern for the health-care industry should be admitting that racism and bias are commonplace within the health profession. In the medical field, most bias is not seen as intentional. Most discrimination is unconscious and occurs without the person thinking or realizing that they are being discriminatory toward another group of people (Allen 1995). Research has shown that implicit bias is normal and pervasive (American Psychological Association 2012). All humans are biased; it is universal (Fiske et al. 2009). Biases develop through everyday social interactions, culture, and media. These biases guide how we interact with one another and often become harmful, especially when we make generalizations or assumptions about a group of people and apply these biases to a single individual (Williams and Cooper 2019). Many racial stereotypes and biases occur automatically, even by people who do not endorse and, in fact, are opposed to racist beliefs (Devine 1989). For example, a study showed that fictional patients who were presented as unemployed and African American were given lower health priority scores and received greater resentment than fictional patients who were described as unemployed and white. Respondents in the study gave lower health-care priority scores, and were more reluctant to contribute to the health-care costs of the fictional African American patients (Williams and Rucker 2000).

In Cincinnati, medical schools can put their ideas into action to address the root causes of underrepresented African Americans in medicine by making a citywide effort to confront disparities in medical education. Revising our courses and curricula is one of the ways to address the problem. As academics, we should make sure our courses value diversity, equity, and inclusion and should reflect on whom we omit and deter from pursuing careers in the field of medicine through the content of our coursework and lectures. Finally, we need to analyze for whom our coursework and curricula are designed and whether they take into consideration students' backgrounds and cultures.

Detect Bias and Discrimination at Medical Schools

More research is needed to identify specific strategies that medical schools can implement, continuously, to detect and respond to patterns of discrimination when it comes to admissions into medical school. It has been recommended that medical schools develop an anonymous reporting system to detect incidents of systematically biased decision-making (Noah 1998). A study found that it was crucial to creating an environment that encourages reporting as part of the workplace by using three strategies for detecting discrimination: direct observation, focus groups, and voluntary reporting (Leape 1997). The occurrence of discrimination in medical schools suggests that reporting should be encouraged at every level. The National Committee of Vital and Health Statistics, (1993), an advisory committee to the Department of Health and Human Services, called for the reporting of discrimination cases in a database that could be open to the public and analyzed by civil rights lawyers who can speak on behalf of medical students that have been discriminated against by the medical profession. The United Nations Human Rights Office has developed a database, the main purpose of which is to combat racism and racial discrimination at the international level. The State of Ohio might create a similar database that could empower its medical schools to fight racism and racial discrimination. This would act as a bridge between medical schools and the public by allowing members of the public to see firsthand which medical schools in the United States are continuing to promote racism and discrimination within their institution.

Another idea for combating racism at medical schools would be for top administrators and faculty to practice self-criticism and self-examination, and to examine what privileges and powers they hold and how they exercise them. Administrators and faculty should self-examine how their biases and privileges take up space and silence others. In addition, administrators and faculty should ask themselves what knowledge are they missing when they do not admit more

African Americans to medical school? And how do they hold themselves accountable for their admissions policies?

Increase the Number of African American Physicians through Mentorship

More research is needed on increasing Ohio's number of Black physicians and other health-care professionals through mentorship and advising (George 2020). Many African American children want to become doctors when they grow up. However, many of these same children never come across a physician with brown skin until they go to college, leaving many children to navigate the pre-med educational requirements on their own. A study conducted by the University of Texas Health Center found that over half of first-year medical students never grew up having mentors or physicians who looked like them in the position that the students wanted to be in. Many respondents in the study reported doing Google searches and asking people whom they did not know, and did not know if they could trust, to mentor them and help them find their way (George 2020). Another study showed that many African American medical students who are first-generation doctors often experience a great deal of racism and receive little support when it comes to seeking advice from people who have been in similar professional situations (Yousry 2021).

A strategy that could be implemented in Ohio which would increase the number of African American physicians in medicine would be to incorporate more mentorship opportunities into pre-med programs and medical schools for people of color who have previously been excluded. Health-care professionals can make sure that African American students are engaging in mentorship activities that question and critique white supremacy and oppression in medicine. Finally, health-care professionals can develop a process where African American youth are connected with mentors who have shared life experiences and who may be able to lessen the effects of racial discrimination.

Representation matters. When young African American boys and girls see positive role models making sacrifices to better their community, it truly has a profound effect on their motivation and perseverance in life. Having mentors and proper advisers who have similar stories and backgrounds as other African Americans who aspire to be physicians, can be a great resource for students to learn how to navigate the waters of medical schools and better prepare students for the medical profession.

Diversifying the Medical and Health-Care Profession

Having a health-care system that is similar to the racial and ethnic population that an individual will serve is crucial during a pandemic. With the US population becoming more diverse within the last 25 years and underrepresented minorities becoming the majority, increasing diversity in the medical profession is in the best interest of medicine during the COVID 19 pandemic. During the last 55 years, several affirmative action policies have been implemented to eliminate health disparities in the medical and health-care profession. Unfortunately, many of these affirmative action policies tended to benefit women more than they did minorities (Williams and Cooper 2019). For instance, the number of females who graduated from medical school (most being white) increased from 6.9 percent in 1965 to 46.3 percent in 2016 (Association of American Medical Colleges 2016). On the other hand, African Americans and Latino women have seen much smaller increases. In 2015, African American women were 5.7 percent and Latino women were 4.6 percent of medical school graduates. Gallegos (2016) reported that the number of applicants (black men) being accepted into medical school has remained stagnant for nearly 40 years. In 1978, 1,410 black men applied to US medical schools. In 2014, that number was 1,337. This data put a spotlight on the fact that it is not enough to just open the doors of opportunity. A great way to implement more diversity in the medical field is to enforce policies that encourage health organizations to hire diverse applicants. This ensures that no matter who walks into a medical setting, there will be an African American physician who can identify with the patient, communicate with the patient, and better serve the patient's needs. Everyone, regardless of race, ethnicity, socioeconomic status, and gender, must be given the opportunity to enter medical school if we are going to protect the future of African Americans and other people of color.

Discussion

This is the first book chapter (to the author's knowledge) that explains why there is a need for more African American doctors in Ohio based on the health disparities that existed before the coronavirus pandemic and the disparities that have continued to exist for all people of color during the pandemic. Understanding that a lack of education can cause

African American students to be less likely to become a physician or to enter medical school is something that cannot be ignored. African Americans need to receive a quality education so they can become future physicians. Mentorship is another area that needs to grow in the medical profession for African American medical students. Having an African American physician that you can trust and share similar life experiences with is a great way to help medical students find their way through medical school.

Finally, the interview with Dr. Dawes reflects the need for more African American doctors. Dr. Dawes explains how we might have seen a decline in the number of deaths due to COVID-19 in the African American community if we already had more African American doctors. Unless we expose more African American students to medicine, we will not be fully prepared to combat the next pandemic or close the health disparities gap.

Conclusion

Eliminating health disparities and racial inequalities in the health-care profession during a pandemic is neither simple nor straightforward. The complexity of this problem is much greater than most researchers can imagine. There is much that we need to learn about COVID-19 and its impact on the African American community. However, one of the most promising ways to ensure communities of color receive health equity during any pandemic is to increase the representation of African Americans in the field of medicine. This will require empathy from those in power and improvements in all aspects of the health-care system. It is not enough just to be aware of the problem. There needs to be an emotional connection among current medical professionals and the students who might be inspired to enter the medical field.

If we are going to make real progress in reducing health disparities, especially during a pandemic, there must be wide social agreement that the lack of African American doctors is unacceptable. As Dr. Dawes did in his interview, medical experts need to share their experiences and tell the story about the lack of African American doctors, so there is a meaningful connection not only between white and Black Americans but for all communities of color, which will allow us to be prepared to handle the next public health crisis.

REFERENCES

AAMC. 2018. *Diversity in Medicine Facts and Figures*. Accessed October 26, 2022. www.aamc.org/data-reports/workforce/interactive-data/figure-18-percentage-all-active-physicians-race/ethnicity-2018.

Allen, Jessie. 1995. "Remedy for Unthinking Discrimination." *Brooklyn Law Review* 61(Winter): 1299–1345.

American Psychological Association Presidential Task Force on Preventing Discrimination and Promoting Diversity. 2012. *Dual Pathways to a Better America: Preventing Discrimination and Promoting Diversity.* Washington, DC: American Psychological Association.

Association of American Medical Colleges. 2015–2016. *The State of Women in Academic Medicine: The Pipeline and Pathways to Leadership* (Table 1) Accessed January 4, 2019. www.aamc.org/data-reports/faculty-institutions/report/state-women-academic-medicine.

"Black-White Disparities in Health Care. AMA Council on Ethical and Judicial Affairs." 1990. *Connecticut Medicine* 54, no. 11: 625–628.

Carlisle, Madeleine. 2020. "How Can You Safely Grocery Shop in the Time of Coronavirus? Here's What Experts Suggest." *TIME magazine,* March 27, 2020. https://time.com/5810782/grocery-store-safety-coronavirus/.

Cort, Malcolm A. 2004. "Cultural Mistrust and the Use of Hospice Care: Challenges and Remedies." *Journal of Palliative Medicine* 71, no. 1: 63–71. https://doi.org/10.1089/109662104322737269.

Devine, Patricia G. 1989. "Stereotypes and Prejudice: Their Automatic and Controlled Components." *Journal of Personality and Social Psychology* 56: 5–18. https://doi.org/10.1037//0022-3514.56.1.55.

Fiske, Susan T., Hilary B. Bergsieker, Ann Marie Russell, and Lyle Williams. 2009. "Images of Black Americans: Then, 'Them,' and Now, 'Obama!'" *Du Bois Review* 6: 83–101. https://doi.org/10.1017/S1742058X0909002X.

Francisco, Courtney. 2021. "Cincinnati Hospital Beds Are Filling Up with Post-Holiday COVID-19 Surge." WCPO Channel 9 Cincinnati, January 14, 2021.

Gallegos, Alicia. 2016. "AAMC Report Shows Decline of Black Males in Medicine" AAMCNEWS. September 27, 2016.

George, Cindy. 2020. "Black Girl White Coat: A Mentoring Program with New MDs." Texas Medical Center. Accessed October 6, 2020. www.tmc.edu/news/2020/05/black-girl-white-coat-a-mentoring-program-with-new-m-d-s-and-momentum/.

Gibson, Chuck. 2020. "An Emerging Trend: Blacks Are Dying from Coronavirus at an Amazing Rate." *Loveland Beacon,* April 14, 2020.

Hamilton, Lynnae A., Paul D. Lyons, Roberta May, Charlie L. Swanson, and Robert Savage. 2006. "African American Community Attitudes and Perceptions towards Schizophrenia and Medical Research: An Exploratory Study." *Journal of National Medical Association* 98, no. 1: 18–27.

Hampton, Robert L., Raymond L. Crowel, and Thomas P. Gullotta, eds. 2006. *The State of the Disparity.* National Association for the Advancement of Colored People. https://epdf.pub/handbook-of-african-american-health.html.

Hoffman, Kelly, Sophia Trawaiter, Jordan R. Axt, and Norman M. Oliver. 2016. "Racial Bias in Pain Assessment and Treatment Recommendations and False Beliefs about Biological Differences between Blacks and Whites." *National Academy of Sciences* 113, no. 16: 4296–4301.

Hostetter, Martha, and Sarah Klein. 2021. "Understanding and Ameliorating Medical Mistrust Among Black Americans." *Advancing Health Equity,* January 14, 2021.

Jaiswal, Jessica, and Perry N. Halkitis. 2019. "Towards a More Inclusive and Dynamic Understanding of Medical Mistrust Informed by Science." *Behavioral Medicine* 45, no. 2 (2019): 79–85. https://doi.org/10.1080/08964289.2019.1619511.

Kennedy, Bernice, Christopher Mathis, and Angela Woods. 2007. "African Americans and Their Mistrust of the Health Care System: Health Care for Diverse Populations." *Journal of Cultural Diversity* 14, no. 2: 56–60.

Kullar, Ravina, Jasmine R. Marcelin, Talia H. Swartz, Damani A. Piggott, Raul Macias Gil, Trini A. Mathew, and Tina Tan. 2020. "Racial Disparity of Coronavirus Disease 2020 in African American Communities." *The Journal of Infectious Diseases* 222, no. 6: 890–893.

Laurencin, Cato T., and Aneesah McClinton. 2020. "The COVID-19 Pandemic: A Call to Action to Identify and Address Racial and Ethnic Disparities." *Journal of Racial Ethnic Health Disparities* 7, no. 3: 398–402. https://doi.org/10.1007/s40615-020-00756-0.

LaViest, Thomas, Kim J. Nickerson, and Janice V. Bowie. 2000. "Attitudes about Racism, Medical Mistrust, and Satisfaction with Care among African Americans and White Cardiac Patients." *Medical Care Research and Review* 57, no. 1: 146–161. https://doi.org/10.1177/1077558700057001S07.

Leape, Lucian L. 1997. "A Systems Analysis Approach to Medical Error." *Journal of Evaluation in Clinical Practice* 3, no. 3: 213–222.

Leonhardt, David. 2022. "Covid and Race." *New York Times,* June 9, 2022.

Londberg, Max. 2020. "These Are the Areas in Hamilton County with the Most Confirmed COVID-19 Cases per Capita." *Cincinnati Enquirer,* April 16, 2020.

Lovelace, Berkely. 2021. "J&J Covid Vaccine Distribution in the Poor, Black Communities Raises Race Questions." CNBC News. March 10, 2021.

Lupkin, Sydney. 2016. "Deep Roots for Lack of Minorities in American Medical Schools." *Medpage Today,* March 15, 2016.

Maloney, Michael. 2020. "The Coronavirus in Cincinnati: The Geography and Demography of It. Cincinnati Health Department." Urban Appalachian Community Coalition. December 2020. https://uacvoice.org

Mills, Emily. 2021. "Coronavirus in Ohio: Summit County Has the Third-Highest COVID-19 Case Rate in the State." *Akron Beacon Journal,* April 9, 2021.

Muttillo, Emily. 2020. "Ohio Kinship Care during the Pandemic." Center for Community Solutions. www.communitysolutions.com/ohio-kinship-care-pandemic/. Accessed March 5, 2021

National Committee on Vital and Health Statistics. 1993. *1. Diversity and Health Care DataBase: A Preamble for Policymakers.* 3–19. DHHS Publication PHS 93-1205.

Nong, Paige, Minakshi Raj, Melissa Creary, Sharon Kardia, and Jodyn Platt. 2020. "Patient-Reported Experiences of Discrimination in the US Health Care

System." *JAMA Netw Open* 3, no. 12: e2029650. https://doi.org/10.1001/jamanetworkopen.2020.29650.

O'Donnell, Jaynee, and David Robinson. 2019. "After Decades of Effort, African American Enrollment in Medical School Still Lags." *USA Today,* February 28, 2019.

Ohio Department of Health. 2022. "COVID-19 Dashboard." July 21, 2022. https:coronavirus.ohio.gov/dashboards.

Pecanha, Sergio, and Yan Wu. 2022. "One Million of Us." *Washington Post,* May 12, 2022.

POZ. 2017. "Unpacking Michael Weinstein's Latest PrEPDenialism." October 10, 2017. www.poz.com/article/unpacking-michael-weinsteins-latest-prep-denialism.

Rao, Vijaya, and Glenn Flores. 2007. "Why Aren't There More African American Physicians? A Qualitative Study and Exploratory Inquiry of African American Student's Perspective on Careers in Medicine." *Journal of the National Medical Association* 9, no. 99: 986–983.

Saker, Anne, and Terri DeMio. 2021. "COVID-19: Barely 5% of Ohioans Vaccinated So Far Are Black, It's Due to a Lack of Supplies, Access, and Trust." *Cincinnati Enquirer,* February 1, 2021.

Schroeder, Kaitlyn. 2020. "Black, Hispanic Ohioans Face Outsized COVID-19 Risk: Why Is That Happening?" *Dayton Daily News,* September 6, 2020.

Tikkanen, Rossa, and Melinda K. Abrams. 2020 "US Healthcare from a Global Perspective: Higher Spending, Worse Outcomes." The Commonwealth Fund, January 30, 2020.

Williams, David R., and Lisa A. Cooper. 2019. "Reducing Racial Inequities in Health: Using What We Already Know to Take Action." *International Journal of Environmental Research and Public Health* 16, no. 4: 606. https://doi.org//10.3390/ijerph16040606.

Williams, David R., and Toni D. Rucker. 2000. "Understanding and Addressing Racial Disparities in Health Care." *Health Care Financing Review* 21, no. 4: 75–90.

Yousry, Farah. 2021. "Black Medical Students Navigate Systematic Racism to Fulfill a Mission. NPR. April 5, 2021. Accessed June 1, 2021. www.wfyi.org/news/articles/black-medical-students-navigate-systemic-racism-to-fulfill-a-mission.

Zuckerman, Jake. 2020. "COVID-19 Hospitalizations Are Hitting Record Highs. Black Ohioans Are Carrying the Heavy Load." *Ohio Capital-Journal,* October 22, 2020.

12 | Old Problems, New Virus: Ableism in Ohio's COVID Pandemic Response

Research and Reflection Article

Kara B. Ayers

This hybrid research and reflection essay by a scholar of disability studies and health equity examines ableism in Ohio's COVID response, drawing on health data, press coverage, and her own experience as a disabled person living through COVID in Ohio.

Introduction

As I learned about the health ramifications of COVID-19, there came a moment I remember vividly, when I realized how deadly this virus could be for me and my husband. We have osteogenesis imperfecta, a disability best known for causing brittle bones. But the same poorly formed collagen that causes our bones to break easily also makes up our lungs. We are more at-risk for all respiratory infections. While the health risks of COVID-19 scared me, the prospects of receiving equitable care should one of us be hospitalized also kept me up at night. In the spring of 2020, I spent many sleepless nights worried about my family's survival. I worried about who would care for our three young children if one parent—or even both of us—died. How long could we stay isolated without help maintaining our home? My sleepless nights continued, so I channeled my anxiety, fear, and fight into the study of COVID-19 and its impact on the disability community.

In this chapter, I reflect upon and analyze the impact of Ohio's COVID response on the disability community. I have integrated a first-person narrative account as I am myself a disabled Ohioan who has lived through this time. My personal reflections appear in *italics* throughout the chapter. Additional perspectives are offered through my lens as a disability researcher. The use of intentional language about disability is important. I have chosen to use both person-first and identity-first language, as both are valid and personal preferences vary.

COVID-19 and Disability in Ohio

The Centers for Disease Control (CDC) estimates that approximately 28 percent of adults in Ohio have at least one type of disability; this estimate represents around 2.6 million or one in four Ohioans who have disabilities (CDC 2021). With the onset of the COVID-19 pandemic, it was immediately clear that disabled Ohioans, especially those who lived in congregate settings, were at a greater risk of death as evidenced by the initial outbreaks within institutional settings. The problems associated with congregate living have plagued people with disabilities for decades. COVID-19 shone a new light on the risks of institutionalization when evidence tied congregate settings to the highest rates of infections and severe outcomes (Constantino et al. 2020). Where a disabled Ohioan lived in March 2020 very directly predicted their odds for survival. Barriers to community living are but one "old problem" this new virus has magnified for people with disabilities. While all Ohioans were undoubtedly impacted by the direct and indirect losses caused by COVID, Ohioans with disabilities have been disproportionately impacted by both the insidious consequences of the disease itself and the ramifications of efforts to stop its rapid spread.

Ohioans with disabilities are not an insignificant sector of the population by size in numbers. Disability is unique, however, in that those who identify as disabled vary largely by type of disability and a wide range of other factors. Because "disability" is such a heterogeneous category, the media sometimes struggles to define it. In March 2020, amid the ever-changing flow of information related to COVID-19, the vague term "preexisting conditions" became ubiquitous as it became clear that the risks of infection and death were higher due to age or disability, among other reasons (Soin et al. 2020). The term seemed to become synonymous with "risk factors" but, more concerning, it seemed implicitly to signify those groups for whom mortality was acceptable. A 2020 Bloomberg news story titled, "99% of Those Who Died from COVID-19 Had Other Illness, Italy Says," seemed to suggest the virus only killed those whom the public perceived to already be on the brink of death. We now know these claims were inaccurate, but they had a snowball effect in their apparent downplaying of the deaths of those with preexisting conditions (Bilinski and Emanuel 2020). Ohioans with disabilities saw the resulting media coverage and social commentary as suggesting that having preexisting conditions or a disability were equivalent to a non-life. This messaging was amplified on social media, which, while not known for its subtlety, went just as far or further in conflating "preexisting condition" with risk factor, and in ignoring the multitude of factors that could actually heighten the pandemic's risk to disabled people.

Some from the disability community have said that COVID-19 resulted in nondisabled people "saying the quiet part out loud" about how very expendable our lives seem to many of them. It was an indescribably terrible feeling to see friends and even some family members claim the virus was a hoax or only a threat to those already sick. People were unwilling to postpone trivial events or wear a mask, even if they did believe that the spread of the virus could mean the deaths of more people. Each time the media mentioned the high-risk category as reserved to people with "preexisting conditions," it felt like a coded message about survival of the fittest. Within just a few weeks, it seemed people began to believe that maybe individuals like me are better off dead if that meant they no longer needed to forgo trips to the mall and their kids' soccer games. I couldn't understand how slogans like "Better Together" were everywhere, but my community was left behind.

Many disabled people expressed how demoralized they felt while on social media, reading the justifications of their predicted future deaths day after day (Abrams and Abbott 2020). In response to yet another news story suggesting COVID-19 posed a risk primarily to those with preexisting conditions, one blogger wrote,

> It's disappointing to see this kind of headline. I know some people will read this and secretly sigh with relief [but] what about us that DO have health conditions? Why is this being shared so matter of fact? Are we not shocked? Sad? Angry that we don't have enough resources? (Turner 2020)

Early, and unfortunately enduring, portrayals of COVID-19 as a virus that was only a serious threat for some have likely extended the trajectory of this pandemic for all. The conceptualization of "preexisting conditions" relies exclusively on a medical model of disability, which considers the symptoms of disability as coinciding with poor health and residing within the individual. While there are some aspects of a person's particular disability, like a weakened immune system or limited lung functioning, that may explain their heightened risk due to health factors, an exclusively medical model approach fails to consider the many social determinants of health that overlie the lives of disabled people. We cannot accurately interpret health information about Ohioans with disabilities without also considering social and environmental factors. A sociocultural model of disability incorporates the lived experience of disability, which still includes disability-related health factors, but through a lens that also considers contributing social, cultural, and political factors. Disability and poor health are not synonymous, but there are many factors that contribute to poor health which are more likely experienced by people with disabilities.

A 2013 public health needs assessment by the Ohio Disability and Health Program (ODHP) reported that Ohioans with disabilities are more likely to smoke daily (47.9 percent) compared to nondisabled people (37.1 percent). They are also more likely to be overweight (44.4 percent) than nondisabled people (30.1 percent); and they are significantly more likely to report fair or poor health status (43.9 percent compared to 8.7 percent). ODHP has contextualized these poor outcomes by noting that there are few smoking cessation or healthy eating programs accessible to Ohioans with disabilities, and that many disabled people report negative experiences with health-care providers (Barnett and Sommers 2017). Those who perceive discrimination on the basis of disability are less likely to seek health care (Moscoso-Porras and Alvarado 2018). Without this important context, it would be easy to wrongly conclude that disability itself causes poor health. This fundamental misunderstanding makes it possible to overlook the structural factors that exacerbated the impact of COVID-19, including the high prevalence of frontline work for people with disabilities, the segregated communities in which they often live, and factors that prevent social distancing, such as the need for help with daily self-care. Health disparities experienced by people with disabilities are related to a history of wide-ranging disadvantages, which are avoidable, preventable, and not primarily caused by underlying disability (Krahn et al. 2015).

Systemic Ableism in Ohio's Public Health System

Systemic ableism, paternalism, and utilitarianism have sustained long-standing health inequities faced by people with disabilities for centuries. They were not new problems, but their overarching presence in the COVID response exacerbated already worse outcomes for disabled people. Ohio is not alone or even unique in its chronically underfunded public health system. It's a major misconception that only the elderly reside in nursing homes. In Ohio, 6,700 people with disabilities, including children and people of all ages, reside in nursing homes, intermediate care facilities (ICFs), and group homes (Frech et al. 2015), which struggled to access personal protective equipment (PPE) for their residents and employees at the start of the pandemic. Prisons, also disproportionately full of people with disabilities, lacked even basic PPE for staff and inmates (Oladeru et al. 2020), despite the obvious risk factors.

Ohio's overuse of institutional settings was a point of political dissension for several years prior to the onset of the pandemic. In April 2020, a federal court ruled on the *Ball v. DeWine* case (formerly *Ball v. Kasich* under the previous Ohio administration), which argued that Ohio was in noncompliance with Title II of the Americans with Disabilities Act (ADA), Section 504 of the Rehabilitation Act, and the Social Security Act. As part of the settlement, Ohio was ordered to offer options counseling to individuals with disabilities residing in congregate settings and those at risk of institutionalization (OACBDD 2020). Options counseling offers people with disabilities a chance to discuss various residential options and potential eligibility for the individual with a professional familiar with the various systems that intersect to provide home and community-based supports in Ohio.

Progress in moving Ohioans with disabilities to more integrated settings has been slow. Hampered by a small but vocal group of parents heavily in favor of institutionalized settings for their children, many legislators have sided with the paternalistic view that individuals with disabilities are better off in controlled, segregated settings. In addition to current law (fortified by the 1999 Olmstead Supreme Court decision, which ruled the unnecessary segregation of persons with disabilities as discriminatory), research is extremely clear that individuals with disabilities are better served in integrated settings (Schwartz et al. 2020). Living in the community is both more cost effective for states and more likely to result in better health, social, and quality-of-life outcomes for individuals (Schwartz et al. 2020). As COVID-19 outbreaks tore through nursing facilities, intermediate care facilities, and group homes, the deadly consequences of this break from best practices was measured in lives lost. In Ohio alone, the virus killed more than 500 nursing home residents in less than three weeks (AP 2020).

Many would conclude that nursing home residents who died from COVID-19 were already on the brink of death prior to infection. This is inaccurate. Unaware that people of all ages reside in congregate care facilities in Ohio, the ableist assumption that disabled lives are less worthy stifled efforts to understand the multiple causes of these outbreaks. Research by Chen, Chevalier, and Long (2021) found most COVID-19 infections could be traced to transmission spread between workers, many of whom worked part-time at multiple facilities. Even months into the pandemic, these high-risk settings still reported shortages of PPE, spotty testing, and little to no effort to mitigate transmission from and among staff. Visitor bans left residents isolated and also without the watchful eye of loved ones, and the virus continued to spread (Abrams and Abbott 2020).

Disabled people are more likely to rent than are our nondisabled counterparts. My husband and I rented for several years until our needs for wheelchair-accessible housing large enough to fit a growing family simply didn't exist among the available rental units. These units were developed with the assumption that disabled people will largely be single or, at most, have one live-in caregiver. We've owned our own home since having our first child. Due to stringent income limits, we don't qualify for any formal assistance programs to help with maintenance or anything at all within the walls of our home. We have creatively problem-solved how to handle tasks like mowing the lawn and are fortunate to have informal supports from family members in response to the occasional need, like a broken water heater or a downed tree limb. COVID-19 meant total isolation for our family. We had to triage the tasks that required the increased risk of letting others into our dwelling. Because I worked from home and my children participated in virtual school, a disruption in Internet service merited the risk; a clogged sink or a burned-out light bulb did not. We calculated our needs carefully and relied on the wide range of curbside and delivery services that helped all Ohioans stay safe, while also increasing overall accessibility to community resources.

Although it was clear early in the pandemic that certain groups and certain settings were at greater risk of infection and death from

COVID-19, some public officials didn't see these greater risks as reason for concern, but rather as a messaging strategy to calm the fears of the majority. During a rally in Swanton, Ohio, in September of 2020, then-President Donald Trump claimed, "It affects elderly people, people with heart problems and other problems. That's what it really affects [...] Take your hat off to the young, because they have a hell of an immune system. But it affects virtually nobody. It's an amazing thing."

The Politicization of COVID-19 and Disability

The politicization of COVID-19 has been particularly damaging for those at heightened risk for the virus. Some policy makers had underlying motives to minimize the threat or danger of COVID-19. Even efforts to communicate accurate information, however, became garbled with conflicting and confusing messages (Van Scoy 2021). Understanding COVID messaging missteps is essential for applying lessons learned from this pandemic response. For people with the type of disabilities that may make it more difficult to read and understand implicit messages, this confusion and rampant misinformation can become yet another health threat.

Ohio's high-profile political figures shared sometimes opposing perspectives despite the state's Republican majority. Ohio Representative Jim Jordan sarcastically tweeted, "How many masks should we wear today?" as counties across the state were deemed to have substantial spread (Moran 2021). Governor Mike DeWine adopted a more concerned stance, relative to counterparts like Jordan. DeWine was one of the first Republican governors to call a state of emergency (Grossman et al. 2020) and consistently messaged the need to practice social distancing and other mitigation behaviors. Governor DeWine was also an outlier in implementing statewide stay-at-home orders. A study found that governors without term limits (unlike DeWine) were 40 percent more likely to issue such orders (Baccini and Bradeur 2021). In 2020, Governor DeWine was in his first term, with a two-term limit.

Governor DeWine was also one of several governors who utilized televised press conferences for daily updates on state case counts and rapidly changing mitigation efforts. During these press conferences, Governor DeWine and invited health officials often emphasized the increased risk of COVID-19 to those with preexisting conditions (Soin et al. 2020). There seemed little connection to how, even with the heightened risk to individuals with preexisting conditions, stopping the transmission of the virus within the community would change the trajectory of the pandemic for everyone (Adams 2020). Repeated reports of outbreaks in congregate settings, like nursing homes and prisons, also implicitly suggested that COVID-19 was a more serious risk to certain subgroups of people, like those who resided in institutions (Soin et al. 2020). Pointing out the disproportionate impact of the virus on these groups without also educating the public about the reasons why became an implicit shorthand for "othering" people killed by the virus (Ktenidis 2020). However, Governor DeWine did note a deep sense of responsibility for policy making that would protect those most at risk of COVID-19. He consistently professed his faith-based obligation to care for the most vulnerable, including those with disabilities (Hancock 2019). This commitment and his aligned actions almost immediately positioned him at odds with his own majority party in his state. Ohio legislators scrambled to explore ways to end health orders, which included stay-at-home orders, mask mandates, and restrictions on in-person school (Hodge and Piat 2021). Political pressure was mounting.

Scapegoating Disability with Paternalism to Avert Safety Measures

After weeks of pressure to reopen the state, Governor DeWine outlined his Responsible Restart Ohio plan on Monday, April 27, 2020. The initial plan included a mask mandate (Borchardt and Balmert 2020). Less than 24 hours later, however, Governor DeWine had amended his stance to make mask wearing a *recommendation* rather than a requirement. Governor DeWine cited a conversation with a mother of a child with autism as a motivating factor for his abrupt change. The mother claimed her child could not wear a mask and would be barred from the community if a mask requirement was enacted. "As governor, it is my responsibility to make the tough decisions. But it is also my responsibility to listen and hear and be respectful of the thoughts and ideas of Ohioans," DeWine said (Hunnell 2020, par. 9). DeWine ultimately reinstated the mask mandate in July 2020, when Ohio cases and deaths surged.

There are many variations of paternalism, which is defined as benevolent interference. Most aim to protect a person in a way that they cannot or will not do for themselves. Some Ohioans have interpreted mask mandates themselves as paternalistic in that they overrule an individual's freedom and forgo consent in the interest of safety. Given DeWine's history of benevolence and his self-identified obligation to care for those whom he describes as "vulnerable Ohioans," his rollback of mask mandates without consultation with actual disabled people (instead of a presumably nondisabled parent) exemplified paternalism as it is often experienced by the disability community.

The resistance to mask wearing has been both confusing and frustrating to observe. As a result of my particular disability (osteogenesis imperfecta), I've endured a wide range of uncomfortable and unequivocally painful experiences. Almost all of them were more aversive than wearing a mask. I sometimes avoid sharing aspects of osteogenesis imperfecta because they can be misconstrued as experiences to pity. I see them as matter of fact and a part of the lens through which I view life. As a child, I slept with heavy, leather and metal leg braces that went past my hips. I still find it uncomfortable to go without shoes because my shoes were welded onto the braces. I had dozens of casts, none of which were waterproof to allow unrestricted bathing. I've healed from more than 70 broken bones, so I still have chronic pain. I have done and not done a number of things in an effort to prevent the worsening of my condition. It has been hard for me to fathom the resistance to what seems such a small thing for almost everyone—to wear a mask—to prevent the worst-scenario outcome of death for others.

As has so often been the case throughout this pandemic, DeWine's abrupt change of course on masks in the spring of 2020 failed to note several realities for the disability community. First, the young person with autism was himself at a disproportionate risk of death from COVID-19 (Kapur et al. 2021). While his inclusion in the community is important, his health and survival did not seem as prioritized as others'. Second, even the earliest iterations of mask mandates included broad exemptions for any individuals with disabilities that precluded putting on, taking off, or wearing a mask. DeWine's original mask mandate included these exclusions (Borchardt and Balmert 2020), which suggests political pressure was likely a key factor in his decision. Beyond a mask exemption, reasonable accommodations, like curbside pickup even when not typically offered, were already supported by the Americans with Disabilities Act. The governor and his staff had previously appeared well versed on such laws (Hancock 2019). By citing concern for a person with a disability as the reason for his reversal, DeWine stood to gain public approval. Constituents of both parties, largely unaware that mask exemptions already existed, praised the governor for his kind foresight in thinking of vulnerable others and acting on their behalf. The paternalistic approach of declaring oneself sensitive to the needs of people with disabilities without any direct consultation with disabled people is unfortunately common in policy making (Boyce et al. 2001). Not mentioned in DeWine's reversal was the heightened health risks that Ohioans with disabilities would now face living in a state without a mask mandate.

Utilitarianism to Ration Care Away from Ohioans with Disabilities

While paternalism seemed to drive some policy making during the COVID-19 pandemic in Ohio, utilitarianism was also at play. Utilitarianism prioritizes the needs and survival of the majority. The principle often guides plans to ration scarce resources. In March 2020, US health-care professionals reported their fears that the need for ventilators would outpace supply, both in terms of available equipment and the capacity of health-care staff (Andrews et al. 2020). Many states began to release crisis care standards or rationing guidelines that directly diverted ventilators, intensive care unit (ICU) beds, and even care *away* from people with disabilities (Andrews et al. 2020). There were reports of people with disabilities receiving pre-filled templates for Do Not Resuscitate orders upon admission to the emergency room with COVID-19 (Chen and McNamara 2020). Although the characteristics correlated with survival of COVID-19 were not yet understood at the onset of the pandemic, early crisis care standards largely assumed that people with disabilities and chronic illnesses would die after consuming valuable resources, like care, ICU beds, and ventilators, while nondisabled people could use those resources to more quickly recover and survive in greater numbers. The US Department of Health and Human Services Office for Civil Rights issued a bulletin that reminded first responders and health-care providers,

> In this time of emergency, the laudable goal of providing care quickly and efficiently must be guided by the fundamental principles of fairness, equality, and compassion that animate our civil rights laws. This is particularly true with respect to the treatment of persons with disabilities during medical emergencies as they possess the same dignity and worth as everyone else. (HHS 2020)

Many states began to roll back their just-released crisis care standards as courts ruled them discriminatory based on disability (Andrews et al. 2020). Ohio had not issued a state plan or guidelines, but only guidance "about standards of care for vulnerable populations in hospital settings" (DODD 2021). Disability Rights Ohio, the state's protection and advocacy organization, applauded the solid foundation of this guidance, but advocated for more clarity and specific protections around health-care discrimination (Disability Rights Ohio 2021). Meanwhile, few, if any, disabled advocates were invited to provide direct input in the development of such guidance.

Crisis care standards weren't the only policies that worried the disability community as the number of COVID-19 cases spiked. Hospital visitor bans intended to reduce the spread of COVID-19 from hospitals to the community meant people with disabilities would be alone if hospitalized. My husband and I are always at risk for hospitalization should we fracture a bone that needs surgery to stabilize. During one such hospitalization as an adult, I waited for hours for a nurse to respond to a call button. When she responded, she complained that people should wait until the morning to ask for help to use the bathroom. An attending physician spoke to me in a childlike tone until my nurse advised him that I am a professor at Cincinnati Children's Hospital. I vowed never to stay overnight in a hospital again without someone by my side to advocate for me. Many disabled people make similar plans for their safety, yet changes to the visitor policy in response to COVID-19 meant facing an overly strained health-care system alone.

Ohio didn't make headlines for an explicitly problematic state plan for rationing scarce resources because, as mentioned above, it didn't release such a state plan at all. The structure of the Ohio Department of Health doesn't allow state guidance to dictate hospital policy making. Instead, Ohio entities, like the Ohio Department of Health or Governor DeWine's office, could only issue guidance in the form of recommendations. The Ohio Hospital Association (2020) released its own guidelines to its member hospitals. As a member organization, the OHA can also only encourage its hospitals, most of which will make their own policies. The guidelines still worried disability advocates (Andrews et al. 2020). They excluded care from people with cystic fibrosis (CF) with seemingly little recognition of the spectrum of this chronic illness and in the absence of any research indicating that those with CF had no chance for recovery from COVID-19. The guidelines made no effort to address known health inequities faced by people with disabilities, ignoring the undertreatment many experience (Abrams and Abbot 2020). Perhaps most concerning, however, was the reality that the individual hospital policies across Ohio would never be accessible to advocates and disability policy scholars for analysis. To date, hospitals have declined to share these policies with advocates. A November 2020 article described Ohio as "extremely close to rationing care," with more than 3,800 hospitalized with the virus (Mosby 2020). At the time of this writing, no hospitals publicly stated a need to ration, but it's also notable that they are not required to share this information. Systems were stressed again with the fourth wave of COVID-19 through the fall of 2021. Hospitals reported they were near capacity and urged people to postpone elective procedures and avoid emergency rooms if possible (Anderson 2021).

Ohio's Prioritization of Vaccines for People with Disabilities

As hospitals in Ohio remained strained through December, hope was also on the horizon in the form of new vaccines. Pfizer and Moderna got emergency use authorization from the Food and Drug Administration (Adedokun et al. 2021). The Ohio Department of Health announced its vaccine rollout plan (Ohio Department of Health, 2021), which included prioritization of different groups for access to the vaccine. In many ways, Ohio followed suit with other states and federal guidance in designating health-care workers and those in long-term care facilities as among those who were first eligible for vaccination (Jain et al. 2021). Yet the state's vaccine plan was unique in its explicit prioritization of those with developmental disabilities and genetic conditions. Unfortunately, Ohio had planned to reach people with developmental disabilities exclusively through service system channels, to which a mere 20 percent of individuals with developmental disabilities are connected (Andrews et al. 2020). This left the vast majority disconnected from the rollout effort. Notably, thousands of Ohioans with developmental disabilities aren't connected to the service system because they've been placed on waiting lists, sometimes for more than a decade, for community-based waiver services (Schwartz et al. 2020).

Despite Down syndrome qualifying under the broader category of developmental disabilities, it was called out on its own for prioritization in group 1B for the state. Many people with disabilities weren't sure where they fit in the state's plan, but people with Down syndrome were technically prioritized twice—and both times, they were placed near the front of the line. Advocacy efforts from the Down syndrome community are largely parent-led. As described by Carey, Block, and

Scotch in their 2020 book *Allies and Obstacles*, parent perspectives often hold more power than disabled voices, especially in paternalistic settings (Carey et al. 2020).

Many of my nondisabled colleagues received their vaccines before I did due to their patient-facing roles with the hospital where I work. In late January 2021, my husband and I were eligible for vaccination under Ohio's 1B priority group, which included individuals with genetic disabilities. The person scheduling vaccines at our county health department had, unsurprisingly, not heard of osteogenesis imperfecta, but I assured her it was a genetic disability and we booked our appointments. The health department is housed in a historical building that is only accessible via a very steep, unevenly paved ramp. We were grateful that health department workers recognized this barrier and brought the vaccines out to the cars of those of us who had called ahead to request this option. I felt some relief after receiving my first shot, but only felt the full gravity of the experience upon receiving my second dose. I am so grateful for the science that persisted in the development and distribution of the COVID-19 vaccine. As I have reflected, the rollout wasn't perfect, but I recognize the enormous privilege in receiving my vaccine in early 2021.

Although Ohio prioritized many with disabilities for vaccination, its plan was not without gaps. Only solid organ transplant recipients were eligible for prioritized status, while bone marrow transplant recipients remained high risk but ineligible. State plans not only varied; they sometimes changed daily. In a collaboration with Johns Hopkins' Disability Health Research Center, the Center for Dignity in Healthcare for People with Disabilities, headquartered at Cincinnati Children's Hospital Medical Center, developed a first-of-its-kind vaccine prioritization dashboard, updated weekly, to help people with disabilities and their caregivers determine how their state defined disability and when they were eligible for vaccination (Epstein et al. 2021). Intellectual disability is characterized by deficits in intellectual and adaptive functioning. The diagnosis is usually assigned by a doctor early in a patient's life. Some states referred to this population as people with cognitive disabilities, further complicating people's ability to determine when they or their loved ones were eligible for the vaccine. In some states, chronic illness was classified as a disability, while in others individual chronic illnesses were broken out by diagnosis to determine eligibility. Deciphering these distinctions in definitions required poring through lengthy state plans. It's unclear how vaccine schedulers and administrators applied the varying definitions in the creation of timetables for vaccine eligibility.

The accessibility of vaccine websites developed and updated by state health departments was also a barrier for many. The vaccine prioritization dashboard was expanded to evaluate how accessible these state websites were for people with disabilities (Johns Hopkins Disability Health Research Center COVID-19 Vaccine Dashboard 2021). Ohio's website ranked eighteenth in overall accessibility, with 185 identified website design errors, many related to easily corrected low-contrast text, which can make it impossible for people with visual impairments to read text online. Despite advocates' requests to the Ohio Department of Health to fix these errors, Ohio's accessibility score and ranking did not change before the dashboard tracking ended on May 19, 2021. It is both disappointing and revealing that none of the concrete suggestions to improve the accessibility of Ohio's vaccine websites were implemented. The inaction suggests the low value placed on equal access.

New Virus, Old Problems for Ohio

Although Ohio's early mitigation efforts were applauded by some health policy experts and physicians (Soin et al. 2020), Ohioans with disabilities were at a greater risk because of their greater likelihood of living in crowded, group settings (Schwartz et al. 2020). As politicians wavered on mask mandates, disability was used as a scapegoat to placate those in political opposition to requirements and confuse those who were not aware individual exemptions were already in place for those who could not wear masks due to disability. A lack of transparency in hospital-level policies on crisis care standards leaves Ohioans with disabilities vulnerable to unfair and discriminatory triage decisions, which can take place at any time. And finally, while well intentioned in prioritizing disability, the influence of proxies (e.g., parents) instead of the direct perspective from people with disabilities was all too clear in Ohio's vaccine rollout plans. Compared to other states, the response could have been worse for disabled Ohioans, but it also could have been much better.

Ohio must expedite the transition of people with disabilities out of congregate settings and into their communities with the utmost urgency. With poor vaccination uptake by nursing home workers, these lives are once again at heightened risk, with breakthrough cases costing the lives of vaccinated residents (Bailly et al. 2021). The institutionalization of Ohioans with disabilities is a life-threatening public health emergency and it must be treated as such.

No matter how well intentioned, paternalism will remain a major barrier to equitable outcomes for Ohioans with disabilities. The direct representation of disabled voices and perspectives must be included at all levels of policy making. Despite advocates' pleas, no representatives from the disability community were appointed to Ohio's COVID-19 Minority Health Commission. Instead, a disability advisory committee was created almost a year after the pandemic's start, adjacent to all other COVID-19 response task forces, with no funding and no direct connection to policy making. The well-known disability rights mantra "Nothing about us without us," doesn't only serve the best interests of the disability community. The inclusion of disabled voices generates best practices that frequently benefit the population at large.

While this chapter has necessarily pointed out the many failings of the COVID response as experienced by the disability community, it's also important to reflect upon the radical efforts of grassroots disability organizations to mobilize in meeting our own needs. I watched with pride as my disabled brothers and sisters from around the world worked together to meet their needs and the needs of their families. They sourced hand sanitizer and life-sustaining medical supplies and arranged socially distanced drop-offs, often with no more resources than a cellular phone. For several weekends during lockdown, I joined a Zoom call with women from around the world with osteogenesis imperfecta. We were previously friends who exchanged pleasantries online and occasionally saw each other at national and international conferences for people with osteogenesis imperfecta. We experienced the pandemic differently in our disparate locations, but we shared so much in common that I always felt less alone after these chats. I have also felt pride in the resilience I've seen blossom in my children. My four-year-old has lived more than half of her life during a pandemic. She now especially relishes trips to the library because she didn't remember the option to go inside! My tween and teen have worn their masks even when they are sometimes alone in doing so in their peer group. We survived and at times thrived throughout an entire year of virtual school! Our family and our community have learned lessons from this experience that I plan to sustain.

Finally, it is inexcusable that in a country and a state rich with resources, we were ever on the brink of rationing resources. The threat of undertreatment during a health crisis is not over for Ohioans with disabilities. It is a reality realized by many who have experienced the ableist gaze or unwelcome comment from a health-care provider. The medical model of disability, often endorsed and evangelized during medical training, must be replaced with a sociocultural model of disability that considers the multiple, dynamic interactions between society and disability (Abrams and Abbott 2020). Rather than accepting closed-door hospital policy making that discriminates on the basis of disability as a grim reality of the current times, we must demand accountability for proper stockpiling, resource sharing, and capacity planning that reflects the inherent dignity and worth of all Ohioans. As Ohio fights to break free from the grip of COVID, it could also simultaneously dismantle the confines of ableism and its negative impacts on those with and without disabilities. For an anti-ableism emergence, however, we first must recognize and remedy the devaluing of disabled lives, deep social injustice, and community exclusion.

REFERENCES

Abrams, Thomas, and David Abbott. 2020. "Disability, Deadly Discourse, and Collectivity amid Coronavirus (COVID-19)." *Scandinavian Journal of Disability Research* 22, no. 1: 168–174.

Adams, V. 2020. "Disasters and Capitalism ... and COVID-19." Somatosphere, March 26, 2020. http://somatosphere.net/2020/disaster-capitalism-covid19.html/.

Adedokun, Kamoru A., Ramat T. Kamorudeen, and Ibrahim O. Bello. 2021. "Authorization of the First COVID-19 Emergency Vaccines: The Matters Arising." *EXCLI Journal* 20: 655–660.

Anderson, Chris. 2021. "Ohio Doctors Sound Alarm on Hospital Capacity for Adult, Pediatric Covid-19 Patients." Cleveland 19, October 14, 2021. www.cleveland19.com/2021/10/14/statewide-covid-19-update-given-by-ohio-department-health-officials/.

Andrews, Erin E., Kara B. Ayers, Kathleen S. Brown, Dana S. Dunn, and Carrie R. Pilarski. 2020. "No Body Is Expendable: Medical Rationing and Disability Justice during the COVID-19 Pandemic." *American Psychologist* 76, no. 3: 451–461.

Associated Press. 2020. "Virus Has Killed 500 Ohio Nursing Home Residents in 3 Weeks." 10tv.com. WBNS, May 8, 2020. www.10tv.com/article/news/local/ohio/virus-has-killed-500-ohio-nursing-home-residents-3-weeks-2020-jun/530-67b55df6-8819-4a43-a39c-67ed255b21da.

Baccini, Leonardo and Abel Brodeur. 2021. "Explaining Governors' Response to the COVID-19 Pandemic in the United States." *American Politics Research* 49, no. 2: 215–220. https://doi.org/10.1177/1532673X20973453

Bailly, Benoit, Luc Guilpain, Kevin Bouiller, Catherine Chirouze, Melissa N'Debi, Alexandre Soulier, Vanessa Demontant et al. 2021. "BNT162b2 mRNA Vaccination Did Not Prevent an Outbreak of SARS COV-2 Variant 501Y. V2 in an Elderly Nursing Home But Reduced Transmission and Disease Severity." *Clinical Infectious Diseases* 74, no. 3: 517–520.

Barnett, M. L., and B. D. Sommers. 2017. "A National Survey of Medicaid Beneficiaries' Experiences and Satisfaction with Health Care." *JAMA Internal Medicine* 177, no. 9: 1378–1381.

Bilinski, Alyssa, and Ezekiel J. Emanuel. 2020. "COVID-19 and Excess All-Cause Mortality in the US and 18 Comparison Countries." *JAMA* 324, no. 20: 2100–2102.

Borchardt, Jessie, and Jackie Balmert. 2020. "Coronavirus in Ohio: GOV. Mike DeWine Reverses Course on Face COVERINGS Mandate for Retail Shoppers." *Cincinnati Enquirer*, April 28, 2020. www.cincinnati.com/story/news/2020/04/28/coronavirus-ohio-gov-mike-dewine-update-covid-19-reopening-businesses/3039122001/.

Boyce, William, Mary Ann McColl, Mary Tremblay, Jerome Bickenbach, Anne Crichton, Steven Andrews, Nancy Gerein et al. 2001. *Seat at the Table: Persons with Disabilities and Policy Making*. Montreal: McGill-Queen's Press-MQUP.

Carey, Allison C., Pamela Block, and Richard Scotch. 2020. *Allies and Obstacles: Disability Activism and Parents of Children with Disabilities*. Philadelphia: Temple University Press.

Centers for Disease Control and Prevention. 2021. *Disability & Health U.S. State Profile Data for Ohio (Adults 18+ Years of Age)*. www.cdc.gov/ncbddd/disabilityandhealth/impacts/ohio.html.

Chen, Bo, and Donna Marie McNamara. 2020. "Disability Discrimination, Medical Rationing and COVID-19." *Asian Bioethics Review* 12, no. 4: 511–518.

Chen, M. Keith, Judith A. Chevalier, and Elisa F. Long. 2021. "Nursing Home Staff Networks and COVID-19." *Proceedings of the National Academy of Sciences* 118, no. 1: e2015455118.

Constantino, John N., Mustafa Sahin, Joseph Piven, Rylin Rodgers, and John Tschida. 2020. "The Impact of COVID-19 on Individuals with Intellectual and Developmental Disabilities: Clinical and Scientific Priorities." *American Journal of Psychiatry* 177, no. 11: 1091–1093.

Disability Rights Ohio. "DRO Continues Fight against Care Rationing Because #AdvocacyMatters." Accessed August 2, 2021. www.disabilityrightsohio.org/news/dro-fights-against-care-rationing-because-advocacymatters.

Epstein, Sabrina, Kara Ayers, and Bonnielin K. Swenor. 2021. "COVID-19 Vaccine Prioritisation for People with Disabilities." *The Lancet Public Health* 6, no. 6: e361.

Frech, Rose, John Honeck, and Kate Warren. 2015. *Ohio at a Crossroads: The Developmental Disabilities System*. The Center for Community Solutions. March 2015. www.communitysolutions.com/wp-content/uploads/2018/04/MajorReport_DD-System_032015_Frech_Honeck_Warren.pdf.

Governor of Ohio. 2021. "Governor DeWine Announces Details of Ohio's Responsible RestartOhio Plan." April 27, 2020. https://governor.ohio.gov/wps/portal/gov/governor/media/news-and-media/covid19-update-april-27.

Grossman, Guy, Soojong Kim, Jonah M. Rexer, and Harsha Thirumurthy. 2020. "Political Partisanship Influences Behavioral Responses to Governors' Recommendations for COVID-19 Prevention in the United States." *Proceedings of the National Academy of Sciences* 117, no. 39: 24144–24153.

Hancock, Laura. 2019. "What to Know about Governor Mike DeWine's First Six Executive Orders." Cleveland.com, January 15, 2019. www.cleveland.com/news/g66l-2019/01/589560b6865486/what-to-know-about-gov-mike-de.html.

Health and Human Services Office for Civil Rights in Action (HHS). 2020. *Bulletin: Civil Rights, HIPAA, and the Coronavirus Disease 2019.* March 28, 2020. www.hhs.gov/sites/default/files/ocr-bulletin-3-28-20.pdf.

Hodge, James G., and Jennifer L. Piatt. 2021. "COVID'S Counterpunch: State Legislative Assaults on Public Health Emergency Powers." *BYU Journal of Public Law* 36, no. 1: 31–50.

Hunnell, Carl. 2020. "DeWine Reverses Masks Policy—Recommended, Not Required." *Richland Source,* April 28, 2020. www.richlandsource.com/news/covid19/dewine-reverses-masks-policy----recommended-not-required/article_22528c32-897a-11ea-8a2e-73933e872278.html.

Jain, Vageesh, Lara Schwarz, and Paula Lorgelly. 2021. "A Rapid Review of COVID-19 Vaccine Prioritization in the US: Alignment between Federal Guidance and State Practice." *International Journal of Environmental Research and Public Health* 18, no. 7: 3483.

Johns Hopkins Disability Health Research Center. COVID-19 Vaccine Dashboard. https://disabilityhealth.jhu.edu/. Accessed August 2, 2021.

Karpur, Arun, Vijay Vasudevan, Andy Shih, and Thomas Frazier. 2021. "Brief Report: Impact of COVID-19 in Individuals with Autism Spectrum Disorders: Analysis of a National Private Claims Insurance Database." *Journal of Autism and Developmental Disorders* 52, no, 5: 2350–2356.

Krahn, Gloria L., Deborah Klein Walker, and Rosaly Correa-De-Araujo. 2015. "Persons with Disabilities as an Unrecognized Health Disparity Population." *American Journal of Public Health* 105, no. S2: S198–S206.

Ktenidis, Antonios. 2020. "Covid-19 and the Implications of Its Ontologically Violent Messages." iHuman. Accessed April 21, 2020. http://ihuman.group.shef.ac.uk/ontologically-violent-messages/.

Moran, Lee. 2021. "Jim Jordan Asked a Snarky Question ABOUT Masks and Twitter Users Did Not Hold Back." *HuffPost,* April 20, 2021. www.huffpost.com/entry/jim-jordan-masks-question_n_607adadce4b001abc4dcaa60.

Mosby, Chris. 2020. "Ohio 'Extremely Close' to Rationing Care Due to COVID-19 Surge." *Patch,* November 19, 2020. https://patch.com/ohio/across-oh/ohio-extremely-close-rationing-care-due-covid-19-surge.

Moscoso-Porras, M.G., and G.F. Alvarado. 2018. "Association between Perceived Discrimination and Healthcare–Seeking Behavior in People with a Disability." *Disability and Health Journal,* 11, no. 1: 93–98.

Ohio Association of County Boards of Developmental Disabilities (OACBDD). "Ball v. DeWine: Information and Updates." Accessed August 2, 2021. www.oacbdd.org/ballvdewine.

Ohio Department of Developmental Disabilities (DODD). "Guidance: Covid-19

Standards of Care for Vulnerable Populations." Accessed August 2, 2021. https://dodd.ohio.gov/wps/portal/gov/dodd/about-us/communication/news/news-guidance-covid-19-standards-of-care.

Ohio Department of Health. COVID-19 Vaccination Program. Accessed July 29, 2021. https://coronavirus.ohio.gov/wps/portal/gov/covid-19/covid-19-vaccination-program.

Ohio Hospital Association. 2020. "Guidelines for Allocation of Scarce Resources." April 5, 2020. https://ohiohospitals.org/OHA/media/OHA-Media/Documents/Patient%20Safety%20and%20Quality/COVID19/Ohio-Guidelines-for-Allocation-of-Scarce-Medical-Resources-CLEAN-FINAL.pdf.

Oladeru, Oluwadamilola T., Tran Nguyen-Toan, Tala Al-Rousan, Brie Williams, and Nickolas Zaller. 2020. "A Call to Protect Patients, Correctional Staff and Healthcare Professionals in Jails and Prisons during the COVID-19 Pandemic." *Health & Justice* 8, no. 1: 1–3.

Schwartz, Steven J., Robert D. Fleischner, Alexander Z. Schwartz, and Emily M. Stephens. 2020. "Realizing the Promise of Olmstead: Ensuring the Informed Choice of Institutionalized Individuals with Disabilities to Receive Services in the Most Integrated Setting." *Journal of Legal Medicine* 40, no. 1: 63–100.

Soin, Amol, Srinivas Vuppala, Gregory Surfield, Ricardo Buenaventura, Mark Malinowski, Akash Rajaratnam, Rahul Madan et al. 2020. "Ohio Response to COVID-19 and Its Impact on Interventional Pain Management Practices." *Pain Physician* 23: S439–S447.

Turner, Gem. 2020. Twitter post. April 16, 2020, 5:59 p.m. https://twitter.com/gem_turner/status/1250906631304609792?s=20.

Van Scoy, Lauren Jodi, Bethany Snyder, Erin L. Miller, Olubukola Toyobo, Ashmita Grewel, Giang Ha, Sarah Gillespie et al. 2021. "Public Anxiety and Distrust due to Perceived Politicization and Media Sensationalism during Early COVID-19 Media Messaging." *Journal of Communication in Healthcare* 14, no. 3: 1–10.

13 | Social Inequality

The Pandemic's Disparate Impact on Food Insecurity among Marginalized Groups

Research Article

Monica M. Adams

This research piece by a scholar and practitioner of social work examines food insecurity during the pandemic in Ohio (and throughout the Midwest) and shows it to be a risk factor for COVID-19-related health complications.

Introduction

The COVID-19 pandemic has put a spotlight on health and wealth disparities in Ohio. In particular, it has drawn attention to the issue of food insecurity, which is not having consistent access to affordable, nutritious foods to sustain an active and healthy life, due to limited resources or access (United States Department of Agriculture 2021a). Food insecurity can be detrimental to an individuals' health and well-being, and it impacts broader society by lowering work productivity and by raising both health-care costs and the cost associated with supplemental food programs. The estimated economic burden of food insecurity is more than $167.5 billion annually (Odums-Young and Bruce 2018, 3). Prior to the pandemic, 10.5 percent of US households were food insecure (Food Research & Action Center 2020). This represents a little over 35 million Americans, including 5.3 million children (Feeding America 2021 United States Department of Agriculture 2020). Some segments of the population are more vulnerable compared to other groups, and economic hardships created by COVID-19 worsened disproportionately among women, and racial and ethnic minorities (Myers and Painter 2017). Therefore, understanding dimensions of social inequality that are unique to women and racial and ethnic minorities and that impact their access to food is critical. While some studies on the issue have examined income inequality between socio-economic class levels (Elmes 2018), less attention has been given to other forms of social inequality unique to these two groups

This chapter, therefore, takes an in-depth look at food insecurity from multiple angles, using Ohio as point of reference. First, different levels of food insecurity and its health implications are discussed, followed by a discussion of the impact of the pandemic on food insecurity nationally and in Ohio. After this, the focus shifts to exploring the issue from the perspective of social inequalities in Ohio and nationwide, and examining how structural racism and structural sexism contributed to women and racial and ethnic minorities being less likely to be food secure before and during the pandemic. This discussion will primarily address how these structural barriers combined with the financial and social impact of the pandemic to inhibit access to needed resources associated with accessing healthy foods (e.g., adequate income, access to grocery stores, social supports). The chapter ends with recommendations for policy changes that would counter the negative impacts of structural racism and sexism with regard to food insecurity.

Food Insecurity and the Impact of COVID-19

Food insecurity has two recognized levels—low food security and very low food security. Low food security is reduced quality, variety, and desirability of food options without substantial disruption to food intake, while very low food security involves one or more household members experiencing disrupted eating patterns and reducing food intake (Staren 2020). One study found that those who were already not food secure prior to the pandemic were more likely to experience very low food security (59 percent) during the pandemic compared to those who were newly food secure (32 percent; Niles et al. 2020). Primarily due to poor nutritional intake, food insecurity has significant health implications, as it can increase the risk for diabetes, hypertension, cardiovascular disease, obesity, and some cancers (US

Department of Health and Human Services and USDA 2015). A study exploring differences in health outcomes between food-secure communities and food-insecure communities located within the same county, found that food-insecure communities had, on average, higher rates of obesity (50 percent), hypertension (43 percent), high cholesterol (31 percent), and diabetes (17 percent) compared to these same conditions in the food-secure communities respectively (31 percent, 31 percent, 27 percent, and 7 percent; Kaiser, Dionne, and Carr 2019). Inadequate access to nutritious foods primarily affects individuals and families with limited incomes and resources, and the pandemic further limited their access to food due to disappearance of income through job loss, and limited availability of foods due to the global disruption of the food production infrastructure (Morales, Morales, and Beltran 2021. This disruption contributed to a sudden increase in food prices (Table 13.1), making it more difficult to afford nutritious foods, even for those enrolled in public assistance programs. Additionally, safety precautions like social distancing and efforts to sanitize public places, including grocery stores, were also barriers to accessibility due to decreased store capacity and hours (Leone et al. 2020). These precautions also contributed to food pantries closing, further limiting access to food for those in need (Dzhanova 2020).

The impact of these negative consequences of COVID-19 can be seen in Ohio, one of the hardest-hit states economically (Davidson 2021). Ohio's prevalence of food insecurity (13.2 percent), pre-pandemic, was already higher than the national average and higher than all other Midwestern states except Missouri (13.2 percent; Feeding America n.d.). This represents just over 1.5 million Ohioans, including 448,600 children (Feeding America n.d.). Ohioans were overburdened by the negative impact of COVID on the economy compared to most states. By June 2020, Ohio was ranked third in the nation with regard to how badly

TABLE 13.1 Comparison of food prices pre- and during pandemic

Food Prices	March 2019–March 2020	March–June 2020
Food overall	+1.1%	+4.3%
Dairy	+3.7%	+2.1%
Fruit/Vegetables	−1.9%	+2.5%
Meat (poultry, fish, eggs)	+2.3%	+10.37%
Beef	+3.8%	+20.4%

residents had been hit financially since the pandemic spread across the country (Garner 2020). A contributing factor was the unemployment rate soaring to 16.8 percent by April 2020, giving Ohio the sixth-highest rate of unemployment in the country (Horan 2020). One study found that over 50 percent Ohioans with low incomes lost employment income due to the pandemic (Ohio Association of Community Action Agencies 2021). Ohio was the only Midwestern state ranked within the top five states projected to have the highest prevalence of food insecurity in 2021, and the only one ranked among the top five states projected to have the highest number of people living in households with very low food security (Feeding America 2021). Because of the economic and social impact of COVID, food insecurity in Ohio was predicted to increase 6.5 percent by 2021, which was over two times the predicted increase for the national average (2.4 percent: Feeding America 2021).

Although food insecurity and poverty are highly correlated (Elmes 2018), it is erroneous to view food insecurity as simply a financial issue at the individual or household level. At the population level, it is a by-product of larger societal issues, such as prolonged periods of high or increasing unemployment and underemployment, declining wages, lack of affordable housing, and the absence of adequate welfare policies (Roncarlo and Potvin 2016). While these issues impact the whole country, they have disproportionately impacted women, and racial and ethnic minorities before and during the pandemic.

The Social Dimension of Food Insecurity

COVID underscored existing disparities in the prevalence of food insecurity among women, and racial and ethnic minorities compared to other vulnerable groups (Wolfson and Leung 2020). These disparities are mostly attributed to social stratification—grouping people based on social demographics (e.g., income, race and ethnicity, sex, and age) in a hierarchical order based on inequalities in wealth, power, and access to resources and opportunities (Robbins et al. 2019). Women and racial and ethnic minorities are overrepresented at the lower end of this social hierarchy. A study that sought to explain the racial inequality in food insecurity in Columbus, Ohio, demonstrated how differences in access to resources contribute to this issue (Table 13.2). The study found that that Blacks had less access to resources associated with food security (Koh et al. 2020).

TABLE 13.2 Comparison of access to resources between Blacks and whites in Columbus, OH

Resources	Blacks	Whites
Income < 25k	65%	31%
Income >100K	3%	21%
College degree	11%	33%
Never drive to shop	34%	14%
Dissatisfied w/access to food	23%	16%
Average shopping distance	4.5 miles	3.87 miles

During the pandemic, people situated at the lower end of the socioeconomic hierarchy continued to have difficulty accessing food, or, in some instances, experienced food insecurity for the first time. Food pantries saw a 55 percent increase in usage, with 40 percent being first-time users (Morello 2021). A study of 1,250 pre-pandemic, food-secure adults found that Black, Hispanic, and Asian participants were more than two times more likely to now be at risk for food insecurity than non-Hispanic whites (Lauren et al. 2021). Within this same study, women (57 percent) were more likely to be at risk than men (42 percent). Structural racism and structural sexism play major roles in the distribution of resources and power throughout the socioeconomic hierarchy, which is why these factors should be included in any discussion on the pandemic's impact on food insecurity.

Structural Racism

Racial disparity in access to affordable, nutritious food pre- and during the pandemic can be best understood through structural racism, which is the sum of societal practices through which racial discrimination creates inequality in the distribution of resources like housing, education, employment, earnings, benefits, and health care (Bailey et al. 2017). Nationally, non-Hispanic Blacks and Hispanics have the highest prevalence of food insecurity among all racial and ethnic groups (USDA 2020). This is also true in Ohio where non-Hispanic Blacks (21.3 percent) are three times more likely, and Hispanics (18.4 percent) are about two and half times more likely to have trouble accessing needed foods compared to non-Hispanic white Ohioans (7 percent; US Census Bureau n.d.). These disparate trends continued throughout the pandemic. For instance, data from the weekly Pulse Survey showed that, throughout the pandemic, non-Hispanic Blacks, and Hispanics were more likely to report "sometimes" or "often not having enough to eat in the past 7 days" compared to non-Hispanic whites in Ohio (Census Bureau n.d.).

One pathway to food insecurity is unemployment, and COVID created even greater disparity in unemployment rates between racial and ethnic minorities and whites. Researchers exploring labor market disruption and job loss compared rates of employment pre-pandemic (February) to during the pandemic (April and May) and found that Hispanics had greater job loss than non-Hispanics, and Blacks had greater job loss than whites (Montenovo et al. 2020). The pandemic also widened the gap in unemployment rates between Black and white Ohioans. Data from the Current Population Survey revealed that, at the onset of the pandemic, Black Ohioans were 1.8 times more likely be unemployed than whites, but, by December 2020, as the state's unemployment rates began to fall across the board, Blacks were three times more likely to be unemployed (Campbell 2021). These differences are partly due to racial and ethnic minorities being overrepresented in industries that experienced significant job loss. Nationally, hotels (42.3 percent), restaurants and bars (48.1 percent), clothing stores (58.9 percent), and amusement parks and casinos (59.9 percent) laid off significant numbers of workers (Pietsch 2020). The construction industry had a threefold increase in unemployment, despite many states allowing construction projects to continue, even during shutdowns (Phillips 2020). Ohio's unemployment rate increased over 200 percent (4 percent to 16.8 percent) within the first two months of the pandemic (Weiker 2020). Some of the most popular industries in Ohio include restaurant work, retail, and construction (Top 200 Popular Jobs 2021). Although almost half of all Ohioans who became unemployed during the pandemic worked in one of these three industries, Black Ohioans were noticeably overrepresented among the unemployed in the areas of construction, retail, and food service (Campbell 2021; Figure 13.1).

It is important to understand that the racial disparity in unemployment rates goes beyond specific industries where people work. While unemployment rates typically decrease as workers' level of education increases, regardless of race and ethnicity, educational attainment has not been a buffer to unemployment for Blacks. For example, Black Ohioans are more likely to be unemployed than white Ohioans with the same level of education (Campbell 2021; Figure 13.2). This unemployment trend in Ohio mimics national statistics that show Black workers as more likely to be unemployed compared to their white counterparts

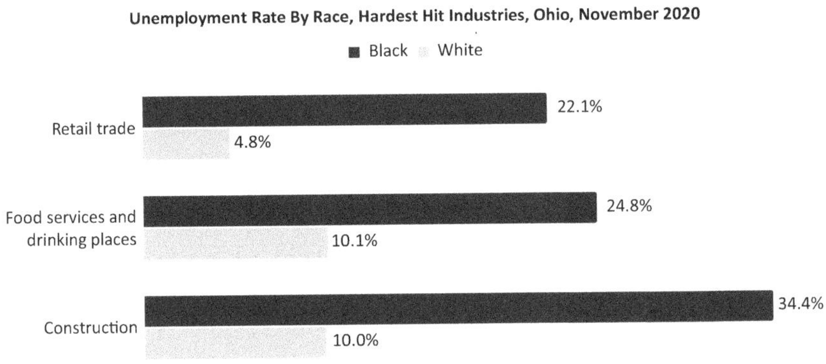

Fig. 13.1. Campbell 2021.

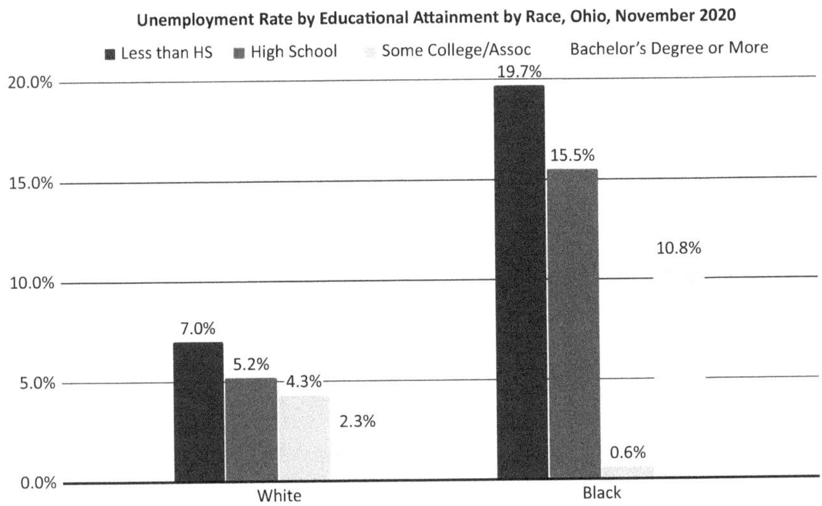

Fig. 13.2. Campbell 2021.

at every level of education, from having less than a high school diploma to an advanced degree (Gould and Wilson 2020).

Structural racism also impacts the neighborhood food environment. Many racial and ethnic minorities live in food deserts, which are geographic areas, typically found in low-income communities, that have limited affordable, nutritious food options. Those living in food deserts may have inadequate access to full-service grocery stores or supermarkets, or no access at all. (Dubowitz et al. 2015; Meyersohn 2020). While these areas are associated with low-income communities, racial segregation in housing opportunities is also a factor. A study conducted by Johns Hopkins University found that, at equal levels of poverty, Black neighborhoods have the fewest and white neighborhoods have the most supermarkets (Bower et al. 2014). In 2020, Ohio was ranked forty-fourth in the nation for housing segregation, with a score of 67 out of 100, where "0" represents total integration and "100" represents complete segregation (United Health Foundation 2021). The state's highest concentrations of racial and ethnic minorities and poor people live in metropolitan areas; many of Ohio's food deserts are found in low-income metropolitan census tracts (Exner 2019; Ohio Development Services 2020; USDA 2021b). In Ohio, racial and ethnic minorities with low incomes are more likely to live in a food desert than their low-income, white counterparts.

Acknowledging the intersection of race and income with regard to the food environment gives us additional insight into how the pandemic disproportionately impacted food insecurity among racial and ethnic minorities. People who live in food deserts are forced either to rely on corner stores or use public transit to access food, and the challenges associated with these options were exacerbated by the pandemic. For example, social distancing protocols and a decrease in demand created cuts in public transit services, which in turn contributed to the potential for overcrowding and increased risk for exposure to COVID-19 (Ezike and Velasco 2020). In Ohio, to limit exposure, the health department issued a recommendation to restrict the number of people using public transit to preserve social distancing (Ohio Department of Health 2021); in some areas of Ohio, bus capacity was limited to just 20 passengers at a time (Kennedy, 2020). Pew Research Center data indicates that low-income and Black or Hispanic people rely on public transportation on a regular basis, making them not only more vulnerable to difficulties accessing food but also to exposure to the virus (Anderson 2020). Those forgoing public transportation and utilizing local corner stores for food shopping had limited options and paid higher prices, as smaller food retailers tend to have less variety of healthy foods and charge higher prices for those they do (Caspi 2017). As mentioned earlier, these prices would have been even higher during the pandemic, further limiting shoppers' already stretched food budgets.

Structural Sexism

Across all racial and ethnic groups, women have been disparately impacted by food insecurity compared to men before and during the pandemic. Prior to the pandemic, women were more likely than men to experience poverty and a lack of food security. Being at risk for both was significantly higher for single mothers (28.7 percent) compared to single fathers (15.4 percent; Feeley 2018; USDA 2021a). This trend continued during the pandemic, with research findings indicating that, among those who were previously food secure, women (57 percent) were more likely at risk for becoming food insecure than men (42 percent; Lauren et al. 2021). Similarly, in Ohio, women (24 percent) compared to men (18 percent), were more likely to report not having enough food or foods they wanted to eat during the pandemic (US Census Bureau n.d.). This difference in how the pandemic has impacted men and women reflects the negative impact of structural sexism, or systemic inequality in the distribution of power and resources based on gender. Similar to how structural racism created a greater burden for racial and ethnic minorities with regard to accessing affordable, nutritious food, systemic sexism created unique experiences that place women at greater risk for experiencing food insecurity (Homan 2019) The next section will focus on differences in power and resources (e.g., income and employment), especially in the context of parenthood and gender roles.

Distribution of Resources through Income

Income has the most obvious impact on food insecurity, considering the high correlation between the two. Identifying structural barriers that limit women's access to income helps us understand why they have shouldered the brunt of the pandemic's negative impact on the economy—so much so, that some have referred to this era not as a recession but as a "she-cession" (Gupta 2020). As a group, women earn less money than men, due in large part to gender discrimination, which has led to women being underrepresented in higher paying managerial jobs, overrepresented in lower paying jobs, and likely to earn less money than men do when performing the same jobs (Barroso and Brown 2021). Occupational segregation based on gender has caused certain jobs traditionally seen as "women's work" (e.g., cosmetology, childcare, medical assistant work) to pay less. According to the US Bureau of Labor and Statistics, industries overrepresented by women were hardest hit by the pandemic, and women in those industries, especially women of color, lost more jobs than men during the pandemic (Boesch and Phadke 2021). By May 2020, women represented more than half (55 percent) of 20.5 million jobs lost nationally and the rate of unemployment for single mothers tripled (Hegewisch et al. 2020). In Ohio, a little over 55 percent of women reported being unemployed by mid-April 2020, compared to a little over 36 percent of men (US Census Bureau n.d.).

An example of job loss with regard to traditional "women's work" would be home health aides who lost their jobs when the agencies that employed them saw decreased demand for service at the outset of the pandemic due to clients' concerns for safety and family members assuming caregiver responsibilities (Sama et al. 2020). Another contributing factor to the gendered disparity in unemployment rates was women assuming caregiver responsibilities for their own younger children when schools closed and for their own older family members. According to data from the Census Bureau's Household Pulse Survey, caring for children not in school or day care was the most frequent reason given by Ohioans for being unemployed (US Census Bureau n.d.). Ohio had some of the most aggressive safety guidelines in the nation at the start of the pandemic. Although the governor received national praise early in the pandemic for his quick response, there were unintended consequences, such as low-income, single mothers having limited childcare options when schools closed. Ohio not only closed schools, it also closed adult and child day care centers to the general public. These closures had a greater impact on single mothers compared to single fathers, because single fathers tend to have a stronger support system (e.g., by cohabiting with a partner who contributes to tasks related to childcare). This inequality in nonfinancial resources will be discussed in the next section.

The gender wage gap also contributed to more women becoming food insecure than men during the pandemic. In 2020, women earned 82 cents for every dollar earned by men, and this gap is even wider for women with minority racial and ethnic backgrounds (American Association of University Women 2020; Barroso and Brown 2021). The average income of Ohio families led by single women is $24,968, while families led by single men earn an average of $41,090 (Campbell 2019). Using the federal poverty line to measure the average family income, and presuming these families had four members, the single-women-headed household would be living in poverty. Also, the income of the single-woman-headed family is about $35,000 less than what was needed in Ohio ($60,000), pre-pandemic, to meet the household's basic needs without outside assistance, while the single-man-headed family falls short by about $19,000. These shortfalls have likely increased during the pandemic as necessities like food, gas, diapers, and toilet paper now cost more due to disruptions to the supply chain and increases in demand (Meyersohn and Tappe 2021).

Distribution of Power through Social Capital

Access to financial resources, while important, is not the only protective factor against food insecurity. Social capital is also necessary to offset some of the load placed on women by COVID-19. If income is viewed as economic capital, then relationships with informal and formal social networks that reflect trust, cohesion, and mutual aid and policies that empower people could be viewed as social capital (Robbins et al. 2019). Studies have shown that social capital can improve food security status (Nosratabadi et al. 2020). It can be a protective factor, or at least can prevent a family from slipping from having low to very low food security by increasing access to resources such as food, clothing, transportation, and shelter. Social capital can empower those with limited or no economic capital (e.g., income) to still get their basic needs met, despite the absence of financial resources. However, the pandemic has illuminated the differences in the quantity and quality of social capital available to men and women. In Ohio, 42 percent of single-man-headed households also include an unmarried partner residing in the household who likely helps with household responsibilities and childcare and may contribute financially, while only 18 percent of single-woman-headed households have this same living situation (Campbell 2019). These differences suggest that single mothers with low incomes have lower levels of social capital than their male counterparts and are likely more reliant on social networks outside of the home such as friends, coworkers, and more formal networks such as social service agencies. However, the pandemic created disruptions to these social networks, further limiting their access to social capital.

For many women with low incomes, relying on social capital helped them manage deficits created by a lack of financial resources. However, extensive and prolonged periods of mandated social distancing during the pandemic disrupted these social networks, diminishing social capital's capacity to protect against food insecurity (Pitas and Ehmer 2020). It became more difficult or impossible to have extended family provide childcare or to access to formal support networks. Due in large part to their often nontraditional working hours and the presence of fewer regulated childcare centers in their communities, low-income mothers tend to rely on relatives for childcare, especially grandparents (Chaudry et al. 2011). However, the fact that older adults were more susceptible to contracting COVID-19 and having poor health outcomes afterward may have contributed to some women with low incomes leaving the workforce during the pandemic, thus increasing their risk for food insecurity (Center for Disease Control n.d.; Courage 2021). Additionally, in-person operations at social service agencies were also suspended, making it difficult for those same low-income mothers to apply for much-needed economic supports. People who lost their jobs in Ohio were not able to apply for benefits in person; they had to apply online or by phone. With most libraries closed, those who did not have a home computer and Internet connection had to apply by phone and endure long waits.

Policy Implications

The immediate health threat of COVID-19 appears to be waning, and the country is slowly returning to a "new normal" socially. However, the financial impact of the pandemic will likely be felt for years to come, making it imperative that those who influence and develop social welfare policies broaden their focus when redressing the factors that made women and racial and ethnic minorities more vulnerable to food insecurity. There are 15 federal nutrition programs that address this issue (e.g., food stamps, Women, Infants and Children [WIC], the National School Lunch Program). During the pandemic, the passage of the Families First Coronavirus Response Act and the Consolidated Appropriations Act increased funding to these programs to provide more resources to Ohio families who were among the hardest hit, financially. However, this additional funding was temporary, and none of the nutrition assistance programs addressed underlying racial, ethnic, and gender disparities in food insecurity, either in Ohio or in the nation as a whole. We need policies to address ongoing social inequalities that lead to women and racial and ethnic minorities shouldering a greater share of the negative outcomes associated with the pandemic and other crises that impact the economy.

An obvious first step in addressing gender and racial/ethnic disparities in food insecurity is to address disparities in poverty by ensuring equal pay across the board, which would increase the incomes of women, and racial and ethnic minorities. For example, if women in Ohio were to receive pay equal to that of their male counterparts (e.g., of similar skill level, education, and hours worked each week), they would see an 18.8 percent increase in pay and a 48 and 34 percent decrease in poverty, respectively, for all women and single mothers, increasing their ability to afford healthy foods (Institute for Women's

Policy Research 2016). Despite federal laws prohibiting discrimination in pay based on gender or race, it is clear discriminatory practices still occur. To address this, the Employer Information Report (i.e., EEO-1 form) should return to collecting demographic pay data to make it easier to enforce equal pay laws. The form had been used for over 50 years to collect employee demographic data, with the exception of pay. The form was revised in 2016 to require employers to include demographic pay data; however, it was revised in 2019, and demographic pay data is no longer collected (Frye 2021). It is also recommended that companies should be more transparent by making pay gaps public and including salary information in all job postings (Frye 2021). Lastly, because marginalized groups have historically been paid less, employers should be banned from including pay history in calculating salary offers (Boesch and Phadke 2021).

Another step toward increasing the pay of these two groups would be identifying and updating policies created during a time of state-sanctioned racial and gender discriminatory practices, which have had lasting negative impacts on the wages for jobs traditionally held by women, and racial and ethnic minorities. The Fair Labor Standards Act (FLSA) should undergo strategic changes to ensure that the Act values all occupations, thus creating equitable wages and protections for historically marginalized groups. For example, Solomon et al. (2019) explain how the FLSA of 1938 improved wages and working conditions for white workers but left many racial and ethnic minorities unprotected, because the Act did not cover domestic, agricultural, and service occupations. Although the Act was later updated to include more occupations, many that are disproportionately held by women and racial and ethnic minorities (e.g. live-in domestic service workers, babysitters, companions for the elderly) remain excluded. Solomon and colleagues point out how the practice of tipping service staff allowed restaurants and railways to avoid paying racial and ethnic minorities at all; their tips were their income. Today, women make up around 70 percent of tipped workers and earn as little as $2.13 per hour (National Women's Law Center 2019). Employers are required to pay the difference if their tips do not make up the difference between their hourly wage and the federal minimum wage. However, evidence indicates that this rarely happens, causing these workers to lose millions of dollars in wages every year. There are growing calls for the sub-minimum wage for tipped workers to be eliminated or at the very least increased to at least half the regular minimum wage (Schweitzer 2021). Eliminating the sub-minimum wage, and paying these workers the full minimum wage would lift women out of poverty and help close the pay wage gap, subsequently decreasing gender disparity in food insecurity (NWLC 2019).

Similarly, the federal minimum wage has not been raised since 2009, and has not kept in step with the cost of living since 1968, which made it difficult for minimum wage earners to meet their basic needs even before the price increases brought on by the pandemic (Kiger 2019). The passage of the Raise the Wage Act of 2021 would increase the federal minimum wage gradually to $15 over a five-year period for everyone, including tipped workers (Fact Sheet 2021). The hope is that this will help close the race and gender wage gap, as nearly half of Black and Latino workers have jobs that pay less than $15 an hour, and 59 percent of minimum wage earners are women (Boesch, Bleiweis, and Haider 2021; Fact Sheet 2021).

Finally, as mentioned above, the pandemic created a situation in which women disproportionately lost their jobs due to caregiver responsibilities. Protections are needed for women who have to simultaneously manage multiple roles, as paid workers and unpaid caregivers. Currently in the United States, there is no national paid leave policy. While eight states (and Washington, DC) have instituted paid family leave benefits, Ohio is not one of them. The Family Medical Leave Act (FMLA), which guarantees unpaid leave for up to 12 weeks, only covers about 60 percent of Ohio's workforce (National Partnership for Women and Families 2022). This is because FMLA only covers workers who have worked at least 1,250 hours for a 12-month period for their employer before their leave begins (US Department of Labor n.d.). Women are more likely to cite caregiving responsibilities as the reason for choosing part-time employment and, in Ohio, women are two times more likely than men to work part-time (Ewing-Nelson 2020; Institute for Women's Policy Research 2015). The ascribed social role of caregiver for women makes it difficult for them to maintain employment for long periods of time and impacts their ability to work an average of 24 hours a week to meet the criteria to be protected under FMLA. The Family First Coronavirus Response Act provided financial support for workers who could not work due to childcare concerns by requiring employers to provide up to 12 weeks of leave (10 of them paid) to all employees, including part-time workers not eligible for FMLA

(Rohen and Wilson 2021). Because this mandate expired in December 2020, FMLA requirements should be updated to permanently include the pandemic-era paid leave mandates, as women continue to require protections from job loss associated with caregiver responsibilities.

Conclusion

The harsh economic and social impact of the pandemic magnified the issue of wealth disparities in the United States. Food insecurity is a multifaceted issue that must be examined in a context that is larger than simply addressing its social consequences (e.g., not having enough to eat). To address the disparities that contribute to more women and racial and ethnic minorities experiencing food insecurity, we must modernize the state and federal policies that impact income. We must also broaden the focus of food insecurity interventions to account for, and redress, structural racism and structural sexism and the unequal distribution of resources and power based on social stratification.

REFERENCES

American Association of University Women. 2020. "Race and the Pay Gap." October 29, 2020. www.aauw.org/resources/research/race-and-the-pay-gap/.

Anderson, Monica. 2020. "Who Relies on Public Transit in the U.S." Pew Research Center, April 7, 2020. www.pewresearch.org/fact-tank/2016/04/07/who-relies-on-public-transit-in-the-u-s/.

Bailey, Zinzi D., Nancy Krieger, Madina Agénor, Jasmine Graves, Natalia Linos, and Mary T. Bassett. 2017. "Structural Racism and Health Inequities in the USA: Evidence and Interventions." *The Lancet* 389, no. 10077: 1453–1463. https://doi.org/10.1016/s0140-6736(17)30569-x.

Barroso, Amanda, and Anna Brown. 2021. "Gender Pay Gap in U.S. Held Steady in 2020." Pew Research Center. www.pewresearch.org/fact-tank/2021/05/25/gender-pay-gap-facts/.

Boesch, Diane, Robin Bleiweis, and Areeba Haider. 2021. "Raising the Minimum Wage Would Be Transformative for Women." Center for American Progress, February 23, 2021. www.americanprogress.org/issues/women/news/2021/02/23/496221/raising-minimum-wage-transformative-women/.

Boesch, Diana, and Shilpa Phadke. 2021. "When Women Lose All the Jobs: Essential Actions for a Gender-Equitable Recovery." Center for American Progress, February 1, 2021. www.americanprogress.org/issues/women/reports/2021/02/01/495209/women-lose-jobs-essential-actions-gender-equitable-recovery/.

Bower, Kelly M., Roland J. Thorpe, Charles Rohde, and Darrell J. Gaskin. 2014. "The Intersection of Neighborhood Racial Segregation, Poverty, AND Urbanicity and Its Impact on Food Store Availability in the United States." *Preventive Medicine* 58: 33–39. https://doi.org/10.1016/j.ypmed.2013.10.010.

Campbell, Emily. 2019. "Ohio's Single-Mom Households More Likely to Live in Poverty than Single Dads, What Does This Mean for Kids?" Center for Community Solutions, October 4, 2019. www.communitysolutions.com/ohios-single-mom-households-likely-live-poverty-single-dads-mean-kids/.

Campbell, Emily. 2021. "Racial Disparities Extend to Unemployment in Ohio." Center for Community Solutions, January 28, 2021. www.communitysolutions.com/racial-disparities-extend-unemployment/.

Cantwell, Maria. 2021. "Fact Sheet." January 28, 2021. www.cantwell.senate.gov/imo/media/doc/Raise-the-Wage-Act-of-2021-Fact-Sheet-FINAL.pdf.

Caspi, Caitlin, Jennifer Pelletier, Lisa Harnack, Darin Erickson, Kathleen Lenk, and Melissa Laska. 2017. "Pricing of Staple Foods at Supermarkets versus Small Food Stores." *International Journal of Environmental Research and Public Health* 14, no. 8: 915–927. https://doi.org/10.3390/ijerph14080915.

Center for Disease Control and Prevention. 2021. "Older Adults Risks and Vaccine Information." August 2, 2021. www.cdc.gov/aging/covid19/covid19-older-adults.html.

Chaudry, Ajay, Juan Pedroza, Heather Sandstrom, Anna Danziger, Michel Grosz, Molly M. Scott, and Sarah Ting. 2011. *Child Care Choices of Low-Income Working Families*. Urban Institute, June 8, 2011. www.urban.org/research/publication/child-care-choices-low-income-working-families.

Courage, Katherine Harmon. 2021. "Day Care, Grandparent, Pod or Nanny? How to Manage the Risks of Pandemic Child Care." NPR, August 21, 2020. www.npr.org/sections/health-shots/2020/08/21/902613282/daycare-grandparent-pod-or-nanny-how-to-manage-the-risks-of-pandemic-child-care.

Davidson, J.D. 2021. "Ohio's Economy among Hardest Hit by COVID-19 Pandemic." The Center Square, April 5, 2021. www.thecentersquare.com/ohio/ohio-s-economy-among-hardest-hit-by-covid-19-pandemic/article_3f3ff67e-9647-11eb-ad26-5fcb59927da7.html.

Dubowitz, Tamara, Collette Ncube, Kristin Leuschner, and Shannah Tharp-Gilliam. 2015. "A Natural Experiment Opportunity in Two Low-Income Urban Food Desert Communities." *Health Education & Behavior* 42, no. 1(suppl.): 87S–96S. https://doi.org/10.1177/1090198115570048.

Dzhanova, Yelena. 2020. "Food Banks Are Closing and Losing Their Workforce Because of the Coronavirus." CNBC, April 29, 2020. www.cnbc.com/2020/04/28/coronavirus-food-banks-are-closing-and-losing-their-workforce.html.

Elmes, Michael B. 2018. "Economic Inequality, Food Insecurity, and the Erosion of Equality of Capabilities in the United States." *Business & Society* 57, no. 6(July): 1045–1074. https://doi.org/10.1177/0007650316676238.

Ewing-Nelson, Claire. 2020. "Part-Time Workers Are Paid Less, Have Less Access to Benefits—and Most Are Women." National Women's Law Center, February 2020. https://nwlc.org/wp-content/uploads/2020/02/Part-Time-Workers-Factsheet-2.26.20.pdf.

Exner, Rich. 2019. "Ranking Every Ohio City, County for Size of Minority Population." Cleveland.com, January 30, 2019. www.cleveland.com/datacentral/2018/01/ranking_every_ohio_city_county_4.html.

Ezike, Richard, and Gabriella Velasco. 2020. "Are Cars a NECESSITY? During COVID-19, Low-Income Households May Consider Public Transit Alternatives." Housing Matters, August 12, 2020. https://housingmatters.urban.org/articles/are-cars-necessity-during-covid-19-low-income-households-may-consider-public-transit.

Feeding America. n.d. "Map the Meal Gap." Feeding America. Accessed May 28, 2021. https://map.feedingamerica.org/county/2019/overall.

Feeding America. 2021. "The Impact of the Coronavirus on Local Food Insecurity." www.feedingamerica.org/research/coronavirus-hunger-research

Feeley, Maris. 2018. "Ending Hunger Is a Gender Equity Issue." Food Research & Action Center, March 20, 2018. https://frac.org/blog/ending-hunger-gender-equity-issue.

Food Research and Action Center. 2020. "Hunger & Poverty in America." https://frac.org/hunger-poverty-america#:~:text=One%20in%20ten%20(10.5%20percent,the%20U.S.%20experience%20food%20insecurity.

Frye, Jocelyn. 2021. "10 Essential Actions to Promote Equal Pay." Center for American Progress, March 24, 2021. www.americanprogress.org/issues/women/reports/2021/03/24/497478/10-essential-actions-promote-equal-pay/.

Garner, Meg. 2020. "Report: Ohioans Rank among Hardest Hit by Covid-19's Financial Impact" *Cincinnati Business Courier*, June 8, 2020. www.bizjournals.com/cincinnati/news/2020/06/08/ohioans-hit-hard-financially-by-covid.html.

Gould, Elise, and Valerie Wilson. 2020. "Black Workers Face Two of the Most Lethal Preexisting Conditions for Coronavirus-Racism and Economic Inequality." Economic Policy Institute, June 1, 2020. https://www.epi.org/publication/black-workers-covid/.

Gupta, Alisha H. 2020. "Why Some Women Call This Recession a 'Shecession'." *New York Times*, May 9, 2020. www.nytimes.com/2020/05/09/us/unemployment-coronavirus-women.html.

Hegewisch, Ariane, Zohal Barsi, and Jeff Hayes. 2020. "Dramatic Decline in Employment Hits Women Even More Severely than Men." Institute for Women's Policy Research, May 8, 2020. https://iwpr.org/wp-content/uploads/2020/05/QF-Breadwinner-Mothers-by-Race-FINAL.pdf.

Homan, Patricia. 2019. "Structural Sexism and Health in the United States: A New Perspective on Health Inequality and the Gender System." *American Sociological Review* 84, no. 3: 486–516. https://doi.org/10.1177/0003122419848723.

Horan, Stephanie. 2020. "States Where Residents Are Financially Hurting the Most during COVID-19—2020 Study." SmartAsset, June 2, 2020. https://smartasset.com/financial-advisor/states-where-residents-are-financially-hurting-covid19-2020.

Institute for Women's Policy Research. 2015. "Part-Time and Full-Time Workers." Status of Women in the States, October 21, 2015. https://statusofwomendata.org/explore-the-data/employment-and-earnings/additional-state-data/part-time-and-full-time-workers/.

Institute for Women's Policy Research. 2016. "The Economic Impact of Equal Pay by State." Women in the States. https://statusofwomendata.org/featured/the-economic-impact-of-equal-pay-by-state/.

Kaiser, Michelle L., Julia Dionne, and Jake K. Carr. 2019. "Predictors of Diet-Related Health Outcomes in Food-Secure and Food-Insecure Communities."

Social Work in Public Health 34, no. 3: 214–229. https://doi.org/10.1080/19371918.2019.1575313.

Kennedy, Eleanor. 2020. "Why Central Ohio's transit service won't look different even as Ohio businesses begin to reopen." *Columbus Business First*. Retrieved October 27, 2022. www.bizjournals.com/columbus/news/2020/04/30/why-central-ohios-transit-service-wont-look.html.

Kiger, Patrick J. 2019. "Minimum Wage in America: A Timeline." History.com. A&E Television Networks, October 18, 2019. www.history.com/news/minimum-wage-america-timeline.

Koh, Keumseok, Michelle L. Kaiser, Glennon Sweeney, Karima Samadi, and Ayaz Hyder. 2020. "Explaining Racial Inequality in Food Security in Columbus, Ohio: A Blinder–Oaxaca Decomposition Analysis." *International Journal of Environmental Research and Public Health* 17, no. 15: 5488–5503. https://doi.org/10.3390/ijerph17155488.

Lauren, Brianna N., Elisabeth R. Silver, Adam S. Faye, Alexandra M. Rogers, Jennifer A. Woo-Baidal, Elissa M. Ozanne, and Chin Hur. 2021. "Predictors of Households at Risk for Food Insecurity in the United States during the COVID-19 Pandemic." *Public Health Nutrition* 24, no. 12: 3929–3936. https://doi.org/10.1017/s1368980021000355.

Leone, Lucia A., Sheila Fleischhacker, Betsy Anderson-Steeves, Kaitlyn Harper, Megan Winkler, Elizabeth Racine, Barbara Baquero, and Joel Gittelsohn. 2020. "Healthy Food Retail during the COVID-19 Pandemic: Challenges and Future Directions." *International Journal of Environmental Research and Public Health* 17, no. 20: 7397–7411. https://doi.org/10.3390/ijerph17207397.

Meyersohn, Nathaniel. 2020. "How the Rise of Supermarkets Left Out Black America." CNN, June 16, 2020. www.cnn.com/2020/06/16/business/grocery-stores-access-race-inequality/index.html.

Meyersohn, Nathaniel, and Anneken Tappe. 2021. "Millions of American Families Are about to Get Hit with Diaper Sticker Shock." KCCI, July 1, 2021. www.kcci.com/article/us-rising-cost-of-diapers/36220981.

Montenovo, Laura, Xuan Jiang, Felipe Lozano Rojas, Ian M. Schmutte, Kosali I. Simon, Bruce A. Weinberg, and Coady Wing. 2020. "Determinants of Disparities in Covid-19 Job Losses." National Bureau of Economic Research, May 11, 2020. www.nber.org/papers/w27132.

Morales, Danielle, Stephanie Moarales and Tyler Beltran. 2021. "Racial/Ethnic Disparities in Household Food Insecurity during the COVID-19 Pandemic: A Nationally Representative Study." *Journal of Racial and Ethnic Health Disparities* 8, no. 5: 1300–1314. https://doi/org/10.1007/s40615-020-00892-7.

Morello, Paul. 2021. "The Food Bank Response to COVID, by the Numbers." Feeding America, March 12, 2021. www.feedingamerica.org/hunger-blog/food-bank-response-covid-numbers.

Myers, Ana McCormick, and Matthew A. Painter. 2017. "Food Insecurity in the United States of America: An Examination of Race/Ethnicity and Nativity." *Food Security* 9, no. 6: 1419–1432. https://doi.org/10.1007/s12571-017-0733-8.

National Partnership for Women and Families. 2022. "Key Facts: The Family and Medical Leave Act." www.nationalpartnership.org/our-work/economic-justice/reports/fmla-key-facts.html

National Women's Law Center. 2019. "The Raise the Wage Act: Boosting Women's Paychecks and Advancing Equal Pay." https://nwlc.org/wp-content/uploads/2019/10/Raise-the-Wage-Act-Boosting-Womens-Pay-Checks-10.22.19.pdf.

Niles, Meredith T., Farryl Bertmann, Emily H. Belarmino, Thomas Wentworth, Erin Biehl, and Roni Neff. 2020. "The Early Food Insecurity Impacts of Covid-19." *Nutrients* 12, no. 7: 2096. https://doi.org/10.3390/nu12072096.

Nosratabadi, Saeed, Nesrine Khazami, Marwa Ben Abdallah, Zoltan Lackner, Shahab S. Band, Amir Mosavi, and Csaba Mako. 2020. "Social Capital Contributions to FOOD Security: A Comprehensive Literature Review." *Foods* 9, no. 11: 1650. https://doi.org/10.3390/foods9111650.

Odoms-Young Angela and Morino Bruce. 2018. "Examining the Impact of Structural Racism on Food Insecurity: Implications for Addressing Racial/Ethnic Disparities". *Family Community Health* 41, no. 41: S3-S6.

Ohio Association of Community Action Agencies. 2021. "2021 State of Poverty Report." https://oacaa.org/wp-content/uploads/2022/01/SOP-2021.pdf.

Ohio Department of Health. 2021. "COVID-19 Guidance Public Transportation Providers." Coronavirus Ohio, March 25, 2021. https://coronavirus.ohio.gov/static/responsible/covid-19-guidance-public-transportation-providers.pdf.

Ohio Development Services Agency. 2020. *The Ohio Poverty Report*. https://www.development.ohio.gov/files/research/p7005.pdf.

Phillips, D. 2020. "Construction Industry Hit Hard by the Coronavirus Pandemic." *U.S. News & World Report*, May 27, 2020. www.communitysolutions.com/racial-disparities-extend-unemployment/.

Pietsch, B. 2020. "20.5 Million People Lost Their Jobs in April. Here Are the 10 Job Types That Were Hardest Hit." *Business Insider*, May 12, 2020. www.businessinsider.com/jobs-industries-careers-hit-hardest-by-coronavirus-unemployment-data-2020-5.

Pitas, Nicholas, and Colin Ehmer. 2020. "Social Capital in the Response to COVID-19." *American Journal of Health Promotion* 34, no. 8: 942–944. https://doi.org/10.1177/0890117120924531.

Robbins, Susan P., Pranab Chatterjee, Edward R. Canda, and George S. Leibowitz. 2019. *Contemporary Human Behavior Theory: A Critical Perspective for Social Work Practice*. New York: Pearson.

Rohen, Jennifer, and Chastity Wilson. 2021. "Let Us Help You Understand What Is Happening with Families First." CLA (CliftonLarsonAllen), April 27, 2021. www.claconnect.com/resources/articles/2021/let-us-help-you-understand-what-is-happening-with-families-first.

Roncarlo, Frederico, and Louise Potvin. 2016. "Food Insecurity as a Symptom of a Social Disease: Analyzing a Social Problem from a Medical Perspective." *Canadian Family Physician* 62: 291–292.

Sama, Susan R., Margaret M. Quinn, Catherine J. Galligan, Nicole D. Karlsson, Rebecca J. Gore, David Kriebel, and Julia C. Prentice. 2020. "Impacts of the COVID-19 Pandemic on Home Health and Home Care Agency Managers, Clients, and Aides: A Cross-Sectional Survey, March to June, 2020." *Home Health Care Management & Practice* 33, no. 2: 125–129. https://doi.org/10.1177/1084822320980415.

Schweitzer, Justin. 2021. "Ending the Tipped Minimum Wage Will Reduce Poverty and Inequality." Center for American Progress, March 30, 2021. www.americanprogress.org/issues/poverty/reports/2021/03/30/497673/ending-tipped-minimum-wage-will-reduce-poverty-inequality/.

Solomon, Danyelle, Connor Maxwell, and Abril Castro. 2019. "Systematic Inequality and Economic Opportunity." Center for American Progress, August 7, 2019. www.americanprogress.org/issues/race/reports/2019/08/07/472910/systematic-inequality-economic-opportunity/.

Staren, Dakota. 2020. "Social Determinants of Health: Food Insecurity in the United States." Healthcare Value Hub, June 2020. www.healthcarevaluehub.org/advocate-resources/publications/social-determinants-health-food-insecurity-united-states

"Top 200 Popular Jobs in Ohio." 200 most popular jobs in Ohio - USAWage.com, 2021. https://www.usawage.com/popular/jobs-state-ohio.php.

United Health Foundation. 2021. *Annual Report.* America's Health Rankings, 2021. www.americashealthrankings.org/explore/annual/measure/Overall_a/state/OH.

US Census Bureau. n.d. "Household Pulse Survey: Measuring Social and Economic Impacts during the Coronavirus Pandemic." Accessed June 5, 2021, www.census.gov/programs-surveys/household-pulse-survey.html.

US Department of Agriculture. Economic Research Service. 2020. Food Security in U.S: Key Statistics and Graphics. https://www.ers.usda.gov/topics/food-nutrition-assistance/food-security-in-the-us/key-statistics-graphics/#insecure.

US Department of Agriculture. Economic Research Service. 2021a. "Food Security in the U.S: Overview." www.ers.usda.gov/topics/food-nutrition-assistance/food-security-in-the-us./

US Department of Agriculture. Economic Research Service. 2021b. "Food Access Research Atlas." USDA ERS—Documentation. www.ers.usda.gov/data-products/food-access-research-atlas/documentation/.

US Department of Health and Human Services and US Department of Agriculture. 2015. "2015–2020 Dietary Guidelines for Americans. 8th Edition." Health.gov, December 2015. https://health.gov/our-work/food-nutrition/previous-dietary-guidelines/2015.

US Department of Labor. n.d. "COVID-19 and the Family and Medical Leave Act Questions and Answers." Accessed June 25, 2021. www.dol.gov/agencies/whd/fmla/pandemic.

Weiker, Jim. 2020. "Ohio Unemployment Reaches All-Time High in April." *Cincinnati Enquirer,* May 22, 2020. www.cincinnati.com/story/news/2020/05/22/ohio-unemployment-rate-april-kentucky-indiana/5242749002/.

Wolfson, Julia A., and Cindy W. Leung. 2020. "Food Insecurity and COVID-19: Disparities in Early Effects for Us Adults." *Nutrients* 12, no. 6: 1648. https://doi.org/10.3390/nu12061648.

14 | Not Returning to Normalized Injustice

Reflections on Teaching and Learning While Living the Pandemic

Personal Reflection

Kim E. Nielsen

In this personal reflection, a scholar of history and disability studies grapples with teaching about ableism and other forms of prejudice to students living with inequalities and vulnerabilities exacerbated by COVID.

"This coronavirus stuff will be over by mid-April," my student predicted during the last week of March 2020. She went on to proclaim confidently, "The president said so. It'll all be fine." My skeptical expression must have been significant enough to convey itself across the video platform we were learning to use with varying degrees of success. Another student, new to a multiple sclerosis diagnosis, turned off her screen; she would later confide that she had started to cry.

Nearly a year later, in January 2021, the next spring semester began. My University of Toledo students and I remained isolated either at home or in dorms, some sequestered with additional family members, all having learned much (but not enough) about synchronous "live" teaching and learning via electronic platforms. We bravely embarked on the semester-long course Eugenics Past and Present, scheduled long before the COVID-19 pandemic. Eugenics is the intentional manipulation of human reproduction and lives in order to "improve" society by eliminating those considered unfit. Eugenic ideologies have produced a range of results, including bullying and hate crimes, coerced sterilization, the denial of medical care, genetic editing, marital fitness laws, and the extreme horrors of the Holocaust. Embedded in eugenics is the ableist assumption that people with disabilities live miserable lives, contribute nothing to society, and face bad futures.

This brief reflection focuses on my experience teaching disability history and analyzing eugenics in the midst of the US coronavirus pandemic. My students and I shared the experience of learning and teaching while daily mired in health-care inequalities, fears related to physical vulnerability and preexisting conditions, economic devastation, ever-expanding family responsibilities, and many profound and traumatic personal losses. The context highlighted the intersections between my own life and the issues I teach, and the intersections of my students' lives with those same issues.

My University of Toledo students are smart, interesting adults committed to improving their lives and the lives of their families. They are disproportionately first-generation college students, and almost all balance working for wages with attending college and performing family care work. Eugenics Past and Present attracted students interested in history, disability studies, and social justice.

The daily personal and large-scale societal pain of the pandemic heightened the lessons that both my students and I took from our semester. Adrienne Rich characterized education as an "ethical and intellectual contract between teacher and student [...] a pledge of mutual seriousness" (Rich 1995, 231). Living out this contract is not easy, for it involves the intellect, emotions, our personal lives, and the larger world of power relationships. Some students, not unreasonably, stepped away from the class contract. They took full-time jobs to support parents who had lost theirs; they supervised the online schooling of nieces and nephews or their own children. Some became immersed in depression or anxiety, or were simply unable to catch up with classwork after being ill with the coronavirus. For those who remained—which took far more effort than the simple word "remained" implies—the pandemic heightened the intensity and importance of our contract. In May 2021, we emerged from the spring semester battered, weary, and with a joint commitment to making lessons known.

The first lesson we learned, and a lesson we relearned daily, was that the trauma of the pandemic heightened our vulnerability to the pain of history and its analysis. As a scholar, teacher, and writer, I seek to convey the joys, the fervor, and the anguish of the past, and I seek to do so without traumatizing my students or myself. The pandemic made this difficult. We began the semester still reeling from the message that "we" should not worry about the pandemic, because it only affected the elderly, those with ongoing health conditions, and those who lived with such people. However, all of us, both in the course and in the world around us, were either in those categories or loved people who were. As we soon learned, no clean line divided the vulnerable from the "safe."

The coronavirus pandemic shone light on contemporary racism, ableism, and economic inequalities profoundly embedded in US history and profoundly unacknowledged. By examining the past, we learned a great deal about our present, and with an intensity we had not anticipated. Like the pandemic, our learning was painful. Our historical and contemporary traumas blurred together.

We analyzed the United States' long history of legal forced sterilizations and marital fitness laws, which targeted disabled people and people of color. Meanwhile, the pandemic was heightening the social isolation of disabled students already isolated by families who rejected them, dating apps that swiped them out of existence, and their inadequate access to mental health care. We read of the national debate generated by Chicago physician Harry Haiselden, who encouraged withholding medical care from disabled infants in the 1910s, and the oft-inadequate health care for most people with disabilities throughout the twentieth century. Simultaneously, our news feeds filled with contemporary national and regional debates about whether or not those with cognitive disabilities or chronic illness should have access to ventilators, other emergency health-care measures, and vaccination. People with disabilities who had lived daily with ventilators for years suddenly feared having theirs taken away.

We read of how ableism and racism were woven together in nineteenth- and early twentieth-century scientific racism, as physicians "diagnosed" African Americans as biologically inferior and undeveloped, which resulted in racist violence and inadequate education, health care, legal protections, and housing. We analyzed the history of World War I veterans' "rehabilitation" programs, which limited the career options of African American veterans to manual labor, presuming that was the height of their capacities. Meanwhile, in news reports across the spring and summer of 2020, we repeatedly learned of another, and then another, incidence of police killing of African American citizens (a disproportionate number of whom were disabled), while many in politics and the public refused to acknowledge such violence as part of a long trend in US history. National protests and local campus protests sought to highlight the injustice. Simultaneously, we saw the disproportionate and devastating effect of COVID on communities of color in both urban and rural regions with long histories of limited access to economic resources and quality health care.

It pained us all to learn about and analyze the eugenic targeting of people dismissed as expendable, while contemporary policies and practices were also targeting many of my students, those they love, and those they work with as expendable. For example, many of my students had health conditions that made them vulnerable and, as a result, they had to choose between the wages they received from going to work or exposure to risk. Their resulting agony required great care in our classroom discussions. As educators, we have responsibility to pay careful attention to those people most targeted. We do so in order to educate and analyze, and, importantly, to avoid harming our students any more than life already does. For many of us, the pandemic highlighted the ways by which education—even the simple demand that students *show up*—can cause harm if we are not careful. The format of our classrooms, our pedagogy, and the materials we study can cause harm. There is no simple solution for this other than care, intentionality, and constant analysis of the power dynamics in which we, and our students, live and struggle.

Despite the global health crisis, my Ohio students embodied hope. Those able to remain insisted on learning, insisted on being taught, and insisted on attempting to make sense of the present within the complex but unavoidable legacies of the past. My students and I emerged from the 2020–2021 school year with an urgent desire that our stories not be lost. Time should not erase the injustice, the courage, the pain, the boredom, and the pet stories of the pandemic; nor should we allow those eager to excuse the Trump administration's willful negligence to gloss over its consequences. What temporarily became our norm is horrific and must not be erased.

We all have stories. Necessitated by a home overflowing with family members, and enabled by the vital-but-sad University of Toledo service of providing Wi-Fi to its campus parking lots, one student spent her semester (including in the cold Ohio winter months) taking classes from her car. The university administration provided emergency laptops to students without them so they could continue their education, greatly aiding one of my students who had been doing all of his coursework on his phone. One student ordinarily lived with and cared for her grandparents, but moved out in order not to endanger them.

She then brought food to their doorstep every day for nearly a month, while working, completing schoolwork, and borrowing a friend's couch and kitchen. Another student, wrestling with intense anxiety, attended every virtual class period with his cat on his lap. Another always kept her camera off, ashamed of her crowded apartment and the poverty it made visible. I shared information on local Toledo food pantries every few weeks, and students updated each other on which pantry had what food available. Two students agonized over the survival of family members in global regions with few medical resources. One student "recovered" from COVID-19 with cognitive impacts that made it impossible for her to finish the course. An unusually high number of students simply disappeared, a national phenomenon not unique to the University of Toledo. One day, a student joined our virtual class from the McDonald's drive-through line, initiating an impromptu and uproarious conversation about our favorite breakfast foods. I remember that conversation as a magical moment of happiness and release.

Of course, educators also have stories. My brother, my much-loved baby brother, asked me if I thought the pandemic had been falsely hyped. He then acquired COVID-19, spent his initial hospital hours in a hallway due to overcrowding, and was given access to a ventilator before being put on an ECMO machine (an artificial heart-lung). He died, and the bulk of my family could not attend his funeral due to safety precautions. I "attended" his funeral via my laptop. Following my already laid-out syllabi, I then taught about how hospitals made decisions, sometimes with great forethought and sometimes horribly, about which COVID-19 patients received ventilators and ECMOs. For the first time in my career, I cried while teaching. My students responded with compassion.

These circumstances temporarily became our norm. As of 2022, the details may have changed, but the context remains our norm. We need to chronicle these stories.

It is too easy to dismiss the corporate injustices and individual experiences discussed here as unique to the pandemic. That, however, lets us ignore our responsibility and erase reality. The dynamics and power structures that were brought to the surface by the pandemic, by public confrontations with racism, by a class on eugenics, and by remote learning all already existed. Economic inequalities, disparate access to health care, social isolation, racism, and the brutal devaluation of people with disabilities were and remain present. Disregard for the lives of the vulnerable already existed, as did our now obvious interdependence and appreciation for the pets that care for us. Our "new" normal is actually the same as before.

As a scholar and educator, now vaccinated and still living in the pandemic, I am trying to learn. My hope is that what was once not apparent to many has boiled to the surface and will remain apparent, so we educators, citizens, and voters can address injustices and exclusions. As voters, Ohio residents, and as people who care about other people, we must address educational, health, and housing inequalities. Ohio students need and deserve the state funding and academic freedom necessary to a quality education. Ohio students need and deserve safe educational spaces in which their lives are not endangered. Ohio legislators must be called out when they fail to meet these needs. If we return to *normal,* we do our students and ourselves a disservice. We must use the lessons of the pandemic to challenge normalized injustices.

REFERENCE

Rich, Adrienne. 1995. "Claiming an Education." In *On Lies, Secrets, and Silence: Selected Prose, 1966–1978,* 231–236. New York: Norton.

15 | Grace and Grief in Uncertain Times

An Account of Love and Dying during COVID

Personal Reflection

Angie Fitzpatrick

This personal reflection by a scholar of gender and culture studies tells a story of profound personal loss due to and during COVID and insightfully contemplates how uncertainty and tension have permeated every level of life during the pandemic.

"They say we will not see the end of this for a couple of months," I wrote to my father on March 14, 2020. There were only 16 confirmed COVID-19 cases in Ohio, and I had just begun to quarantine with my husband and two young children in our cozy Toledo home, naively thinking we could use this time to catch up on housework and bond as a family. At the time, my father was living in a nursing home in Wahpeton, North Dakota, where he was convalescing after multiple back injuries. Overweight, over 65, and suffering from preexisting health conditions, including chronic obstructive pulmonary disease (COPD), Dad was by all accounts one of the vulnerable Americans that we wanted so desperately to protect with our masks and lockdowns. My mother, a stage-four colon cancer survivor undergoing chemo treatment in Fargo, North Dakota, was also at risk. Beneath the surface of my cautious optimism that we could "flatten the curve" and perhaps even find a silver lining in this pandemic, I felt a persistent sense of dread that someone I loved would become a COVID-19 casualty. Still, I never could have imagined that before the year's end I would watch my parents die, just days apart.

The weekend of March 14, 2020, I was supposed to be in Rochester, Minnesota, accompanying my mother to her cancer treatment appointments at the Mayo Clinic. I had long looked forward to this trip because it would be the first time in the four years since her cancer diagnosis that I would present for her medical appointments. I had left North Dakota in 2003 to attend graduate school in Ohio, where I have now lived most of my adult life. As her oldest child, I felt an immense sense of responsibility for supporting her and my siblings through her ongoing health crisis and it had pained me to watch from the sidelines. When word of a deadly novel coronavirus began to circulate just days before my planned visit, I canceled the trip with a heavy heart and promised to see her as soon as it was safe. Devastated that the pandemic had robbed us of our time together, we were also scared that we might not see each other again. While I could hunker down in my house and wait out the pandemic, Mom was now in an impossible position. Seeking cancer treatment put her at risk of contracting coronavirus, but if she stopped treatment, the cancer would kill her.

Mom and I would exchange COVID-19 data points and safety tips in our family's group text, where we were the only two who seemed to grasp the seriousness of the pandemic and the necessity of mask mandates and lockdowns. I repeatedly stressed the need for my mother to isolate herself from the family as much as possible and for family members to wear masks all the time to protect Mom. Knowing full well that either the virus or the cancer would get her, Mom could not bear to isolate herself and so she babysat her grandkids and attended mask-optional family gatherings. I watched these scenes play out in family posts on Facebook with a sense of disbelief from my location in Ohio, where I avoided indoor contact with anyone outside of my pod and religiously wore my mask.

Then, early in July my mother was hospitalized for cancer complications, so my husband and I packed our two young children into our minivan and made the trek from the northwest corner of Ohio through Indiana, Illinois, Wisconsin, and Minnesota to just over the border into North Dakota. We had no clue what to expect during our journey. Would we be safe sleeping in a hotel? Could we safely use public restrooms? How would we keep the kids from touching anything at the gas station? The further west we went, the fewer masks we saw and the more our discomfort grew. It was startling to transition from the shelter of Toledo where mask mandates were enforced, businesses had modified their space to promote physical distancing, and most folks did their best in public to keep that distance. We had entered this pandemic under the thoughtful, data-driven leadership of Governor Mike DeWine and Dr. Amy Acton, the former director of the Ohio Department of Public Health. Though the lockdown in Ohio had been lifted under political pressure from the conservative right, we felt compelled to continue following public health protocol. Yet the more my mother's health declined, and the more we realized this year could be her last, the more difficult it became to avoid travel.

When my youngest sister decided to get married in September, while our mother was still alive, I felt strongly about being present for what could very well be the last big family hurrah in our mother's lifetime. However, as the big day drew closer, it became clear that my sister had no pandemic safety protocols in place for the wedding. Instead of bowing out, I leaped into action, buying reusable masks for the wedding party and disposable masks for guests. Then, in an ironic twist of fate, my sister tested positive for COVID-19 the day before the ill-advised wedding. So, too, did my other sister, brother-in-law, stepfather, and other guests who all had attended an indoor bachelorette party the week prior. (Luckily, my immunocompromised mother was spared.) None of my relatives could believe they had gotten the virus. "I always wear a mask!" they exclaimed. I thought back to their Facebook posts over the last couple months, which had featured photos of them at indoor parties with family, laughing and eating as if the world were not on fire. I thought back to the many times I, too, had felt a false sense of safety at certain social events and let my mask fall away. I sobbed on our way home to Ohio, not only because we had so narrowly escaped the clutch of COVID, but also because it felt so futile to fight it.

It should not have surprised me when my father tested positive for the virus at the end of October 2020. I had watched the number of cases grow around the world, including within my personal networks in Ohio and North Dakota. Still, my sisters and I trusted that the safety measures in place at Dad's nursing home would protect him from the virus. Surely the nursing home staff, who knew better than anyone else the importance of protecting the elderly, were practicing social distancing, good hygiene, and masking both at the facility and out in the community. But also, I had been so occupied with my mother's ongoing health crises that I had not given much thought to my father. I would call him occasionally to give him updates on the grandkids and exchange speculations on the outcome of the upcoming presidential election. He could never talk for long—years of heavy smoking had led to severe COPD and he found it difficult to sustain a conversation, even with supplemental oxygen. I had plans to visit him, but, because of the unpredictability of my mother's health and the pandemic, I never made it there.

By November, both of my parents were on their deathbeds in a small hospital in downtown Fargo, North Dakota. Mom had entered hospice care and Dad was admitted to the COVID-19 intensive care unit (ICU). He was having difficulty breathing and needed to be placed on a bilevel positive airway pressure machine, or BiPAP for short. The BiPAP is a type of ventilator that delivers more oxygen to the body than a standard oxygen tank, and if this machine could not help Dad recover, he would need to be intubated. Dad had told us for years that he did not want any "heroic measures" to save his life, so when the hospital asked my sister if they should intubate, she had to say no.

I was in my campus office in Ohio when my sister called to give me the news about Dad. Though Mom had just entered hospice care, she was stable, and the hospice care team thought we had a least a couple of weeks before she would pass away. I called hospice for daily updates on Mom, waiting for the more advanced end-of-life signs to appear before I made the westward trek again. I was not expecting this call from my sister, and it broke me. The weight of trying to keep myself and my family safe, of traveling hundreds of miles through a contagious countryside to be with my family, of waiting by the phone for news of Mother's imminent death, of knowing that sooner or later I would probably test positive for COVID-19 myself ... it was all too much. I could feel my heart pounding out of my chest, my legs gave way under me and I collapsed onto the floor, sobbing into the phone along with my sister. A few days later, I arranged with my husband and my employer to spend as much time as I needed in North Dakota so I could be present for my parents' final days.

When I first arrived, the hospice nurses were kind and gentle. They spoke about death in tender terms and took care of my mother without any fear of what lay ahead for her. Their presence was calming, and I found myself striking up a conversation whenever they came into the room. It was hard to be alone with Mom, who had already started to change. She had grown quiet and pale, and her once full figure seemed to be melting away under the hospital blankets. She wanted the room kept dark and quiet, as if our silence could protect us from what was coming. None of us wanted to say that final farewell.

She was like that for weeks. The nurses asked if we could think of any reason why Mom might be hanging onto life so fiercely. A fighter by nature, we thought she might be waiting to meet her great-grandson, and my grandson, who had just been born a few weeks prior in Ohio. One day she asked where the baby was. When I replied that she would not be seeing him, she was confused and heartbroken. Traveling across the country with a newborn baby during a pandemic seemed so foolish, but I knew that my mother needed to meet this baby, just as she needed to see my sister get married. So, my oldest son and his fiancée made the long drive from Ohio to Fargo and my mother got to feel her great-grandson rest on her chest. After that visit she withdrew even further into herself and we knew her time with us would end soon.

At the other end of the hospital, my father had made the decision to go on palliative care. The coronavirus had caused irreparable damage to his lungs and he would never again breathe without the help of a ventilator. When I stepped into his room on the ICU where he was awaiting transfer, I was struck by how much the large BiPAP mask changed his face, as if he had become a pandemic cyborg. Using a small whiteboard to communicate, his first request was to take a photo of him holding a message for his sisters. Like many Americans, they had spent the last four years fiercely debating politics. A vehement opponent to former President Donald Trump, my father's message read, in part: "Seems the monster you so joyously supported has caused my death and too many others." It was a heartbreaking scene and at the same time it made me laugh to see Dad still throwing punches from his deathbed.

Visiting him was a stark contrast to time spent with Mom. In between jokes and thoughtful musings, Dad would rattle off requests for his last meal: cinnamon gum, vanilla milkshake, burger, fruit and cottage cheese. He stayed up late into the night with my oldest sister, singing his favorite oldies from under the enormous BiPAP mask. Nurses would occasionally come in, administering small doses of morphine to keep him comfortable while his lungs struggled to keep up. He was as full of life as one could be in that situation, so we were all surprised when he did not wake up from his loud snoring slumber the next day. As the hours passed, we grew increasingly concerned and asked the care team to check his vitals. We discovered then that Dad's oxygen level was at 65 even though the BiPAP machine was still going strong. When the nurse seemed as perplexed as we were, we realized that though it felt like death was all around us, they were not prepared for death on this floor, because it was the kind of unit where people usually recover and return home. Overwhelmed by the influx of patients with COVID-19 complications, the hospital space and staff were stretched to the limit, and so they made space in this unit for people like my father who would never recover and never return home. That afternoon, we played Dad's favorite songs, said a prayer, kissed him goodbye, and the doctor turned off the BiPAP. He took two final heavy breaths and was gone. After the others left, I waited by his side until the staff came to tell me that they needed to hurry if we wanted Dad to get a space in the hospital mortuary, where spaces were quickly filling up.

My mother passed away three days later, in the dark still of the night, as my grandmother and I held her in our arms. It seemed fitting that she should transition out of this life both with the woman who brought her into the world and with the first life she had brought into the world. We spent the next few days planning her service and final resting place with funeral home staff who had been working around the clock under a deluge of COVID-19 causalities. I watched Mom's funeral from the floor of my basement in Toledo, Ohio, where I held my own sweet children while my husband battled COVID-19 under isolation in the spare bedroom upstairs. He had developed symptoms after dining indoors with family from northern Michigan over the Thanksgiving weekend. When he reported that the fatigue and shortness of breath had become unbearable, I drove through the night, praying that I would not lose another loved one so soon. He survived with nothing more than a lingering cough, as did his COVID-positive family members, including his 94-year-old grandmother. As much as I felt relieved to avoid more death, I also felt angry that my father had not been so lucky.

Navigating the pandemic made the loss of my parents that much more difficult. I had spent the last half of 2020 traveling between Ohio and North Dakota, anxiously trying to keep one step ahead of the coronavirus. Most of that time was spent in hospital rooms, the one space in North Dakota where I felt safe because at least there I could count on people to wear masks. I saw firsthand the courage of the pandemic heroes we had come to praise, the health-care workers who showed up day after day to care for us and our loved ones. And I also witnessed their vulnerability and fear. Every hospital had a strict visitation policy to protect patients and staff. The hospital systems in Fargo, North Dakota, allowed one visitor per patient per day, while palliative care patients were allowed four visitors per day. Hospital staff and security diligently monitored the visitor list to ensure no one violated hospital policy. The hospice unit where my mother lived out her final days permitted three visitors per day, a limit difficult for my large family. As the eldest child,

I became the visitation coordinator and spokesperson, setting the visitation schedule for Mom's room, apologizing when one of my siblings broke the visitation rules, and requesting flexibility in the policy as needed. It was a miserable role to play and became a source of tension between me, my family, and the hospice staff. When Dad entered palliative care, I assumed the same role for him, carefully doling out those precious last moments to make sure we could all say goodbye. On the day he died, my nephew and his girlfriend were visiting, along with me and my older sister, which made four visitors—the total allowed for that day. Once we realized he was actively dying, the supervising nurse allowed us to swap out the visiting grandchildren for the children, so that my siblings and I could be together with our father in his final moments.

This act of generosity was a welcome relief from the increasingly tense exchanges I had with the hospice nurses, who frequently reminded us that we were lucky to be visiting at all considering that the hospital was nearly at capacity with COVID-19 cases. When it became clear that my mother was actively dying, I asked the nurse in charge if they would make an exception and allow us one extra visitor so that my mother's four children could be by her side as we had done with my father just days before in the other unit. The nurse denied my request and again reminded me that we were lucky to have any visitors during a global pandemic. I fought back my rage as I reminded her that my father had just died from that deadly disease. How dare this nurse rob me and my family of our precious time with our dying mother? That rage lived in my chest for months afterward, protecting me from the pain of my loss. Thinking back now, I realize that the nurse and I were just two women, trying to stay alive in a world where death and dying were all around us. In these uncertain times, full of loss and grief, we need grace for ourselves and for others.

Afterword: Pandemic Lessons from Dr. Amy Acton

> *"On some positions cowardice asks the question, is it safe? Expediency asks the question, is it politic? Vanity asks the question, is it popular? But conscience asks the question, is it right? And there comes a time when one must take a position that is neither safe, nor politic, nor popular but he must take it because conscience tells him it is right."*
>
> —Martin Luther King Jr., "A Proper Sense of Priorities," speech delivered February 6, 1968, in Washington, DC

Ohio under COVID *co-editors Michelle McGowan and Danielle Bessett interviewed Dr. Amy Acton in November 2021. Amy Acton, MD, MPH, served as Director of Health for the Ohio Department of Health (ODH) at the outset of the COVID-19 pandemic, and was honored with the JFK Library* Profile in COVID Courage Award *for her service. Their conversation has been edited for length, content, and clarity.*

Bessett: Can you briefly walk us through what you see as the history of COVID-19 in Ohio from when you first became aware of it through the present?

Acton: My first recollection of the pandemic was at the very end of December in 2019—hearing a news story about a "weird pneumonia" in China. It was in Wuhan, which, coincidentally, is Ohio's sister state. Looking back, there were so many serendipities that helped me figure out what was going on, but the first clue came from hearing this early interview with an epidemiologist from the World Health Organization. I could

> tell that she was very concerned. There was a level of something in her voice that just stood out to me. I think when you have the kind of rough childhood I had, while I sometimes feel clueless about ordinary life, I've found that I'm very good in a crisis. And as a preventive medicine physician, I tend to read the environment for threats and cues and notice subtle things that people often don't pay much attention to.

Shortly after that story, when I was coming through the airport returning from visiting family over the holiday, I saw signs were up for colleges welcoming students back from abroad, including from China. Later, I shared this on a national call as a possible risk group—college students. Here in Ohio we have a lot of students and faculty who travel during the break.

I remember saying in a press conference: "At the beginning of a pandemic, you look a bit like Chicken Little—and that by the end of a pandemic, you feel like you didn't do enough." So I'm very grateful that our team took it seriously and in early January [2020] we kicked into gear.

In the beginning, our leadership team would sit in on government calls for updates from the CDC [Center for Disease Control and Prevention], ASTHO [Association of State and Territorial Health Officers], the FDA [Food and Drug Administration], and the White House. As I watched the disease progress I, like you, saw the scenes of Wuhan as a ghost city, and recognized that this is basically our New York City—bigger than New York City—and those images really stood out in my mind.

The Japanese *Diamond Princess* cruise ship was another big moment. It turned out that we had Ohioans in places all over the world trying to return home. We had Ohioans on the Nile River cruises that were getting attention, on the boat in California that was kept off the shore, and in those long lines in our airports coming back from Europe.

And our team was also watching the White House press conferences, which had, over time, become increasingly confusing as experts began to contradict one another. I remember a particular day in mid-January, jumping out of my chair saying, "Something's not going right here." As it spread to places like Italy, I found myself literally Googling the word "pandemic" even though I taught Introduction to Global Public Health, and thinking to myself, "Is it me, or are people not naming things the way you're supposed to name it?"

Our first PUIs [persons under investigation] were two university students who returned from winter break in China and they were so scared. I flew with some of the Governor's team to help and do a press conference. The students were being isolated in a secret location. I remember there were stirrings of anti-Asian sentiment on campus and in the town, and so we worked with the administration and local health director—they just did such an amazing job navigating this and made sure the students were getting food and social support.

We had no testing then. If you tried to send a test to the CDC, it would take eight, ten, fourteen days to get results. We were one of the last states to get testing since two of our three reagents didn't work. So we weren't able to diagnose our first cases until March [2020]. We now have retrospective evidence of cases from as early as January [2020]. Fortunately, those two students were negative [for COVID], but from then on, our infectious disease specialists and local health departments worked nonstop, seven days a week.

I had another early experience with my colleague in the State of Washington who had the first nursing home outbreak and then the town lost their entire fire department to quarantine. You began to see those ripple effects. He said, "If I had only had two more weeks to get ready ..." And that really stood out to me. We all now know the story of "flattening the curve," that two weeks makes all the difference—St. Louis versus Philadelphia during the 1918 flu. One city prepares and one doesn't, and they have tremendously different trajectories. So that logarithmic effect of being on the preventive side was another lesson.

My team went into full emergency preparedness mode. We built a website: coronavirus.ohio.gov. We started working on a hotline. Thank goodness we did because when things really picked up, they moved fast. We did a formal pandemic "Table Top" drill with the head of our National Guard and the entire [Ohio] Cabinet in early February [2020]. We created a small emergency operating center on the thirty-first floor of the Riffe office tower and began to troubleshoot scenarios with leaders from hospitals, nursing homes, prisons, schools, the legislature, businesses [...] we started to build extensive relationships. That also turned out to be key.

ODH was staffed at around 1,150 people, most of whom work on 175 other programs unrelated to infectious disease and emergency preparedness. Ohio has 113 local health departments, all very different from each other, so we were starting to row and create a rhythm that they could always count on meeting at a certain time a few times a week to give them updates and to hear what they were seeing on the ground. Our team was already exhausted by February [2020] but they were so determined. I will never be able to say enough how fortunate we are for our public servants and how proud I was to be a part of a team where everyone worked together under the most difficult of situations. Everyone stepped up to new responsibilities and respite was rare.

After we did get negative results for those first two PUIs, I heard stories. We started looking at influenza-like illnesses. We were having tons of nursing homes with outbreaks and people dying but they weren't testing positive for flu or other things on the viral panel. We began to explore testing wastewater. But again, no test results yet. Yet we highly suspected the virus was already here.

I was also fortunate that I ended up being the SHO [State Health Officer] representative for the Midwest to ASTHO, which is the professional organization for my position. That turned out to be really valuable as we were able to coordinate with all of the states around Ohio.

So, the last week of February [2020] I traveled to the ASTHO board meeting in [Washington] DC. We were briefed by the CDC and ASPR [Office of the Assistant Secretary for Preparedness and Response] experts. One person really stood out to me: Dr. Bob Kadlec, a renowned expert in bioterrorism and infectious diseases for multiple administrations. He had just come back from an update on the *Japanese Princess* and was visibly upset. You could feel the tension in the room from these folks who were on the inside. It was just so obvious we were on the precipice of something.

And then we went to a meeting in the Executive Building at the White House. The stock market had crashed for the second time, so my phone was lighting up from the Governor's Office. By then, everyone was definitely paying attention. Mick Mulvaney was there, the President's Chief of Staff, and my colleagues were taking turns going around the room making comments, mostly about preparing for the virus. I was sitting next to a woman from the President's communication team, who happened to be from Ohio.

I don't know what it was, but when it got to me, most everything technical had already been said. I don't know where these words came from, but I remember saying to Mick Mulvaney and everyone, "I think this is the 'higher angels' moment. This is the FDR, Churchill, Lincoln moment."

I personally felt such a longing to know the truth, and I suspect that was how most Americans felt by then. The people knew there was something bad happening, but no one would just say it. Yet this was the time to lead this like a war: a war on an invisible, common enemy. Invisibility is what makes it hard. And that's one of the worst travesties of this virus because I think at that moment, had we been able to name it and wage war on it, and get us all on the same team around the world, the trajectory would have been profoundly different.

Everyone in the room got really quiet. I can't even tell you how somber this was. It was like the launching point before heading off to battle.

And then I remember getting on an airplane and flying back to Ohio, so exhausted. I was instantly turned around and put in a van to go to MetroHealth in Cleveland to join the Governor. We were scheduled to visit their special isolation unit for really dangerous infectious diseases like Ebola. On the ride there, I got a call from the Health Commissioner for Columbus, on behalf of the Mayor saying, "The Arnold Classic is coming. What do you think we should do?" As we traveled up I-71, all of my staff were on phones and laptops, trying to assess the situation while writing talking points. I had to keep incredibly focused. I knew this was the turning point. By the time we arrived, I remember even the reporters were getting really anxious.

The night before, President Trump had done a press conference that signaled a new chapter. He had to address the concerns of Dr. Nancy Messonnier [then-Director of the CDC's National Center for Immunization and Respiratory Diseases], who had gone on air earlier that same day and said to people, "This is serious. You need to go home and talk to your children and tell them that things are going to be disrupted. Life is not going to be the same."

And so the Governor and I—much to this Governor's credit—said, "We don't have all the answers yet. But we're going to tell you what we know, as we know it." We made a commitment to have daily press conferences, and we picked 2 p.m. because we thought that would give the reporters time to get to press. So that's how it got started.

Professor Villegas from Kenyon [College] would later study 60 days of press conferences. He determined our pressers functioned as a "sacred, ritual holding space." Ohioans affectionately called them "Wine with DeWine and Snackin' with Acton." Creating that holding space in a crisis is one of the most important lessons I've learned from this experience.

With no organized federal leadership, many scientists had gone underground because they were getting attacked or felt at risk if they spoke up. It turned out many of them were veterans of previous pandemics. They called themselves the "Red Dawn." And so when we went out and we started telling the truth, all the scientists started calling us.

Another pandemic serendipity was that I hired a new chief of communications four days before the pandemic began. It turned out her brother, Rajeev Venkayya, was a physician who had gone to my medical school, and had actually helped write the Pandemic Playbook in George W. Bush's White House. What were the chances of that? He and Dr. Carter Mecher helped me with many of the strategies and metaphors we used early on with Ohioans, such as the layers of Swiss cheese analogy.

So, coming back from Cleveland we began considering The Arnold and went straight to meet with the Columbus Mayor and his team at the Governor's Office on "30." We knew that at the Biogen Conference in Boston, two people had gone in unknowingly with COVID, and they sent 70 people out sick, many by ambulance. My chief of staff's wife was actually there describing ambulances pulling up to the hotel. This was one of many clues of the virus's asymptomatic and rapid spread. That evening we held a press conference, and I remember Arnold Schwarzenegger spoke via the Governor's cell phone.

The Arnold was the very first of many hard-got, heavily-debated decisions. Limiting mass gatherings is one of the first steps in the playbook. We knew this could be a super-spreader event: 80 countries, 250,000 spectators, across several jurisdictions. The locals could have written their own orders with the Mayor. But it was complicated to get that many health departments lined up and time was of the essence. We were looking at a potential $50 million loss to the economy. It was a really tough decision, but fortunately we were able to work with the event organizers to scale it way back. We didn't stop it completely, but we limited spectators. As we now know, many such mass gathering events from professional sports to conferences would soon follow suit as players and attendees fell sick.

That was the beginning of making very hard decisions in Ohio, and in this country, but they were never made in a vacuum. We had so many experts at the table. I can't tell you how much I respect all those involved for helping make the courageous calls. They helped save lives.

Even then, people started thinking that I had unusual premonition skills, but truth be told, so much of it was common sense and knowing this pandemic playbook. It turns out that after 9/11, George W. Bush read John Barry's book *The Great Influenza*. Homeland Security, Congress, everyone realized a pandemic was one of the gravest security risks to our country. It's not just the virus, which is the big lesson in all of this. It's so much more. They predicted there would be attacks on our grid. There would be unrest of all sorts, because people would feel untethered. As I've often said, there's a contagion worse than the virus: it's fear and ambiguity and our intolerance for this huge unknown. And for every decision made, there would be cascading consequences.

If you think of 9/11, there were those four days where everything fell away. No one on the street was a stranger—really, no one in the world. I had never felt that before. I just knew, in some strange way, there was this chance that we might all have that energy of bonding again. And then, what could you do with that energy? You have to give people something to do, a way to help, a way to act. And that became the essence of our press conferences.

McGowan: I'm wondering if there's anything about any particular features of Ohio as a place, whether challenges or assets, that you think shaped the Ohio case and the Ohio response.

Acton: The benefit from our work beginning in January [2020] was that Ohio was way ahead of the game: we had prepared and we worked as a team. Honestly, we're very lucky to have such an experienced governor that had held many roles. He is by nature a prosecutor. When he felt we didn't get enough information, he would just grill everybody. We never rested; there was not one day, not even a Sunday, that we weren't up by six in the morning on phone calls from dawn till the end of the day when they would forcibly drag him away to eat—never did we stop asking hard questions and trying to gather information.

The message from the feds who we thought would be running this was "Governors, it's on you. Go for it." We were very lucky in Ohio. Our Governor had always wanted this job, he loves Ohio, and he's respected by other governors. So the governors got on phone calls with other governors. And I can tell you on those calls there was no ego; there was none of the drama we'd later come to see in the press. Everything fell away. Nobody wanted their people to die. At the beginning, everyone was so humble and would share what their scientists were telling them, not out in public but behind the scenes. Our Governor specifically reached out to all our neighboring states and our big city mayors. The Midwest states in our region rowed together really well. And all of the state health officers—we would do late night calls to share what we were learning and help one another.

I really love that about us, and you could almost see, if you go back and if someone ever lays out the policy, you'll see these states inching forward following this pandemic playbook. The series of policy moves were those brakes you're pulling in the worst emergency to try to gain control, to contain the virus. We had *Hunger Games* for PPE [personal protective equipment]. Our hospitals were outbidding our hospitals. Our boats were being stolen at port—we had to pull everyone together and say, "Let's quit outbidding each other. Let's figure out a way to bid together." And all these people were rowing, and I think Ohio was especially good at that.

And we were creating that holding space in those press conferences. There was so much Ohio Buckeye Pride in those early days. You could really see people wanting to help. I really credit our communications team: they quickly came up with "In this Together." Then Ryan Vesler of Homage, the T-shirt company, came up with the slogan for "Not All Heroes Wear Capes," which quickly became an Ohio theme during the pandemic, and that T-shirt went viral, ultimately raising tons of money to help homeless youth. Stories of our citizens' efforts went global.

The other great thing about Ohio is how we innovated: we had no data modelers on staff, so we had to invent things. We ended up getting volunteer scientists from different agencies, universities, and hospitals. They became something we called "The Force," and they all worked together to do some of our original numbers. We ended up having some of the best predictive analytics because of that. We have great universities and businesses who helped us with the PPE and creating policy. So at Public Health, we were running the response guided by the most important question I teach my students: "Who's at the table?" Everyone answered the call. We truly have such great resources in Ohio.

Bessett: Could you talk about the communication strategies you used as the Director of Health for the Ohio Department of Health to address the constantly evolving public health situation that unfolded during the pandemic?

Acton: Well, another one of the serendipitous backstories: one part of my formal training with the CDC was to go to a weekend-long intensive communications

> seminar in the fall of 2019. I have an aging dog who requires elaborate booby-trapping of our house to prevent accidents. As fate would have it, I tripped over a dog gate and fractured my pelvis in several places, so the trip was nixed.

Truth be told, I am probably more of an introvert by nature and, like many, still feel some nervousness every time I approach the podium. I'd been trained in my residency on crisis communication. You learn the Cs: the "be clear, concise, credible, consistent" goals of communication. And of course, as a Director, you do a lot of public speaking. My team had already recognized that I was sort of "unwrangleable" in terms of reading very scripted speeches as I need to look people in the eye to feel connected. I learned early on that I couldn't teach without first having an authentic relationship.

So my unconscious approach to communication was to talk as I always do—as a professor with a class or a doctor with a patient. I trained in pediatrics before preventive medicine, so often you have to describe very hard things to people in really stressed environments. My kids said of the pressers, "That's just Mom." So the person you see on TV, for better or worse, was me. And it speaks volumes that they let me be who I am. I've been told I didn't have that prepared spin to me, and that was probably a blessing because I talked to Ohioans as we're talking right now. I felt a relationship. I distinctly remember the feeling of just wanting to reach through that dark, empty camera lens to the people on the other side. And it wasn't originally that obvious to me that people were following it as closely as they were because it was the Ohio News Network at 2 p.m. No one's really watching that, right?

And in the beginning, before we were sequestered, we were in the room with the press. I give them so much credit: remember, they were going through this too. They had children to manage, and parents in nursing homes, and were facing all the same things as the people at home watching. We were all learning about the virus together.

We were buying precious time. No doctor knew how to treat this and mortality rates were high. There were no medicines. We didn't know what worked yet. We had no PPE and not enough ventilators. There was little testing. There were even shortages of embalming fluid. The hospitals knew that they could be overloaded. Hospitals are built for the capacity of flu season, and they were already near max capacity. So they knew that they could be overrun and have to start rationing care, which then affects all of our care. We all watched as Italy and New York City faced "who lives or dies" choices and filled morgue trucks. Deploying morgue trucks is one of the many unexpected duties of a director of health, and ours were on standby. Stopping of elective surgeries—that was something hospitals needed—and then teams catalogued outpatient equipment. Soon we were figuring out how to move a ventilator from a veterinary practice to a hospital. There's also all those wraparound things to consider. How do we keep small businesses viable while you're doing something like this? What do you do in a homeless shelter? And there's always the cascading consequences of every decision; this was part of the plan and so you have to keep tweaking your policies.

In the beginning, you're still hoping that you can keep the virus from getting widespread and employ the strategies of things like social distancing, washing your hands, and masking. You try to box the virus in through quick identification and quarantine. They're all imperfect tools before you have a vaccine. But if you layer them, they're like layers of Swiss cheese. The strategies all have holes. While they aren't perfect, you end up with an almost vaccine-like ability to function as a society. We've seen this when we were able to keep schools [open] with masks, social distancing, and all the other measures such as testing, contact tracing, and good ventilation. We eventually were able to keep infection pretty low in Ohio schools before we got to the place where vaccines were available. And so, those kinds of metaphors became helpful, we thought, to people.

The *New York Times* op-ed video studying our press conferences in May 2020 did a fascinating, linguistic-style analysis and came up with three leadership themes that we need to take seriously when we face a humanitarian crisis of this nature: brutal honesty, vulnerability, and empowerment. It was an elaborate analysis including pronoun choice, and I'd love to say I was that deliberate! But it was something that we just intuitively did.

I had this gut sense that we needed to pull each other up onto this life raft. No one person was going to do it alone. I thought, "I have 11.7 million patients: How are we all going to keep each other afloat?" I imagined each of us reaching out and grabbing whoever was within reach and pulling them up to safety. And so that was why I said constantly, "Please go check on your neighbor. Go make a meal for the nurse who's working that extra shift." While we would have certain key things that we agreed upon to get across, like the numbers for the day, the rest varied with the circumstances of what people in Ohio were experiencing.

One of my most famous quotes was when we did the stay-at-home order: "I'm not afraid, I'm determined." Turns out that was something my husband said to me that morning when I was leaving. My husband's a coach and an elementary school teacher. And so again, that wasn't scripted, but it was spontaneous, coming out in the moment, and it was beautiful.

Courage doesn't mean you never feel fear. But in Ohio, we had a higher purpose. The Governor and I would often quote Winston Churchill: "When you're going through hell, keep going!"

And I had that white coat, and the white coat became a symbol of sorts that tied everything together. It never varied. I realized I needed to stay very consistent. I didn't have time to shower so that helped! But in those pockets, I would carry all of these trinkets and things Ohioans sent us. Art drawings of COVIDs from kids, letters from Ohioans, a needlepoint angel [...] I intend to share all that someday.

Thanks to the *New York Times* editors, I now realize how powerful those concepts of leadership and communication were—the Governor and I, along with the team, felt the full responsibility and owned it—it is not the norm to be brutally honest, including what you don't know, to acknowledge the vulnerability of what we were all feeling. And it is wise to ask more of people—not just for sacrifices but by empowering them to lead.

Brutal truth: No order can flatten the curve. *Ohioans flattened the curve*—through their collective actions. They tried to support business by keeping up gym memberships and ordering carryout. They tipped extra. They reached out to their neighbors and frontline workers. They learned to Zoom. They invented innovation after innovation, and fought hard to adapt to unprecedented challenges. Every little act was helping. We did it together.

And that's one of the hard things about this, I think. First of all, you have to understand this is a war. You don't get to choose "no war." It's a given there will be suffering and casualties. You are fighting to minimize the losses, and are fighting for our way of life back.

You have to respect the enemy. We often don't respect nature. This is your science fiction nemesis—this virus. Asymptomatic spread. Very virulent and supercontagious, with this terrible multisystem inflammatory response. We were discovering one awful thing after another.

So the choice? We can stumble through it. Or, we can try to run an offense as best we can, using all the levers that we have at our disposal, which far exceeds even what's under the roof of government. And so we did things early. We pulled together nonprofits and philanthropies in Ohio to help prevent people such as the homeless from falling through the cracks; to deliver food and prevent evictions. We created a zone system where we divided our state into thirds and three hospital CEOs agreed to work with nursing homes and prisons; they don't have to do that. But they agreed to do [it] to try to keep everybody rowing.

Disruption creates opportunity. Walls fall away. Things you can't ever get done start happening. And so that's the kind of energy I think we generated in the beginning. It was Ohioans at their best, and honestly I have to say it was a privilege of a lifetime to help hold that space.

Bessett: You had to contend with outright hostility and threats of violence. Do you have any thoughts on this and would you be willing to share your experience of these attacks?

Acton: For me there was a very distinct moment when things turned, and it was in a press conference right around Easter and Passover. The Governor said something kind about celebrating a virtual Seder because he knew that I'm Jewish. My husband is Christian, he's Episcopalian. So my family—we celebrate both holidays. I remember jokingly saying, "I make a mean matzo ball soup."

Shortly after, the tone of the protests changed. Faces were pressed up on the glass panes of the statehouse, literally six feet from the Lieutenant Governor—very thin panes of glass, which we ultimately saw broken during later protests—giant guns, Guy Fawkes masks, and screaming so loud while we were recording that I had to address it live with the people of Ohio.

While there were many peaceful protesters with legitimate concerns about our policies, something about matzo ball soup ended up being the final straw that unleashed a new level of hate, a reason for legislators to use words like "globalist." This coincided with President Trump's calls to "Liberate" and "Activate." Much has been written by others about just how intentional and organized this was.

The Governor was very assertive in saying that was unacceptable, that the buck stopped with him. Sadly, we've now seen this scene play out everywhere. But at the time it was shocking, and that's when a lot of the anti-Semitic and other hate themes became a part of it in Ohio. That's what you saw at my house.

Truth be told, I really didn't have time to let in either the good or bad. You are just so focused on the work—on saving lives and restoring our ability to live our lives. My instinct, when there were the first protests at my house, was to go outside and talk to people. But once there were guns involved, you can't do that. I saw there were people who had lost businesses who were devastated, and I wanted to hear what was going on. I wanted to know what they were up against. I wanted to take that information and bring it back into our meetings and talk about: What are we doing? What's the legislature doing for small businesses? Instead there was a false pitting of the economy versus health, which is very unfortunate.

Our well-being is all one thing in my book: the social determinants of health. Economic policy is health policy. Education policy is health policy. Transportation policy is health policy. Housing policy is health policy. We needed to do all of it well. Our mission was to get all of us thriving and on the other side of this as fast as possible. We actually had a team that began working on how to reopen in March [2020], even as we were still in the process of following the playbook to stop the spread. By April [2020], we were also working with Scott Gottlieb's recommendations from the American Enterprise Institute as well as plans from the National Governors Association and the White House COVID task force.

I had executive protection assigned very early on. I owe them so much. It turns out, as we now know, there were very, very credible threats against the Governor and me. There was a lot of chatter on the dark web. I learned just recently that there was a safe house set up for my family. My boys who are out of college and work in California were getting threats at their jobs. We had 24-7 state highway patrol in our driveway, which looks really strange in our small neighborhood.

I was worried. Our neighbors were incredible, our Mayor came, people sat in my yard in silent solidarity, but you worry about it getting violent. You just don't know what can happen in circumstances that can escalate like that. We've had an open door policy in our house. We didn't want to live in that kind of fear, and so it has definitely changed our lives and how we have to think to this day. The neighbors ultimately commissioned an artist to make a Peace Pole for our yard and I hope to give it to a museum someday.

When I stepped down, there was a talk show host who had been saying things: that he would punch someone like me in the face, and he did a 20-minute diatribe about it. In post-genocide Rwanda, where I've done global health work, it wasn't that the president just gets taken out one day and neighbor turns on neighbor. It was a slow process—then their social media was radio—it was a slow "othering" of people and the gradual changing of tenor and civility in how we treat one another.

It gets turned up slowly over time, and that builds to a moment when people are easily influenced and turn.

And that's the kind of rhetoric that's unacceptable to our public servants who work tirelessly during this pandemic doing the best they can. They are professionals. They're people. They're citizens. They're your neighbor, and that's been a tragedy of this. But it is crucial to remember, it was such a small group of people.

McGowan: In contrast, we also saw public outpourings of support for you and your approach as a Public Health official through social media, art, and phrases you used in your daily briefings with the Governor being turned into slogans. How do you make sense of these responses, and what did they reveal to you about Ohioans during the pandemic?

Acton: Our mail rooms that are larger than the whole first floor of my house—you could not walk in the Governor's or ODH's for how many things Ohioans sent. The goodwill, the things they made, the things they sent out of the show of solidarity, how they made meaning out of the unthinkable during a pandemic.

Just a few examples: I remember a cape that was an Ohio pennant flag and the other side was Wonder Woman fabric, because we were saying that "not all heroes wear capes." I got a baseball bat from a company in Ohio that had my name engraved on it with a funny note that said, "Don't recommend using this on the protesters." There was "ACTon Love, Not Hate" signs done by a mom and her boys that went viral in Ohio, a play on my last name which I would have never thought of. And so we started saying things like "act on love, not hate," "act on kindness, not fear." The slogans happened organically: the "Don your mask, don your cape," "Act on love," "We're all in this together."

If our leaders can help us to know that we are all in the same boat, that will be a big step forward. And acknowledge there are people really suffering and legitimately upset. I mean, there are bad actors, and then there are people that are just confused and suffering profound losses. Unfortunately, there are people that get power out of scaring people and use that fear to other ends.

But there is so much goodwill out there to be had. There is such a silent majority of people trying to row together. It is up to our leaders to remember that, and intentionally evoke our higher angels. If enough of us do the right thing, most of the time, all of us will get through.

Bessett: As Director of Ohio's Public Health Department, you had to contend with hesitancy to trust medical professionals. And I wonder if there's anything that is new or unique to the COVID pandemic in relation to mistrust of science, medicine, and public health?

Acton: The silent victories of public health make it really hard to make your case even though it's super cost effective and there's millions of things we do every day that keep Ohioans safe. We live, on average, twice the life expectancy we did 100 years ago. For all of prior human history, we were expected to live to our forties max. Of the thirty years gained in the last century, only five were due to the very high-tech things I learned in med school—sick care.

The truth is, we live longer, healthier lives due to things that we can only solve collectively. We don't think about the fact that we turn on our tap water and it is safe to drink. Safe food, infectious disease control, highway safety, child labor laws, racoon rabies control, lead abatement, the list goes on and on. We don't realize that only one-third of what affects our health is in our individual control. We absolutely must take responsibility for what we can do as individuals, but we're also undeniably *interdependen*t. There's nothing like a zoonotic disease to make the case, really, that there's nothing that separates us on this planet. And that's not a bad thing; it's just a true thing. It's the concept of One Health—the health of animals, humans, and the environment are inextricably connected.

So I think making the case for public health has always been hard. Because when we do it well—when we knock it out of the park and prevent the bad things from happening—then we don't see the problem. These are the "silent victories" of public health. And clearly, we're going to have to do a much better job of communicating this.

My real hope is for the establishment of a 9/11-style commission to study the lessons of this pandemic. I've been advocating for this. Really study what we did. What went right? What didn't go right? It's so important. We're going to want to move on. Obviously, we're exhausted. I'm exhausted. We're going to want to just put it behind us. But the truth is, what we can learn from this will help us with all disasters and with so many other things that would proactively give us health and make us stronger as a country.

We're going to have to mourn. We're going to have to create literal memorials. And then I think we'll also grieve together at some level because it will become more and more apparent all the time—what we have all lost. By the end of this, no one will have gone unscathed.

We'll also celebrate some things that I think we are yet to see. I think of "Generation C"—Generation COVID—the young people coming of age. I imagine them teaching the lessons of "The Great Pandemic" to their great-grandchildren. They've had to deal with COVID and unprecedented chaos and challenges. They are also compassionate and caring and collaborative: they have the potential to be catalysts and change agents, and they're very excited to be part of rebuilding something different. We can intentionally foster individual and community resiliency.

Part of the playbook acknowledged that other countries might take advantage when people in America are polarized, whether it's the politics of the day, or something like a pandemic. Unfortunately, bad actors will use things that divide to gain power, to disrupt and undermine us, which then is undermining our very democracy. So I think we must look at how these structures, such as social media, can be misused—and also ask, how could they be used for good? It will be important to help us stay better informed because obviously we're not getting our information in the same way on three channels as we used to.

Some of this preceded COVID. This pandemic was uniquely hard because, as a country, we didn't own it at the top, and we didn't name the common enemy, and we didn't all row together from the very beginning using all of government in partnership. We had to do it in this state-by-state way. Viruses don't know borders. So my hope is that in the future, we will lead the pandemic differently, and lead collaboratively as a world. Because once again, we had a common enemy: you don't get this chance very often, where all of humanity is on the same team.

Bessett: We were wondering if you can talk a little bit about the mounting and competing pressures you experienced in your tenure at ODH, and how you experienced it, especially toward the end of your time there.

Acton: It was getting harder and harder. There was a movement afoot across the country—the response was starting to be less strategic and there was a really false and a very unfortunate pitting of the economy versus health. Many of my colleagues were losing their jobs just when they were most needed.

There were always known to be cascading consequences with each policy and decision and a constant need to adjust to what you learn about the virus. What we did has to be remembered within the context of what we now know. But in the early pandemic, so much of it was still unfolding. This was "break glass time" while we gained control of an unprecedented threat to our health and national security.

And so instead of a very controlled return to business and life that would allow us to maximize how we lived with the virus, instead of being disciplined and sticking to the reopening plans and using data and being really strategic, there started to be increasing pressure on states to open up haphazardly, not recognizing the risks because we'd done such a good job averting the worst. In Ohio, we had prevented a very high first wave, which also led to people saying, "Her numbers are wrong" because we're not seeing them, the "silent victory" catch-22 of public health once again.

We had bought time to learn how to live with COVID. I recently read the mortality rate in March was around 25 percent and fell to 5 percent by June of 2020. We were on the path to successfully adjusting as a world to face an unprecedented threat.

I remember on March 15 [2020], on *Meet the Press,* Chuck Todd asking Dr. Anthony Fauci: "This doctor in Ohio, is she right?" And Dr. Fauci, who himself appeared to be navigating a great deal, acknowledged, "Yeah, she's probably about right with these numbers." So the modeling, while not exactly perfect, was in the ballpark and is what we ultimately saw by late fall of that year. But being right--it's just not something you feel good about if you're not able to use it to your preventive, get-ahead-of-it advantage.

So this pressure was mounting around the country and from the legislature. The Governor never asked me to step down, it's so important to say. It was my decision. I had let his team know it was getting increasingly difficult for me professionally, and for my family and my team. I felt the noise was now distracting from the work. But it wasn't the protests. In the end, it was the politicization of the pandemic.

There was particular pressure around an order wanted by a legislator the weekend before I stepped down [June 11, 2020]. I remember going for a long walk with my husband, saying to him, "I just can't sign my name to it." And that's the thing: it's not just a figure of speech. Only the Director can sign an order. The question was: can I sleep at night with my decisions?

I took an oath of office to protect and serve all Ohioans. It doesn't matter if you're a Republican or Democrat or Independent: as Director of Health, all 11.7 million Ohioans are my patients. If you can imagine, there is the tension of the responsibility and loyalty that you feel—the want to be very supportive of the administration and work closely with the legislature—yet also, as a physician, what is different is that you take a Hippocratic Oath to "do no harm." There are many shades of gray; these aren't black and white policies.

How do you know when you've crossed your line, honor that, but still keep trying to help? That was my dilemma and led to my offer to the Governor: "I want to keep helping in any way I can. I'll be there to advise you for as long as you need it." I loved working with him, I think that showed, and that day we announced [my resignation] broke my heart. Truthfully, there really hasn't been a day since that my heart hasn't broken watching the pandemic and politics unfold. But as I see clearly now, it wasn't going to end with that order. And so I find other ways to help. I haven't stopped fighting COVID.

A pandemic is uniquely challenging: you can only compromise to a point when it's life or death. Ohioans, and our country, need us to work together during a humanitarian crisis. A threat of this scale, scope, and duration challenges us to transcend politics and row together for the common good.

On behalf of my service, and that of my team and all of the frontline healthcare workers—in my mind, on behalf of *all the Ohioans* who worked so hard to row together—I was humbled to receive a John F. Kennedy [JFK] Library Profile in COVID Courage Award. JFK wrote *Profiles in Courage* about eight senators who had to make really hard calls. It's about wrestling with doing the right thing even when you stand to lose everything: your job, your reputation, your friends—perhaps even your life. We seem to be living in similar times.

I think there's a compass we all build within ourselves that is a combination of the values and the lessons learned, but it's also using your gut intuition. It's a combination of all things, but I felt like I had a very strong compass that helped me predict some of the things that helped Ohioans—and helped me to know when I could no longer effectively do that.

I'll say it for the rest of my life: it was an absolute honor to serve Ohioans and to work on behalf of the Governor and with my fellow Cabinet members. And I now have such a renewed respect for the tens of thousands of public servants who work tirelessly, day in and day out. We need to realize how much we need these professionals whose work is so often invisible to us.

I just happened to be the visible one—the tip of the iceberg—at an unprecedented moment in our history. I was an ordinary person in an extraordinary time.

McGowan: You've mentioned several times throughout this conversation the idea of the pandemic playbook that was originally created under the George W. Bush administration. I'm wondering if you can say a little bit more about it how you think the pandemic playbook ought to be reinvented in light of our pandemic experience with COVID.

Acton: Reinventing the pandemic playbook is something I'm very passionate about. We're still in it, so that makes it a very tricky time where people don't even have the bandwidth, let alone maybe the political will to look in a mirror yet. I feel really good I can sleep at night with every choice I've made, but I know we'll learn things from it we would do differently.

If I had the ideal little manual to have walked into this with, it would say things like, "Who's at the table?" and it would recommend a much broader representation of talent. For instance, people in the future might intentionally evoke the arts community to help make meaning of the chaos. Ohioans made tons of art to cope that I hope to someday share, such as this one picture of a little girl that's lying on the ground with [a] drawing of a chalk cape flowing behind her: our Ohio mantra that "Not All Heroes Wear Capes."

And then there was the story of Bonnie Bowen, the ninety-year-old woman who went on a Facebook page to share paintings: Day One of the pandemic in Ohio, Day Two [...] she did these whimsical watercolors that kept people going. She did this for over a year, and then she got sick with COVID herself. And literally 250,000 prayers came in to her—you can't tell me that that didn't help her get to the other side. One of my favorites was a *Laverne and Shirley*-themed cartoon of the Governor, Lieutenant Governor, and me that ended with an ask: "Stay Home, Stay Kind, Stay Hopeful Ohio!"

The Surgeon General, Dr. Vivek Murthy, has a book out on the fact that loneliness is an epidemic underlying so many public health issues. Realizing that, we would go into this with a different understanding of the fact that people are going to feel so untethered and unmoored. In early March [2020], I remember driving to the Statehouse with traffic going just like a normal day, knowing that life was about to change dramatically: these would be Wuhan-looking streets in two weeks. What do you say? What are the words you're going to use to say that to people? How are you going to make meaning out of that?

And so I suspect the playbook will have whole new and different kinds of communications. I expect we'll have updated viral mitigation strategies and new kinds of ways that data systems will talk to each other. I think that will be a really exciting thing. But who is at the table is key. There will be all kinds of talent that wasn't at the table, I hope, far beyond virologists and epidemiologists, whether officially or unofficially.

Leaders have had to persevere for a really long stretch. We must intentionally create space for someone to endure having that ultimate responsibility, whether you're a President of the United States or a school superintendent. Being a leader during a humanitarian crisis of this scale, scope, and duration doesn't work like the usual politics, and it doesn't work like the normal running of a business. And that's a big problem.

So I'm hoping those kinds of really interesting conversations happen, that papers get written by every discipline and sector: medical anthropology, sociology, history, business, the military, theology, law, philanthropy, nonprofit [...] how much would you have brought to the table had you been a member of a team? It's just different. We need all of these disciplines at the table.

And we need strategies to better address health disparities and help groups that are at a higher risk of succumbing to a virus or falling between the cracks—people who are homeless, in group homes, nursing homes, prisons, differently-abled, immunocompromised, or distrusting of the medical system to name just a few. And yes, we need to address racism as a public health issue. And vaccine hesitancy. And a myriad of diseases of despair, and the underlying epidemic of isolation and loneliness that predates the pandemic: so much was merely *unveiled* by COVID.

I think the original playbook was very well conceived and it evolved over the years with every President. For example, people had long studied that schools are the last thing to shut down, but here's why you do it and when you do it. But it had never been fully executed on this scale, and our modern circumstances created unanticipated issues.

We faced new challenges like postponing an Ohio primary election. So now there are legal case studies around, "Is that a good or bad thing to do? And why?" All of our decisions and policies were hard-got and well debated. We tried so hard to keep that election open. Frankly, we were killing ourselves to solve it: there were huge shortages of poll workers because they tend to be elderly and were at the greatest risk. Could the teachers at home like my husband work the polls? And how do we keep them safe? It looked like we might just pull it off, but at the last moment, the CDC ruled we were down to 50 (then 10) people as a mass gathering, and that made it impossible to run the polls. We realized people were going to have to unfairly choose between their health versus the right to vote. These are complicated decisions, not just a health director's decision, but really nuanced things for our society.

One of the things I learned from Governor Larry Hogan early on was that he had involved his National Guard in Maryland. Managing the pandemic is a tremendous logistics challenge. The Ohio National Guard is uniquely equipped for helping manage a war on a virus--Ohioans serving Ohioans.

We need very visible, very nonpartisan responses to a humanitarian crisis, to prevent it from becoming polarized and get tested leaders that people may have memory of, or trust for, out front and visible. I kept imagining Colin Powell or a bipartisan partnership of past presidents to run the national and global effort. In Ohio, past Governors Dick Celeste and Bob Taft joined forces to help us develop testing.

I imagine there'll be another type of leadership structure considered because pandemic problems are nuanced and complex, and best solved with a cross-systems, cross-sectors, more lithe approach. We had to spontaneously create innovative solutions with hospitals and nursing homes and prisons and entities that are not normally part of my jurisdiction, but in a pandemic you have all those systems trying to row together. We need to modernize Public Health with regional health strategists and cross-sector teams, utilizing cutting-edge data tools and analytics, outstanding communications, and empowered to address the social determinants of health. I think we need to consider public-private partnerships to ensure community health and well-being, similar to how we address the economy. We need to consider *human* and economic development engines.

And there's going to have to be a very intentional trauma-informed lens to this playbook. What can you do preventively? Just like we try to do things before people go to war: what could I have been saying or doing to prevent collective trauma? There's a whole body of science behind that.

We have such tremendous talent in Ohio. I think that if we study Ohio very well, we can capture lessons learned and then try to advocate nationally for a reinvented playbook.

McGowan: Is there anything else that you'd like to share with us in our time together today?

Acton: These days, I find myself pondering the challenges and opportunities that lie ahead: How do we weave the fabric of our lives––our families and communities––back together? How do we emerge from the pandemic?

One of the themes that has come up in my talks with students is about how they must develop their own compass to navigate life. I talk about Joseph Campbell, who studied all world religions, mythologies, and stories across history and cultures and wrote *The Hero's Adventure*. Many artists were inspired by his work, such as George Lucas in creating *Star Wars*. He taught that everyone's life is a hero's adventure, and all of us inevitably travel a journey into the dark forest where you must face your fears, slay some dragons, and––if you're lucky, and you don't get killed––you emerge with the gold: the very thing that your society needs.

And so I find myself talking to students a lot because they're always very interested in what their life is going to be and fear that they have somehow messed up already and that they're lost. And of course, I'm brutally honest: "You will get lost. You're going to feel lost now and again, all the way to the end. But your compass gets better over time." We talk a bit about how you can intentionally hone your own compass with clues discovered by paying close attention to choices, and not just from noticing when things go well, but especially by paying attention during the times when they don't. I've come to believe that right in the middle of everything we deem bad, within every crisis, lie the seeds of opportunity. It never fails. I would talk about this with my staff at ODH. Always baked in the middle of these awful things is the next breadcrumb clue of your path, perhaps some new innovation that you haven't yet seen. These disruptions inherently have pearls in them.

I recently shared with Denison [University] students [Friedrich] Nietzsche's belief that suffering is essential for the soul. What's really striking about this time in history is that, until recently, we have had this feeling of relative safety, that the plagues of old are gone. You know, all these things that we keep at bay and feel we have control over. I don't think all this suffering and struggling we're doing is for naught. During the beginning of the pandemic, we intentionally tried to help people tolerate the intolerable. This pain we're having is a part of opening our hearts and our souls and our minds to new ways of thinking about things.

So I would say, this pandemic and the crisis of it, the disruption of it [...] while there is much loss and there is much we will legitimately mourn, there is a great opportunity for growth in ourselves, and for growth as humanity. I really see this as this moment where all of us are reassessing what are our priorities and our strengths. Public health is about creating the conditions in which we can all flourish and contribute to our fullest potential. A vital life vitalizes others—and this energy spreads. Everyone is kind of reckoning with this—no one has gone unscathed.

As we emerge from the pandemic, we need leaders more than ever who will help us sort through this experience and make meaning out of it, that help us realize we are being called to do more. I felt called to this moment. I distinctly felt it, on one of those cold mornings in the dark at 4 a.m. I had this sudden, complete feeling that everything that had ever happened in my life was exactly what I needed: all the good stuff and bad stuff, my childhood. For some reason my unique life—a journey that didn't look like a straight path—suddenly made perfect sense and gave me the exact skills I needed to serve.

But that's really happening for everybody right now. We're all going to have to make meaning of this, for ourselves, and collectively. We're all going to have to discover what moral courage means for us and choose democracy again, choose civil life again, and choose common good and common purpose again.

REFERENCE

King, Martin Luther Jr. 1968. "A Proper Sense of Priorities," speech delivered February 6, 1968, in Washington, DC. www.aavw.org/special_features/speeches_speech_king04.html.

Editors and Contributors

Amy Acton served as Director of Health for the Ohio Department of Health at the outset of the COVID-19 pandemic, and subsequently served as a senior health adviser to the Ohio Governor's administration. Dr. Acton has more than 30 years of experience in medical practice, government and community service, healthcare policy and advocacy, academic and nonprofit administration, consulting, teaching, and data analysis.

Jordyn Adams is a graduate student in Communication at the University of Cincinnati. She studies identity and its relationship to health communication.

Monica M. Adams is Assistant Professor of Social Work in the College of Community and Public Affairs at Binghamton University. Her research builds on 25 years of social work practice and concerns health disparities with a focus on food insecurity as a social determinant of health, and socio-environmental factors contributing to disparity in the prevalence of obesity among marginalized populations.

Mahwish U. Ahmad is Associate Staff Ethicist at the Cleveland Clinic within the Center for Bioethics and also teaches as Assistant Clinical Professor in the Department of Bioethics at Case Western Reserve University. She specializes in catering to the ethics needs of the transplant center at the Cleveland Clinic, while researching organ donation ethics, ethical considerations of transplant eligibility, disparities in transplant access, and informed consent and patient safety.

Lora Arduser is Associate Professor in Technical and Professional Writing at the University of Cincinnati where she directs the Professional Writing program. She specializes in the rhetoric of health and medicine, which focuses on understanding the effectiveness of discourse in medical and healthcare-related settings.

Julie Aultman is Interim Dean of the College of Graduate Studies, Director of Medical Ethics and Humanities, and Professor of Family and Community Medicine at Northeast Ohio Medical University. She teaches and mentors health professions students, works with non-profit organizations in urban and rural communities, and promotes ethical decision-making among community stakeholders to improve health equity.

Kara B. Ayers is Associate Professor of Pediatrics in the College of Medicine at the University of Cincinnati and a faculty member in the Division of Developmental and Behavioral Pediatrics at Cincinnati Children's Hospital Medical Center. Her research agenda connects to her identity as a disabled person and includes pursuing health equity for people with disabilities, supporting parenting with a disability, and exploring the impact of media on shaping the narrative of disability.

Deborah Barnbaum is Professor of Philosophy, with a focus in bio-ethics, at Kent State University, and an associate graduate faculty member at the Northeast Ohio Medical University. Her specializations include the ethics of clinical research; in that capacity she serves on data safety monitoring boards for two National Institutes of Health (NIH) clinical research collaboratives, as well as two stand-alone NIH-sponsored clinical trials.

M. Forrest Behne is Policy Director for the COVID Prison Project, where he and his colleagues track data and policies to monitor COVID-19 in prisons and jails in the US. He is a Policy Analyst at the Center for Health Equity Research in the UNC School of Medicine at the University of North Carolina at Chapel Hill, and his research interests include the intersection of mass incarceration and public health and the health inequities of systems-impacted communities.

Danielle Bessett (she/her) is Professor of Sociology at the University of Cincinnati, Ohio, and faculty affiliate of both the Department of Women's, Gender, and Sexuality Studies and the Medical Scientist Training Program at UC. She specializes in the sociology of medicine, gender, and reproduction and co-leads the Ohio Policy Evaluation Network (OPEN), which promotes rigorous, interdisciplinary research to assess Ohioans' reproductive health and well-being.

Vanessa Carbonell is Associate Professor of Philosophy at the University of Cincinnati, where she directs the undergraduate programs in Philosophy as well as the Bioethics certificate and BA in Medicine, Health & Society. She specializes in moral theory, but has also written about ethical issues in clinical care, health policy, and medical technology.

Joshua S. Crites is a Staff Ethicist, Regional Ethicist (West), and Codirector of the Cleveland Fellowship in Advanced Bioethics at the Cleveland Clinic. His current work and scholarship center around ethics consultation (particularly quality assessment and standardization in ethics consultation), ethics education for healthcare professionals and trainees, and ethical issues related to healthcare delivery during a pandemic.

Danielle Czarnecki is Visiting Assistant Professor of Sociology at Case Western Reserve University. Her research focuses on issues related to reproduction, medicine, gender, technology, and religion.

Diego F. Cuadros is Assistant Professor of Geography and Geographic Information System Mapping at the University of Cincinnati. He is interested in health geography and quantitative epidemiology, particularly in the study of socioeconomic drivers of disease distribution.

Chayanika Devi is a Research Associate at Azim Premji University in Bangalore, India. Her interests focus on the issues and challenges faced in the health sector. The topics that she has been working on are diverse and include land use and land cover, smart city planning, forest vegetation mapping, and seismic survey GIS application.

Haley Fite is a graduate student in Communication at the University of Cincinnati. They study technology with an emphasis on social media and the policies that shape these platforms.

Angie Fitzpatrick is Director of the Catharine S. Eberly Center for Women at the University of Toledo. Her advocacy and research focus on women, education, and labor. She is an Ohio transplant originally from North Dakota.

Kimberly K. Garchar (she/her) is Associate Professor of Philosophy at Kent State University and an affiliated graduate faculty member at Northeast Ohio Medical University. Her areas of research specialization include clinical ethics, especially death and dying; ethical theory; and American pragmatism.

Zac Ginsberg is a faculty member in the Departments of Trauma, Critical Care Surgery, and Emergency Medicine at Duke University Hospital, who worked during the first wave of the pandemic in southwest Ohio. His research focuses on disaster preparedness and hospital resiliency.

Hillary J. Gyuras is Senior Research Associate at the University of Cincinnati with the Ohio Policy Evaluation Network. Her research focuses on the politicization of sexual and reproductive healthcare and seeks to center the voices of those impacted by abortion restrictions.

Molly Jasina is an undergraduate student majoring in Neuroscience and minoring in Linguistics at Ohio State University. She writes about her social identities and experiences as an Asian adoptee.

Blair Kramer is a graduate student in Communication at the University of Cincinnati. She studies political discourse and its effects on interpersonal communication.

Elizabeth Lanphier is Assistant Professor in the Ethics Center at Cincinnati Children's Hospital Medical Center, and the Departments of Pediatrics and Philosophy at the University of Cincinnati, as well as a nonresident Research Fellow with the Institute for Philosophy and Public Policy. Elizabeth's research focuses on shared and collective responsibility, particularly for healthcare rights and access, and narrative and trauma-informed practices in medicine and ethics.

Christopher Laycock is a graduate student in Communication at the University of Cincinnati. His research interests focus on the intersections of health, identity, and video game etiquette.

John A. Lynch is Professor of Communication at the University of Cincinnati, where he researches bioethics, public memory, and the rhetoric of science and medicine. His most recent book, *The Origins of*

Bioethics: Remembering When Medicine Went Wrong, was published in 2019 by Michigan State University Press and received the 2020 Book Award from the Association for the Rhetoric of Science, Technology, and Medicine.

Neil J. MacKinnon is Provost and Executive Vice President for Academic Affairs at Augusta University and Professor of Population Health Sciences at the Medical College of Georgia. He maintains an active research program on health policy, including COVID-19.

Michelle L. McGowan is Senior Associate Consultant II in the Biomedical Ethics Research Program at Mayo Clinic and Visiting Scholar in the Department of Women's, Gender, and Sexuality Studies at the University of Cincinnati. Her research focuses on the ethical and social dimensions of reproductive health policies and practices, with a particular emphasis on the justice implications of the accessibility of abortion care.

Kim E. Nielsen is Professor of Disability Studies and History at the University of Toledo. Her research focuses on US disability history, with a focus on gender, biography, institutionalization, and law.

Alison H. Norris is Associate Professor in Ohio State University's Colleges of Public Health and Medicine. As an epidemiologist who studies reproductive health and infectious diseases, she employs multidisciplinary methods to investigate access to contraception and abortion, prevention of unwanted pregnancy and sexually transmitted diseases, and knowledge and stigma about sexual and reproductive health topics. She co-leads the Ohio Policy Evaluation Network (OPEN).

Kathryn Poe is a public policy professional currently working at Equality Ohio on LGBT+ issues. They graduated from Capital University with a BA in Creative Writing, and have worked on a number of other advocacy issue areas including high-cost medications, pediatric rare disease, disability access, end-of-life issues, and LGBTQ+ health.

Prabalini Rajendram was previously Assistant Professor of Medicine and staff physician in the Department of Critical Care in the Respiratory Institute at the Cleveland Clinic in Ohio and now works at Memorial

Sloan Kettering Cancer Center in New York. Her research focuses on ethical issues in critically ill people and on the care of the oncologic critically ill population.

Shelby Singh is a graduate student in Communication at the University of Cincinnati. She studies interpersonal communication with a focus on stigma.

Daniel Skinner is Associate Professor of Health Policy at Ohio University's Heritage College of Osteopathic Medicine, in Dublin, Ohio. Skinner's research interests include the politics of health and health care reform; hospital-community relations; addiction; and the rhetoric of health and medicine.

Mikaela H. Smith is Research Scientist at the Ohio State University with the Ohio Policy Evaluation Network. Her research focuses on inequities in state reproductive healthcare policy, with a special interest in public opinion and policy.

Jonathan Spelman is Assistant Professor of Philosophy at Ohio Northern University. He specializes in theoretical and practical ethics and has written about issues in bioethics, environmental ethics, and food ethics.

Katherine Sorrels is Associate Professor of History and affiliate faculty in Judaic Studies at the University of Cincinnati. Her research concerns modern European and North American history of medicine, disability, and the Jewish experience. She is Chair of UC's Taft Health Humanities Research Group.

Sarah K. Richter serves as the Principal of Alternative Programs for Mt. Healthy City Schools and is the creator and Principal of the new Mt. Healthy Virtual School in Cincinnati, Ohio. She is an educator of 21 years specializing in secondary mathematics education, educational leadership, and curriculum & instruction. She has recently completed her doctorate with research on Students with Limited or Interrupted Formal Education (SLIFE) and trauma-informed schools and is continuing her educational career in serving diverse communities of learners in urban settings.

Rachel V. Tucker is a doctoral student in Communication at the University of Connecticut. Her research focuses on how stigmatized sexual health conditions, identities, and experiences are shaped by understandings of gender and sexuality, and how they are managed, particularly through the use of information and communication technologies.

Dirichi Umunna is a graduate student in Communication at the University of Cincinnati. She works on media, globalization, and feminism, with a focus on communication research that amplifies inclusive discussions about Africa.

Edward V. Wallace is Associate Professor in the Department of Africana Studies and affiliate faculty in the College of Medicine at the University of Cincinnati. He specializes in the area of health disparities where his focus is on racial and ethnic health inequality, health policy, and minority health.

Index